LAW AND INSTITUTIONS OF MODERN CHINA

LAW AND INSTITUTIONS OF MODERN CHINA

Critical Concepts in Law

Edited by Sanzhu Zhu

Volume III
Constitution and basic laws of the
People's Republic of China

Routledge
Taylor & Francis Group

LONDON AND NEW YORK

First published 2011
by Routledge
2 Park Square, Milton Park, Abingdon, Oxon OX14 4RN

Simultaneously published in the USA and Canada
by Routledge
711 Third Avenue, New York, NY 10017

*Routledge is an imprint of the Taylor & Francis Group, an informa
business*

British Library Cataloguing in Publication Data
A catalogue record for this book is available from the British Library

Library of Congress Cataloging-in-Publication Data
Law and institutions of modern China : critical concepts in law / Edited
by Sanzhu Zhu.
    p. cm.
    Includes bibliographical references and index.
    1. Law–China. I. Zhu, Sanzhu.
    KNQ68.L39 2011
    349.51–dc22

                                                                    2010050164

ISBN: 978-0-415-56545-5 (set)
ISBN: 978-0-415-56691-9 (Volume III)

Typeset in Times New Roman
by Wearset Ltd, Boldon, Tyne and wear

Publisher's Note
References within each chapter are as they appear in the original complete
work

FSC
www.fsc.org

MIX
Paper from
responsible sources
FSC° C004839

Printed and bound in Great Britain by
TJI Digital, Padstow, Cornwall

CONTENTS

CONTENTS

ACKNOWLEDGEMENTS

The publishers would like to thank the following for permission to reprint their material:

Washington University Law Quarterly for permission to reprint William C. Jones, 'The Constitution of the People's Republic of China', *Washington University Law Quarterly*, 1985, 63, 4, 707–35.

Palgrave Macmillan for permission to reprint Yu Xingzhong, 'Western Constitutional Ideas and Constitutional Discourse in China, 1978–2005', in Stéphanie Balme and Michael W. Dowdle (eds), *Building Constitutionalism in China* (Palgrave, 2009), pp. 111–24.

Northwestern University School of Law, *Journal of Criminal Law and Criminology* for permission to reprint Shao-Chuan Leng, 'Criminal Justice in Post-Mao China: Some Preliminary Observations', *Journal of Criminal Law and Criminology*, 1982, 73, 1, 204–37.

Cambridge University Press for permission to reprint Hualing Fu, 'Criminal Defence in China: The Possible Impact of the 1996 Criminal Procedure Law Reform', *The China Quarterly*, 1998, 153, 31–48. © School of Oriental and African Studies.

Law and Contemporary Problems for permission to reprint Tong Rou, 'The General Principles of Civil Law of the PRC: Its Birth, Characteristics, and Role', trans. Jonathan K. Ocko, *Law and Contemporary Problems*, 1989, 52, 2, 151–75.

Berkeley Business Law Journal for permission to reprint Mo Zhang, 'From Public to Private: The Newly Enacted Chinese Property Law and the Protection of Property Rights in China', *Berkeley Business Law Journal*, 2008, 5, 2, 317–63. © 2008 by the Regents of the University of California.

Cambridge University Press for permission to reprint Minxin Pei, 'Citizens v. Mandarins: Administrative Litigation in China', *The China Quarterly*, 1997, 152, 832–62. © School of Oriental and African Studies.

Cambridge University Press for permission to reprint James V. Feinerman, 'New Hope for Corporate Governance in China?', *The China Quarterly*, 2007, 191, 590–612. © School of Oriental and African Studies.

Disclaimer

The publishers have made every effort to contact authors/copyright holders of works reprinted in *Law and Institutions of Modern China: Critical Concepts in Law*. This has not been possible in every case, however, and we would welcome correspondence from those individuals/companies whom we have been unable to trace.

Part 11

CONSTITUTION AND CONSTITUTIONALISM

28

THE CONSTITUTION OF THE PEOPLE'S REPUBLIC OF CHINA

William C. Jones

Source: *Washington University Law Quarterly* 63:4 (1985): 707–735.

The 1982 Constitution of the People's Republic of China,[1] like its many predecessors, purports to establish a government that appears quite recognizable to Westerners. It bears an obvious relation to both the United States[2] and Soviet constitutions,[3] though it has some unusual characteristics. Power is said to belong to the people, but it is exercised by what looks like an indirectly elected parliament, the National People's Congress.[4] Congress enacts—or formally approves—legislation. But in addition, it elects the President, who is the head of state; the Premier, who is head of the government, that is, the bureaucracy; and the top officials in the courts, the procuracy, and a number of other organizations.[5] Congresses at lower levels, such as the provinces and counties, exercise similar powers at their levels. That is, they choose the local administrative chiefs such as governors in the case of provinces, mayors, countyheads, etc. They also choose the presidents of the courts and the chief procurators at their levels.[6] Citizens are guaranteed the usual political rights such as freedom of speech, assembly and religion,[7] as well as the new social and economic rights such as the right to remunerative employment, retirement benefits and the like.[8]

The most unusual feature is Congress. It is not really a parliament in the usual sense, both because it is too large (around 3,000 members)[9] and because it meets too seldom (once a year) actually to initiate legislation on its own.[10] In fact, it is not intended to initiate legislation. Its primary function is to elect and remove the important officials of government, including a standing committee that can act as Congress when the latter is not in session.[11] The actual control of the government is in the hands of the Premier and the top officials of the ministries. Legislation is supposedly the task of the Standing Committee of the National People's Congress.[12] The Premier, government officials and Standing Committee are responsible to Congress, but only in an ultimate sense: Congress selects them and can remove them from office.[13] There is no parliamentary responsibility in the sense of a system whereby a government that fails to get a majority in parliament on a

3

vote of confidence falls. The process of election of Congress is unusual. The Constitution provides that citizens elect representatives to local people's congresses directly.[14] These congresses elect delegates to the congress of the next superior level and so on up the line to the National People's Congress. At present there are only three levels in the process: the local congresses, provincial congresses (or the equivalent), and the National People's Congress.[15] Thus, citizens vote directly for members of local congresses. These congresses elect the members of the provincial congresses, and the latter choose the members of the National People's Congress.

In other words, the constitution purports to establish a rather interesting system of government. One might wonder how a large number of problems that seem to be presented will be resolved. For instance, how will the Chinese solve the problem of divided control between the local congresses and top level officials in Peking? The problem is most obvious in the case of the courts. While, as indicated, local courts are appointed by local congresses and are responsible to them,[16] appeals from their decisions lie to the higher courts and in some cases to the Supreme People's Court in Peking. These higher courts are charged with supervising the lower courts.[17] Who controls? The courts or the Congresses? The same problem exists in all ministries because all ministries exercise ultimate control over local levels, and yet local officials are said to be responsible to the local congresses that appoint them.

Such questions, and many others, are interesting for students of government, but unless there are some radical changes in China, we shall never know the answers. The constitution seems to bear no relation to the actual government of China. Citizens enjoy neither civil[18] nor economic rights.[19] Congresses are in fact rubber stamps that do as they are told by whoever is in power at their level.[20] The meetings of a congress are ceremonial occasions. No doubt they afford a welcome opportunity for their members to travel, see friends, and make contacts. Perhaps they are significant as meeting places for important people because congress members are normally persons of some significance. In that way they may serve as significant parts of the actual government of China.

But it is fairly clear which governmental structures exercise power in China, at least in a formal sense, and the National People's Congress and the local congresses are not among them. China is a country that is governed by a highly centralized bureaucracy that is more or less under the control of the Communist Party.[21] The Army remains a great power that is not usually directly involved either in the government or Party, but that may become so at any time. Of course it is not clear at all just how control is exercised either within the Party or by the Party on external organizations such as ministries, to say nothing of the Army. The situation at the lower levels is especially murky, but it is difficult to understand how things work even at the more visible top levels. Deng Xiaoping is nominally an official who is chairman of a committee that supervises the Army; he is subordinate, on paper, to Congress. He has never held the very top posts in either the government or Party. Yet it is quite clear that if Deng were to go to

E Mei Shan to contemplate nature and observe the sacred monkeys for an extended time, E Mei Shan is where the government of China would be. Congress could continue to hold performances in Peking or not. It would not affect the way things ran. For that matter, the Politburo could continue to hold its meetings and make pronouncements, but unless it was clear that Deng agreed, it would not be wise to rely on these actions.[22]

What is true of the 1982 constitution was also true of its predecessors. The written constitution was not the place to start if one wanted to know what the government of China was really like. One might say that the written constitution had little to do with the actual constitution, that is, the real structure of government. Though it should be said that the 1975 and 1978 constitutions were a little closer to reality than the rest, because they both emphasized the importance of the Communist Party.[23] In other respects, however, they shared the remoteness from reality of their fellows. In view of this, it is tempting simply to dismiss Chinese constitutions as trumpery designed to provide an occasion for flights of oratory at the time of their adoption.[24] There is much to be said for this point of view. Indeed, it may be the only rational position to take on the question of the content of Chinese constitutions.

This is not to say that written constitutions play no role in the Chinese polity. They clearly have one function: The adoption of a constitution is a signal that a significant change has taken place in the government or in society, and that it is conceived to be long-lasting. The first constitution, the so-called "Common Program" in 1949, signified that the Communists had won the civil war against the Nationalists and had formed a completely new government for China. The 1954 constitution showed that the new government regarded itself as firmly established. Military and political control were complete. There was no significant problem with foreign or domestic enemies, and the foundations of a socialist state had been laid. The 1975 constitution indicated that what might be called the leftist faction believed that it had won decisively the bitter intra-party struggle of the Cultural Revolution and was in a position where the adoption of a new constitution would solidify its control. The 1978 constitution indicated how mistaken the leftist faction was, and affirmed what was apparently believed to be the permanence of the coalition that overturned the "Gang of Four." This belief was in turn pretty firmly exploded by the end of the same year in the Third Plenum of the Eleventh Session of the Central Committee. This signaled the establishment of Deng's primacy. The change was confirmed by the 1982 constitution whose promulgation purports to indicate a complete rejection of the Cultural Revolution and all "leftist" ideas and a return to the good old days of the 1950s. If the former pattern continues, then the failure to promulgate a new constitution when Deng passes from the scene might indicate a belief—or perhaps just a hope—of the ruling powers that they would continue to govern. Or it might mean that a fight was going on and it was not yet clear who had won. Of course something might have happened to the Chinese polity and it might mean that a more impersonal and permanent system of government had been established. Whatever

5

happens, the promulgation of a new constitution, or the failure to promulgate one, will be an event of great political significance.

There is not much question that constitutions play this role in China. The question is, do they have any other significance, since they do not establish or describe the apparatus of government nor determine the rights of citizens. It seems pretty clear that they perform at least one additional, though related, function. Apart from merely signaling a change in power or in the political and economic conditions of the country, constitutions also tend to show the direction that their promulgators plan to take in governing China. This will take the form both of indications of actions that the new government plans to take and of a basic ideological statement. The result is that constitutions can indeed be regarded as the source of law in the People's Republic of China just as they are declared to be.[25] But the term "constitution" has a different meaning from the one normally given to it in the West. The constitution is not written for the ages. It is a statement of current policy. When the policy changes, the law ipso facto changes. Indeed the change in the operative rule may antedate the change in the wording of the constitution. For instance, when, in the 1950s, the ownership of agricultural land was converted from cooperative and individual property to commune or collective property, and then in the late 1970s and 1980s was changed back again, it was because the rulers of China believed that collective or individual operation of the land, as the case might be, was the best way to solve the problem of increasing agricultural production at that time. Once this decision was made, an appropriate system of land ownership was adopted. Eventually the constitutions were changed to reflect the new policy. But the law in an operative sense had changed long before. Policy in China *is* law. It does not merely influence law.[26]

Presumably this is a perfectly correct way of looking at law and the constitution in a Marxist society. Law is an instrument that the ruling class uses to exert social control. It is an aspect of the superstructure.[27] The only real law is dialectical materialism. The governing structure in a country like China is the Communist Party, which establishes—and disestablishes—institutions as seems desirable in order to achieve the ultimate goal of communism. A constitution is a general summary of present policy. Laws are more particularized statements of policy. For this reason, an ideological statement is even more important than a concrete statement of economic or social policy because it serves as the basis of such policies. Particular policies must be appropriate to the current stage of society's development. This stage will be made clear in the ideological statement. For example, the most important change in the 1975 constitution from the 1954 constitution was the change in the phrase "China is a people's democratic state"[28] to "China is a state of the dictatorship of the proletariat."[29] This indicated that there had been a change in the nature of the state and society. Even more important, it was regarded as emphasizing the fact that there would be a continuation of the class struggle against, among others, enemies at home. And in turn this meant a continuation of the Cultural Revolution. On the other hand, the

6

switch to the phrase "People's democratic dictatorship" in the 1982 constitution[30] signals the elimination of the class struggle, and that indicates that the Cultural Revolution will not be revived. At least in the current stage of development, the policy of advancing the Four Modernizations rests on this foundation. The various measures in furtherance of foreign trade, including the Joint Venture Law[31] and the individual responsibility system, are aspects of the Four Modernizations campaign. Thus the ideological statement is the basis of a general statement, which serves as the basis of concrete statutes.

Of course, one cannot regard any of these ideological or policy statements as permanently binding, but if a statement is fairly recent and seems to be in accord with current conditions and attitudes, it is a good indication of where the leadership expects to go. A clear statement of policy may, in consequence, be of considerably more value than a more detailed set of rules. As a result, the preamble is generally the most important part of the constitution. Thus the statements in the preamble to the 1982 constitution that emphasize the importance of modernization and the necessity to make use of foreign capital and almost to eliminate class struggle[32] may be rather more significant to a person who is contemplating a joint venture than a whole portfolio of legal materials of the usual type.

A description of Chinese constitutions is, therefore, a description of the way the documents called constitutions relate to the social, economic and political conditions that existed when they were promulgated and to the actions taken and contemplated by those who promulgated them. It has a continuing relationship with those conditions, and changes accordingly. A Chinese constitution must, in consequence, be seen as part of a process and can only be understood if one has some sense of this development. This has been true since the very beginning of the People's Republic of China.

The People's Republic of China came into existence formally in 1949 immediately after the enactment of the Common Program.[33] The Common Program was, as indicated above, a response to the victory of the Communists in their long war with the Nationalists. Its purpose was to solemnize this victory and to indicate where the country was to go. The main task of the new government was to assure its control and to eliminate the effects of decades of war and neglect. At the same time the government was committed to Marxism-Leninism-Mao Zedong Thought. It wished to establish the basis for socialism in China, but without scaring people. The program began by declaring that China was a people's democratic state that carried out the people's democratic dictatorship on the basis of an alliance of workers and peasants.[34] The tasks of the new nation were to complete the war of liberation,[35] to destroy the special rights of imperialist countries in China, and to confiscate bureaucratic capital and return it to the ownership of the democratic society. The nation should gradually change feudal and semifeudal ownership into a system whereby the farmers owned the land. It should protect rights and advance China from an agricultural into an industrial country.[36] It must establish equality of the sexes[37] and eliminate counter-revolutionary and imperialist Guomindang antirevolutionary activity. In necessary cases, it must, according to law, take away the political rights of persons involved in such activities.[38] In foreign affairs, China is united with those countries which love peace and freedom and particularly the Soviet Union and the People's Democracies.[39] There were a number of more particular provisions connected with the establishment of new social conditions such as the necessity for workers to participate in management.[40]

The policy was carried out pretty much as written. By 1954, all significant opposition was quelled except in Taiwan; a successful war had been fought against the United States; the economy was rehabilitated and progressing; nationalization had begun.[41] As the preamble to the 1954 constitution announced, "the necessary conditions have been created for planned economic construction and gradual transition to socialism." Thus the time was ripe for a new constitution— the first to be given the name of "constitution." The preamble stated that during this time of transition to socialism, there was to be a "broad people's democratic united front." State ownership, cooperative ownership, individual ownership, and capitalism could all exist, though it was implied that capitalism was only temporary. In foreign affairs, "China has already built an indestructible friendship with the great Union of Soviet Socialist Republics and the People's Democracies."

In the body of the constitution, China was again defined as a "people's democratic state led by the working class and based on the alliance of workers and peasants."[42] Article 4 is perhaps the most significant. It provides: "The People's Republic of China, by relying on the organs of state and the social forces, and by means of socialist industrialization and socialist transformation, ensures the gradual abolition of systems of exploitation and the building of a socialist society." Several sections follow in which it is stated that different groups, such as individual workers and capitalists, will be "helped and guided" to enter into cooperatives or state-controlled activity.[43] Capitalists are forbidden to engage in "unlawful activities which injure the public interest, disrupt the social-economic order or undermine the economic plan of the state."[44] "Feudal landlords" and "bureaucratic landlords" continue to be deprived of political rights. Treasonable and counter-revolutionary activities are suppressed.[45]

Socialist transformation, in the sense of a change in ownership relations, came very quickly thereafter. By 1958 almost all agricultural land had been collectivised and all industry had come under state control. The individual sector of the economy had ceased to be of much importance.[46] In some ways it was time for a new constitution. Indeed, the issue was raised by Mao Zedong.[47] But the completion of the transition to socialism (if that is an accurate description of what happened) was almost immediately succeeded by a number of disturbances that delayed the adoption of a new constitution.

The two most important occurrences were the Great Leap Forward in 1958[48] and the Cultural Revolution in 1966.[49] These two events were very complex. Opinions vary enormously as to what caused them and what they mean. There is no space to discuss these matters here. There is, however, one element that is common to both of these events that has been very important for Chinese constitutional development. This is the issue of the persistence of and the necessity for the class struggle in China after the goals of nationalization of the economy and the establishment of political and military control had been achieved.

There is no question that the exploiting classes in the usual sense of the term had been eliminated. Many members of those classes—landlords, capitalists, officials in the former government, etc.—had been killed or imprisoned. Their ownership rights in the means of production had been confiscated and their organizations were destroyed. But China's revolution was not complete. Both agricultural and industrial production were far too low. What should be done to improve them? If one believed that the class struggle was essentially over, then the emphasis would be on physical conditions. One might feel that the chief obstacles to China's march towards socialism were essentially the objective material conditions of poor transportation, a low educational level, poor technology, and lack of skilled personnel and of capital to make improvements and the like. In short, one might concentrate on what could be called "productive forces."

On the other hand, if one believed that the basic problem was always political and that development comes from changing ownership relationships, or, one might say, the class struggle, then the problem was to locate the class that must be struggled against. One could, of course, continue to badger the survivors of the old exploiting groups and their descendants. And, as a matter of fact, the constant harassment of persons with a bad class background was a feature of Chinese life until quite recently. But it is obvious that this is not enough because these people had little power. Who did? High officials and members of the Communist Party. If these people were harboring feudal or bourgeois thoughts, they must be struggled against. They had become an exploiting class.[50] But ultimately—according to one very influential view—the battle was subjective. We must all struggle to rid ourselves of restrictive feudal or bourgeois thinking, to rid ourselves of the ego.[51] If these political problems were attacked first, the solution to economic and social problems would appear.

Of course, it does not do to regard the upholders of these views as completely separate. All Marxists believe in the importance of the class struggle and that political questions, as they understand the term, are very important. No one in China questions the necessity for improved irrigation and the use of computers. But there are great differences in emphasis and these differences are reflected in the constitutions that have been promulgated since 1975.

It is not clear just who was in control of China in 1975, but it is pretty clear that the group favoring emphasis on the class struggle was in control of the media. Apparently this group also controlled the government sufficiently to cause a new constitution reflecting their views to be promulgated, because the preamble made it very clear that this constitution was the product of those who emphasized the class struggle. It provided:

> Socialist society covers a considerably long historical period. Throughout this historical period, there are classes, class contradictions and

class struggle, there is the struggle between the socialist road and the capitalist road, there is the danger of capitalist restoration and there is the threat of subversion and aggression by imperialism and social-imperialism. These contradictions can be resolved only by depending on the theory of continued revolution under the dictatorship of the proletariat and on practice under its guidance.[52]

These ideas are pervasive in the 1975 constitution. It is what might be called a very Maoist document.[53] Almost all traces of the former social system had disappeared.[54] The Communist Party is the core of leadership of the whole Chinese people. "The working class exercises leadership over the state through its vanguard, the Communist Party of China."[55] References to capitalists and other parties had disappeared. Essentially the only property relationships that are recognized are collective or state property,[56] though very grudging permission is given for private plots and handicrafts.[57] The emphasis is on struggle. Administrators must "put proletarian politics in command, combat bureaucracy, maintain close ties with the masses and wholeheartedly serve the people. Cadres at all levels must participate in collective productive labour."[58] "The proletariat must exercise all-round dictatorship over the bourgeoisie in the superstructure, including all spheres of culture."[59] Article 13 more or less describes and endorses the Cultural Revolution. It provides:

> Speaking out freely, airing views fully, holding great debates and writing big-character posters are new forms of carrying on socialist revolution created by the masses of the people. The state shall ensure to the masses the right to use these forms to create a political situation in which there are both centralism and democracy, both discipline and freedom, both unity of will and personal ease of mind and liveliness, and so help consolidate the leadership of the Communist Party of China over the state and consolidate the dictatorship of the proletariat.[60]

The standing committees of local congresses are replaced by "revolutionary committees."[61] In regard to legal procedure, the constitution provided that: "The mass line must be applied in procuratorial work and in trying cases. In major counterrevolutionary criminal cases the masses should be mobilized for discussion and criticism."[62]

It is difficult to determine the extent to which China was actually governed by these precepts, but there is no question that between the time when the constitution was adopted in 1975 and the death of Mao in September 1976, the "leftists" who, as indicated above, seem to have controlled the media, made strenuous efforts to promote these views. During the summer before Mao's death, there was a vigorous campaign against Deng Xiaoping and his doctrine of emphasizing "productive forces."[63] There was a lot of favorable publicity given to the Cultural Revolution with perhaps a hint at its revival.[64] This period is included in what the present government calls ten years of turmoil. It could also be classified as a period in which the doctrine of viewing the class struggle as the key link was the keystone of official government policy.[65]

Almost immediately upon Mao's death, things began to change. The group—later characterized as the Gang of Four—who had presumably been behind this constitution were imprisoned and new people began to take over.[66] One of the first notable changes in policy involved education.[67] The entire system of university admissions was changed. In the early 1970s admission was, in theory, based primarily on work experience and political reliability and not on academic qualifications as we understand the term. The course of study emphasized practice more than theory and the length of time spent in the university was shortened. In 1977, soon after the fall of the Gang of Four, this was changed to a system that based admission on an extremely competitive examination more or less of the western type. The courses of study became much more academic and longer. There were changes in other fields as well. Foreign contacts were encouraged and imports increased.[68] There were purges of those who had sided with the Gang of Four, and there was a "reversal of verdicts" of those who were said to have been unjustly accused of various things—usually counter-revolutionary activity—during the Cultural Revolution.[69] The government was a rather strange alliance. It included both Deng Xiaoping and Hua Guofong, the man who had replaced him after his downfall in April 1976.[70] In the midst of all this, the 1978 constitution was promulgated.[71] It reflected the unresolved conflicts in the government.

The new constitution retained the general ideological line of the 1975 constitution, but there were some modifications. Thus, in the preamble, China is still said to be a country under the dictatorship of the proletariat and the Cultural Revolution is still a great victory. But there is a slight relaxation in the cry for the class struggle. Intellectuals are now included in the worker-peasant alliance by means of the "mass line," which was to be expanded and strengthened as a sort of united front. The big task is to preserve the revolution and to make China a modern country by the end of the century by achieving the Four Modernizations.

In the text there is the same compromise. Most of the language is the same as in the 1975 constitution, but some changes have been made. For instance, the rural people's commune is no longer defined as "an organization which integrates government, administration and economic management."[72] Instead, it is a "socialist sector" of the economy.[73] In the article on improving production, instead of saying that the state by "grasping revolution ... improves the people's material and cultural life step by step ...,"[74] the 1978 constitution says that the state "adheres to the general line of going all out, aiming high and achieving greater, faster, better and more economical results in building socialism ... and it continuously develops the *productive forces* so as to consolidate the country's independence and security and improve the people's material and cultural life step by step."[75] The term "productive forces" was anathema to the Gang of Four

11

because it indicated that one was not emphasizing the importance of the class struggle as the key to development.

The 1978 document also eliminated the statement that the proletariat must "exercise all-round dictatorship over the bourgeoisie in the superstructure."[76] Education and science again became primary aims of the state.[77]

There were some structural changes as well. The procuracy was restored[78] as well as the use of "people's assessors" in the trial of cases.[79] The accused had a right to a defense, and while the masses were to be drawn in for discussion and suggestions in major counter-revolutionary or criminal cases,[80] there was no statement that the mass line must be generally used.[81] In the part dealing with the legislature, the powers given to the National People's Congress and to its standing committee are set out in much more detail[82] than in the 1975 constitution.[83] It was believed by some that these provisions strengthened Congress.[84]

It is hard to say whether any of these changes in the language of the constitution would have had any effect whatever on the actual government of China even if the constitution had remained in effect. But as it happens, before the year 1978 was out, the political situation changed radically. The Third Plenum of the Eleventh Central Committee Meeting of the Party was held in December.[85] Its report announced the end of the class struggle and made the Four Modernizations the country's main task. This meeting signaled the basic victory of Deng Xiaoping and his group in the struggle for control of the Party—though mopping up operations still go on. In August 1980, the Central Committee of the Communist Party recommended the establishment of a committee to revise the constitution.[86] Soon thereafter the National People's Congress established a constitutional revision committee.[87] The 1982 constitution is what they came up with. In June 1981, at the Sixth Plenum of the Central Committee, Hua Guofeng resigned as Party Chairman and Hu Yaobang, a follower of Deng, was selected to replace him.[88] These events indicated that the Deng group was in firm control of both the Party and the government, at least at the top levels.

In the period since Deng took power, the most visible aspect of political life in China has been the emphasis on the Four Modernizations. Or, one might say, industrialization at almost any cost. This campaign, if one can call it that, pervades every aspect of Chinese life. In fact, though not in name, collective ownership of agricultural land is being scrapped in favor of a sort of limited individual ownership under the label of the "individual responsibility system."[89] Foreign investment is sought eagerly and foreigners are even permitted to develop and, in effect, to own China's natural resources such as oil.[90] Internally, private capitalism at a low level, such as handicraft industry, hauling, restaurants, etc., is permitted.[91] It is reported that shares will soon be sold in Chinese enterprises and that both Chinese and foreigners will be permitted to buy them.[92] In other words, private and even foreign ownership of the means of production is now permitted (although considerable intellectual energy is expended to deny this). Education is also being emphasized and changed. Its chief goal now is to produce high-quality experts in large numbers. Education is now an elite system that relies on competitive examinations, foreign experts and foreign training for its staff, a complete reversal of the radical egalitarian theories of Chairman Mao. The new officials in the Party and government, at least at the top levels, tend to be people with university educations.[93]

In valuating these changes, it is instructive to look back at the campaign that was conducted against Deng Xiaoping during late 1975 and 1976.[94] That is roughly the period between the promulgation of the 1975 constitution and the death of Mao. This campaign began with the attack on Deng's theories of education. It was alleged that he advocated that there be more attention to theory, less to practice. He advocated down-playing the worker-peasant teams. He was accused of having said, "The greatest tragedy of these years is that study has been abandoned and everything is work and trade."[95] He is supposed to have said that universities should train scientists and cadres and "universities" which train people to become peasants and workers should be abolished.

The general attack on Deng's ideas that followed in the next few months quoted speeches in which Deng is alleged to have criticized campaigns as a waste of time that harmed old Party members who were falsely accused of being revisionists. He objected to the criticism of intellectuals. He emphasized science and technology. In general he advocated the development of productive forces as opposed to the class struggle. He said, quoting Mao, "The criterion of good or bad is whether production force is released or tied down."[96] He advocated purchasing foreign technology on credit, using Chinese resources to pay for it. He advocated the use of material incentives both in industry and agriculture to raise production.

Thus the positions for which Deng was criticized have become the official program of the Chinese government and the basis of the 1982 constitution. This could have been predicted: So long as Deng and his group are in power, this will continue to be the program (unless they change their minds). If what have been his opposition are in power, one can expect a shift in emphasis from productive forces to the class struggle. At any rate, these are the principles that govern China now and they form the basis of the new constitution just as the ideology of previous groups has governed the constitutions they promulgated and the policies they followed.

The ideological message of the 1982 constitution is very clear. The preamble begins with the usual history of the struggle of the Chinese people against feudalism and imperialism. However, it emphasizes China's long and glorious history and the role of Sun Yat-sen in over-throwing the Manchus. These are both new features of the standard history. Then there is a summary of the history of the People's Republic of China. The Cultural Revolution—emphasized in the 1975 and 1978 constitutions—is ignored. In sum, the "people's democratic dictatorship led by the working class and based on the alliance of workers and peasants, which is, in essence, the dictatorship of the proletariat, has been consolidated and developed."[97] The basic task at this stage is to achieve the Four Modernizations.[98] The class struggle is basically over. It is essential to rely on workers, peasants and intellectuals in achieving modernization; there must be a "broad patriotic united front."

In the constitution's text, this message is continued. Article 1 states that China is a people's democratic dictatorship. This phrase is apparently a code term that means that the class struggle is down-played. It is especially valuable for intellectuals and former capitalists—two groups very important for the Four Modernizations—who can be classified as "people" or even "workers," but who are a little difficult to characterize as "the proletariat." If these groups participate in the dictatorship, then they are less likely to be targets of it. In the case of the dictatorship of the proletariat, anyone who is not a member of the proletariat is a likely target for dictatorship. The consequences can range from inability to get work or an education to execution as an enemy.

The Four Modernizations are not mentioned by name in the text, but their spirit governs. In the 1975 and 1978 constitutions, the state administers the individual economy in an effort to eliminate it. Now the individual economy is a complement to the "socialist public economy," and "the state protects the lawful rights and interests of the individual economy."[99] Article 14 summarizes the present economic program:

> The state continuously raises labour productivity, improves economic results and develops the *productive forces* by enhancing the enthusiasm of the working people, raising the level of their technical skill, disseminating advanced science and technology, improving the system of economic administration and enterprise operation and management, instituting the socialist system of responsibility in various forms and improving organization of work.[100]

State and collective enterprises are given some independence.[101] Foreign investment is allowed.[102] The state awards achievements in scientific discoveries. Article 25 provides: "The state trains specialized personnel in all fields who serve socialism, increases the number of intellectuals and creates conditions to give full scope to their role in socialist modernization."[103]

All of this is in line with the preamble and with what Deng preached before he got to power and practiced thereafter. In other words, China is a state that is dedicated to the principles of Marxism-Leninism-Mao Zedong Thought, but which at the present time must concentrate on building up its productive forces. When the aims of the Four Modernizations are achieved, China will presumably be able to advance to a stage closer to socialism. Because the intellectuals by that time will be in control of both Party and state, their positions would seem to be assured, so that this would be socialism with a very different face from that contemplated in 1975 and 1978.

The activities of the government since the 1982 constitution was promulgated are in accordance with these aims. And that is perhaps one of the points to notice about Chinese constitutions. To say that policy is law is not to say that China's political system is lawless, or unpredictable, or subject to the whim and caprice of its leaders. The official policy of a country like China is normally hammered out after lengthy discussions. Once established, it is likely to continue for a long while. If a group that is in power wishes to change policy, there will probably be many signals. And if an opposing group comes to power, it is likely that one will know beforehand much of what it plans to do. Still, there is more uncertainty and more change than there is in a system such as that of the United States, in which policy tends to be crystallized into "law." The policy against over-concentration in industry is held in varying degrees of esteem by different administrations, but none has felt it possible formally to repeal the antitrust laws. But in China, every policy, every law, can be completely changed within a very short time.

Such changes are now going on. What will happen next? If past practice continues, then this constitution will remain in force as long as the present group remains in power, unless its policies should change considerably. In the event of a significant political or policy change, there would be a formal constitutional change. This would presumably be of no surprise to the Chinese, who are at least as aware as we are of the transitory nature of their constitutions. Indeed, they sometimes say as much. A member of the Chinese People's Political Consultative Conference is supposed to have said in regard to the 1982 constitution: "Will the new constitution become a mere scrap of paper as the 1954 constitution became ...?"[104] The Chinese must also be aware of the fact that institutions of government such as the courts and congresses have no real power and that a constitutional guarantee such as a guarantee of freedom of the person or the right to have a trial uninfluenced by "Administrative organs, public organization or individuals"[105] and the like, is pretty empty. Officials must, in other words, be aware of the facts that not only can all their policies and laws change if they lose out in a power struggle, but also they themselves run a serious risk of personal harm if this should happen. It has already happened to these officials during the Cultural Revolution—and before, for that matter. It seems reasonable to assume that they do not wish for it to happen again. Consequently, they seem to have a great desire for stability, and they have attempted to make this constitution different from its predecessors in order to get that stability. They have attempted to substitute law, as we understand the term, for policy. They have done this by means of certain provisions in the constitution itself,[106] and by means of a vigorous campaign for the "rule of law" in China.[107]

It is difficult to know what significance to give to these or any other institutional changes in Chinese constitutions, because all we have to go on are the constitutions themselves and the Chinese commentaries. The Chinese commentators make no effort to ask how things will actually work. Instead they write about Chinese constitutions in the way an American might write about a new state constitution. They discuss every institution as if it functioned exactly as one would expect from reading the text. This is almost never true. It often seems that none of the institutions that are dealt with at length in the constitutions have any importance at all. Consequently, what does it matter if there are changes in the functions that are supposedly given to the institutions? It would matter, of course, if there were a strong desire on the part of very powerful people to have the changes mean something. There are hints in the new constitution and its official commentary that this may be the case now. What seems to be intended is to create institutions that will have some actual power and thus to create a government that is at least distanced from the Party, if not completely removed from its control.[108]

The outlines of such a government are anything but clear. They may not always be clear to the authors. One clue to what is intended may be found in the seven changes in governmental institutions in the new constitution that are said by the draftsmen in their official commentary to be particularly significant.[109] These changes were:

1 The power of the National People's Congress is increased because more power is given to its standing committee. Because the standing committee can meet frequently and is much smaller than the Congress as a whole, it can exercise power effectively. This is something that the Congress cannot do.

2 The position of President of the Republic is restored.

3 A military affairs control committee is established. It is appointed by the Congress and responsible to it. Formerly the armed forces were under the Party's control (at least that is what the constitutions said).

4 The Premier is made responsible to Congress for the actions of the government. Each ministry operates under a system whereby the minister is responsible for the action of his ministry to the Premier. A system of auditing is instituted both at the national and local levels in order to strengthen the supervision of fiscal matters.

5 The local government authorities have been strengthened under central leadership. The congresses of provinces and cities under direct rule exercise supervisory authority over local governments, which operate under a system whereby the chief administrator is responsible.

6 The communes have been deprived of all political functions, which now go to the "township." This clarifies political responsibility.

7 Certain high officials, such as the President and members of the Standing Committee of the National People's Congress, may not serve more than two terms.

These provisions seem to be designed to create an hierarchical system of government with the apex in the Premier. Each unit has a head who is responsible to the next higher level and so on up to the top. The Premier is in turn nominally responsible to the National People's Congress, but in fact this means that he is responsible to the Standing Committee. The Committee will, in all probability, be more or less self-perpetuating because, in view of the indirect nature of the electoral process, radical changes in the composition of the Congress are unlikely, and the Standing Committee is clearly intended to control Congress. Hence what one has is very similar to the system of the government in an American corporation. The organization is run by its permanent bureaucracy, the President and his subordinates, but there is a very real power of ultimate supervision by a self-perpetuating board of directors. In China, however, there is the troublesome memory of a long-term power holder—Mao Zedong—that is no doubt fresh in people's minds. So no one is permitted to stay in a top job for more than two terms. One curious aspect to this system is that it is, in some ways, more in harmony with the theories of Sun Yat-sen than the government that now exists in Taiwan.[110]

Dr. Sun believed that political power should be distinguished from governmental power. A strong government was not to be feared so long as the government is ultimately controlled by the people in the exercise of their political power. Government consists of making, enforcing and interpreting rules as well as recruiting personnel for government and investigating its work. The mass of the people cannot do these things. But the people can control the government by exercising four political powers: suffrage, initiative, referendum and recall. In a country as large as China, they cannot exercise powers directly as they might, perhaps, in a Swiss canton. Hence they act through the people's Congress. The Congress is not a legislature. It does not make laws in the usual way. Rather, it elects the leaders of the government, one branch of which makes laws (the legislative yüan). The people, acting through their representatives, the Congress, can elect or remove all top officials. The people can initiate legislation or have it referred to them for approval (referendum). But the initiative and referendum are as extraordinary in China as they are in the United States. Normally people simply elect top officials of the government and supervise their work by getting periodic reports. This is, of course, the way the National People's Congress is supposed to work.

There are also, to be sure, many differences between the 1982 constitution and the ideas of Dr. Sun and his followers.[111] Still, if one looks only at what the constitution says about the political as opposed to economic institutions of China and at what it says about international relations, one cannot help wondering about the possible influences of Dr. Sun—who has never been repudiated by the Communists. At the present time, even those economic provisions of the constitution that encourage individual farmers to control the land they farm and benefit from it seem to be a sort of echo of Dr. Sun's famous program of giving land to the tiller. Dr. Sun attempted to assimilate western democratic ideas and institutions into traditional Chinese ideas and institutions in order to create a system that would work in China. If the present constitution is in fact influenced by Dr. Sun, its draftsmen are emphasizing the Chinese tradition as the foundation of their government. There seems to be some hint of this in the preamble in the midst of many protestations of loyalty to Marxism-Leninism.[112] Connecting the present government to Chinese tradition is an obvious way of giving the government a basis for existing independent of the Party.

Regardless, however, of whether the leaders of China are the ardent followers of Marxism-Leninism-Mao Zedong Thought that they purport to be, or closet devotees of the Three People's Principles, it is still not clear that the governmental institutions described in the constitution will ever operate independently of the Party. The Party at the present time is not, after all, a small band of enthusiastic revolutionaries. It is an enormous bureaucracy with tens of millions of members. For thirty-five years, membership in the Party has been the principal road to power and the perquisites of power such as housing, food, education, health care, travel, and the like.[113] The vast majority of persons now living in China have never known anything else. All of the persons who are in the top positions in the government are also important Party members. The two things go together. It is hard to see those Party members who are, for example, Standing Committee members, getting rid of Party control of the electoral process. Though it was suggested recently by one of the most authoritative observers of China that the current Chairman of the National People's Congress, Peng Zhen, who was vice-chairman of the committee that was said to have drafted the constitution, is attempting to make the Standing Committee of the National People's Congress a rival power-center to the Politburo of the Communist Party because Zhen is not a member of the Politburo. He is said to have significant support.[114] If this is an accurate assessment, it is interesting. Even if it does not mean that power has shifted from the Party to governmental institutions, Zhen's attempt would mean that they, particularly the Standing Committee, have become fora in which battles for Party control might be fought. Hence they would acquire some real life as opposed to the merely formal existence they have had heretofore. Of course such importance, even if it exists, may be short-lived. Mao Zedong created extra-Party organizations, notably the Cultural Revolution Small Group and the Red Guards, when he had apparently lost control of the Party apparatus. He used these new organizations to destroy the leaders of the Party (sometimes in a very literal sense).[115] But once this was accomplished, he simply put his men into control of the Party. The new organizations disappeared or ceased to have much power. Moreover, if there is some sort of struggle for power going on now between Deng and Peng, it is a struggle between two octogenarians. It is not clear that its outcome will have any long-term significance. Although of course it may.

There is another development that might make the institutions created by this constitution different from those created by its predecessors. That is the development of a legal profession. China has never had a significant legal profession in the western sense outside of the Treaty Ports such as Shanghai where there were extraterritorial courts. Even the vestiges of a western (or even Soviet) system pretty much disappeared after 1958. There were courts, but it is not clear what function they fulfilled. There was clearly no general system of criminal courts in a western sense. Nor were there lawyers.[116] Beginning in the late 1970s, however, there has been a determined movement to change this situation. Laws and law books proliferate. Law departments are being established or re-established in universities. University-level institutions and special courses

18

are being formed to give training in law to judges, most of whom were military men and had no legal training.[117] If this activity continues, it will mean that there will be a very large number of people in a well-entrenched bureaucracy—the courts and procuracy (though will the security administration continue to dominate?)—who have been trained to think in terms of law as something independent of policy. There will be other trained lawyers throughout the bureaucracy. This is already true of the foreign trade organs.

It would be foolish to suppose that all of these individuals will have acquired a passionate fondness for civil rights and due process, although it is clear that at least those who have studied law in law departments have had access to western legal materials, including constitutional law materials.[118] It does seem possible, however, that they will serve to form a core of resistance to rapid change outside the normal channels, such as to something like the Cultural Revolution. If one wished to rid oneself of an opponent, a "trial" for counter-revolutionary acts would be used rather than a mass meeting. The "trial" of the Gang of Four is of interest in this context because previously trials were not used in purges of Party leaders.[119]

Despite this apparent desire for change and the measures that seem to have been taken to bring it about, it is far too early to say whether the new constitution will in fact effect some changes or simply go the way of its predecessors. Much depends on how long Deng stays in power and on who succeeds him. To make any predictions on how the Chinese constitution will fare in the midst of these events, one must be able to predict the immediate future of Chinese politics, and few would wish to attempt that.[120] All that one can say is that from 1949 to the present, Chinese constitutions have not played a western role of describing and prescribing the forms and powers of governmental institutions and the rights of citizens, although they purport to do so. Rather, they have signaled political and ideological change. The more recent changes have involved a bitter and violent dispute over the issue of the continuation of the class struggle thirty years or so after liberation. Those who oppose continuation of the struggle are now in power. They have attempted in every possible way to prevent a reversal of their programs. Doubtless the most important method that they have used is the traditional one of purging the party and replacing supporters of the old group with their own people.[121] They have devoted much attention to building up mass support. But they have also attempted to make some institutional changes in the Chinese government that may make it more resistant to change. And they constantly emphasize the importance of law as opposed to policy, and have sponsored the development of a legal system and a legal profession. Only time will tell what they have accomplished.

Notes

1 I have used the following sources for the Chinese texts of the constitutions: 1949 Common Program, 1 XIAN FA ZELIAO XUANBIAN, SELECTED MATERIALS ON CONSTITUTIONAL LAW [hereinafter referred to as CONSTITUTIONAL MATERIALS]; the 1954

constitution is found in *id.* at 150; the 1975 constitution is found in *id.* at 293; the 1978 constitution is found in *id.* at 303; and the 1982 constitution is found in the official pamphlet edition, which contains the report of the drafting committee. I have used the following English translations from which all translations in the text are taken: Common Program, FUNDAMENTAL LEGAL DOCUMENTS OF COMMUNIST CHINA 34 (A.P. Blaustein ed. 1962); 1954 constitution, SELECTED LEGAL DOCUMENTS OF THE PEOPLE'S REPUBLIC OF CHINA 1 (J. En-pao Wang ed. 1976); 1975 constitution, *id.* at 65; 1978 constitution, official translation in separate booklet published by Foreign Languages Press (1978); 1982 constitution, official translation in separate booklet published by Foreign Languages Press (1982).

2 Most constitutions are modeled to some extent on the United States Constitution because it is one of the oldest and easily the best known. The similarities with the Chinese constitution lie primarily in the structure of the constitution. In both, the powers of the most important organs of government are set out in general terms, and the organs are similar: Congress, the Administration and the Judiciary. Yet there are differences, particularly in the Administration where, in China, the existence of the bureaucracy is recognized (arts. 30–32). And there are some additional institutions in China such as the Central Military Commission (art. 93) and the Procuracy (arts. 129–133). China is a unitary rather than a federal state, so the treatment of local matters is quite different. Still, the document as a whole is close to the form of the United States Constitution and it includes a bill of rights. *See infra* note 7.

3 The principal similarity of the Chinese constitution to that of the Soviet Union seems to me to lie in the presence of ideological statements and the prominence of economics, in other words, the clear recognition of Marxism as the official doctrine of the state. Thus, the preambles in both constitutions refer to the struggle to overturn capitalism and to establish socialism. Both define themselves as socialist states. China: "The People's Republic of China is a socialist state under the people's democratic dictatorship led by the working class and based on the alliance of workers and peasants." Art. 1. The U.S.S.R.: "The Union of Soviet Socialist Republics is a socialist all-people's state expressing the will and the interests of the workers, the peasants, and the intelligentsia, and of the working people of all the nations and nationalities of the country." Art. 1. The Soviet constitution devotes chapter II to the "Economic System." The Chinese constitution devotes thirteen articles in its first chapter, "General Principles," to economics. Arts. 6–18.

There are also institutional similarities. The Chinese procuracy is obviously of Soviet origin. *See* Ginsburgs & Stahnke, *The Genesis of the People's Procuracy Procuratorate in the People's Republic of China.* THE CHINA Q. 1 (1964); *The People's Procuratorate in Communist China: The Period of Maturation, 1951–1955, id.* at 53 (1965); *The People's Procuratorate in Communist China: The Institution Ascendent, 1954–1957, id.* at 82 (1968). The use of standing committees of larger bodies, such as a congress, to do the real work of those bodies, is also a common feature of the two constitutions. See the provisions on the Presidium of the Supreme Soviet, arts. 119–124. The Standing Committee of the National People's Congress is dealt with primarily in articles 65–69.

4 Art. 59. The actual process of election is controlled by the Election Law for the National People's Congress and Local Congress of 1979. CONSTITUTIONAL MATERIALS, *supra* note 1, at 336, amended by Fifth National People's Congress, Dec. 10, 1982, translated in SUMMARY OF WORLD BROADCASTS, PART III: THE FAR EAST, (Dec. 18, 1982 FE/7212/C/1) [hereinafter cited as SWB].

5 Arts. 62 & 79. The term that the Chinese now translate as "President" [*Zhuxi*] is normally translated as "Chairman," as in "Chairman Mao." I do not know the reason for the change.

6 Art. 101.

7 Art. 33 provides that all citizens are equal before the law; art. 34 gives the right to vote, and to be elected, to all citizens over 18 years old, except to those "deprived of political rights according to law;" art. 35 gives rights of "freedom of speech, of the press, of assembly, of association, of procession and of demonstration;" art. 36 gives freedom of religious belief; art. 37 declares that the freedom of persons is inviolable, that no one can be arrested except by order of the court of procuracy, and that unlawful searches of the person are prohibited; art. 38 guarantees personal dignity; art. 39 protects against unlawful searches of houses; art. 40 guarantees the confidentiality of correspondence; art. 41 gives the right to criticize and make complaints to officials.

8 Art. 42 declares that citizens have the right and duty to work; art. 43 declares working people have the right to rest; art. 44 says the state will prescribe a system of retirement for workers and staff in enterprises and organs of the state; art. 45 declares that citizens have the right to material assistance from the state and provides for the blind and other disabled persons; art. 46 declares that citizens have a right to an education.

9 The number varies from session to session. See C.E. WENG, CONTEMPORARY CHINESE POLITICS 109 (2d ed. 1958) [hereinafter cited as WENG].

10 The point is made by the Chinese themselves. See, e.g., Wang, The New Constitution Strengthens the Standing Committee of the National People's Congress, in A GUIDE TO THE CONSTITUTION OF THE PEOPLE'S REPUBLIC OF CHINA [Zhonghua Renmin Gongheguo Xian Fa Jianghua] 110 (1983) [hereinafter cited as CHINESE CONSTITUTION.]

11 Arts. 61 & 67.

12 Art. 67. There are some statutes that only Congress can enact—notably amendments to the constitution, arts. 62(1) & 64.

13 Art. 62(5)–(8) (power to appoint); art. 63 (power to dismiss).

14 Art. 59.

15 Art. 5 lists the level below the national level; art. 97 sets out the election process. See also FOREIGN BROADCAST INFORMATION SERVICE (FBIS), Electoral Law of the PRC for the NPIC and Local People's Congresses of All Levels, in DAILY REPORT 12 (Jul. 27, 1979).

16 Arts. 101 & 128.

17 Art. 127.

18 It is perhaps enough to cite the case of Wei Jingsheng, one of the leaders of the short-lived "Peking Spring" movement, when some young people expressed themselves very freely in making criticisms of the government. Wei was sentenced to 15 years on what seem to me to have been trumped-up charges. See Jones, Due Process in China: The Trial of Wei Jingsheng, 9 REV. OF. SOC. L. 55 (1983). To be sure, this was before the 1982 constitution, but freedom of speech was also guaranteed in the 1978 constitution, art. 45, and the people who put Wei in prison are the people who still govern China and who promulgated the 1982 constitution. Wei is still imprisoned. For reports on a number of political prisoners, see AMNESTY INTERNATIONAL, CHINA: VIOLATIONS OF HUMAN RIGHTS 5–51 (1984). One might also note the "Cultural Pollution" campaign of 1983–84. See Schram, Economics in Command? Ideology and Policy Since the Third Plenum, THE CHINA Q. 418, 437–48 (1984). This was used to dampen discussion in at least one university. But citation is otiose. Some of the "freedoms" are so qualified in the text that they are meaningless. Thus, art. 36 guarantees freedom of religion but states that "Religious bodies and religious affairs are not subject to any foreign domination... ." In practice, this means that many persons cannot practice their religion, notably Roman Catholics and Tibetan Buddhists.

19 China is a poor country and does well to keep its citizens from starving to death. It does not always succeed in that. "Retirement" as such is not guaranteed to farmers and perhaps some kinds of workers. All are supposed to get material assistance when they are old. Art. 45. But one hears that one of the reasons peasants are not cooperating with the birth-control program is that they believe sons are the only dependable

social security. It might be added that China has a significant unemployment problem, although it is disguised by such terms as youth waiting for assignment. *See, e.g.,* WENG, *supra* note 9, at 255.

20 The Chinese would of course deny this. I can only say that I have never seen any evidence of independence. Even Professor Weng who has tried to find examples of independent action regards Congress as pretty subservient. *See* WENG, *supra* note 9, at 111.

21 This does not mean that every order from the center is automatically obeyed nor that local organizations have no independence. As a matter of fact, they are often quite resistant and hard to control. But the organizational chart is quite clear. And by and large the center gets what it wants.

22 He is Chairman of the Central Military Commission, which was created by the 1982 constitution, art. 93. This position is subject to the National People's Congress. Art. 63(3).

23 1975 CONST. art. 2; 1978 CONST. art. 2(24).

24 There is quite a lot of that. *See, e.g., PLA Delegates Discuss New Constitution,* SWB (Dec. 3, 1982, FE/7199/C/99):

… said that inclusions of provisions for building socialist spiritual civilization is of great significance. He said communist ideology is the core of socialist spiritual civilization of which Lei Feng was an exemplar … every PLA fighter should emulate Lei Feng, foster a deep love for the motherland and the people, and for labour, science and socialism, display the communist spirit and be a vanguard in building socialist spiritual civilization… .

See also the reactions of Chinese People's Political Consultative Conference observers at the National People's Congress: "all an historic event …," "an achievement gained through a struggle and a summary of experience," "It is paid for with blood." FBIS, Report CPPCC meeting in Renmin R:Bao, in DAILY REPORT K8 (Dec. 9, 1982). Peng Zhen in presenting the constitution to Congress said, "When our one billion people all cultivate the consciousness and habit of observing and upholding the constitution and fight against all acts violating and undermining the Constitution this will become a mighty force." SWB (Dec. 7, 1982, FE/7202/C/16).

25 The preamble, in its last paragraph, states that the constitution "is the fundamental law of the state." It must be taken by all as "the basic norm of conduct." One of the articles by Wang Zhengzhao and Lin Yuhui in a book on the constitution prepared by the People's Daily Press, CHINESE CONSTITUTION, *supra* note 10, at 12, which is entitled *The New Constitution is our Country's Basic Law.* It says that the constitution is the basic law because (1) its content sets out the basic principles of law such as the necessity for constructing socialist modernization, the nature of the state, and the economy, but it does not go into detail; (2) any law that is in conflict with it is without effect; and (3) it is enacted and amended in a different way.

26 The 1954 constitution recognized the existence of state, cooperative, individual, and capitalist ownership, art. 5. The formation of cooperatives was encouraged, arts. 7 & 8. But individual ownership of land by peasants is protected, art. 8. It was anticipated that no more than one-third of the peasant households would form "lower-level producer cooperatives," in which the individuals retained ownership but farmed cooperatively and split the profits, by the end of 1957. However, in 1955 Mao decided that the pace should be accelerated and the country was almost completely collectivized by 1957, having passed through cooperatives into socialist collectives in which there was no individual ownership and peasants were rewarded for their work. Communes that unified political and economic control appeared in 1958. *See* M. MEISSNER, MAO'S CHINA 140–60, 230–41 (1977) [hereinafter cited as MEISSNER]. But the constitutional provisions on land ownership were not changed until 1975. The 1978 constitution stated that there were two types of ownership of the means of production: state

ownership and collective ownership (communes), art. 5. Within the commune there was ownership by: the commune, the production brigade and the production team. Farming of private plots for personal needs subject to predominance of the collective economy was permitted, art. 7. In 1977, prior to the time the constitution was promulgated, "household contracting" had begun in some areas. Under this system the procurement contract was made with an individual household rather than a team or brigade. Once its quota was met, it could dispose of the surplus for its own benefit. The system has many variations. By 1982 it dominated in China. The changes were effected by a series of Central Committee Documents. The constitutional change recognizing (more or less) individual responsibility was promulgated in December 1982. 1982 CONST. art. 14. For a summary of these developments, see Walker, *Chinese Agriculture During the Period of Readjustment 1978–83*, THE CHINA Q. 783, 786–89 (1984).

27 *See* Wang Shuwen, *The Basic Characteristics of the New Constitution*, CHINESE CONSTITUTION, *supra* note 10, at 21. He states that constitutions are important component parts of the superstructure. According to Lenin, there are two types: the "real constitution" and the "written constitution." The real constitution determines the nature, content and character of the written constitution. Wang then indicates how the four written constitutions (the Chinese never call the Common Program a constitution) reflect their real constitutions. The only good ones are those of 1954 and 1982. The latter reflects the conclusions of the Third Plenum such as the four basic policies and the Four Modernizations.

28 1954 CONST. art. 1.

29 1975 CONST. art. 1. This change in phrasing was the principal subject of the publicity in favor of the 1975 constitution when it was promulgated. *See* Cohen, *China's Changing Constitution*, 76 THE CHINA Q. 794 (1978) [hereinafter cited as Cohen].

30 Art. 1.

31 Enacted July 1, 1979, translated in SWB (July 16, 1979, FE6/63/C/22).

32 The preamble to the 1982 constitution keeps the concept of the class struggle, but only just. After making it clear that the exploiting classes no longer exist as a class, it states that the class struggle will have to go on for a long time against foreign and domestic enemies. However, in the official commentary, it is pointed out that according to the 1981 census, 99.97% of those over 18 years old had the right to vote and be elected. In other words, they were not "exploiters" who had been deprived of their political rights. The exploiting classes have diminished greatly in size. Still the country has to fight the enemy within and without. So, dictatorship is preserved. *Id.* at 56.

33 The Common Program was enacted by the Chinese People's Political Consultative Conference on September 29, 1949. 1 COLLECTED LAWS AND REGULATIONS OF THE CHINESE CENTRAL PEOPLE'S GOVERNMENT [Zhongyang Renmin Zhengfu Faling Huipian] 17 (1945–50). The People's Republic of China came into being on October 1, 1949. Central People's Government Announcement of the People's Republic of China, *id.* at 28.

34 Art. 1.

35 Art. 2.

36 Art. 3.

37 Art. 6.

38 Art. 7.

39 Art. 11.

40 Part IV, Economic Policy, arts. 26–40, sets out the government's policy, which is, essentially, to permit and encourage capitalism under state control, while making the state economy the principal factor. Art. 32 deals with workers' participation in management.

41 MEISSNER, *supra* note 26, at 59, 60, 73–80, 92–97.
42 Art. 1.
43 Art. 7 states that the state encourages, "guides and helps" the development of cooperatives, which are "the chief means for the transformation of individual farming and individual handicrafts." Art. 8 provides that the state "guides and helps" individual peasants to form cooperatives. The policy of the state in regard to rich peasant economy is to eliminate it. Under art. 9, handicraft workers are to be "guide[d] and help[ed]" into cooperatives. Under art. 10, the good aspects of capitalist industry and commerce are permitted but the state "encourages and guides their transformation into various forms of state-capitalist economy."
44 Art. 10.
45 Art. 19.
46 D. PERKINS, MARKET CONTROL AND PLANNING IN COMMUNIST CHINA 13–17 (1966).
47 JOINT PUBLICATIONS RESEARCH SERVICE, MISCELLANY OF MAO TSE-TUNG THOUGHT [Maoze dong sixiang wan sui] (1949–1968) PART I, 138 (Feb. 20, 1974). It is reported that Mao said on December 12, 1958, "The issue of integrating politics and the commune, for example, was not passed by the People's Congress, nor is it in the constitution. Many parts of the constitution are obsolete, but it cannot be revised now. As for surpassing the U.S., we will formulate a written constitution."
48 The Greap Leap is discussed in MEISSNER, *supra* note 26, at 204–52.
49 The Cultural Revolution is discussed in MEISSNER, *supra* note 26, at 309–58.
50 See the discussion of "old classes" in Whyte, *Inequality and Stratification in China*, 64 THE CHINA Q. 698–705 (1976).
51 See report on Jiang Qing by Roxanne Witke in COMRADE CHIANG CH'ING 339 (1977): Chiang Ch'ing concluded her remarks on a cherished subject, the problem of the Ego. That subjective aspect of revolutionary transformation was always (and most emphatically in our interview) at the forefront of her consciousness, and seemingly was her sense of the heart of the Cultural Revolution. Making revolution, she said in effect, was simultaneously an introverted and extroverted experience, a personal and public affair. Conflicts were not only external—between the enemy and ourselves—or internal—among ourselves, as Chairman Mao had argued. They must be waged *within* oneself—*against* the so-called Ego.
52 1975 CONST. preamble.
53 Though there is some question whether or not Mao approved of it since he did not attend either the meeting of the Party Central Committee prior to the meeting of the National People's Congress at which the constitution was promulgated, or the Congress itself. *See* M-h Yao, *The Fourth National People's Congress and Peiping's Future Direction* in THE NEW CONSTITUTION OF COMMUNIST CHINA 324, 327–8 (M. Lindsay ed. 1976).
54 There is no reference to capitalism or, for that matter, to landlords except as persons deprived of political rights. Art. 14.
55 Art. 2.
56 Art. 5.
57 Art. 7. Private plots are permitted so long as the "development and absolute predominance of the collective economy of the people's commune are ensured." Art. 9 permits ownership of income from work, savings, houses, and "other means of livelihood."
58 Art. 11.
59 Art. 12.
60 Art. 13.
61 Art. 22.
62 Art. 25.
63 The discussion of the campaign against Deng Xiaoping is based upon *Two Systems, Lessons of Teng's Crimes*, CHINA NEWS ANALYSIS (1976). *See also* B. BRUGGER, CHINA: RADICALISM TO REVISION 1962–1979, 170–96 (1981).

64 *See, e.g., The Great Cultural Revolution Will Shine Forever*, PEKING REV., at 14 (July 2, 1976), *The Making of a Young Actress, id.; Advance Along the Road of the Great Proletarian Cultural Revolution, id.* at 16.

65 *See, e.g.*, the translation of the official commentary to the 1975 constitution in SELECTED LEGAL DOCUMENTS OF THE PEOPLE'S REPUBLIC OF CHINA 93–95 (J. En-Pao Wang ed. 1976), where it is said that "our main task is to ... persist in continued revolution ..." and a statement of Mao Zedong is quoted: "... there are still classes, class contradictions and class struggles... ."

66 See B. BRUGGER, *supra* note 63, at 194–96, 201, 202.

67 *See* Pepper, *Chinese Education After Mao: Two Steps Forward, Two Steps Back and Begin Again?*, THE CHINA Q. 1 (1980).

68 See, for instance, the statement about a 26.8% increase in exports in the first half of 1979 and the establishment of new institutions to encourage trade and the import of technology, in *Quarterly Chronicle and Documentation*, THE CHINA Q. 881, 886 (1979).

69 *See Quarterly Chronicle and Documentation: (b) The Campaign Against Lin Piao and the 'Gang of Four'*, and *id.* (c) *The Leadership*, THE CHINA Q. 157, 158, 173 (1979).

70 Deng was rehabilitated and reappeared as Vice-Chairman of the Party by mid-1977. B. BRUGGER, *supra* note 63, at 202–03.

71 The 1978 Constitution is discussed in detail in Cohen, *supra* note 29.

72 1975 CONST. art. 7.

73 1978 CONST. art. 7.

74 1975 CONST. art. 10.

75 1975 CONST. art. 11.

76 1975 CONST. art. 12.

77 1978 CONST. art. 13.

78 1978 CONST. art. 43.

79 1978 CONST. art. 41.

80 *Id.*

81 1978 CONST. art. 22.

82 1978 CONST. art. 25.

83 1975 CONST. art. 17 & 18.

84 Cohen, *supra* note 29, at 809–12.

85 The Third Plenum is discussed in B. BRUGGER, *supra* note 63, at 218–19.

86 Proposal of the Central Committee of the Chinese Communist Party Regarding the Revision of the Constitution and the Establishment of a Constitutional Revision Committee [*Zhongguo Gongzhan Dang Zhongyang Weiyuanhui Guanyu Xingai Xianfa He Chengli Xianfa Xingai Weiyuanhui*] of August 30, 1980, in CONSTITU-TIONAL MATERIALS, *supra* note 1, at 375.

87 Resolution of the Third Session of the Fifth National People's Congress of the People's Republic of China Regarding the Revision of the Constitution and the Establishment of a Constitution Revision Committee [*Zhonghua Renmin Gongheguo Ti Wu Jie Quanguo Renmin Daibiao Da Hui Ti San Ze Huiyi Guanyu Xingai Xianfa He Chengle Xianfa Xiugai Weihuanhui*] of September 10, 1980, CONSTITUTIONAL MATERIALS, *supra* note 1, at 379.

88 *See Quarterly Chronicle and Documentation*, THE CHINA Q. 547, 548 (1981).

89 *See* Schell, *A Reporter at Large: The Wind of Wanting to Go It Alone*, THE NEW YORKER 65–73 (Jan. 23, 1984) [hereinafter cited as Schell]. *See also supra* note 26. The Chinese would, of course, deny that land farmed under the individual responsi-bility system is "owned" by the cultivator because it cannot be sold or even rented. Even if the peasants were not busy finding ways around these prohibitions—as one assumes they are—the rights they do have constitute ownership as this term is

defined in the RESTATEMENT OF PROPERTY § 10 comment b (1936). The recent *Circular of the Central Committee of the Chinese Communist Party on Rural Work During 1984*, THE CHINA Q. 132 (1985), allows households to enter into contracts to use land for 15 years or more. This is "ownership" by almost any definition. While land "may not be bought or sold, may not be leased to a third party and may not be transferred as building plots for housing or for any other non-agricultural use," *id.*, the contract can be transferred with the consent of the collective. *Id.* It is said that the peasants expect the leasehold to become "property" after 15 years and in the meantime there is a brisk trade in them. Kueh, *The Economics of the 'Second Land Reform' in China*, THE CHINA Q. 122, 128 nn. 10–12 (1985).

90 The Joint Venture Law is available in both English and Chinese in 1 CHINA'S FOREIGN ECONOMIC LEGISLATION 1 (1982).

91 *See* Schell, *supra* note 89, at 43–58.

92 As to possible foreign ownership of shares in Chinese concerns, see *Peking firms may seek Hong Kong listing*. South China Morning Post, July 6, 1984, at 1.

93 *See* WENG, *supra* note 9, at 251–54.

94 This is based on CHINA NEWS ANALYSIS No. 1044 (June 18, 1976). *See also* B. BRUGGER, *supra* note 63, at 177–95.

95 CHINA NEWS ANALYSIS, No. 1044 (June 18, 1976).

96 *Id.*

97 1982 CONST. preamble.

98 The Four Modernizations are: industry, agriculture, defense, and science and technology.

99 1982 CONST. art. 11.

100 1982 CONST. art. 14.

101 1982 CONST. art. 16.

102 1982 CONST. art. 18.

103 1982 CONST. art. 25.

104 FBIS, DAILY REPORT K8 (Dec. 9, 1982).

105 Art. 126.

106 Consider for example the treatment of art. 5, which provides that "no law ... shall contravene the Constitution," and all "state organs, the armed forces," etc., "must abide by the Constitution and the law." Both the Congress, art. 62(2), and its Standing Committee, art. 67(1), are to enforce this apparently. The problem of constitutionality is discussed in one standard commentary under the chapter heading "The new constitution strengthens the stipulations for defending the constitution" [*Xin Xianfa Zhajiangle Xianfa Bao Zhangde Guiding*]. The authors list four ways in which the new constitution provides this protection: (1) it strengthens the supervisory power of the Congress and its Standing Committee; (2) it gives the standing committee power to declare acts and regulations unconstitutional; (3) it provides that all agencies and citizens must respect the constitution; and (4) it requires a supermajority of Congress to amend the constitution. There is no discussion of how all this will work. There seems to be a feeling that if there are words in a statute that say someone has a "right," then he does. *See* W. ZHAOZHE & C. YUNSHENG, GUIDE TO THE NEW CONSTITUTION [*Xin Xianfa Jianghua*] 224–27 (1983).

107 *See supra* note 19. *See also The Use of the Legal Weapon*, CHINA NEWS ANALYSIS (June 18, 1984).

108 The 1982 Party Constitution, adopted three months before the State Constitution, is in harmony with this view. It provides in the preamble that "The Party must conduct its activities within the limits permitted by the Constitution and the laws of the state." 25 BEIJING REV. at 8 (1982). In 1980 when this constitution was being drafted, Deng Xiaoping, in a speech delivered to the Political Bureau of the Party, stated that the Party should be separated from the government. The Party would establish

general principles but would strengthen the state structure. Policy would not be a substitute for government. HSIA & JOHNSON, THE CHINESE COMMUNIST PARTY CONSTITUTION OF 1982: DENG ZIAOPING'S PROGRAM FOR MODERNIZATION (1984).

109 Speech by Peng Zhen printed in Chinese edition of 1982 constitution, *supra* note 1, at 66–69.

110 The Constitution of the Republic of China (Taiwan) provides for direct election to the Legislative Yüan—the body that actually legislates, art. 64, as well as to the Congress, art. 26. As indicated in the text, Dr. Sun wanted elections only to the Congress, which was to elect the Legislative Yuan. *See* P.M.A. LINEBARGER, THE POLITICAL DOCTRINES OF SUN YATSEN 89–121, 209–23 (1937) and W.Y. TSAO, THE CONSTITUTIONAL STRUCTURE OF MODERN CHINA 96–113, 130–45 (1947). The Tsao book reprints the translations of the texts of the Chinese Constitution of 1946 (in force in Taiwan), *id.* at 275, and the draft constitution of 1937, much closer to Dr. Sun's ideas, *id.* at 238.

111 The most obvious difference is that Dr. Sun proposed to have the government administration divided into five divisions, or Yüan: Legislative, Judicial, Administrative, Examination and Control. Y-S SUN, SAN MIN CHU-1 144–49 [Lecture Six]. The first three divisions are taken from the U.S. Constitution and the last two from traditional Chinese institutions. The table of organization for the government established by the 1982 constitution of the People's Republic of China envisages a Congress which formally enacts legislation that is actually drafted by its standing committee and special committees subordinate to it, not a Legislative Yüan that is quite separate. The government supervised by the congress has three or four parts: the State Council (equivalent to Dr. Sun's Administrative Yüan); Central Military Commission; People's Courts; and People's Procuracy. (The last two are treated together). On the other hand, one of the principal features of Dr. Sun's program for China was the idea of "tutelage." China was not yet ready for direct elections nationwide because it had no experience with democracy. Hence the Guomindang controlled the country and conducted elections first at the local or county level. When all the counties in a province were electing their local government, the province was then ready to have province-wide elections. When half the provinces were democratic, there could be elections to Congress. LINEBARGER, *supra* note 104, at 210–214. The system of indirect elections established in the 1982 constitution is certainly compatible with this, although it is not exactly the same. It is curious that the idea of a standing committee of the People's Congress, which was rejected by the drafters of the Guomindang constitution, was strongly advocated—for much the same reasons given by Peng Zhen—by Professor Tsao, who seems clearly to be a disciple of Dr. Sun. TSAO, *supra* note 110, at 112–13.

112 See preamble provisions on China's long history and Sun's role in overthrowing the Manchus.

113 *See* WENG, *supra* note 9, at 135.

114 L. LaDanay, *China's New Power Centre?*, FAR EASTERN ECON. REV. 38 (1984).

115 *See* H-Y LEE, THE POLITICS OF THE CHINESE CULTURAL REVOLUTION 1–10 (1978).

116 For my views on the system as of 1975, see Jones, *A Possible Model for the Criminal Trial in the People's Republic of China*, 24 AM. J. COMP. L. 229 (1976). See Peng, *Importance of Improving China's Legislation*, BEIJING REV. no. 35, 16 (1984), for an official view of the legal situation in China since liberation.

117 *See, e.g.*, Li, *Legal Education Surges Ahead*, 26 BEIJING REV. 22 (1985); *Spare-time college helps train judges*, China Daily, Feb. 18, 1983; *Socialist legal system making good progress, id.*, Dec. 12, 1983; *Major plan adopted to train jurists, id.*, Jan. 7, 1984.

118 For example, CONSTITUTIONAL MATERIALS consists of five volumes and includes most of the major constitutional documents of the western world, including the

Magna Carta, The Petition of Right, the U.S. Declaration of Independence and Constitution, and the Declaration of the Rights of Man. It had an initial press run of 15,000 copies and was freely available throughout the country.

119 As a "trial" it was a farce, but it was interesting that the Chinese used a public show trial to get rid of defeated opponents. Previously, people just disappeared. Sometimes they were publicly attacked, but there was no trial-like proceeding. For the early purge of Gao Gang and Rao Shushi, see F. TEIWES, POLITICS AND PURGES IN CHINA 166–210 (1979). Two prominent leaders were accused primarily of "factionalism" and trying to seize power. They were accused anonymously at the Fourth Plenum of the Seventh Central Committee Meeting in 1954, and were publicly attacked at the National Conference of the Party in 1955. Sometime in between Gao committed suicide. There was a "verdict," but no trial. The Teiwes book discusses all of the important purges up to the Cultural Revolution.

120 Of course if one had to guess, it would be that what is likely to emerge is something like the system in the Soviet Union: stable, but very authoritarian and controlled, and rather corrupt. The Soviets are said to believe that China will have to adopt their system, though of course they do not characterize it as I have. See T. Oka, China charts its own course, The Christian Science Monitor, June 30-July 6, 1984, at 14 (int'l ed.).

121 This present campaign to "consolidate" the Party has in fact been characterized as a purge by one well-informed observer. See HSIA & JOHNSON, supra note 108, at 30–31.

THE DEVELOPMENT OF CONSTITUTIONALISM IN THE TRANSITION OF CHINESE SOCIETY

Dingjian Cai

Source: *Columbia Journal of Asian Law* 19:1 (2005): 1–29.

I The transitions and crises of Chinese society

China's economy has been growing at a rate of approximately 8% annually over the last decade, and its GDP has reached about ¥13.65 trillion. These dramatic economic developments have been accompanied by great changes in people's lives, especially in the cities. In contrast to the "proletarian" status they held in the communist past, citizens now hold private interests in real property, business enterprises, and personal investments.[1] Many people now enjoy a happier, higher quality of life than they ever knew in the past. Especially in the country's developed regions, lifestyles and consumption patterns have reached an international standard. The achievements of China's economic development are indeed remarkable.

Nonetheless, with economic development come social problems. With a Gini coefficient recently reaching 0.5,[2] the income gap between the haves and the have-nots in China continues to widen. In addition, unemployment plagues the Chinese economy.[3] In some extreme cases, living conditions have not improved but have in fact deteriorated.[4] Pressing issues of national concern include environmental destruction, stagnation—even decline—of education and public health services, and increasingly problematic issues surrounding public security in rural areas.

A series of contentious social problems has appeared over the course of China's modernization. A large floating population has become a significant minority in the cities, and urban residents often discriminate against these migrants. Adolescents succumb to addiction, prostitution, and destitution. Public order in China's vast rural areas is breaking down. Traditional administrative organs and governmental authorities have weakened, whereas modern governance is far from established. The relationship between peasants and those in authority is often unstable, with social order maintained mainly by administrative punishment and coercive measures. Sharp and violent conflicts sometimes break out between peasants and local government representatives.

Like so many other elements of Chinese culture, corruption has changed with the times, despite extensive central government campaigns to stamp it out. These changes in the nature of corruption in China may be described in four general ways. First, corruption is more widespread than it was before. It concerns not only a small handful of government officials, but almost every government agency. It is often considered normal for official to take unfair advantage of their authority and resources.[5] Second, several cases have indicated a high degree of collusion among a large number of cadres. The Ma De case[6] in Heilongjiang province, for example, involved hundreds of government officials. Third, signs indicate that corruption is reaching increasingly higher levels of government. According to statistics released by the Central Discipline Review Commission and the Ministry of Supervision, 166,795 cases were investigated in 2004 alone. As a result of those investigations, 170,850 people were punished: 5966 were county-level officials, 431 were municipal-level, and sixteen others were provincial-level.[7] Fourth, the problem of judicial corruption is more severe now than it has been in the past. In 2004 alone, two members of a Higher Level People's Court and two officials in a Higher Level People's Procuratorate, both provincial-level institutions, were investigated for corruption and bribery.[8] In the same year, 35,031 government officials were tried for corruption and bribery, and more than 1275 of those bribery and appropriation cases involved more than ¥1 million.[9]

The mechanisms of social justice in China have lost their ability to function. First, inequitable policies perpetuate the unfair distribution of wealth. For example, preferential treatment towards particular regional economies leads to significant disparities in regional economic development.[10] Additionally, officials discriminate against private enterprises, especially where foreign trade is concerned. Some local governments ignore guidelines and standards regarding labor and, as a result, investors obtain disproportionately high profits while "bloody factory" and "bloody mine" scandals prevail.[11] Government regulators permit inadequately qualified companies to be listed on the stock market to rope in capital from ordinary shareholders. To a great extent, the prosperity of Chinese cities is due to direct administrative interference from the government, while the greater Chinese masses, including a disproportionate segment of rural peasants and disenfranchised urban residents, end up footing the bill.[12]

The unfair allocation of resources is the result of three major social forces. First, state-owned assets have been carved up as a result of severe upheavals accompanying the restructuring of these assets. Second, inappropriate allocation policies have led to unfair income distribution. Those economic areas monopolized by government entities—finance, telecommunications, and air travel, for example—enjoy disproportionately high profits. Managers in state-owned enterprises set their own salaries, and not surprisingly they usually decide to pay themselves a salary hundreds of times higher than that of ordinary workers. A third source of inequality is in the realm of education. Instead of guaranteeing that each rural child receives an education, the government instead diverts resources to guaranteeing a high standard of education in cities. Consequently, unequal distribution of educational resources is widespread: while universities continue to expand, they do so at the expense of providing basic educational services to primary and secondary schools in the countryside.[13] In addition, discriminatory admissions policies based upon testing standards that vary by geographic region perpetuate severe inequities.

Serious problems also abound regarding injustice in the legal system. Exorbitant litigation fees keep many parties with legitimate grievances from having their day in court. Some trans-regional disputes over economic matters cannot be settled because of endemic local protectionism. Corrupt judges perpetuate greater injustices, which in turn lead to an increasing number of appeals and petitions to higher authorities.[14]

In addition to the improper exercise of discretion in the judiciary, China's social realm bears witness to widespread discrimination and injustice as well. Due in part to the labor surplus in China's market economy, employment discrimination is rampant. In many cities, shopkeepers explicitly state that anyone not meeting certain height requirements need not apply for employment. These discriminatory practices are based on a number of criteria, including region of origin, official residence status, gender, age, socioeconomic class, and appearance.

In sum, social stability has not kept pace with economic development or improvements in living conditions. Indeed, social conflicts have become even sharper precisely because of the discrepancy between economic development and social justice. New conflicts arise while old problems remain.

The incidence of people filing administrative petitions, or "letters and visits," has increased dramatically as well. The National Letters and Visits Bureau received 214,508 petitions in 2001, 370,219 in 2002, and 488,974 in 2004.[15] In the past, complaints concentrated on such issues as non-payment of social security benefits for employees of state-owned enterprises, collection of illegal fees in rural areas, and crude implementation of central policies by local officials. Complaints are now about judicial injustice and corruption, expropriation of rural land, and the increasing problem of forced evictions (拆迁, *chaiqian*). Other problems include illegitimate village elections, increased social discontent, and occasional mass protests.

Meanwhile, new social problems have gained prominence. The unemployment rate among recent college graduates has increased as they enter the labor market at unsustainable rates.[16] Other problems include villagers' fights for self-governance and their struggle to protect local natural resources.

Still more problems spring from the degradation of traditional morality and culture. The role of Confucianism in Chinese society has been a constant point of contention since the mid-19th century. In the post-Mao "reform and opening" era, people have lost faith in communism, while the central authorities continue to reject Western values. This moral vacuum leads to the exclusive pursuit of individual interests and personal wealth.

In the annals of comparative history, crises of the sort that China now faces have usually indicated the birth of constitutionalism. They are usually precipitated by inequitable distribution of resources in transitional periods, which in turn motivates the quest for the rule of law. This quest increasingly gains momentum which, while possibly constituting a real crisis for Chinese society, may be the very force for promoting constitutionalism within China.

II Bottom-up efforts for constitutionalism

With economic development come new demands for political participation. As personal assets increase and economic entities privatize and multiply, individual interests and civil society are taking shape. Individual interests lead to individual quests for civil rights. Chinese citizens have begun to fight for their rights spontaneously and consciously via such avenues as social groups, media outlets, judicial organs, and political deliberative forums. This vibrant activity illustrates the impact of social forces on the political regime of China. The quests for human rights, democracy, and rule of law become the bases of constitutionalism. These forces include the following factors.

A Spontaneous political participation

1 "I want to be a representative"

In March 2003, when elections were held for representatives in Shenzhen's People's Congress, a remarkable event happened: twelve ordinary citizens registered as candidates and two of them were ultimately elected.[17] This had a great impact on Chinese politics and received intense attention from national media outlets, legal scholars, and the public in general.[18] Similar volunteer candidates appeared in Beijing and Hubei province. In Beijing, for example, twenty two citizens registered for the election by the end of 2003, and three of them were elected.[19] In Qianjiang, a city in Hubei province, forty one citizens, including twelve peasants, ran in the local election.[20] Such efforts are remarkable in the development of Chinese democracy.

Why have such phenomena become the highlights of democratic development in China? Campus elections became regular events in the beginning of the reform era;[21] those elections, however, were primarily regarded as merely the idealistic political actions of students, whereas the events surrounding the 2003 elections arose from the spontaneous quest to vindicate the interests of ordinary citizens, including peasants. As one commentator said, "If the elections in Peking University were idealistic, this time they rose from practical interests and claims."[22]

Typically, candidates for National People's Congress representatives are appointed by the Communist Party and hence "elected" in accordance with the Party's plans. Until recently, no independent candidates were allowed to participate in the process. The reason for the recent emergence of these independent candidates is that the volunteer candidates want to protect their economic rights by enhancing their political status. The candidates are often white-collar professionals who have benefited from the market economy with above-average incomes, and who maintain close relationships with the electorate.[23] Most of them are motivated by an awareness of the problems of community management, and wish to resolve these problems as People's Congress representatives. In the past, responsibility for resolving these issues fell to the government and relevant work units. Now, however, with the withdrawal of the government from many areas of civic life, it is up to the residents themselves to work out a solution. An intermediary is therefore necessary for these individuals to communicate and cooperate with the government. Representatives of the People's Congress have become such intermediaries: they speak for the residents and fight for their interests.[24]

What is the constitutional significance of such spontaneous political participation? It is in fact a manifestation of the reformist trend toward an electoral system, and a challenge to the appointment mechanism of the Communist Party. Some experts maintain that such bottom-up initiatives in Shenzhen are activating internal democratic mechanisms inherent in China's Constitution, indicating a middle class initiative and willingness to participate in politics and to protect their political rights.[25] With the development of the socialist market economy, such "Shenzhen phenomena" demonstrate the inevitability of establishing democratic mechanisms in China.

2 The representatives are speaking out

For a long time, becoming a representative of the People's Congress has been a political favor bestowed by powerbrokers in the Communist Party. To a great extent, being a representative was a matter of Party appointment, rather than of the will of the voters. As a result, representatives had no reason to feel accountable to their constituency, and few critical or opposing opinions were expressed in the People's Congress. In general, the institution had been considered a "voting machine."

This has changed dramatically in recent years. Representatives' accountability has been enhanced through recent electoral processes, especially among those representatives nominated by their constituency. Such representatives therefore dare to speak out.

For example, in March 2004, before the convention of the National People's Congress ("NPC"), Zhou Xiaoguang, the representative of Yiwu city in Zhejiang province, placed advertisements in local media outlets inviting her constituents to submit suggestions for government action. This is a remarkable move toward greater responsiveness and accountability among representatives, and such instances are hardly isolated. In recent years, increasing numbers of representatives from throughout the country have been speaking out for their electorate. When the People's Congress convenes, representatives propose bills reflecting their constituents' interests and requests, and after the session, they visit those constituents to assure them that their rights are being protected.[26] Wang Yuancheng, for example, identifies himself as a national representative of migrant workers.[27] During the convention in Beijing, he visited several construction sites to acquaint himself with the opinions of migrant workers, and proposed to the National People's Congress a number of bills guaranteeing employment rights. A national representative from Hunan province, Wang Tian, spent ¥10,000 to hire legal experts for assistance in drafting an NPC bill.[28] Simultaneously, legal experts, NGOs, and lawyers offer their legislative services to representatives, an emerging phenomenon similar to lobbying in Western countries.

Conversely, representatives who do not perform their appropriate functions are forced to resign or are dismissed by the government.[29] Being a representative is no longer solely a political honor, but has become a position with genuine duties and obligations. Both the growth of representatives' accountability and the increasing awareness of the electorate signal hope for the development of China's mechanism of democratic representation.

3 Public participation: hearings

Prior to 1996, the concept of a hearing was alien to most Chinese people. In that year, the Law on Administrative Punishment required that a hearing be held before the imposition of any sanction concerning citizens' property in excess of a small fine.[30] In the following year, the Price Law required a public hearing before any price increase of certain important services or products.[31] The problem, however, was that such requirements were seldom enforced. That changed on January 18, 2001, when Qiao Zhanxiang, a lawyer in Hebei province, challenged the state to implement the long-neglected hearing system. He claimed that the Ministry of Railways had raised train fares during the Spring Festival of 2001 without a prior public hearing, a violation of the Price Law and an infringement upon his legal rights. He applied to the Ministry for an administrative reconsideration of the price hike, as well as a review of the legality of the State Planning Commission's Reply on Questions Regarding the Implementation of Government-Guided Pricing on Train Fares. The Ministry accepted—and later rejected—the appeal. Despite the fact that Qiao's appeal ultimately failed, it had a significant impact on the role of public hearings in Chinese civic life. When the Railway Ministry wanted to raise fares again during the 2002 Spring Festival holiday season, the State Planning Commission held a public hearing and broadcasted it live on CCTV. Were it not for Qiao's appeal the previous year, such a hearing would probably never have occurred. Similarly, his appeal raised awareness among ordinary Chinese citizens of their rights in the government decision-making process. Since then, extensive public hearings have been held on such issues as price fixing, administrative punishment, and urban planning.

Public hearings are held not only on administrative matters, but on legislative issues as well. According to the 2000 Law on Legislation, the public can take part in hearings on important legislation. The first legislative hearing was held in Guangzhou in 2000, and the practice soon spread to other regions. By the end of 2004, legislative hearings had become commonplace in local people's congresses, having been held in more than twenty provinces.[32]

Both administrative and legislative hearings have been established as important mechanisms of public participation in state affairs. With such a system, democracy is no longer some unattainable realm of civic life, but is instead becoming a process in which every citizen may be directly involved.

B Media oversight and public opinion

Among the most dramatic changes in recent years in the active role played by the Chinese media and public opinion, including communication via the Internet, in monitoring government activities and protecting civil rights. The 2003 Sun Zhigang case,[33] for example, is a prominent example of cooperation between the media and legal experts. Three graduate students of law appealed to the NPC Standing Committee, calling for constitutional review of the State Council's Detention and Repatriation Measure Regarding Vagrant and Mendicant People. Under nationwide media pressure, the State Council abolished the measure. This is only one of many cases in recent years in which media scrutiny facilitated protection of civil rights.

Other cases that fell under the media spotlight include the Shenyang "Liu Yong case,"[34] the "BMW case,"[35] the Hebei "Entrepreneur Sun Dawu Illegal Financing case,"[36] the Bazhou city "Police False Imprisonment, Murder and Concealment of the Body case,"[37] and Hunan's Jiahe County "Violent Demolition case."[38] The resolution of these cases in the public interest would not have happened without media oversight. In addition, the media has published accounts of many other instances of corruption and liability-triggering accidents, resulting in many government officials being held accountable under the law.[39] Media and public opinion have become influential social forces and have dramatic influence over government decisions.

Not all the impacts of media scrutiny are positive, of course. Especially in judicial cases, media exposure might prove to be a harmful intervention into the realm of fair adjudication.[40] In general, however, the media's emerging role as watchdog is an important contribution to China's democratic development. Heretofore, public opinion and the media had never been so powerful as to influence legislation or government action. It is important, therefore, to acknowledge the positive role that the media plays in the process of democratization, while simultaneoulsy recognizing that a small number of media outlets may abuse their prerogatives. Though not all media outlets exercise the appropriate degree of judgment, Chinese society nevertheless needs the voice of the media and public opinion. The emergence of independent media supervision of the government is an important force for the development of constitutionalism in China.

C Constitutional protection of civil rights

1 Challenging the system of constitutional review

The Chinese Constitution has long been regarded not as a legal vehicle for the protection of citizens' rights, but as merely a political document. The 2001 Qi Yuling case, however, breathed some life into this document. The Supreme People's Court ("SPC") issued a historical judicial interpretation, holding that the defendant in this case should bear civil liability for infringement upon the constitutional right to an education, via violation of the right of name.[41] The role of constitutional rights in the realm of Chinese law has since become a popular topic in both academic and popular discourse. Though some legal experts question whether this is a real constitutional case,[42] its significance lies in the fact that it was the first interpretation from the SPC explicitly endorsing lawsuits with constitutional claims.[43] This is a significant stride toward the actualization of constitutional rights.

The Qi Yuling interpretation initiated a domino effect, with a series of cases concerning constitutional rights brought in the following years, the most notable of which were the "Three High School Graduates vs. the Ministry of Education case"[44] and the "Hepatitis B Carriers case."[45] Unlike the Qi Yuling case, an application of the Constitution to protect individual rights in a civil matter, the "High School Graduates vs. Ministry of Education case" was a deliberate attempt by lawyers and academics to activate constitutional review: it was impact litigation with Chinese characteristics.

The petition submitted to the NPC Standing Committee by three JSD students following the Sun Zhigang case is one effort in which citizens succeeded in challenging the system of constitutional review. In the petition, they asked the Standing Committee to review the constitutionality of the 1982 Detention and Repatriation Measure. Ultimately, the government abolished the measure, in part because of constitutional complaints by citizens; this is unprecedented in the history of the PRC.[46] Its success is significant both theoretically and practically. In the past, constitutional review was no more than a topic in constitutional law classes; few citizens knew what the phrase even meant. One of the rationales for bringing this petition, therefore, was to compel the Standing Committee to activate the mechanism.[47] Though the parties involved failed to meet this goal, it still served as an important lesson in constitutional law for Chinese leaders: that the Constitutional imposes a constraint on state power. It also sparked interest in constitutional issues among ordinary citizens. Constitutional review has now become a topic of public discourse, and citizens are learning how to protect their basic rights via this mechanism. This case has greatly enhanced the authority of the Constitution.

The key factors that contributed to success in this instance are: First, the parties seized the opportunity when the leadership was "highly emphasizing the Constitution"[48] and made strategic use of this discourse. Second, the apparent conflicts between the 1982 Measure and the 2000 Law on Legislation provided a strong basis for their petition.[49] Finally, the media played a key role in this process: its extensive coverage of this case exerted great social pressure on the government.

Emboldened by the qualified success of the Sun Zhigang case, reformers subsequently filed a series of complaints. For instance, tens of thousands of Hepatitis B carriers demanded that the State Council undertake a constitutional review of the Provisional Statute of Civil Servants, in which the Standard of Civil Servant's Health Examination is purportedly discriminatory. Similarly, other complaints filed by female civil servants demanded constitutional review of a statute articulating gender-based disparities in the retirement age. Thousands of citizens appealed to the Standing Committee regarding the constitutionality of the State Council's Management Measure on Housing Demolition and related local regulations.[50] During the constitutional amendment process in March 2003, the NPC passed an amendment on the protection of private property, directly advancing citizens' constitutional rights and bolstering ordinary citizens' appeals to the Constitution in attempts to protect their private property. For instance, a Beijing resident tried to protect his house from demolition by posting the Constitution on his front door.[51] Another case involves the protection of villagers' constitutional rights in Guangzhou's Xiaoguwei village.[52] Though not all of these efforts succeeded, they were still significant in that they attempted to cite the Constitution in the vindication of citizens' rights.

These cases show that the Constitution, formerly a document significant only for politicians and therefore detached from ordinary citizens, now has a real potential to become a powerful legal weapon to constrain the government and protect individuals' constitutional rights.

2 Anti-discrimination litigation

Similar to the challenges to the system of constitutional review, anti-discrimination lawsuits have become another venue in which legal experts promote constitutionalism. According to the Constitution, the authority of constitutional review belongs to the legislature, namely the NPC and its Standing Committee. The problem with this mechanism, however, is that the NPC has not exercised this authority. An alternative to this dilemma, therefore, is for litigants to assert constitutional rights via administrative litigation. Under the Administrative Litigation Law, citizens can bring lawsuits only in relation to concrete rather than abstract administrative actions—in other words, they may complain about the specific application of laws and regulations to them, but not about the content of laws and regulations themselves. As a result, constitutional review of laws and regulations through the court system is not permitted. Issues relating to discrimination, however, are directly related to constitutional rights, and so they become areas where breakthroughs in constitutional litigation may happen.

Employment discrimination on the basis of residence or migrant status is common in contemporary China. The field is rife with instances of discrimination based on immutable characteristics such as gender, height, and physical attractiveness. These issues concern citizens' basic constitutional rights. Though anti-discrimination litigation is not recognized by law as falling within the scope of acceptable cases, the constant occurrence of this type of litigation is catalyzing systemic progress.

China's first anti-discrimination case was *Jiang Tao v. The People's Bank of China*.[53] In December 2001, the Chengdu Branch of the People's Bank of China advertised in local media to recruit clerks. In the advertisement, it stated certain qualifications for the position, including education level and major area of study. In addition to these qualifications, it specified a minimum height requirement of 168 centimeters for men and 155 centimeters for women. Jiang Tao, a graduate from Sichuan University's School of Law, was 165 centimeters tall and therefore automatically ineligible for the position. He considered this a form of discrimination in violation of his constitutional right to equal protection.[54] The Wuhou District Level People's Court dismissed the case on May 21, 2002 on the grounds that it did not fall within the scope of acceptable administrative cases, and that, because the bank had cancelled the height requirement after the suit began, Jiang's claim was rendered moot.

In a similar July 2002 case, eight law students from Sichuan University brought suit against the management committee for the park at Emei Mountain.[55] The committee set the admission fee for local students at ¥10, whereas the price of admission for other students was ¥80. The students saw this as discrimination on the basis of home region and brought suit against the committee. Their suit asked for an apology as well as an injunction against such regional pricing discrimination. The local court dismissed the case on the rationale that it lacked a legal basis.

The most influential case in this regard was *Zhang Xianzhu v. The Wuhu City Bureau of Personnel*.[56] In June 2003, Zhang ranked first on both written and oral exams for the recruitment of civil servants in Anhui Province. The personnel bureau rejected his application because Zhang is a Hepatitis B carrier. He appealed to Anhui's Office of Personnel for administrative reconsideration, but the appeal was promptly dismissed. Zhang then filed suit in local court, accusing the personnel bureau of discrimination against Hepatitis B carriers. The court ruled on April 2, 2004 for the plaintiff, but failed to specify any concrete remedies.

In these ways, members of the legal profession have tried to protect citizens' constitutional rights through administrative litigation. Though no verdict of any substance has emerged from these cases, the efforts have proven profoundly influential in, for example, the revision of discriminatory rules regarding health examination standards in 2004.

D Autonomous local democratic reforms

Since the implementation in 1987 of a system of village self-governance, rural areas have seen the rise of grassroots democracy in the form of elections, management methods, and supervisory practices. Farmers are participating in comprehensive experiments in democracy, and their enthusiasm toward these democratic practices has greatly facilitated the development of grassroots democracy. The NPC's 1998 Organic Law on Village Committees promoted village elections and self-governance. After the establishment and development of village elections, people then began to seek ways to directly elect township or county leaders.

Entire regions, therefore, began to experiment with democratic election reforms, including the introduction of public recommendations for township leaders and party committee chairs.[57] In some places, even county-level leaders were nominated and elected directly. Simultaneously, other democratic reforms within the party system were carried out, establishing a standing body of the Party's Congress and allowing for the direct election of representatives in county-level party congresses. Two consecutive direct elections of township leaders were carried out in Sichuan's Buyun County in 1998 and 2001.[58]

The problem with such local practices, however, is that they are not codified in law and therefore cannot be carried out extensively. This nonetheless has become an unstoppable trend in some places. According to some investigations, about 40% of Sichuan's townships had competitive elections for township and party leaders in 2002.[59] In September 2003, for instance, Pingba, a township in Chongqing, implemented a reform on direct elections of party and township leaders.[60] Indeed, this phenomenon is spreading: in April 2004, seven towns in Yunnan's Shiping County and ten towns in Luxi County elected their own township leaders.[61] Direct, open, and competitive elections are becoming an irreversible trend in China.

Of course, obstacles persist in the development of grassroots democracies, especially in village elections. These obstacles generally take the form of either local cadres or other troublemakers attempting to exert undue influence on the electoral process. They may prevent elected village heads from exercising their authority, block democratic decision making among villagers, void democratic oversight processes, or make it difficult for the village's finance committee to function properly. In some extreme cases, the very security and property of elected village heads are threatened, some of whom are even beaten or illegally imprisoned. Many villagers struggle against these unlawful interferences via petitions or collective protests. The development of grassroots democracy, therefore, requires legislative support from the government. The NPC should draft and enact a national law on village elections, thereby defining electoral procedures, guaranteeing fairness of the elections, and providing for the punishment of any illegal interference.

E Establishing a rule-of-law government

The development of constitutionalism in China requires more input from the government itself than from the public. Constitutional reform should be a two-pronged effort. First, political institutions should be diverse and open, with extensive opportunities for public participation. Second, governmental actions need to be constrained. A rule-of-law government operates according to the law: openly, transparently, and efficiently. Recent years have seen little progress on the first front, but significant progress on the second.

1 Building a transparent and constrained government

The Wen Jiabao administration made explicit the goal of establishing a rule-of-law government. The State Council's March 2004 Outline of Promoting Governance According to the Law stated that a rule-of-law government should be established within ten years.[62] Though it is still too early to judge the feasibility of this proclamation, the past year has been one of noticeable progress.

First, information regarding governance is increasingly open to the public. Almost all departments of the central government, as well as those at the provincial and lower levels, have established websites to facilitate the free flow of information from government to citizen. State Council ministries have established a "spokesman" system allowing publication of relevant information. Shanghai has local laws concerning the openness of government information, requiring that all normative documents of governmental departments be put on record in the Shanghai Institute of Archives, a database accessible to the public.

Second, the decreased scope of administrative licensing regulations and the transformation of governmental functions also indicate a shift to a less intrusive government. Administrative permission was formerly one of the major functions of government offices. The practice had become so extensive that the government played a role in significant aspects of citizens' social, economic, and private lives. Such officially sanctioned intervention inevitably led to graft and corruption, with bribes and special favors being doled out for licenses and government approval. Some administrative licenses required complicated application procedures, yet applications often sat in limbo in government offices. Ultimately, many citizens came to feel that the system of administrative licensing amounted to little more than a black box into which applications were placed, and an indeterminate amount of time later, a license was mysteriously produced—or not.

Such a labyrinthine system is a breeding ground for corruption and rent-seeking behavior. Administrative licensing had, to a large extent, become a serious obstacle to the transformation of governmental functions. The 2003

Administrative Licensing Law[63] was designed to solve such problems. It identifies the scope of administrative licenses and accordingly restricts their application. The law states that no administrative license should be required for matters that can be addressed independently by citizens, enterprises, and other organizations, or that can be addressed by competitive market mechanisms, guilds, or other intermediary organs. Other reforms include the articulation of administrative licensing requirements, simplification of procedures, and strengthening of supervisory mechanisms. Despite varied opinions on the matter, the author is of the opinion that the law has had a great impact upon the transformation of governmental functions, the reform of administrative management, and ultimately the establishment of a rule-of-law government. In line with the State Compensation Law, Administrative Punishment Law, and Administrative Reconsideration Law, this legislation is a significant step forward in the process of China's political and legal reform.

2 Accountability of government officials

The current administration has taken significant steps towards establishing a responsible government. A rule-of-law government should be, first of all, a government with accountability, subject to public supervision. The public should hold government officials responsible for their actions. Specifically, any breach of duty or malfeasance ought to result in that official's resignation or dismissal. Under a top-down regime, government officials are more responsible to the party in charge of promotions than they are to ordinary citizens. As long as that party is satisfied, an official will remain in power, regardless of any breach of duty or degree of popular dissatisfaction.

To embody the credo of governance for the people, the current government is devoted to establishing a service-oriented model of governance. As a result, a system of accountability has been established and officials have been dismissed as a result of unfortunate events under their watch. Proof of this mechanism's efficacy was seen in the wake of the SARS crisis of 2003. The activities of the Minister of Public Health and the mayor of Beijing were investigated, and as a result of their inept crisis management, they were forced to resign as part of an attempt to restore the government's credibility.[64] It was not until 2004, however, when the State Council published the Outline for Comprehensive Promotion of Administration According to Law,[65] that such mechanisms were established extensively. Mid-April saw a spate of forced resignations around China arising from mismanagement of local disasters. In the wake of a December 2003 mine explosion claiming more than 200 lives in Chongqing Municipality, Ma Fucai, general manager of the China National Petroleum Corporation, was forced to step down from his post.[66] Former county head Zhang Wen resigned from his post after the trampling death of thirty seven people during a February 2004 lantern festival in his Beijing suburb.[67] After fifty three people died in a fire in the Zhongbai Shopping Mall in Jilin, Gang Zhanbiao, the mayor of that city, was forced to resign.[68] From these events emerged the rule that responsible government officials must resign if a catastrophe results in a significant number of deaths on their watch. Since April 2004, about 200 officials, some at the provincial level, have received sanctions for their failure to effectively manage fatal accidents.

Accountability has become one of the means by which the rule of law is established among government officials in China. A position in the government is no longer an "iron rice bowl," but an occupation with great responsibilities. As a result, this establishes a channel for the public supervision of government officials.

3 "The Storm of Audits"

Previously, independent voices were not allowed in the Chinese government. It was a government of top-down personal rule, requiring absolute obedience, not to the law, but to the senior leadership. Therefore, government administration according to the law was impossible.

This has changed in recent years. Respect for the law has increased, and the independence and autonomy of those cadres charged with checking government power have been enhanced. This was illustrated in June 2004 when General Auditor Li Jinhua disclosed to the NPC Standing Committee serious legal infractions and instances of corruption in at least forty one central government departments and twenty one infractions at the provincial level.[69] These illegal activities included the use of shoddy materials to construct a dike on the Yangtze River, the National Sports Bureau's abuse of ¥131 million of Olympic funds, and the National Electric Company's potential loss of ¥3.28 billion due to mismanagement. In 2005, the Auditing Bureau continued to disclose financial impropriety. The 2005 audit disclosed the misuse, typically by budget inflation and embezzlement, of ¥9.06 billion, 6% of the total amount audited by thirty eight central ministry organs during the 2004 fiscal year. In several audits of universities, hospitals, and scientific research institutes, it was found that water conservation efforts and antipollution projects in key drainage areas were poorly regulated and capital was seriously misused.[70]

These shocking reports drew such attention that the media named them "the storm of audits." General Auditor Li Jinhua was thus highly lauded and praised by the public, who dubbed him the "Iron Auditor."[71] The report garnered such intense support because it daringly revealed the unlawful activities of government officials. Further, these problems primarily concerned sitting ministry officials with real power. Finally, these problems were made known to the public as well as the relevant government bodies.[72]

The "Storm of Environmental Protection," occurring shortly after the audits and their fallout, is another example of state organs functioning independently and lawfully. The State Environmental Protection Administration announced on January 18, 2005 that more than thirty construction projects in over ten provinces and cities were illegal.[73] These projects were initiated without first undertaking the requisite environmental impact assessments, and so were suspended.[74]

One government organ's disclosure of another's problems was rare in the past. Typically, such problems would be reported to the relevant leader and resolved through internal negotiations. At most, an official would be criticized, but no publicizing of the conflicts was allowed; to allow otherwise would be to undermine the legitimacy of the government. Significantly, these recent actions indicate that a handful of state organs are daring to supervise others according to the law, and this, to some extent, reflects the advantages of an open and transparent form of governance. Moreover, it indicates the evolution of an increasingly powerful rule-of-law model of governance, and the establishment of mutual checks and balances.

It is noticeable that this trend began with state organs that, in the past, wielded little if any real power. To establish their legitimacy, these offices have relied upon the letter of China's law. This desire for legitimacy within the government itself is among the motivations underlying these governmental organs' struggle for a supervisory role.

III The possibility for the development of constitutionalism in China

Since the initiation of reform and opening in the late 1970s, China's protection of its citizens' civil rights has been an evolving process. In the 1980s, this process began with a movement to correct the miscarriages of justice resulting from large-scale trampling of individual rights during the Cultural Revolution and other political campaigns. In the 1990s, the civil rights movement was a consequence of a two-pronged desire: first, to protect economic rights—most notably consumer rights—and second, to remedy government misdeeds in the form of administrative litigation. The beginning of the 21st century, however, has witnessed the expansion of citizens' grievances regarding social and cultural rights to include issues of environmental protection, historical heritage preservation, and education. Protection of constitutional rights has become a focus of serious attention over the past few years. The right to freedom of movement, embodied in the millions of migrants within the country, continuously challenges such fundamental government policies as the system of household registration (戶口, *hukou*). Citizens have begun to demand equal rights in the arenas of work and education, and to fight against discrimination in employment. Moreover, the desire to participate in China's political processes has become greater, from the fight for public hearings, to the calls for constitutional review, to campaigns for the position of representatives in people's congresses. Gradually, citizens have come to demand the rights promised them in their country's Constitution.

Many researchers have expressed reservations about the extent to which civil society's campaigns for constitutional reform will be effective. Some claim that these efforts are meaningless because of the lack of real political reform. However, the efforts outlined in this essay are not only necessary but also effective.

What is constitutionalism? If it is, in essence, constraint on the exercise of state power, then the next question is where these constraints come from. These checks on state power come from a variety of state organs, as well as from the people. Does the realization of civil rights rest on radical political reform, or is it possible to gradually realize these rights through citizens' efforts via the current constitutional and legal framework?

Political reform is admittedly necessary for the construction of a constitutional framework. Nonetheless, the success of a country's political reform rests upon the spontaneous endeavors of its citizens. There will be no real constitutionalism, but instead a revolution similar to those of China's imperial history, without the conscious pursuit of basic rights by China's citizens. All in all, constitutionalism is a compromise between the government and the people—or in some cases, other political forces. The process of exercising constitutional rights is actually a form of negotiation with the government. An active constitutional movement among the citizenry proves that dialogue is possible between the government and its people, and this dialogue has resulted in some effective outcomes.

The SPC's interpretation in the 2001 Qi Yuling case opened the door to constitutional litigation, indicating that the Supreme People's Court was willing to protect constitutional rights via adjudication. The petition from the three graduate students of law directly led to the abolition of a State Council regulation. This was an education in constitutional law for the public. Though no legal basis exists for employment discrimination litigation of the sort recounted above, certain local courts have accepted such cases despite this deficiency in the current legal framework. Although the rulings of the courts were not satisfactory in the height discrimination case of 2001[75] and the park ticket pricing case of 2002,[76] the fact that local courts are willing to accept such cases at all is itself an indication of progress.

Zhang Xianzhu's Hepatitis B discrimination case[77] is more significant in this regard. Not only did the court accept the case, but the plaintiff obtained a favorable ruling. Moreover, this case, coupled with other complaints filed by Hepatitis B carriers, pressured the Ministry of Personnel and the Ministry of Public Health to revise the General Standards of Health Examination in Recruiting Civil Servants in August 2004, eliminating some discriminatory standards. Public pressure is widely considered to have been a significant factor in the impact of this first successful anti-discrimination case.[78]

The government has taken significant steps forward to protect private property as well. The waves of demolition throughout China prior to 2004 led to large-scale protests.[79] Citizens from throughout the country filed constitutional complaints with the NPC Standing Committee, prompting constitutional review on the rules of demolition. The Central Office of the State Council then issued a notice to curb the scale of demolition and strengthen the management of construction projects. The notice called for the Ministry of Land Resources, the Ministry of Construction, and relevant public organs in the provinces to revise unreasonable rules, raise the level of compensation offered to homeowners, establish stricter procedures, and provide mechanisms for public hearings. These measures have abated conflicts on this issue.

These cases illustrate how citizens' efforts to promote constitutionalism have met with a certain degree of success. These claims have the potential to influence the establishment of China's rule of constitutional law, the spread of constitutional concepts, and the promotion of academic research. For instance, while the petition that three legal academics submitted to the NPC Standing Committee after Sun Zhigang's death failed to trigger the constitutional review that it called for, it, coupled with public outcry surrounding the event, did prompt the establishment of the Review and Registration Office on Regulations in May 2004.[80] In 2003, the Standing Committee also reacted positively to citizens who had campaigned to become People's Congress representatives in places such as Guangzhou and Beijing. The revised Electoral Law of 2004 added a procedure for primary elections, providing all citizens with an equal opportunity to win candidacy. This is in remarkable contrast to the prior process, in which the electoral committee appointed candidates behind closed doors. Such public participation in governance is a necessary first step in the process of realizing constitutionalism as an element of China's legal system.

Three motivating factors underlie the development of constitutionalism in modern China. First, the development of the market economy strengthens citizens' awareness of their benefits and rights. Their desire to vindicate property rights is motivated not by any political ideology, but by self-interest. Consequently, civil society actors push for an ever-expanding adherence to the law on the part of government officials. This constitutes an instinctive impulse to promote the implementation of the Constitution, and it makes constitutional protection practical and sustainable.

Second, the current regime's "government of the people" ideology, coupled with its introduction of clauses protecting human rights and private property into the Constitution, has broadened the size of citizens' platforms when pursuing their constitutional rights. Because they use the rhetoric of those currently in power, their constitutional claims obtain legitimacy and legal authority. The Chinese government has responded positively to a variety of reasonable and legitimate claims from civil society, improving the legal system and institutions accordingly.

Third, the media and public opinion play critical roles. In their efforts to vindicate the rights guaranteed under the Constitution, citizens use the media and public opinion to pressure the government. Some officials fear the media, and some of them even lobby the media to suppress negative disclosures of government problems. One of the reasons for this emergence of the media's role as the government's watchdog, rather than its lapdog, is the commercialization of news suppliers. These commercialized news corporations sell their products through attention-grabbing reports and articles, and therefore focus more on high-profile cases. In addition, the market economy has given rise to a group of journalists with a social conscience and sense of social responsibility. They have become the vanguard of media supervision of the government, as well as the disclosers of government corruption.

This is not, however, to say that simply because of grassroots efforts in pushing for constitutionalism, China can immediately jump to a constitutional society, change its political system, and avoid potential social crises. Civil society has not yet become a sufficiently strong force in the push for China's development of constitutional law. Furthermore, the foundation for constitutional change must be laid by basic reforms within the political system. In the absence of changes reaching to the very root of political society, the room for civil society's campaigns for constitutionalism is very limited, and these campaigns can be suppressed at any change in the political climate. This is not to deny the utility of those efforts; on the contrary, they are an indispensable part of the social forces striving for the success of constitutionalism in China. Citizens' failure to consciously pursue their constitutional rights and push for grassroots democratic reform, coupled with the absence of a strong civil society, were some of the most important reasons why China failed to establish a true, active system of constitutional law in the 20th century.

Individual quests to protect their constitutional rights contribute positively to China's political reform. As the nation's market economy develops, the need to protect citizens' rights will invite legal reform and institution building. To take one example, the controversies surrounding demolition and eviction concern the question of whether citizens can litigate to protect property rights to their houses and apartments. It also concerns judicial review of the power of local governments. As such, judicial independence becomes yet another element vital to strengthening citizens' legal and constitutional rights, and constitutional reform aimed at improving the status and independence of the judiciary becomes inevitable.

Government responses to appeals for the vindication of citizens' rights, which take the form of improved institutions, are also beneficial to the establishment of constitutionalism. The dialogue between government and citizens not only helps alleviate social conflicts and avoid crises, but also equips the government with the ability to communicate with citizens and civil organizations. Through this medium, the government may negotiate with interest groups to reach compromises.[81] This ability is integral to a democratic government able to communicate effectively with citizens and respond to their appeals through institutionalized mechanisms, leading to "virtuous interactions" instead of "vicious interactions."[82] Lawful appeals to vindicate citizens' rights can become a feedback mechanism to help the government legitimize its rule in a democratic way.

The hope for constitutionalism in China rests upon continuous efforts to increase virtuous interactions between members of civil society and the government. The government should regard civil organizations' demands for the protection of individual rights not as "unstable elements" to be oppressed, but as an accumulating series of opportunities to improve China's legal system and institutions. This would put the country on the track of developing constitutional democracy through legal means. On this track, civil society forces are important and basic, but the key role is still lies with the government.

Notes

1 Household saving totaled ¥7 trillion in 2001 and ¥11 trillion in 2004.
2 According to research by the Chinese Academy of Social Science's Institute of Economics, in 2004 the Gini coefficient had reached 0.454, while statistics released by Fudan University's Institute of Economics reported a coefficient of 0.5.
3 According to statistic released by the PRC's Ministry of Labor and Social Security, at the end of the third quarter of 2004, 8.21 million urban residents were registered as unemployed, constituting an unemployment rate of 4.2%. This figure does not include unregistered residents and "ahead-of-schedule" retirees who were forced to retire with relatively low wages in their forties and fifties.
4 According to the Human Development Report published by the United Nation Development Program, when China's annual per-capita GDP ranked 123rd in the world, its Human Development Index ranked 111th. This indicated that China had reached a higher standard of human development with a lower per-capita annual income. China ranked 96th in both categories in 2000, while in 2001, it ranked 102nd in per-capita GDP, yet 104th in the Human Development Index.
5 Officials' salaries, bonuses, and benefits vary widely among the various organs of government. As a result, it is occasionally the case that cadres in local departments of education inflate students' fees and embezzle the surplus funds, police department officials use money collected through fines to fund bonuses and purchase supplies, and municipal court officers finance their own salaries and supplies through the court fees they collect.
6 Ma De was the former Chairman of the Communist Party's Committee of Suihua city, Heilongjiang province. He accumulated more than ¥5 million and an additional US$25,000 by selling official titles to people. 256 officials were involved in this case. *See* 刘畅, 绥化马德卖官案 侦查终结 透视绥化畸形官场生态 [Liu Chang, *The Investigation of Ma De Case in Suihua Concludes, Perspective on Suihua Official Corruption Emerges*], 中国青年报 [CHINA YOUTH DAILY], Aug. 25, 2004, at A3.
7 Li Zhilun spoke at the State Council's third working meeting on corruption on February 16, 2005.
8 They were Wu Zhenhan, President of the People's High Court of Hunan Province; Ding Xinfa, President of the People's Procuratorate in Shanxi province; Xu Yandong, President of the People's High Court in Heilongjiang province; and Xu Fa, President of the People's Procuratorate in Heilongjiang province. *See* 2005: 两会热门词汇 – 编织体系反腐的天罗地网 [*2005: Popular Vocabulary of Two Congresses – Knitting a Meshwork of Systemic Anti-Corruption*], 工人日报 [WORKERS DAILY], March 11, 2005, at 11.
9 The President of the Supreme People's Procuratorate spoke at the third meeting of the tenth National People's Congress on March 9, 2005.
10 The development strategy in the eastern costal regions during the 1980s, for example, bestowed considerable economic privileges upon these regions, attracting cheap labor and business elites from the country's central and western provinces. This resulted in an imbalance of human resources among the country's regions.

11 "Bloody factory" and "bloody mine" scandals involve factories and mines in which the work conditions are abominable. Miners typically work for low compensation over ten hours per day under conditions that violate national and international labor laws.

12 The key to "managing the city" is to obtain land at a low price, then sell it to exploiters. Both the exploiters and local government representatives snatch huge profits.

13 Chinese universities have expanded aggressively in recent years, especially in the field of graduate studies. This flood of graduate students consumes scarce educational resources.

14 Petitions on the grounds of judicial impropriety account for one of the four major categories of petitions in China. The other categories are claims of benefits for laid-off state workers, petitions against demolition orders, and complaints about land expropriation in rural areas.

15 Petitions filed by groups increased dramatically. In 2003, the National Letters and Visits Bureau saw a 41% increase in the number of petitions filed by a group from the previous year; there was a corresponding 44.8% increase in the number of appeals filed by an individual. The largest petitioning group contained more than 800 people. Simultaneously, these petitions are becoming increasingly violent.

16 *See* 调查报告: 我国大学毕业生平均就业率为 73% [*Survey Report: National Employment Rate Among University Graduates at 73%*], 新 华 网 [XINHUA NET], May 24, 2005, *at* http://news.xinhuanet.com/edu/2005–05/24/content_2993650.htm (last visited Feb. 19, 2006).

17 Hereinafter, "registering" means that citizens take the initiative to sign up for and run in elections, organize their own campaigns, and compete against other appointed candidates.

18 *See, e.g.,* 2003 年深圳竞选实录, [2003: RECORD ON THE SHENZHEN ELECTION] (唐娟 & 邹树彬编 [Tang Juan & Zhou Shubin eds.], 2003) [hereinafter RECORD ON THE SHENZHEN ELECTION].

19 Ten of the twenty-two volunteers had college degrees, six were homeowners, and six were professionals such as scholars or lawyers. Some of them wanted to protect their rights, others wanted to challenge the Election Law in order to promote election reform, and still others represented activists in the public sphere. *See* 中国基层民主发展报告 [REPORT ON THE DEVELOPMENT OF GRASSROOTS DEMOCRACY] 25 (李凡编 [Li Fan ed.], 2004).

20 Among the forty-one volunteers, there were twelve peasants, eleven teachers, five village heads, four legal practitioners, and nine workers. Due to lack of support from the organizers, all of them failed.

21 Between 1980 and 1986, elections were held in universities throughout China, with particular prominence in Beijing, Wuhan, and Hunan.

22 *See* RECORD ON THE SHENZHEN ELECTION, *supra* note 18, at 363.

23 Four of the candidates in Shenzhen were representatives of the Community Home Owner Committees, two were migrant or laid-off workers, and the two others were a school president and an engineer.

24 *See* RECORD ON THE SHENZHEN ELECTION, *supra* note 18, at 346.

25 黄卫平 [Huang Weiping], *Preface* to RECORD ON THE SHENZHEN ELECTION *supra* note 18, at 1, 2.

26 Former NPC representative Yao Xiurong actively helps citizens solve problems. He has accepted more than 1000 citizen appeals. Beijing representative Wu Qing used the Constitution to protect civil rights everywhere. Shenyang representative Feng Youwei and Hubei representative Yao Lifa exposed government problems and disclosed corruption.

27 Wang Yuancheng actively calls for the rights of migrant workers. When asked about his motivation, he said that he simply wanted to be "a representative with a sense of justice and a conscience." He explained: "I am just trying to fulfill my responsibility

as a representative." *See* 王元成代表口述: 农民工代表的心愿 [*The Dictation of Wang Yuancheng: Wishes of Migrant Workers*], 光明日报 [GUANGMING DAILY], March 7, 2004, at B2.

28 Wang Tian proposed a draft of The Law on Large Business Companies to the NPC in March 2003.

29 In 2003 in Ningbo, Zhejiang province, more than 100 representatives were required to resign because they were unable to fulfill their duties. *See*, "建议代表辞职"起争议 ["*Suggesting that Representatives Resign" Gives Rise to Controversy*], *at* http://www.e-cpcs.org/yhyj_readnews.aspx? id=2218&cols=2612 (last visited Feb. 19, 2006).

30 中华人民共和国行政处罚法 [Law on Administrative Punishment] art. 42 (promulgated by the Standing Comm. of the Nat'l People's Cong., Mar. 17, 1996, effective October 1, 1996) 03/1996 全国人民代表大会常务委员会公报 [STANDING COMM. NAT'L PEOPLE'S CONG. GAZ.] (P.R.C.), *available at* http://news.xinhuanet.com/legal/2003–01/22/content_701464.htm (last visited Feb. 20, 2006).

31 中华人民共和国价格法 [Price Law] art. 23 (promulgated by the Standing Comm. of the Nat'l People's Cong. Dec. 29, 1997, effective May 1, 1998) 07/1997 全国人民代表大会常务委员会公报 [STANDING COMM. NAT'L PEOPLE'S CONG. GAZ.] 783 (P.R.C), *available at* http://news.xinhuanet.com/legal/2003–01/22/content_701763.htm (last visited Feb. 20, 2006). The requirement covers prices for public utilities, natural monopolies, and other goods and services subject to government "guidance pricing" or mandatory pricing.

32 Since 2002, Peking University's Center for the Study of the People's Congress and Foreign Legislation, cooperating with the NPC Legal Committee's Domestic Law Office, has held frequent domestic and international symposia on legislative hearings, which have greatly promoted the development of legislative hearings in China.

33 At 10 PM on March 17, 2003, Sun Zhigang, a young college graduate who had recently moved to Guangzhou in search of work, was detained by the police because he didn't have his identification with him. Three days later, he died in a police clinic. This was disclosed by the Southern Metropolitan News (南方都市报, *Nanfang Dushi Bao*) and had a great impact on the public. Not only was there public outcry over the police's action, but this event led to questions about the legality of the measure promulgated by the State Council in the 1950s pursuant to which he had been detained. As part of an initiative targeting vagrants, this measure granted police the authority to detain those citizens not carrying identification papers.

34 Liu Yong was accused of being the ringleader of the Shenyang Mafia and sentenced to death. His lawyer claimed that the police had tortured him to extract a confession, and the appeals court changed the sentence to death subject to a two-year suspension. This was greatly criticized by the public. Many believed that the crimes he committed were so appalling that he should be sentenced to death regardless of police procedural impropriety. Under the pressure of public opinion, the Supreme People's Court finally sentenced him again to death without suspension. *See* 最高人民法院判处刘涌死刑 [*Supreme People's Court Sentences Liu Yong to Death*], 人民网 [PEOPLE'S DAILY ONLINE], *at* http://www.people.com.cn/GB/shehui/8217/29349/ (last visited Feb. 7, 2006).

35 A citizen of Shenyang named Su Xiuwen killed a peasant with whom she had quarreled while driving her BMW, but she was only sanctioned mildly by the court. The disclosure of this case on the Internet aroused public suspicion about courtroom justice. The public opinion was that Su was granted leniency because of her wealth and power. Upon review of the case, however, the court still held that this was a traffic violation and not murder. *See* 刘鉴强, "宝马案" 疑云, [Liu Jianqiang, *"BMW Case" Suspicions*], 南方周末 [S. WEEKEND] Jan. 8, 2004, at A5.

36 Farmer-entrepreneur Sun Dawu was arrested for the crime of illegal financing, but the public was moved by reports depicting him as an advocate of charity. Furthermore, the difficulties procuring financing that Sun faced as a peasant entrepreneur were common knowledge. Consequently, Sun was sanctioned mildly and quickly released from prison. *See* 万静波, 亿万富翁孙大午的梦和痛, [Wan Jingbo, *The Dream and Pain of Billionaire Sun Dawu*], 南方周末 [S. WEEKEND], Nov. 6, 2003, at A2.

37 In Bazhou city, Hebei province, a policeman falsely imprisoned a person, tortured him to death during an interrogation, and then buried the corpse to conceal his crime. Police investigated the case after media disclosure. The policeman in question was sentenced to life imprisonment. While this case resembled in the past, the common sentences were typically no more than three to five years of imprisonment with probation. The severe sanctioning of a policeman in this case indicated an evolving respect for the lawful rights of citizens. *See* 人民检察院公布 4 超挂牌督办重大渎职侵权案件 [*People's Procuratorate Announces Four Major Cases of Supervisory Malfeasance and Dereliction of Duty*], 人民网 [PEOPLE'S DAILY ONLINE], *at* http://www.people.com.cn/GB/shizheng/1027/2945054.html (last visited Feb. 19, 2006).

38 Due to public pressure, the central government sent special teams to inspect and investigate allegations of forced eviction, resulting in the resignation of two main county leaders. *See* 建设部, 湖南省委严查嘉禾拆迁案县长书记被撤, [*Construction Bureau, Hunan Provincial Party Committee Investigate the Jiahe Forced Eviction Case, County Magistrate, and Party Secretary Removed*] (June 4, 2004), *at* http://news.sina.com.cn/c/2004–06–04/20442719546s.shtml (last visited Feb. 19, 2006).

39 Other cases include a fake lottery case in Shanxi, in which the salespeople bribed government officials and kept the lottery's grand prize—cars—for themselves. The media disclosed this and the persons involved bore criminal liability. *See* 杨永明原想独吞四辆宝马 [*Yang Yongming Wanted to Keep All 4 BMWs*], 新京报 [NEW CAPITAL NEWS], May 9, 2004, at A18. In the "Inferior Milk Powder case" in Anhui province's Fuyang county, it was discovered that there were 55 different brands of inferior milk powder in the Anhui market, all of which were unlicensed. After CCTV broke this story, it attracted Premier Wen Jiabao's attention. The counterfeiters and involved officials bore criminal liability; some associated leaders were forced to resign. *See* 阜阳奶粉案五被告分别被判 4 至 8 年 5 人提出上诉 [*Five Accused in Fuyang Milk Powder Case Get Four to Eight Years in Prison, All Five to Appeal Decision*], 人民网 [PEOPLE'S DAILY ONLINE], Jan. 7, 2005, *at* http://www.people.com.cn/GB/shehui/1061/3103482.html (last visited Feb. 19, 2006).

40 In the Liu Yong case, the appellate court confirmed the defense lawyer's claim regarding police use of illegal evidence. This is an improvement in China's legal system because in the past courts did not review procedural matters in appeals. However, media scrutiny prompted political leaders to intervene in this case, thus inhibiting the prospect of independent adjudication. The negative effect of media supervision is especially severe in circumstances where judicial independence has not been established, the quality of judges is still low, and intervention from leaders at higher levels is frequent.

41 A junior college accepted plaintiff Qi Yuling in 1990 after her graduation from middle school. However, the daughter of a local official impersonated Qi and attended college in her place. In 1999, when Qi discovered the fraud, she filed an administrative lawsuit, claiming identity theft and violation of her right of education. She appealed to the Shandong Higher Level People's Court after she failed in the first instance. Subsequently, the Shandong Higher Level People's Court asked for advice from the Supreme People's Court, which issued a judicial interpretation. *See* 宪法因何而美丽 [*How the Constitution is Beautiful*], *at* http://www.chinalawinfo.com/xin/index3.asp?code1=179 (last visited Feb. 19, 2006); *see also* Shen Kui, *Is It the Beginning of*

the Era of the Rule of the Constitution? Reinterpreting China's "First Constitutional Case", 12 PAC. RIM L. & POL'Y J. 199 (2003).

42 The query mainly concerned whether this was a constitutional case. Some argued that this was a case in tort, rather than a claim of constitutional rights. *See* 童之伟，宪法司法适用研究中的几个问题, [Tong Zhiwei, *Several Problems About Judicial Implementation of the Constitution*], *in* 公法 [PUBLIC LAW] 324, 331–33 (信春鹰编 [Xin Chunying ed.], 2002).

43 In a 1955 interpretation, the SPC prohibited courts from convicting defendants of crimes on the basis of language in the Constitution; in a 1986 interpretation, the SPC listed the norms courts may cite in support of their judgments but failed to mention the Constitution. Both of these documents have been widely interpreted in the Chinese legal community as making the Constitution non-justiciable.

44 On August 23, 2001, three high school graduates filed an administrative lawsuit against the Ministry of Education on the grounds that the universities' 2001 recruitment plans infringed upon their right to equal education. The claim was based on the assertion that a Qingdao student needed significantly higher results on the standardized entrance examination than a Beijing student for university admission. *See generally* 俞梅荪，从教育部当被告的两案看招生制度创新的迫切性, [Yu Meisun, *On the Exigency of Renovating the College Recruiting System, Judging From the Two Cases Where the Ministry of Education is the Defendant*], 大纪元 [THE EPOCH TIMES], Apr. 23, 2004, *available at* http://www.epochtimes.com/gb/4/4/23/n519496.htm.

45 On November 20, 2003, a petition signed by 1161 citizens demanded constitutional review of a regulation barring Hepatitis B carriers from recruitment as civil servants and called for more protection for Hepatitis B carriers. The petition pointed out that the regulation excluded 120 million Hepatitis B carriers from positions as civil servants, infringing upon their constitutional rights of labor and equal protection. *See generally* "乙肝歧视"第一案、张先著胜诉 [Plaintiff Zhang Xianzhu Wins The First Case Of Discrimination Against Hepatitis B], 野草先锋 [Ye Cao Xian Feng], Apr. 3, 2004, *at* http://www.yecao.net/html/20044324116–1.html (last visited Jan. 14, 2006).

46 It cannot be said that the case was completely successful. Legal scholars aimed to establish a system of constitutional review in China through this case. However, their efforts only served to cause the government to abolish this regulation.

47 According to the Constitution, the Standing Committee has the authority to explain and interpret the Constitution.

48 Leading up to this case, the new leadership had increasingly emphasized the importance of the Constitution, notably in 2002 when Hu Jintao gave a speech at the Great Hall of the People's Congress during the twentieth anniversary of the 1982 Constitution. This was the first speech by the General Secretary of the Party addressing the Constitution. In a 2004 constitutional amendment, protection of human rights and private property were introduced into the Constitution. After the amendments, the central government called for cadres of various levels to study the Constitution. Though it may be argued that these actions are motivated more by politics than by policy, they reflect the new leadership's emphasis on the document; such emphasis provides a broader platform and legitimate grounds for citizens to protect their constitutional rights.

49 The Article 8 of the Law on Legislation stipulates that only the NPC can make laws that impose constraints on individual liberty. *See* 中华人民共和国立法法 [Law on Legislation] art. 8 (promulgated by the Standing Comm. of the Nat'l People's Cong., Mar. 15, 2000, effective July 1, 2000) 03/2000 全国人民代表大会常务委员会公报 [STANDING COMM. NAT'L PEOPLE'S CONG. GAZ.] 112 (P.R.C), *available at* http://www.cnlawservice.com/chinese/law&regulation/flcx/a003.htm (last visited Feb. 22, 2006).

50 In his capacity as a prominent law professor with a longstanding interest in and distinguished expertise on the topic, the author has received appeals for judicial review of

the Measure on Housing Demolition from residents of Zhejiang, Beijing, and Shanghai, some of which were signed by thousands of inhabitants. However, the author has never brought a housing demolition case to court and is not qualified as a plaintiff under Chinese law.

51 When the police came to demolish his house, Huang Zhenyun referred to the new amendments as guaranteeing "protection of private property" and "protection of human rights." Yet the house was demolished within the month. The media covered this case and it had a great impact on the constitutional movement in China. *See* 田雨, 李薇薇 & 沈路涛, 宪法走进寻常百姓家, [Tian Yu, Li Weiwei & Shen Lutao, *The Constitution Enters the Homes of Ordinary People*], 人民日报海外版 [PEOPLE'S DAILY OVERSEAS ED.], Dec. 4, 2004, *available at* http://www.people.com.cn/GB/paper39/13547/1213154.html (last visited Feb. 20, 2006).

52 Faced with coercive demolition, residents hired lawyers to protect their constitutionally guaranteed property rights. Each household placed a Constitution in front of their homes. *See* 黄培坚, 广州大学城拆迁中的冲突 [Huang Peijian, *The Conflicts of University Demolition in Guangzhou*], 经济观察报 [ECON. OBSERVER] Aug. 14, 2004.

53 *See* 王磊, 选择宪法, [WANG LEI, THE CHOICE OF CONSTITUTION] 86 (2003) [hereinafter THE CHOICE OF CONSTITUTION].

54 The People's Bank of China is a state-owned bank, and so its employees are civil servants.

55 THE CHOICE OF CONSTITUTION, *supra* note 53, at 90.

56 *See* 唐建光, 乙肝病毒携带者维权运动 [Tang Jianguang, *The Rights-claiming Movement of Hepatitis Carriers*], 中国新闻周刊 [CHINA NEWS WEEK], Nov. 24, 2003, *available at* http://www.chinanews.com.cn/n/2003–11–24/26/372556.html (last visited Feb. 20, 2006).

57 "Public recommendations" are quasi-elections in which the electorate recommends the candidates. For instance, in an election for the head of a county, candidates must be elected by cadres of the county, village heads, and representatives of the villagers; then the People's Congress at the county level will vote to elect the head of the county. The candidate pool varies by region.

58 At the same time, Sichuan's Nancheng county in Qingshen township began its own experiment with electoral democracy. In Shenzhen, a "two ballot system" was introduced in January 1999. The voters elected the candidates, and the representatives of the People's Congresses elected the township leader from that candidate pool.

59 赖海榕, 竞争性选举在四川省乡镇一级的发展, [Lai Hairong, *The Development of Competitive Election in the Towns of Sichuan Province*], *in* 战略与管理 [STRATEGY AND MANAGEMENT] 57, 57 (2003).

60 The election failed because of the upper government's interference on the eve of the polling day. *See* 王巧丽, 一场夭折的乡镇直选, [Wang Qiaoli, *A Failed Direct County Election*], Oct. 20, 2003, *available at* http://www.e-cpcs.org/oldweb/jqhd_d.asp?id=1227 (last visited Feb. 20, 2006).

61 Some villagers even resorted to excessive measures to protest flawed elections; they were often imprisoned for disturbing social order or elections.

62 温家宝, 全面推进依法行政实施纲要, [WEN JIABAO, OUTLINE OF PROMOTING GOVERNANCE ACCORDING TO THE LAW] (2004), *available at* http://news.xinhuanet.com/zhengfu/2004–04/21/content_1431232.htm (last visited Feb. 7, 2006).

63 *See* 中华人民共和国行政许可法 [Law on Administrative Licensing] (promulgated by the Standing Comm. Nat'l People's Cong. Aug. 27, 2003, effective July 1, 2004) 05/2003 全国人民代表大会常务委员会公报 [STANDING COMM. NAT'L PEOPLE'S CONG. GAZ.] 439 (P.R.C.), *available at* http://news.xinhuanet.com/zhengfu/2003–08/28/content_1048844.htm (last visited Feb. 21, 2006) [hereinafter Law on Administrative Licensing].

64 These two leaders were forced to resign for not openly and truly informing the public of the disease.

65 *See* Law on Administrative Licensing, *supra* note 63.

66 *See Local drilling company chief sacked for SW gas blowout*, PEOPLE'S DAILY ONLINE, May 14, 2004, *at* http://english.people.com.cn/200405/14/eng20040514_143332.html (last visited Feb. 21, 2006).

67 *See Two police jailed over Miyun stampede case*, XINHUA, Nov. 26, 2004, *available at* http://www.chinadaily.com.cn/english/doc/2004–11/26/content_395220.htm (last visited Feb. 21, 2006).

68 *See Leaders held responsible for accidents*, CHINA DAILY, May 6, 2004, *available at* http://www.chinadaily.com.cn/english/doc/2004–05/06/content_328434.htm (last visited Feb. 21, 2006).

69 *See* 李金华, 审计长作 2003 年度审计工作报告 (全文), 2003 [LI JINHUA, 2004 AUDIT REPORT TO THE STANDING COMMITTEE OF THE NPC (COMPLETE TEXT)], *available at* http://news.xinhuanet.com/zhengfu/2004–06/24/content_1543949.htm (last visited Feb. 21, 2006).

70 *Id.*

71 Li was elected in the 2004 China Economic Annual Figures with a 70.83% vote, far exceeding other candidates. *See* 新浪财经, 经济年度任务: 李金华为何成大热, [NEW WAVE FIN. & ECON., LI JINHUA BECOMES A BIGSHOT], *at* http://www.yrsri.cn/xinwen-zhitongche/ReadArticle13.asp?ID=49 60&BoardID=99999 (last visited Feb. 21, 2006).

72 *See* 文平, 李金华拨动法治政府的琴弦 [Wen Ping, *Li Jinhua Plays the Strings of a Rule-of-Law Government*], 人物 [PEOPLE MAG.], Feb. 2005.

73 *See* "环保风暴" 给 "经济过热" 降温 [*"Storm of Environmental Protection" Cooled the "Overheated Economy"*], 21 世纪经济报 [THE ECON. REP. OF 21st CENTURY] (Jan. 31, 2005), *available at* http://cn.news.yahoo.com/050131/346/28kny.html (last visited Feb. 21, 2006).

74 This was the first time in the history of the 2003 Environmental Impact Assessment Law that large-scale projects were ordered to halt and their names publicized. It was a rare public disclosure and broke with the customary way of dealing with such issues. *See* 孙展, 访环保总局副局长潘岳: 环保已到最紧要关头[Sun Zhan, *Interviewing Pan Yue, Vice Minister of State Environmental Protection Administration: Environmental Protection Has Come at a Critical Moment*], 中国新闻周刊 [CHINA NEWS WKLY.], Jan. 20, 2005.

75 *See* THE CHOICE OF CONSTITUTION, *supra* note 53, at 86.

76 *Id.* at 90.

77 Tang, *supra* note 56.

78 Zhang Xianzhu, considered the spokesman of more than 100 million Hepatitis B carriers in China, has enjoyed broad mass media support. The Justice Department and CCTV recognized him as one of the Ten Persons of the Law in 2004. *See* 张先著当选 2004 年度中国十大法治人物 [*Zhang Xianzhu Chosen in the 2004 National Ten People of the Law*], 芜湖日报 [WUHU DAILY] (Dec. 7, 2004), *available at* http://www.yfzs.gov.cn/gb/info/XXDT/2005–01/03/1712035975.html (last visited Feb. 7, 2006).

79 In one notable incident, a citizen self-immolated to protest demolitions in Beijing. Similar cases have occurred in Nanjing.

80 This office conducts preliminary review of statutes submitted to the Standing Committee. If a statute is considered to be in conflict with the Constitution or law, the office requires that the Legal Committee report it to the NPC Standing Committee, which makes the final decision.

81 A government which does not negotiate and compromise with its people cannot be a good, representative government, and can even be a tyranny controlled by the private interests of a few people.

82 "Virtuous interactions" are ones in which (1) the government takes appeals from civil society seriously; (2) appeals for the vindication of individual rights are resolved through legal (and eventually judicial) means; and (3) reasonable mass public appeals are absorbed through improved institution building, while unreasonable appeals are alleviated through dialogue and explanation. In "vicious interactions," the government views all appeals from civil society organs as a sign of dissatisfaction with the state, and hence suppresses them. This suppression causes further dissatisfaction and resistance, which leads to even harsher suppression. In such a pattern, reasonable, lawful appeals may escalate into serious conflicts between citizens and the state.

30

WESTERN CONSTITUTIONAL IDEAS AND CONSTITUTIONAL DISCOURSE IN CHINA, 1978–2005

Yu Xingzhong

Source: Stéphanie Balme and Michael W. Dowdle (eds), *Building Constitutionalism in China*, New York: Palgrave, 2009, pp. 111–124.

I Introduction

Since its inception in 1949, the People's Republic of China (PRC) has enacted four constitutions, and a quasi Constitution called the Common Program of the Chinese People's Political Consultative Conference (1949). These constitutions have served the government well in legitimizing its domination and in promoting its political programs. But due to the lack of effective enforcing mechanisms, they had almost no direct relevance to the daily life of the Chinese people.

Since 1999, however, the Constitution seems to have been animated by some magic touch. Judges began to invoke constitutional provisions to justify court decisions on civil matters; ordinary citizens began trying to use the Constitution to curb unlawful government annexation of private properties; government officials also began arguing for greater respect for the Constitution in order to promote social stability.

This sudden rise of constitutional consciousness is the outcome of diverse forces in China's political and social arena. These forces each have had their own agenda for promoting the Constitution. For instance, some government officials want to use the Constitution to strengthen official party ideology; some judges want to use the Constitution to expand the sphere of influence of the judiciary; some scholars see constitutionalism as a way of modernizing and pursuing better governance; and some individuals use the Constitution as a means to fight against injustice.

Many of these political-economic factors have been explored in depth. But one factor needs to be more fully explored—that is, the influence of Western constitutional theories on Chinese constitutional scholarship in the reform era. This includes both American constitutional thought and, to a lesser extent, continental European constitutional thought as well.

This chapter attempts to look at this factor by examining how Western constitutional theories have been introduced into China by various scholars and how they have actually influenced Chinese constitutional mentality since 1978. It begins with a brief discussion of the nature of Chinese constitutional discourse. It then analyses several areas of China's emerging constitutional thinking in which Western scholars have played a significant role. The chapter concludes by pointing out some of the limitations of current Western constitutional theories as they are understood and utilized in China.

II Chinese constitutional thinking in transition

A four-thousand year history of rewarding the good and punishing the evil has naturally fostered a strict and powerful legal tradition in China (see Bodde and Morris 1967; Chu 1961; Zhang 1986). In their competition for position of authoritative ideology in Chinese history, Confucians, Taoists, Moists, and Legalists respectively praised or devalued the idea of governing by law, resulting in a cluster of vague ideas and statements about law that were to become eternal sources of disputes and misunderstandings for Chinese as well as foreign scholars (Alford 1986; see, e.g., Unger. 1976). These ideas and statements, however, never went beyond the theme of whether it is wise to use law, and if it is, how law should be used, to reward or punish (see Liang 1987).

Thus, despite its long legal tradition, China did not have much to offer to the world constitutionally speaking. It is often claimed that the Chinese word for "constitution," "*xianfa*," was imported from Japan (as many modern terms were). The word "*xian*" did in fact exist in classical Chinese—it meant "law, order, or edicts" and had some normative implications. But it did not mean "constitution" in modern sense, in the sense of the laying out of government structure and the protection of individual rights. There is a chapter in one of *The Classics*, the *Shu Jing* (*The Classic of History*), which describes something resembling a Constitution. The chapter is called "*Hong Fan* (The Great Plan)," and it contains an exposition of nine categories of government affairs. It was, however, not well-known or followed by any ruler in the course of dynastic politics. There was also very little discussion, if any, in *The Classics* about individual rights. And the idea of using an authoritative legal document to lay out the structure of government never emerged.

Modern constitutional discourse in China began in the 1830s when China was witnessing earth-shaking changes in its traditions. But the first Constitution in China did not appear until more than seventy years later (see Xie 2004, 2–4; see also the chapter by Xiaohong Xiao-Planes earlier in this volume). Subsequent traumatic events—such as wars with foreign powers, civil wars, upheavals and revolutions—gave this discourse an uneven history. It began as a hope for a powerful modern state, but was cut short by a series of revolutions, and then resumed after the communist revolution of 1949 with a somewhat reconfigured political ideology (see the chapter by Glenn Tiffert in this volume). Following the founding of the PRC in 1949, China's constitutional discourse has gone from focusing on Marxist ideology in the early 1950s; to promoting indigenous constitutional ideas during the Cultural Revolution; to encouraging a more liberal appeal in promoting economic reform in the opening-up era.

Entering the 21st century, constitutional discourse in China is witnessing unprecedented prosperity and diversity (see, for example, Han 2006; see also Tong Zhiwei, this volume). From 1978 to 1988, China's legal reform focused primarily on criminal law and criminal procedure, as the tasks facing legal reformers were mainly related to establishing and maintaining social and political order during the reform and opening-up period. Beginning in 1985, China began focusing on reforming its economic institutions. With the deepening of these economic reforms, there appeared a great need for legal rules concerning business transactions and investments. A large number of laws regulating civil law relations were made to meet these new needs.

But since 1998, in order to address changed circumstances and respond to foreign and domestic calls for rule of law and greater protection of human rights, China has directed its attention increasingly to better administration and better protection of individual rights, thus opening a new page in the history of its legal reform. In 1998, at the 15th Congress of the Chinese Communist Party (CCP), the CCP leadership promised to establish the country as a "a socialist country with the rule of law." The government has made enormous efforts to promote law and legal institutions: including sending people abroad to study; running cooperative training programs with Western countries; and supporting research projects on constitutionalism, human rights, and public law. Frequently heard now is that the rule of law means the rule of the Constitution. In 2003 Xiao Yang, then President of the Supreme People's Court (SPC), said that the authority of the Constitution must be upheld (Xiao 2003). Hu Jintao, the President of the PRC and the General Secretary of the CCP, has also made speeches demanding that government officials act within the Constitution (see Hu 2003). All in all, the Chinese government has appeared very supportive of fostering constitutional consciousness in Chinese society.

The unprecedented rise of constitutional consciousness in China has been a natural outcome of this process. It has been a rise in which PRC constitutional scholars have played a very significant role. There has been a proliferation of books, articles, conferences, and websites on constitutional law and constitutionalism in China. Academic discourse on issues such as the rule of law, the supremacy of the Constitution, fundamental constitutional principles, constitutional protection of human rights, constitutional supervision, right to education, equality, nondiscrimination, and various other rights have contributed to this rise of constitutional consciousness. The status, prestige, and influence of constitutional law scholars also has risen accordingly. The argument that the rule of law means the rule of Constitution especially has put the Constitution at the forefront of legal reforms. In 2003, for example, constitutional law scholars in China appealed to the National People's Congress Standing Committee for constitutional review of

Custody and Repatriation regulations following the Sun Zhigang incident (see chapter by Keith Hand in this volume). More recently, academic constitutional discourse has compelled the National People's Congress (NPC) to revise the draft Property Law (*Zhonghua Renmin Gongheguo Wuquan Fa*) (2007).

In all these discussions and debates, Chinese constitutional scholars have conscientiously looked to American and continental European constitutional ideals for inspiration. It is no exaggeration to say that Chinese constitutional discourse has been significantly "Westernized."

III Western influences on constitutional discourse in China

As described above, notions of constitutionalism deriving from the West entered China more than one hundred years ago, but did not really meet with full acceptance until the end of the 20th century. Today, many well-known works by Western constitutional scholars have been translated into Chinese. These include Bruce Ackerman's *We the People* (1991); Ronald Dworkin's *Taking Rights Seriously* (1977) and *Law's Empire* (1986); Friedrich Hayek's *The Constitution of Liberty* (1960) and works by Cass Sunstein and Richard Posner (American influence has been especially predominant in Chinese constitutional discourse). All of these are foundational references for Chinese post-graduate students working in areas of legal theory and constitutional law.

While translating and introducing Western books and articles, Chinese constitutional scholars have also incorporated into their own writings the ideas and principles of these liberal constitutionalists. One good example of this is found in the work of Professor Li Buyun of the Law Institute of the Chinese Academy of Social Science. As an advisor to the ad hoc Constitutional Revision Working Group, Li has lectured to the top leaders in China on constitutional issues. During the early 1990s, Li spent a considerable period of time at Columbia Law School, exchanging ideas with Louis Henkin, Andrew Nathan, Randle Edwards, and other American scholars. These discussions formed the basis of a series of influential articles he later wrote on the fundamental concepts and principles of constitutionalism—articles that advocated including principles of human rights, rule of law, democracy, and constitutional freedoms into Chinese constitutionalism.

For example, in an influential article entitled "An Outline for Implementing the Strategy of Governing the Country in Accordance with Law," Li (1999) argued that the Chinese vision of rule of law is marked by ten major characteristics. These include a comprehensive legal system, sovereignty of the people, protection of human rights, checks and balance on power, equality before law, supremacy of law, administration according to law, judicial independence, due process, and obedience to law by the party, most of which are obviously liberal values. In another much-read article entitled "Several Theoretical Issues in Constitutional Studies," Li (2002) wrote: "there are two core issues in constitutionalism: one is to constrain state power and regulate its limits and procedure. The other is to provide for the rights of the citizens." In both these articles, Li's arguments are obviously following mainstream American constitutional thought.

All in all, there is now a large literature in China discussing major liberal constitutional notions and how they might contribute to constitutional theories in China. Particularly prominent among these are the notions of rule of law, of individual rights, of judicial review, of limited government, and of the nature of a democratic civil society. As we explore below, all of these discussions have drawn heavily from the work of Western scholars.

A Albert Venn Dicey, Friedrich Hayek, and Chinese discourse on the rule of law

Since Aristotle, many Western thinkers, such as Grotius, Spinoza, Hobbes, Locke, Rousseau, and Montesquieu, have contributed to the notion of the rule of law. The most thorough and explicit explanation of the concept, however, was given by the British constitutional scholar, Albert Venn Dicey. According to Dicey (1981, 110), "rule of law" means first of all that "the absolute supremacy or predominance of regular law as opposed to the influence of arbitrary power, or even of wide discretionary authority on the part of government." Second, it also means "the equal subjection of all classes to the ordinary law of the land administered by the ordinary law courts ... which excludes the idea of any exemption of officials or others from the duty of obedience to the law which governs other citizens or from the jurisdiction of the ordinary tribunals" (Dicey 1981, 120). Building on Dicey's formula, Friedrich Hayek (1944, 54) provided an even clearer formulation of rule of law, maintaining that "[s]tripped of all technicalities this means that the government in all its actions is bound by rules fixed and announced beforehand—rules which make it possible to foresee with fair certainty how the authority will use its coercive powers in given circumstances, and to plan one's individual affairs on the basis of this knowledge."

The particular notions of "rule of law" advanced by Dicey and Hayek have significantly influenced Chinese constitutional discourse. In the 1980s, Chinese governmental officials, scholars, and the general populace showed great interest in the idea of "rule of law." The government and many legal scholars saw it as a strategy for governing the country; commoners began to use it to seek justice in protecting their own rights. Slogans like "rule the country in accordance with law," "managing water resources in accordance with law," and "managing forestation in accordance with law" could be seen everywhere in China. In newspapers, magazines, and scholarly works, there appeared a large number of articles about "rule of law" and "running the country in accordance with the law." Suddenly, rule of law became quite fashionable—if not obsessively so.

Of course, interest in rule of law was not then new for the Chinese. Ever since the late Qing reforms of the 19th century, the Chinese have been trying to understand the meaning of and uses of "rule of law" (see Wang 2002). But the

Chinese interest in rule of law that began in the 1980s was different from this earlier pursuit. The late Qing reformers were skeptical about rule of law, or they only had a rough idea as to its meaning. They were not certain whether rule of law could be used to change China, to emancipate the Chinese people, or to make China into a strong country. They were not certain whether it was worth pursuing.

By contrast, since the late 1980s Chinese interest in rule of law has proceeded with unquestioned certainty regarding its virtues. The Chinese regard the concept of rule of law, however vaguely defined, as an absolute good, and as the only possible way for China and the Chinese people to enjoy modern, workable government. At the beginning of the 21st century, it seems to be China's only option for fulfilling its ambition of modernization. Despite disagreement over the concept of the rule of law, it is now seen by Chinese scholars and government officials as the highest ideal for what is described as China's ongoing "transitional period."

At the same time, the introduction of classical liberalism and modern legal philosophies over the last two decades has also considerably reshaped Chinese scholars' understanding of law and legal institutions in the West, and provided new theoretical lenses for them to evaluate the existing legal system of China. In the aftermath of the Cultural Revolution, which is often associated with "rule of man," the idea of the rule of law, as advocated by Western liberal scholars became all the more attractive, and was wholeheartedly embraced by Chinese scholars. There was a proliferation in the literature on rule of law and related issues in Chinese magazines, periodicals, and books (see generally Chen 1999–2000).

Hayek, in particular, is one of the most frequently referenced theorists in this literature. Professor Deng Zhenglai of Jilin University, for example, has devoted most of the last twenty years studying Hayek. His ideas on Hayek have greatly influenced young Chinese political and legal scholars. Deng has translated most of Hayek's writings into Chinese, of which Hayek's *The Constitution of Liberty* (1960) has become particularly widely read by Chinese scholars and students. Deng also wrote extensively and systematically on Hayek's theories of society and law. In two articles published in 2002. Deng went to great lengths to discuss what he called Hayek's "theory of the Common-Law state with rule of law, based on spontaneous ordering and an evolutionary dynamic of law," arguing authoritatively that Hayek's theories on rule of law present a model of rule of law that is distinct from that of the continental law tradition that China is pursuing. What is implied in this argument is that state-sponsored continental legal transplantations may not have been as effective as has been thought, and there is thus need to look at Anglo-American traditions of rule of law as well (see Deng 2004, 245–367).

B Ronald Dworkin and the emergence of "Rights Talk" in China

Perhaps the most obvious sign of Western, and particularly American, influence on Chinese constitutional discourse can be seen in the growing Chinese acceptance of "rights talk." Ancient China did not have a concept of rights. Again, as was the case with constitutionalism, rights talk or rights theories entered China only in late 19th century, when China began to be more actively engaged with foreign cultures. Classical Western theories on natural and individual rights first became popular among the new Chinese intellectuals of the early 20th century, but they were soon replaced by theories of legal positivism that arose in the West as a reaction against classical, natural-rights theories.

After the founding of the PRC, a Marxist conception of rights took center stage. Marxism saw rights as correlative to duties, and as class oriented, with collective rights being much more significant than individual rights. Even where it recognized constitutional rights, Marxism argued that such rights were overshadowed by the interests of the state and the collective.

This is in sharp contrast with the liberal conception of right that see fundamental, individual rights as somewhat absolute "trumps" over more collective interests. Most famously, Ronald Dworkin has argued that there should be some institution serving as a check and balance on the majoritarian legislature to guarantee that in the pursuit of the majority will, the legislature does not violate the basic rights of individuals. In Dworkin's words, fundamental rights should take precedent over even the most democratic of processes when those processes threaten such rights (Dworkin 1977, 184–205).

Since the reform era, "rights" has become a buzzword for Chinese legal scholars, lawyers, and government officials. This, of course, was not achieved in one stretch. There were doubts and debates over whether China should adopt arguments made by Western rights advocates that the science of law is the science of rights. Some, like Zhang Wenxian, believed that legal studies should focus on rights (see Zhang 2002). Others like Zhang Hengshan, argue that legal science is the science of duties (see Zhang 1989). Eventually, the rights argument triumphed—not only in the academic world but also in the political world. After a decade-long debate, the protection of fundamental, individual rights has now been written into the PRC Constitution.

Dworkin is the most important intellectual resource in this rights talk movement.[1] Many of his books—including *Taking Rights Seriously* (1977) and *A Matter of Principle* (1986)—have been translated, by and large accurately, into Chinese. Articles discussing his theories of law and theories of rights have appeared in Chinese legal periodicals since the late 1970s. There has been an enormous amount of literature in Chinese devoted to the study of his legal and constitutional thought. Dworkin's name has become so popular that even scholars outside the legal world know about him. The first translation of *Taking Rights Seriously* was a best seller in China. In 2002, when he was invited by the Qinghua Law School to visit China, he was treated like a deity. A seminar organized by an academic bookstore in Beijing was attended by over one hundred selected intellectuals (see *Gongfa Pinglun* 2002).

Dworkin's theories of rights and law have influenced several generations of Chinese constitutional scholars. *Taking Rights Seriously* was first introduced to China by Pan Handian, a senior scholar and translator, who translated some excerpts from that book in 1980. In 1981 Professor Shen Zongling's book,

Contemporary Western Legal Philosophies, devoted a chapter to Dworkin's natural law theory. Later on, scholars like Zhang Wenxian (1987) have offered more detailed and updated studies of Dworkin's notion of law as integrity and interpretation.

By 2005, rights-based arguments had become firmly implanted in Chinese soil. Younger generations of Chinese legal scholars now talk about rights as if they were homegrown truths. Government officials are also able to refer and appeal to rights in their policy debates.[2] There is no doubt that such rights talk— and in particular Dworkin's thinking about rights—has exerted tremendous and lasting influence on Chinese legal and constitutional thinking.

C Marbury v. Madison *and the judicialization of the Constitution*

In China, there has recently emerged a kind of constitutional "judicial activism" that is also a reflection of American influence on Chinese constitutional discourse. In China's political system, the constitutional position of the judiciary has traditionally been very weak. In particular, the power to supervise the enforcement of the Constitution has traditionally and formally vested in the hands of the NPC, not those of the courts. The NPC is the supreme organ of the state power. It has the power to legislate and to supervise the work of the executive, judicial, and procuratorial organs. The SPC, by contrast, is appointed by the NPC and works under its formal supervision. To many, it would seem to be somewhat "impudent" for the SPC to review and sit in judgment of the constitutionality of laws passed by its constitutional superior.

In fact, prior to 1999, there was not a single instance of constitutional review by the PRC judiciary. There were not even any provision for such review. And the courts accepted this arrangement. In 1955, the SPC declared the use of constitutional provisions in criminal adjudication inappropriate (see SPC 1955). In 1986, the SPC again made it clear that the Constitution should not be cited in adjudicating cases (see SPC 1986). As a result, many of the fundamental rights (and duties) specified in the Chinese Constitution remain true only on paper.

Since 1999, however, Chinese courts have become more willing to implicate constitutional norms into their decision making (see also Balme, this volume). One particularly dramatic case of this was the *Qi Yuling* case. In that case, the SPC, in defiance of its previous constraints, adopted a proactive attitude that expanded the scope of its interpretive jurisdiction to include the PRC Constitution's guarantee of a "right to education."[3] This has been labeled the "first constitutional case" in the history of the PRC. It caused heated debate over the so-called "judicialization" of the Constitution.

The *Qi Yuling* case was actually a civil case involving the defendant's misappropriation of the plaintiff's name. Having passed the provincial entrance examination for specialized vocational schools, the plaintiff, Qi Yuling, was admitted to Jining Commercial School in Shandong Province. Yet the admission letter for Qi was picked up by her classmate, Chen Xiaoqi, who then enrolled in the Jining

School under Qi's name. Upon graduation, Chen then took a job under Qi's name and worked for ten years before her false identity was discovered by Qi Yuling herself. Qi then brought a lawsuit in the Intermediate People's Court of Zaozhuang in Shandong province, claiming misappropriation of her identity (the civil version of identity theft) and violation of her right to an education. The trial court awarded her RMB 35,000 for Chen's misappropriation of her name, but declined to provide remedy for the violation of her right to education, saying that she had waived that right by subsequent actions.

Qi Yuling then appealed that decision to the High People's Court of Shandong Province, arguing that her subsequent actions could not be construed as waiving her civil-law right to education. Because of the complexities of the case, the High Court filed an inquiry to the SPC seeking direction as to the right to education question. In a surprise reply, the SPC (2001) directed to the High Court that the plaintiff's "right to education" was a *constitutional* right under Article 46 of the PRC Constitution, and that as a constitutional right it could not be waived.

This was the first time that a Chinese court had ever cited a constitutional provision in issuing a judicial interpretation. Not surprisingly, it generated a good deal of political and legal controversy. Some saw this as China's first case of judicial review, and believed that the SPC, in expressly citing to Qi Yuling's constitutional rights in this case, has opened a new chapter in PRC constitutional development. On the other hand, many critics argued that the SPC was wrong to cite a constitutional provision in this case—first, because that case is clearly a civil law case, to which the General Principles of Civil Law rather than the Constitution were applicable; and second, because the Constitution itself was not justiciable.

In the midst of this debate, an article by an SPC Judge—Huang Songyou, one of the drafters of the SPC interpretation—publicly defended that interpretation by comparing it to the famous American case of *Marbury v. Madison* (1803), which established judicial review as a part of the American Constitution. Huang noted how in that case, the Supreme Court of the United States pioneered the practice of judicializing of the Constitution by declaring that legislation that contradicts the Constitution can be annulled by the courts. In doing so, they made constitutional interpretation an ordinary part of the judicial process. He argued that *Marbury* has become an international trend, and that China, with the deepening of its ongoing reforms, also needs to begin referencing constitutional provisions in order to more effectively uphold the law (Huang 2001).[4]

D Benjamin Constant and the nature of popular sovereignty

While Anglo-American influence has been particularly dominant in contemporary Chinese constitutional discourse, continental European influence, especially French influence, is also present. In the early part of the twentieth century, French constitutional thinkers were more inflential in China than Anglo-American thinkers: Rousseau, Montesquieu, Voltaire, Dedroit, to name just a few, had very significant and lasting influence on both intellectuals and revolutionaries in China. In the present era, however, for some reason French thinkers seem to be less influential than their Anglo-American counterparts. Nevertheless, Foucault, Bourdieu, and Derrida are part of the compulsory reading list for the students of philosophy and cultural criticism, while two other French thinkers, Benjamin Constant and Alexis de Tocqueville, seem to be enjoying a growing popularity among political scientists and constitutional scholars in China.

Benjamin Constant's influence comes from his critique of Jean-Jacques Rousseau's notion of "popular sovereignty." Rousseau had argued that the sovereignty of the state stems from the *collective* general will, and that as such it is both unlimited and superior to individual will. This vision has reigned over official Chinese political mentality for almost a century. In critiquing Rousseau, many scholars rejected his "popular" basis of sovereignty due to certain totalitarian features. Constant, on the other hand, was much more nuanced in his critique. For Constant, the principle of popular sovereignty is beyond debate. But he also argued that such sovereignty must in essence be constrained by the independent needs and existence of the individual.

Like Rousseau, the current political culture of China sees China's popular sovereignty as inviolable and unlimited. Constant's argument thus provides a subtle reminder that the sovereignty of the state over its individual citizens may not be as total as Chinese politicians are wont to assume. For constitutional scholars in China, Constant is thus appealing because he viewed political power as a necessary evil that must be limited.[5] His arguments are used to advance the idea that government's power can be limited by constitutional principles, by institutional arrangements that check and balance power, and by external factors such as the independent rights of individuals.

In China, Constant's arguments win him followers, particularly among those who are keen on constitutional reform. Professor Li Qiang of Beijing University, for example, is among those who are most enthusiastic about Constant's ideas. He believes that Constant figures very significantly in the history of the development of liberty. He argued in a preface he wrote to the Chinese translation of Constant's most famous political writings on liberty and constitutionalism that even though Constant could not be said to be good at speculative thinking, he had the sensitivity of a man of letters and the pragmatism of a statesman. He also pointed out that Constant's political ideas, especially ideas on totalitarianism and liberty, are extremely profound and had lasting impact on ideas of liberalism that emerged later (see Li 1999).

E Alexis de Tocqueville and democratic development

Another French thinker who has attracted many followers in China is Alexis de Tocqueville.[6] The Chinese translation of his *Democracy in America* appeared in 1988 and is constantly quoted by Chinese political scientists and legal scholars (see Tuokewei'er [Alexis de Tocqueville] 1988). Tocqueville is an important intellectual source for China's further democratic reform. For example, Mao Shoulong, a constitutional scholar in the People's University of China, has argued that *Democracy in America* presents great opportunities for Chinese readers to understand patterns of democratic development, both in mature democracies and in developing democracies as well (see Mao [undated]). Mao argued that although China is not an ideal democracy, democracy is developing there. It is simply that China's democratic revolution is still ongoing. For this reason, China must draw on the experience of democratic revolutions in other countries of the world.

Tocqueville's ideas on centralized power in a democratic society, on the "tyranny of majority," and on the merits of civil society have been widely accepted and quoted by Chinese scholars. One scholar, Gong Qun (2005), has argued that the principle of majoritian decisionmaking leads to rule by majority, and that the rule by majority often results in a dictatorship of the majority. Chen Binghui (2004b) has argued that Tocqueville's concept of tyranny of the majority has become a common topic in contemporary theories of democracy. As he sees it, many scholars have come to reject democracy based on their misinterpretation of that concept, but in fact Tocqueville was not opposed to democracy—his argument is that one must adhere to democratic principles of government decisionmaking while at the same time preventing the emergence of a "tyranny of the majority." Tocqueville is also regarded as one of the first persons to recognize the role of civil society in promoting freedom and democracy. His argument that a relatively independent and pluralistic civil society is an indispensable component of a constitutional government's capacity to restrain political power has been carefully studied in China (see, for example, Chen 2004d).

IV Asian values, Chinese characteristics and the limitations of the influence of Western constitutional theories

But the current Western influence on Chinese constitutional discourse is limited by a tension between universalism and cultural relativism. On one hand, liberal constitutionalism is often portrayed as a universal paradigm upon which China is expected to build its constitutional and legal framework, design its constitutional enforcement mechanisms, and implement its substantive principles. On the other hand, there is a constant urge in China demanding "Chinese-ness" in whatever the Chinese are engaged in doing. Any "constitutionalism with Chinese characteristics" or "Chinese constitutionalism" will have to struggle with this tension, and whatever hybrid form of constitutionalism that is able to emerge out of this tension will take time to appear.

Since the latter half of the 20th century, constitutional studies in many Asian countries have become conscious of the special constitutional identities of their respective cultures. There is also some discussion about a "pan-Asian" version of constitutionalism. So far, however, no systematic theory of constitutional law that could be adequately called "Asian constitutionalism" has emerged. Despite Lawrence W. Beer's effort to articulate a constitutionalism practiced in Asian countries that might be different from the liberal constitutionalism embraced by the United States and other Western democracies, the notion of an "Asian constitutionalism" has not gone beyond the application of liberal constitutionalism to Asian historical and cultural backgrounds.

The idea of a (pan-) Asian constitutionalism thus remains a vague consciousness among a few, mainly Asian, constitutional scholars. Han Dayuan, an enthusiastic advocator for Asian constitutionalism in China, argues that Asian constitutionalism is defined by a conspicuous intellectual trend that moves away from "Western Centrism" in constitutional thinking and captures the distinctive theories and practices of constitutionalism in Asian countries. Yet he also acknowledges that the main values that Asian constitutionalism embraces—such as rule of law, democracy, and protection of citizens' rights—are drawn from liberal constitutionalism. If there is anything distinct about Asian constitutionalism, perhaps it lies in the constitutional emphasis its advocates attach to the role that economic development, state building, and community values play in the constitutional framework. But these roles can also be seen simply as complements to liberal constitutionalism, which would make Asian constitutionalism merely a variant of liberal constitutionalism, rather than a brand new version of constitutionalism.

In the Chinese context, the idea of an Asian constitutionalism is more like a close cousin to Western constitutionalism—related to the household, but living in a different house. One major conviction of many Chinese reformer s is that China can keep its unique national and cultural identity intact in the process of modernization. The government has long been pressing for a socialist system and a socialist market economy with "Chinese characteristics." This goal has even been incorporated into the Chinese Constitution and its laws. But the question of what, exactly, these "Chinese characteristics" are is yet to be worked out. If anything significantly different from liberal constitutionalism eventually appears, it will not be called "Asian constitutionalism," at least in China, but "constitutionalism with Chinese characteristics," because of China's obsession with Chinese-ness and indifference to the larger concept of "Asia," which often reminds the Chinese of the bad experience of Japanese invasion in the 1930s and 1940s.

V Conclusion

The introduction of Western constitutional theories into Chinese political and legal culture has obviously affected the way that Chinese constitutional scholars and reform-minded officials have thought about China's future constitutional development. Anglo-American influence already has brought about significant changes in Chinese constitutional law. Continental influence is also obvious, but its practical impact is yet to be as keenly felt. The impact of Western constitutional theories, however, is still limited. The concern with Chinese-ness, a lack of effective enforcement mechanisms, and the interest of the party and the state, all work to reduce the effectiveness of these theories.

Notes

1   A Chinese-character Google search of Dworkin's name (*Dewojin*) retrieved over 42,900 items on May 26, 2007.
2   A Chinese-character Google search of the term "rights" (*quanli*) retrieved over 75 million items on May 26, 2007.
3   Article 46 of the PRC Constitution provides: "[c]itizens of the People's Republic of China have the duty as well as the right to receive education. The state promotes the all-around moral, intellectual and physical development of children and young people."
4   In December 2008, the Supreme People's Court (2008) formally annulled its *Qi Yuling* Interpretation (the court's final judgement for Qi Yuling, however, was not affected).
5   A Chinese-character Google search of Constant's name (*Gongsidang*) retrieved over 17,200 items on May 26, 2007.
6   A Chinese-character Google search of Tocqueville's name (*Tuokewei'er*) retrieved over 388,000 items on May 26, 2007.

Bibliography

Books, Chapters and Articles

Alford, William. 1986. The inscrutable occidental? Implications of Roberto Unger's uses and abuses of the Chinese past. *Texas Law Review* 64:915–972.

Bodde, Derk, and Clarence Morris. 1962. *Law is imperial China*. Philadelphia: University of Pennsylvania Press.

Chen, Albert. 1999–2000. Toward a legal enlightenment: discussions in contemporary China on the rule of law. *UGLA Pacific Basin Law Journal* 17:125–165.

Chen Binghu. 2004b. Minzhu yu duoshu de huanzhi: iedu Tuokewei'er de munzhu lilun [Democracy and tyranny of the majority: an Interpretation of Tocqueville's theory of democracy]. *Xiamen Daxue Xuebao*, no. 2:29–34.

Chen Jiansheng. 2004d. Lun Tnokewei'er "Yi Shehui Zhiyue Quanli" sixiang [Regarding Tocqueville's idea of "Restriction of Power by Society"]. *Hannon Dexut Xurbaa Shehui Koxur* Bar no. 2:188–192.

Deng Zhenglai, 2004. *Guize, zhixu, wuzhi [Rules, order, and ignorance]*. Beijing: Sanlian Shudian.

Dicey, A.V. [Albert Venn]. 1981. *Introduction to the study of the law of the constitution.* Indianapolis: Liberty Classics.

Dworkin, Ronald. 1977. *Taking rights seriously*. Cambridge, MA: Harvard University Press.

Gong Qun. 2005. Lun baohu shaoshu de quanli [The rights of minority]. *Zhongguo Renmin Daxue Xuebao* no. 3: 95–101.

Han Dayuan. 2006. Liang qian ling wu nian xianfa xueshu yanjiu huigu [Constitutional scholarship in 2005]. *Faxuejia* no. 1.

Hayek, Friedrich A. 1944. *The road to serfdom*. London: Routledge.

Hu Jintao. 2003. Quanmian guanche shishi xianfa, wei quanmian jianshe xiaokang shehui tigong jianshi falu baozhang [Fully enforce the constitution to provide solid legal guarantee for full construction of a society with minimum satisfaction]. In *Dangzheng ganba xianfa jiaoyu duben*, ed. Gu Angran and Qiao Xiaoyang, 1–5. Beijing: Zhonggong zhongyang dangxiao chubanshe.

Huang Songyou. 2001. Xianfa sifahuan jiqi yiyi [The judicialization of the constitution and its significance]. *Renmin Fayuan Bao*, August 13.

Li Buyun. 1999. Shishi yifa zhiguo zhanlue lungang [An outline for implementing the strategy of governing the country in accordance with law]. *Xuexi Yu Tansuo* no. 3: 65–71.

Li Buyun. 2002. Xianfa xue de jige lilun wenti [Some theoretical problems concerning the study of constitutional law]. *Zhongguo Shehui Kexueyuan Yanjiu Shengyuon Xuebao* no. 6: 19–25.

Li Qiang. 1999. Gongsidang yu xiandai ziyou zhuyi [Benjamin Constant and modern liberalism]. In *Gudai ren de ziyou yu xiandai ren de ziyou: Gongsidang zhengzhi lunwen xuan [Liberty of the ancients and of the moderns: the political theory of Benjamin Constant]*, by Benjamin Constant, 1–12. Beijing: Shangwu yinshuguan.

Liang Zhiping. 1987. Zhongguo fa de guoqu. xianzai yu weilai: yige wenhua de jiantao [The past, present, and future of Chinese law: an exploration from a cultural perspective.] *Bijiaofa Yanjiu* 17:21–36.

Mao Shoulong. Undated. Lun *Meigua de Minzhu* "Xuyan" Daodu [Introduction to the Preface of *Democracy in America*]. http://article.chinalawinfo.com/article/user/article_ display. asp?ArticleD=30265.

Supreme People's Court (PRC). 1955. *Zuigao Renmin Fayuan guanyu zai xingshi panjue zhong buyi yinyong xianfa zuo lunzui kexing yiju de pifu [Reply of the Supreme People's Court on not citing the constitution as the basis for determining guilt or sentences in criminal judgments]*. Issued July 30 Reprinted In *Xin zhongguo sifa jieshi daquan*, 420–421 Beijing: Zhongguo jiancha chubanshe

Supreme People's Court (PRC). 1986. *Zuigao Renmin Fayuan Guanyu Renmin Fayuan zhizuo falu wenshu ruhe yinyong falu guifanxing wenjian de pifu [Reply concerning how People's Courts are to cite legally normative documents when producing legal documents]*. Issued October 28.

Supreme People's Court (PRC). 2001. *Guanyu yi qing fan xingiaingquan de shouduan qingfan xianfa baohu de gongmin shoujiaoyuquan de jiben quanli shifon ying chengdan minshi zeren de pifu [Response regarding whether one who violated the constitutionally protected basic right to education of the citizen should bear civil obligation]*. Reprinted in *Zuigao Renmin Rayuan Gongbao [Gazette of the Supreme People's Court of the People's Republic of China]* no. 5:158–161.

Tuokewei'er [Alexis de Tocqueville]. 1988. *Lun Meiguo de Minzhu [Democracy in America]*. 2 vols. trans. Dong Guoliang. Beijing: Shangwu yinshuguan.

Tyler, Tom. 1990. *Why people obey the law*. New Haven: Yale University Press.

Unger, Roberto Mangabeira. 1976. *Law in modern society: toward a criticism of social theory*. New York: Free Press.

Wang Jian. 2002. Xifa dongjian: zhongxi falu gainian duiying guanxi zaoqi jishi de kaocha [Legal transplantation from the West to the East: a study of the corresponding meaning of legal concepts between the West and China in the late Qing Dynasty]. In *Qinghua Fazhi Lunheng*, ed. Gao Hongjun. Vol. 2, 296–359. Beijing: Qinghua daxue-chubanshe.

Xiao Yang. 2003. Weihu xianfa de zhishang quanwei [Defending the supremacy of the constitution]. In *Dangzheng ganbu xianfa jiaoyu duben [A constitutional reader for the party and government cadres]*, ed. Gu Angran and Qiao Xiaoyang, 268–274. Beijing: Zhonggong zhongyang dangxiao chubanshe.

Xie Weiyan. 2004. *Cong xianfa dao xianzheng [From constitutions to constitutionalism]*. Jinan: Shandong Renmin chubanshe.

Zhang Hengshan. 1989. Fa de zhongxin hezai?—Ping "quanli benwei" shuo [What is the focus of Law?—A critique of the "rights-orientation" thesis]. *Zhengzhi yu Falu* no. 1:6–9.

Zhang Jinfan. 1986. *Zhongguo fazhi shigang [An outline of China's legal system]*. Beijing: Zhongguo zhengfa daxue chubanshe.

Zhang Wenxian. 2002. Cong yiwu benwei dao quanli benwei shi fa de fazhan guilu [The Developmental Pattern of Law: From Obligations to Rights]. *Zhongguo Lilun faxue yanjiu xinwen wang [Legaltheory.com.on]*. December 24, 2002. http://www.legaltheory.com.cn/info asp?id=854. Accessed May 9, 2008.

Zhang Wenxian. 1987. *Dangdai xifang fazhexue [Contemporary western legal philosophy]*. Jilin: Jilin renmin chubanshe.

Treaties and Legislation

Zhonghua Renmin Gongheguo Wuquan Fa [Property Law of the People's Republic of China]. Adopted 2007.

Part 12

CRIMINAL PROCESS
AND JUSTICE

31

CRIMINAL JUSTICE IN POST-MAO CHINA

Some preliminary observations

Shao-Chuan Leng

Source: *Journal of Criminal Law & Criminology* 73:1 (1982): 204–237.

China's trial of the Gang of Four and six other members of the "Lin-Jiang cliques" has attracted world-wide attention. Chinese press has pictured the trial as a landmark: the end of a lawless era, a successful test of the new legal system and a demonstration that all are equal before the law.[1] Contrary to Chinese leaders' expectations, however, many observers have considered the trial as essentially a political rather than legal exercise.[2] On the other hand, the holding of this trial appeared to reflect, among other things, Beijing's desire to publicize its commitment to legality, and the controlled and selected reporting of the court sessions has given the outside world glimpses of the judicial process under China's new and emerging legal order.

This article attempts to provide a preliminary and general survey of the procedure through which criminal justice is administered, in law and in practice, in post-Mao China. Special attention will be given to the applicability of certain universal principles of the conception of the rule of law in relation to criminal cases, e.g., public trials, presumption of innocence, equality before the law, right to defense and appeal, judicial independence, etc.

I China's recent legal development

Until mid-1979, the People's Republic of China did not have a code of substantive or procedural criminal law, although there were a few statutes governing criminal justice such as the Act for Punishment of Counterrevolutionaries of 1951, the Act for the Punishment of Corruption of 1952, the Arrest and Detention Act of 1954 and the Security Administration Punishment Act ("SAPA") of 1957.[3] The single most important reason for the PRC's lack of codification in its 30-year history appeared to be Mao Zedong, whose bias against bureaucratization and preference for the mass line accounted mainly for Beijing's past emphasis on the societal (informal) model of law over the jural (formal) model and on the politicization of the legal process.[4]

There was a period in the mid-1950s when the ascendency of the jural mode was marked by the adoption of a state constitution, organic legislation for the courts and procuracy, and a series of substantive and procedural laws. Effort was also made to draft civil, criminal and procedural codes. China's progress toward a stable legal order, however, was brought to an abrupt end by the Anti-Rightist Campaign of 1957–58, the result of which was the disruption of the codification effort and the assumption of a dominant role in law enforcement by the Party and the police at the expense of the judiciary and the procuracy.[5] The jural model suffered another serious setback during the Cultural Revolution of 1966–69 when "smashing Gong-Jian-Fa (police, police, and courts)" became the slogan of the day. There is little question that the decade immediately preceding the death of Mao and the subsequent arrest of the Gang of Four in late 1976 was the most regressive period of China's legal life. The current Chinese leadership, in fact, has attacked Lin Biao and the Gang of Four for creating a state of lawlessness and "feudal-facist" rule during the years of 1966–76, subjecting tens of thousands of innocent people to cruel persecution.[6]

The purge of the Gang of Four and their followers and the commitment to the modernization of Chinese society by post-Mao leaders have created a new setting for the revitalization and improvement of China's legal system. In the interest of restoring order and morale and of attracting domestic support and external assistance for the modernization program, the Chinese leadership has taken a number of steps to strengthen the Chinese laws and judicial system so as to provide a secure, orderly environment for economic development. A new constitution was adopted in March 1978 to restore many provisions on legality and individual rights contained in the 1954 constitution but omitted in the 1975 document. Among those revived are the rights of the accused to defense and to an open, public trial and the participation of the people's assessor in the administration of justice.[7] In the judicial field, the new constitution also reinstitutes the procuracy, victim of the Cultural Revolution, and reestablishes the requirement for the police to have the approval of the judiciary or the procuracy before making an arrest.[8] Another institutional development was the restoration of the Ministry of Justice in 1979 by the Standing Committee of the National People's Congress ("NPC") to handle judicial administrative work and to manage and train judicial cadres.[9]

As part of the overall plan to win back popular confidence and to right the wrongs of its predecessor, the post-Mao leadership released in June 1978 some 110,000 persons who had been detained as "rightists" since 1957.[10] It also decided in early 1979 to restore political and civil rights to members of former "class enemies:" as long as former landlords and rich peasants and their descendants "support socialism," they would no longer be discriminated against.[11] Moreover, the Chinese government has taken measures to rectify the injustice and repressions allegedly committed by the Gang of Four and their followers. As reported by President Jiang Hua of the Supreme Court, by the end of June 1980 the people's courts at various levels had reviewed over 1.13 million criminal conviction cases handled during the Cultural Revolution and had redressed more than 251,000 cases in which people were unjustly, falsely and wrongly charged and sentenced.[12] On the legislative front, progress has been made with considerable speed. The NPC adopted in July 1979 seven major legal codes: Criminal Law ("Chinese CL");[13] Criminal Procedure Law ("Chinese CP");[14] the Organic Law of Local People's Congresses and Local People's Governments;[15] the Electoral Law for the NPC and Local People's Congresses; the Organic Law of People's Courts;[16] the Organic Law of People's Procuratorates;[17] and the Law on Joint Ventures with Chinese and Foreign Investments. This has been followed by a nation-wide campaign to publicize the new legal system and the enactment of other laws and regulations. For instance, four new laws were adopted by the NPC in September 1980: the Nationality Law, the (revised) Marriage Law, the Income Tax Law Concerning Joint Ventures, and the Individual Income Tax Law. According to Peng Zhen, Vice Chairman of the NPC Standing Committee and Director of its Commission for Legal Affairs, work has been advancing in formulating a civil law, a civil procedural law and a number of economic regulations.[18] It should also be noted that the NPC Standing Committee has passed a resolution that all laws and decrees enacted since the founding of the People's Republic in 1949 remain effective if they do not conflict with the present constitution and other laws and decrees.[19]

In the meantime, legal education, research and publication have been accelerated by the current leadership with equal vigor. According to a recent report, there are eighteen universities in China with legal departments. In addition, four institutes of politics and law (Beijing, East China, Northwest and Southwest) have resumed operation. Some 2,000 new college students were enrolled in 1979 for legal study. Proposals have been made to add law departments to more universities, to reestablish the Central South Institute of Politics and Law, and to establish a new Northeast Institute of Politics and Law and a new South China Institute of Politics and Law.[20] Aside from university legal departments and special institutes of politics and law, there are a number of political and judicial cadre schools as well as part-time colleges and short-term training classes to provide students with legal education.[21] Research and publication in the legal field not only have been resumed but also are gaining new respectability. Books on the constitution, the Chinese CL, the Chinese CP, and other legal subjects have been published. Several new legal journals have appeared, better known among them being *Faxue yanjiu* (Studies in Law) and *Minzhu yu fazhi* (Democracy and the Legal System).[22] To popularize legal knowledge, the socialist legal system has frequently been discussed by PRC news media. Indeed, hardly a day passes now without some new legal materials appearing in the Chinese press or other publications.

II The resurrected judicial system

With the coming into effect on January 1, 1980, of the Chinese CL, the Chinese CP and the Organic Laws of Courts and Procuratorates, the PRC's system of criminal justice has entered a new era of operation and development. As in the mid-1950s, the current judicial structure consists of the courts, the procuracy and the police designed to complement and restrict one another. Compared to the 1954 Organic Law of the People's Courts, the new Court Law has made only a few changes. The court system is still composed of the Supreme People's Court, the higher people's courts, the intermediate people's courts and the basic people's courts. In addition, there are special courts that include military courts, railway transport courts water transport courts and new forestry courts. Some 3,100 people's courts at various local levels are reported to have been in operation throughout the country.[23] With minor modifications, the new Court Law reiterates the 1954 provisions concerning judicial independence, equality before the law, public trials, the right to defense, people's assessors, judicial committees and the two-trial (one appeal) system.[24]

One significant change in the revised Court Law is to make the court accountable only to the people's congresses and free the court from direct supervision by local governments. According to articles 35 and 36, the presidents of the people's courts at all levels are elected and recalled by the corresponding people's congress and their vice presidents, presiding judges and other judges are appointed and removed by the standing committees of the corresponding people's congress.[25] Under the 1954 Law, the vice presidents and other officials of the local courts were appointed and removed by the people's councils at the corresponding levels.[26] Another noticeable feature of the revised Law is to provide the Supreme People's Court with additional power. While the authority to interpret the constitution and laws in the PRC is reserved for the Standing Committee of the National People's Congress,[27] the Supreme People's Court is bestowed with the power to give "explanations on questions concerning specific applications of laws and decrees in judicial procedure" in addition to its adjudication functions.[28] The requirement adopted by the NPC in 1957, that all death sentences must have the approval of the Supreme People's Court,[29] is also incorporated into the new Organic Law of the Courts as Article 13.

The New Organic Law of the People's Procuratorates retains the same structure of the procuracy established by the 1954 organic enactment, namely, the Supreme People's Procuratorate, local people's procuratorates and special people's procuratorates. Parallel to that of the local people's courts, the hierarchy of the local procuratorates consists of three levels: (1) people's procuratorates of provinces, autonomous regions, and municipalities directly under the central authority; (2) branches of the above and people's procuratorates of prefectures and counties directly under the provincial governments; (3) people's procuratorates of counties, cities, autonomous counties, and district directly under the city governments.[30] In other respects, the new Law on the procuracy introduces some important innovations on the basis of Chinese conditions thus departing from the Soviet model on which the 1954 statute was closely patterned.[31] First, it drops the controversial principle of "vertical leadership" adopted in 1954 under which local procuratorates were free of control by local state organs and were responsible only to higher level organs of the procuracy.[32] Instead, the new law applies the principle of dual leadership making the procuratorates at all levels accountable to the people's congresses and their standing committees at corresponding levels and at the same time placing local procuratorates in their work under the leadership of the procuratorate at the next higher level.[33] As in the case of court officials, the power to elect or recall chief procurators and to appoint or remove deputy chief procurators and other procurators at various levels is vested in the corresponding people's congresses and their standing committees respectively.[34]

Second, the new Law removes the 1954 provisions for the power of general supervision whereby the procuracy could supervise the legality of the actions of all state organs.[35] The procuratorates are now permitted to deal with state functionaries only when the latter violate the Criminal Law.[36] "Ordinary cases concerning breaches of Party or government discipline but no violation of the Criminal Law," in the words of Peng Zhen, "shall all be handled by the discipline inspection departments of the Party or the organs of government."[37] Article 1 of the new Organic Law defines the procuratorates as "the organs of the state supervising the administration of justice."[38] In that capacity, the procuracy is empowered to carry out investigation of criminal cases, oversee the activities of the police in the criminal process, institute prosecution, scrutinize the trial activities of the courts and supervise the execution of judgments and the activities of correctional institutions.[39] Reflecting the current political need in China, the procuracy also has the power to "exercise procuratorial authority with regard to cases of treason, of attempts to split the country and other major criminal cases of serious disruption of the unified implementation of state policies, law, decrees and administrative orders."[40] The independence of the procuracy is restored in Article 9 which reads: "People's Procuratorates shall exercise their procuratorial authority independently in accordance with the law and shall not be subject to interference by other administrative organs, organizations or individuals."[41]

There is little doubt that the adoption of the long-awaited Chinese CL and Chinese CP is a very significant development in the Chinese system of justice for these measures define punishable acts and penalties and regularize the sanctioning process in the PRC. The Chinese CL is devised to protect, first of all, the socialist order and next, the people's personal rights, as indicated in the following words of Article 2:

> The tasks of Criminal Law of the People's Republic of China are to use criminal punishments to struggle against all counterrevolutionary and other criminal conduct in order to defend the system of the dictatorship of the proletariat, to protect socialist property owned by the whole people and property collectively owned by the laboring masses, to protect citizens' lawful privately-owned property, to protect citizens' rights of the person, democratic rights, and other rights, to maintain social order, order in production, order in work, order in education and

research, and order in the lives of the masses of people, and to safeguard the smooth progress of the socialist revolution and the work of socialist construction.[42]

Under the general provisions of the new Chinese CL Law, punishments are classified as principal and supplementary. The principal punishments are: (1) public surveillance, a special Chinese practice, which ranges from three months to two years of work with pay; (2) detention of fifteen days to six months during which time appropriate pay is given for work done and one or two days leave is granted each month; (3) fixed-term imprisonment from six months to fifteen years; (4) life imprisonment; and (5) the death penalty. The supplementary punishments include fines, deprivation of political rights and confiscation of property.[43] The specific provisions of the Law stipulate eight types of offenses and their punishments. They are: (1) counterrevolutionary offenses; (2) offenses endangering public security; (3) offenses against the socialist economic order; (4) offenses infringing upon the personal and democratic rights of citizens; (5) offenses of encroachment on property; (6) offenses against public order; (7) offenses against marriage and the family; and (8) malfeasance.[44]

As in the Soviet Union, severe sanctions are provided for counter-revolutionary crimes in the PRC. Nevertheless, the new Law differs from past practice and defines in clearer terms a long list of acts of counterrevolutionary offenses, including conspiring with a foreign state to jeopardize the security of China, plotting to overthrow the government or split the country, inciting an insurrection, committing espionage or supporting the enemy, and highjacking ships or aircraft.[45] Capital punishment is imposed only for those counterrevolutionary offenses "when the harm to the country and the people is especially serious and the circumstances especially evil."[46] The other grave offenses listed in the Criminal Law as punishable by the death penalty are homicide, robbery, arson, rape, dike-breaching, planting explosives, embezzling public property, etc.[47] Similar to the requirement of the Court Law, Article 43 of the Chinese CL stipulates that "except for judgments of the Supreme People's Court, all sentences of the death penalty shall be submitted to the Supreme People's Court for approval."[48] It also reinstates a provision, a unique PRC innovation, to suspend in most cases the death penalty for a two-year period during which reform through labor will be carried out to see if the offender shows evidence of repentence.[49]

To prevent the recurrence of flagrant abuses of the past, the Chinese CL prohibits extortion of confessions through torture or gathering a crowd for "beating, smashing and looting."[50] There are also penalties against false charges, perjury, unlawful incarceration and illegal searches or entries.[51] The Law further protects citizens from slander and libel, including the use of wall posters.[52]

As one may note, the application of analogy and retroactivity in China's past criminal legislation has been a main subject of concern and criticism.[53] The new Criminal Law eliminates the use of retroactivity by stipulating that offenses committed before the date of its promulgation (January 1, 1980) shall be dealt with in accordance with the laws, decrees and policies at the time when the infractions occurred.[54] However, the new Law does retain the principle of analogy with certain restrictions, as Article 79 provides: "A crime that is not expressly provided for in the Special Provisions of this Law may be determined and punished by reference to the most closely analogous article of the Special Provisions of this Law, but the matter must be submitted to the Supreme People's Court for approval."[55]

The retention of analogy in the Chinese CL, although with tighter control than before, is open to criticism.[56] Some observers also think that the definition of counterrevolution is still somewhat vague.[57] Despite these flaws, the presence of the Chinese CL itself constitutes a significant advancement in post-Mao China's move toward legality.[58] The same can be said about the promulgation of the Chinese CP, whose provisions will be analyzed in detail later.[59] It is generally agreed that by and large the 192-article Chinese CL and the 164-article Chinese CP are impressive and concise pieces of legislation. Together they prescribe appropriate legal standards to guide judicial work and the framework for "due process" to protect the individual. Their enforcement, on the other hand, is certainly no easy task especially in view of the shortage of trained personnel in the legal field.[60] Along with several others, the two Laws officially came into force in January 1980. Nevertheless, in accordance with the proposal of the Supreme People's Court and the Supreme People's Procuratorate, the NPC Standing Committee decided in April 1980 that if there should be a shortage of judicial personnel to deal with criminal cases, the time limit for handling them as stipulated in the Chinese CP could be extended up to the end of 1980. To prepare for the overall enforcement of the Chinese CP across the country in 1981, the Committee also called upon the courts, procuratorates, public security organs and judicial administrative departments at all levels to draw up, in the light of actual conditions, specific plans to implement the Chinese CP by stages and at different times within 1980 except for a few remote areas.[61]

In the following pages, the process through which criminal justice is administered in China and the major issues pertinent to the judicial procedure are examined.

III Pretrial proceedings

According to the Chinese CP, "the public security organs are responsible for investigation, detention, and preparatory examination in criminal cases. The people's procuracies are responsible for approving arrest, conducting procuratorial control (including investigation) and initiating public prosecution. The people's courts are responsible for adjudication. No other organ, organization or individual has the right to exercise these powers."[62] In criminal proceedings, the court, the procuracy and the police should "take facts as their basis and law as their criterion"[63] and should "have a division of labor with separate responsibilities and coordinate with each other and restrain each other in order to guarantee the accurate and effective enforcement of the law."[64]

The pretrial proceedings of the Chinese criminal process are composed of two principal parts: (1) arrest and detention and (2) investigation. To prevent illegal arrests and prolonged detentions, proper procedure and strict time limits are set by the Procedure Law as well as by the revised Regulations Governing Arrest and Detention promulgated in February 1979 to replace the old enactment in 1954.[65] In carrying out an apprehension or in making an arrest, the police must produce a warrant. The family of the detainee or the arrested should be notified of the reasons for the action and the place of confinement within 24 hours. Interrogation must start within twenty-four hours after any apprehension or arrest, and the detainee or the arrested must be immediately released if no legitimate ground is found. When the public security organ deems it necessary to declare a detainee arrested, the matter should be submitted to the procuratorate for approval within three days or, in special circumstances, seven days. The procuracy must either sanction the arrest or order the release of the detainee within three days.[66]

During the stage of investigation, the tasks include interrogation of the accused and witnesses, search and seizure, examination of evidence and preparation of the indictment. Mindful of past abuses, the Chinese CP stipulates that in collecting various kinds of evidence throughout the entire judicial process, the police, judges and procurators are strictly forbidden to extort confessions by torture, threat, enticement, deceit or any other illegal means.[67] At the time of search, except in emergency situations, investigators shall show the searched a search warrant.[68] The Chinese CP further provides that detention of an accused pending investigation should not exceed two months. If necessary, a one-month extension may be granted by the procuratorate at the next higher level.[69] A procuratorate is required to decide whether or not to prosecute a case sent to it by police within one month to one and a half months.[70]

In practice, the shortage of trained personnel and persistence of negative and erroneous views about the law have hampered the full implementation of the provisions of the Chinese CP. Some police and judicial cadres regard the law as a hindrance tying their hands and feet in the fight against crimes.[71] Others cling to the old prejudice that the suspect in a criminal case is guilty and should be dealt with as such.[72] Consequently, it is not too surprising to find the frequent occurrence of illegal arrests and detentions and unlawful search and seizure in Chinese society.[73] What has happened to some political dissidents is only a part of this phenomenon.[74]

Educational and other efforts have been made by the PRC to combat the negative attitude toward the law. A 1979 textbook on the Chinese CP, for example, warned against the unlawful practice of prolonged detentions and the use of "continuous interrogation" and other forms of "disguised torture" to extract a confession from the accused.[75] A 1980 article in the *Enlightenment Daily* also took pains to explain the reasons for banning torture in extracting confessions.[76] Still, violations have been taking place. In one case, an African student in Beijing was allegedly arrested by the police, held in prison six days and tortured because of his supposed relations with several Chinese women.[77] In another case a policeman in Shanghai was reported to have illegally detained and cruelly beaten a stranger just over a minor dispute.[78] According to the information of the Supreme People's Procuratorate, between January 1979 and June 1980 procuratorial organs at various levels accepted and heard more than 10,000 cases in infringement upon citizens' personal and democratic rights, such as illegal detention, illegal search, extorting confessions by torture, etc. More than 8,000 such cases have already been handled and over 9,000 persons have been found guilty of violating the law and discipline.[79]

As part of Beijing's effort to publicize its legal system, prominent Chinese jurists in a radio broadcast answered questions concerning the recent trial of the Gang of Four and six others. One of the procedural issues raised was why Jiang Qing and other defendants were only brought to trial recently after having been under detention for several years. In his explanations, Zhang Youyu, Vice President of the Chinese Academy of Social Sciences, said that more time was needed to conduct investigation for this important case and to reconstruct China's badly damaged judicial system and put it back into operation:

> The reason for the delay of the trial until now is that the case was of such extraordinary and grave nature and required us to do tremendous work in thoroughly and meticulously checking and verifying the evidence. Moreover, during the ten turbulent years legal organs at all levels in our country had been destroyed and all the laws were abrogated. It was in 1978—2 years after the downfall of the Gang of Four— that the new Constitution was formulated. Also, it took quite some time to set up the organization, train cadres and make other legal preparations.[80]

IV Trial proceedings

According to Article 100 of the Chinese CP, when the procuratorate finds conclusive and sufficient evidence for prosecution of the accused, it will initiate a public prosecution by the filing of an indictment with a court.[81] The indictment shall include basic information about the accused, facts and evidence of the offense, and article or articles of the law violated.[82]

A trial, as stipulated by the Chinese CP, is divided into four stages: (1) investigation, (2) debate, (3) appraisal by the collegiate bench, and (4) judgment.[83] Except for minor cases, trials are conducted in cases of original jurisdiction by a collegiate bench of a judge and two assessors. In cases of appeal or protest, a collegiate bench of three to five judges is required.[84] All cases are heard in public except those involving minors, state secrets, or personal intimacy.[85] However, at panel discussions held by NPC Deputies in September 1980, a delegate from Tianjin pointed out that the overwhelming majority of the courts in China lacked the necessary facilities and funds for conducting public trials.[86] Western observers also criticized the recent trial of the Gang of Four as not an open (public) one because of the exclusion of foreigners and severe restrictions on Chinese attendance.[87] Jurist Zhang Youyu, on the other hand, argued that the limitation of the trial attendance to representatives of selected Chinese groups was fully in accord with the general practice of all states to restrict the number of people attending a court session. As for the exclusion of foreigners, he contended, it was necessitated by the grave nature of the case and the involvement of many important state secrets.[88]

A *Right of defense*

Article 41 of the constitution states: "the accused has the right to defense." To elaborate on this point, the Chinese CP provides that besides exercising the right to defend himself, an accused may have for his defense a lawyer, a relative, a guardian, a citizen recommended by a people's organization or the unit he belongs to, or an advocate appointed by the court for him.[89] The responsibility of an advocate is to present "materials exonerating or extenuating the accused and offers his recommendation for mitigation or remission of punishment and to safeguard the legitimate rights and interests of the accused."[90]

While the Chinese CP permits laymen to act as counsel, its preference is definitely lawyers, who have the right to study case materials and visit and correspond with the accused in custody.[91] Writers on Chinese law have also suggested that lawyers are better equipped than the others to act as defenders.[92] It should be noted here that before the PRC's move toward a stable legal order was abruptly reversed by the Anti-Rightist Campaign of 1957–58 there were some 3,000 lawyers and 800 legal advisory offices across the country. Now, with the legal profession being rebuilt, China reportedly has 3,000 lawyers working at 380 legal advisory offices.[93] According to the Provisional Regulations on Lawyers adopted by the NPC Standing Committee on August 26, 1980, lawyers are "state legal workers" and have the duty to "protect the interests of the state and the collective and the legitimate rights and interests of citizens."[94] In addition to graduates of law facilities, persons with special training in law or practical experience in legal work are also qualified for lawyer certificates if they meet the requirements and approval of the provincial departments of justice.[95] The Regulations list a number of functions for lawyers, ranging from providing legal advice and drafting legal documents, to participation in litigation, mediation, or arbitration. In performing their functions, lawyers are expected to "act on the basis of facts and take the law as their criterion" and must be "loyal to the cause of socialism."[96] At the same time, they are to "enjoy the protection of state's law" and be free from interference of any unit or individual in the course of their work.[97] Chinese lawyers practice collectively in legal advisory offices, which are led and supervised by state judicial organs. The expenditures of the offices are covered by the state and their incomes are handed over to the state. Moreover, lawyers are also organized into revived Lawyers' Associations, whose tasks consist of "protection of lawyers' legal rights, promotion of exchange of work experience, facilitation of development of lawyers' work and expansion of contacts between Chinese and foreign legal practioners."[98]

One major problem facing the Chinese lawyer in defending a criminal suspect is the traditional prejudice against legal defense. During the years when the PRC was experimenting with the lawyers system, many people regarded the presence of a lawyer at a criminal trial as troublemaking and even traitorous.[99] This hostile attitude appears to be persisting in China today. For instance, one reader complained to a legal journal that "the negative views on lawyers that some judicial cadres have continued to harbor are the main reason for the difficulty of finding defense attorneys."[100] In an article entitled "Correctly Understand and Support the Defense Lawyer System," a Beijing radio commentator stated "in some places some comrades still do not quite understand the meaning and role of lawyers. Therefore, they take a rather strong dislike to defense lawyers, and, in some places, even openly prevent lawyers from performing their duties. All this is very wrong."[101] In a forum on the question of "restoring and strengthening the lawyer system" sponsored by *Democracy and the Legal System* and the Shanghai Legal Society, several speakers emphasized the importance of removing mistaken ideas and lingering fears about defense counsel.[102] One author went to considerable lengths to show that it would be erroneous to "view a lawyer being on the side of the enemy" or to "assume defendants being necessarily the same as criminals."[103]

Another touchy issue is whether PRC lawyers can function independently and how far they may go to defend their clients. One Chinese lawyer is quoted by *Beijing Review* as saying: "There is no such thing as absolute independence. We are government functionaries and as such, must handle affairs strictly in accordance with state laws.... . I think we practise law more independently than those hired by big firms or wealthy people."[104] China's First Vice-Minister of Justice also spoke of the difference between Chinese and Western lawyers. According to him, lawyers in capitalist countries act only in terms of their clients' interest while lawyers in China must proceed from a "proletarian stand" in their work.[105] Commentaries from other Chinese legal sources further suggest that in doing their job as defense counsel "proletarian lawyers" should not act like "bourgeois lawyers" who are willing to manipulate facts and bend the law to win a case and help an accused escape criminal responsibility.[106]

Given the various constraints, it is little surprise that defense lawyers in China generally play a passive role in court proceedings. They tend to confine their defense to pleading for leniency and are reluctant to challenge the prosecution or to exercise such rights as cross-examining state witnesses and calling witnesses of their own as provided by the Chinese CP.[107] At a robbery trial in Beijing open to foreign observers, the defense lawyer was reported to have spoken only once during the three-hour session, when he asked for a lighter penalty because of the defendant's confession and contribution. No attempt, however, was made either to examine the two witnesses or to ask questions of the police and the prosecutor.[108] This pattern has been repeated in other reported trials and the two trials witnessed by the author, including the one attended with fellow members of the American Bar Association Delegation in the Shanghai Intermediate Court on June 9, 1981.

In the recent trial of ten former radical leaders, five defendants did appoint or accept the court's appointment of two defense lawyers each, while Jiang Qing and four others did not accept or request the appointment of defense counsel.[109] Judging from the limited office news release, the lawyers appeared to be not too active during trial proceedings and made statements for their clients only at the time when the court was concluding the debates on each defendant. There are no reports of objection to the prosecution's questions, or cross-examination of witnesses, or evidence presented by the defense.[110]

A uniform line of defense was essentially used by the attorneys for Chen Boda, Li Quopeng, Jiang Tengjiao, Wu Faxian and Yao Wenyuan. The lawyers basically agreed with the state that the defendants had committed serious crimes but argued that they were not "principal culprits" and should be given lenient punishment because of their guilty pleas and repentent attitudes.[111] Minor exceptions, however, were taken to some specific charges made by the prosecution against the accused. Li Zuopeng's lawyers, for instance, pointed out that as shown in the court investigation, he did not participate in drawing up the project for the armed coup, nor was there any evidence showing that he had taken a direct part in the counterrevolutionary activities of engineering the coup.[112] Lawyers for Chen Boda said the defendant should bear "an unshirkable responsibility" for making a speech to "trump up" a case against the party organization of eastern Hepei Province. Nevertheless, they argued that there was no evidence to show that his speech alone caused the death of thousands of people and the persecution of tens of thousands.[113] Yao Wengyuan's lawyers also said that it "could not be established" that Yao was involved in a plot by two other members of the Gang of Four, Zhang Chunqiao and Wang Hongwen, to stage an armed rebellion in Shanghai in October 1976, as charged in item forty-six of the indictment.[114]

B Presumption of innocence

The real importance of the presumption of innocence, as observed by a group of international jurists, lies not in the abstract principle but in the extent to which in actual practice an accused person is in a position to "assert the principle against an over-eager prosecutor or police official who may find it easier to build up a case by intimidation of the accused, based on an assumption of guilt, than by laborious collection of independent evidence."[115] In the past the assumption of guilt and emphasis on confessions have been the prevailing mode of the PRC's criminal justice.[116] One noticeable change found in the current Chinese CP is the premium now placed on facts and hard evidence. Article 31 of the Chinese CP stipulates that evidence can be used as the basis of judgment only after it has been verified. In collecting various kinds of evidence to prove the innocence or guilt of the accused, use of illegal means including extortion of confessions by torture is strictly forbidden.[117] The Law also provides that in all cases "stress should be laid on evidence, investigation, and study, and credence should not be given too readily to confessions. The accused shall not be convicted without evidence other than his confession but he may be convicted when there is conclusive evidence even without his confession."[118]

However, there appears to be still considerable resistance to the adoption of the presumption of innocence in China's criminal procedure.[119] During 1956–57 some liberal Chinese jurists did urge the acceptance of this principle, but it was rejected as a "reactionary bourgeois doctrine" in the ensuing Anti-Rightist Campaign. The official line was that to assume the accused innocent in penal prosecution would only mean "the protection of guilty persons from punishment" and "the restriction of the freedom of the judicial organs and the masses in their fight against counterrevolutionary and other criminal elements."[120] Since 1979 the debate on this principle has been again revived among Chinese legal circles. This time, nevertheless, it has been conducted on a broader scale and in a more open atmosphere.

Among the proponents of the presumption of innocence, some advocate its critical assimilation into the Chinese criminal process. Despite certain contradictions that this principle contains, they argue, China should selectively absorb its spirit and essence and reject its "dregs" and unreasonable elements so as to insure the protection of the innocent and keep wrong or unjust judgments to a minimum.[121] Others even go a step further to urge the adoption of the presumption of innocence as one of the basic principles of China's criminal procedure without qualifications. They justify their stand not only in terms of the importance of this principle in guiding the correct handling of cases but also in terms of its compatibility with the socialist legal system. First of all, according to them, the principle of presumption of innocence is a true expression of materialism, because it insists that a judgment can only be made by reliable, objective evidence rather than by subjective views inherent in the feudalistic tradition of "presumption of guilt." Moreover, what the presumption of innocence stands for is in complete accord with a number of principles in the Chinese CP such as "seeking truth from facts," "taking facts as the basis and law as the criterion," "putting emphasis on evidence and investigation and not giving ready credence to confessions," etc. Therefore, the incorporation of the presumption of innocence into Chinese law, in the eyes of its advocates, would have the benefits of reinforcing the aforementioned democratic principles and facilitating the full realization of the PRC's socialist legality.[122]

Those who hold an opposite view on this issue may also be divided into two groups. The hardliners brand the presumption of innocence as a legacy of the capitalist countries, used by the bourgeois class as a means to oppress the people. Unscientific and reactionary, it violates the fundamental spirit of the Chinese CP. To adopt this principle would create much confusion, tie the hands of law enforcement personnel, and leave many criminals unpunished.[123] Some even raise the following question: If the defendant is "innocent," why has he been arrested and a public charge preferred against him?[124]

Others tend to take a more moderate position by saying that there is no need for socialist China to adopt either the feudal principle of presumption of guilt or the bourgeois principle of presumption of innocence although an analysis of both may be useful. The primary responsibility for Chinese judges in a criminal trial, as suggested by the argument, is to investigate the facts and evaluate the evidence with an open mind and from all sides so that the accused's guilt or innocence can be rightfully proven and a correct verdict can be rendered.[125] This position seems to reflect somewhat the current official line, even though the debate on the presumption issue is continuing. In a New China News Agency reported interview on the trial of the Gang of Four, jurist Zhang Youyu explained the Chinese attitude toward the principle of presumption of innocence. According to him, China's criminal procedure operates neither on the presumption of guilt nor of innocence but adheres to the principle of "basing ourselves on facts and taking law as the criterion." In so doing, "we can insure the correctness of the judgment and avoid an erroneous judgment arising from preconceived ideas. The exercise of this principle can avoid wronging the innocent and allowing the guilty to go unpunished. This complies to the social system and concrete conditions of China."[126]

C Question of judicial independence

The 1954 Organic Law of People's Courts had, as does the current Law, the provision that "the People's Court administer justice independently and are subject only to the law."[127] Unfortunately, those legal scholars and practioners who took this provision seriously were branded in the late 1950s as "rightists" challenging Party leadership.[128] As a result, in the ensuing years Party control over judicial work continued to be so dominant that the Party committee examined and approved cases tried by the court at the same level. This system has come to be known as "Shuji pian" (approving cases by the secretary) since the Party committee frequently delegated the decision making authority to its secretary in charge of political-legal affairs.[129]

Several problems arising from this past practice have been pointed out by critics in the post-Mao era. First, it is impossible for the Party committee (i.e., its political-legal secretary) to have time to investigate all the cases, thus often resulting in either unreasonable delays of administering justice or making careless and erroneous decisions. Second, the Party committee's direct involvement in concrete court cases has tended to weaken the spirit and enthusiasm of judicial personnel in their work. Third, this has had the effect of rendering court trials a mere formality and causing the people to lose confidence in the PRC's legal system.[130]

In view of all this, the Central Committee of the Chinese Communist Party explicitly abolished the practice of examining and approving cases by Party committees in an instruction issued in September 1979 on the full implementation of the Chinese CC and the Chinese CP.[131] President Jiang Hua of the Supreme Court also urged at a criminal trials conference in August 1980 that the Party Central Committee's instruction be resolutely carried out. According to him, it was necessary for Party committees to examine and approve cases during the war and in the early years of the People's Republic. After the principle that "the People's Court administer justice independently according to the law" was established in 1954, the practice of examining and approving cases by Party Committee should have been gradually changed. However, for various reasons it was not done. Now, the Party Central Committee's decision to revoke the system of examining and approving cases by Party Committee is a major step of reform to insure "independent court trial according to the Law" and "proper Party leadership over judicial organs in principles and policy lines and not in concrete and routine matters."[132]

Along the same line other official statements and legal writings have tried to reconcile the principle of judicial independence with the principle of Party leadership, by allowing some functional freedom for judicial organs without relinquishing the leadership of the Party. To begin with, the Chinese point out that insofar as their judicial system operates within the framework of Party leadership, it would be wrong to equate the socialist principle of "administering justice independently" with "the separation of the three powers" and "the independent judiciary" proclaimed by the bourgeoisie.[133] Equally mistaken, from their perspective, is to interpret Party leadership to mean substituting the Party for the courts and interference by Party committees in the details of judicial operation.[134] Moreover, they stress the fact that insistence on the principle of "administering justice independently according to the law" is entirely consistent with the strengthening of Party leadership in legal work:

> Our country's law is made by the National People's Congress under the guidance of the Party. It embodies the will of the people and the policy of the Party. Determination to carry out the law is determination to carry out the people's will and the Party's policy. Therefore, independent adjudication by the courts according to the law really stands for accepting Party leadership and not seeking independence from the Party... . With the strengthening of the socialist legal system, Party leadership over the people's courts must be strengthened, not weakened. This leadership, however, is exercised primarily to strengthen the Party's political-ideological guidance so as to make the people's courts to see the right direction in the complicated class struggle and resolutely implement the Party's political line, principles, and policies... . In the meantime, Party committees must also be required to select and train a large group of proletarian judges, who are loyal to the law, to the system, to the people's interests, as well as to true facts.[135]

By following the above prescriptions and refraining from handling concrete cases, Party committees are said to be in a position to assert more effective leadership in the legal field, as they can concentrate on what is essential without getting bogged down by trivial matters.[136]

In spite of all this, there is evidence that Party officials have continued to interefere in the performance of adjudication functions by the judicial organs. At a panel discussion held by NPC delegates in September 1980, Yang Xiufeng from Tianjin suggested, among other things, that the PRC must guarantee the independence of the People's court in administering justice:

> Some cadres do not grasp the principle of independent trial according to the law and adopt an attitude of passive resistance. Others even interfere with the courts' judicial authority and seek to replace the law with words. In some cases, judicial cadres who have held firmly to principles and handled cases according to the law have been transferred or replaced. Such a situation must resolutely be rectified.[137]

In an informal discussion session sponsored by the *Enlightenment Daily* in October 1980, Ma Rongie, Editor of *Studies in Law*, also called attention to the continued practice of substituting the Party for the government in judicial work. This usurpation, as he observed, manifests itself principally in two areas: (1) in some localities, the election, appointment and removal of presidents and judges of the people's courts and chief procurators and other procurators of the people's procuratorates are actually decided by Party committees, contrary to the provisions of the Organic Laws of the Courts and the Procuracy. Ma cited a case in which the president and vice president of a municipal intermediate court were removed by the first secretary of the municipal Party committee because of their refusal to bend the law to change a judgment. (2) The supposedly abolished practice whereby cases are examined and approved by Party committees is still in effect in certain localities.[138]

The same problem was raised by an article in the *Beijing Daily* on January 23, 1981, which pointed out the revocation of the practice of reviewing cases by Party committees "has been passively resisted by some comrades and overtly challenged by others." Two instances were cited. One responsible person of a certain county party committee interfered in a trial and unjustifiably dismissed the chief procurator from his post. Another county Party committee seriously infringed upon the right of a court to conduct adjudication independently and refused to carry out the verdict so as to prevent the close of case.[139]

To combat unlawful interference in judicial work and to overcome the passive attitude of some judicial personnel, Chinese leaders like Ye Jianying and Jiang Hua have called for fearless judges and procurators ready to sacrifice their lives for the dignity of the legal system.[140] While there are reports about courageous and model judicial workers on the one hand, there are also reports concerning those judicial cadres who have been slow, reluctant, or unable to carry out their duties on the other. In Pingding county of Shanxi province, a demobilized soldier was reported to have been unjustly arrested, tortured and sentenced to prison during 1976–78 because of his criticism of Dazhai and its leaders. Even after his release he failed in his attempts to have the verdict reversed by the courts. Finally the intermediate court of Jingzhong did so in August 1980 after a rehabilitation meeting called by the Pingding County CCP committee had completely exonerated him.[141]

In a letter to a law journal, one reader reported another victim of unjust imprisonment in Quingpu County near Shanghai. Even after the facts became known, the county court continued to delay any action to "rehabilitate" him for fear of the opposition of certain Party committee members. Only after the repeated urging of the municipal higher court did the county court eventually reverse the verdict.[142] Writing to the same journals, two members of the people's court in Jingan district of Shanghai complained that a legally effective judgment of their court could not be executed due to the resistance from some cadres in the branch office of the China Shipping Fuel Supply Company.[143]

D Equality before the law

Article 5 of the Organic Law of the People's Courts as well as Article 4 of the Chinese CP provide that in judicial proceedings all citizens are equal before the application of law, irrespective of their nationality, race, sex, occupation, social origin, religious belief, education, property status, or duration of residence.[144] The same principle of equality was stipulated in the 1954 constitution[145] and in the 1954 Organic Law of the People's Courts.[146] However, it never took root in Mao's China and was repudiated as a bourgeois concept in the 1957–58 Anti-Rightist Campaign. During the Cultural Revolution the radicals attacked Peng Zhen for, among other things, advocating this anti-Party principle.[147] In fact, Chinese justice under Mao put so much stress on an individual's class background that persons from the "enemy" class usually received harsher sanctions for the same offense than those among "the people."[148]

The post-Mao leadership, on the other hand, has attempted to change the past policy both in law and in practice. As mentioned before, Beijing declared in early 1979 that former landlords, rich peasants, and their descendants would no longer be discriminated against "[a]s long as they support socialism."[149] According to the author of a legal article, conditions in China are now ready for the application of the principle of "equality before the law." "The broad masses of the working class have already become the masters of China; the political dominance of the exploiting class has been overthrown; private ownership of the means of production has been eliminated; public ownership under socialism has been established; the toiling masses have achieved economic equality. All this has wiped out the social roots for inequality before the law."[150] In administration of criminal justice, another author writes in the Red Flag:

[T]he criterion for measuring the penalty for a criminal is determined by the extent of harm to society caused by the nature of the crime and the criminal offense itself as well as by the extent of the offense. It is not determined by whether his class element is good or bad, whether his years of revolutionary experience are long or short, or whether his work position is high or long.[151]

Since the law in China reflects the will of the Party and the people of the whole country, Peng Zhen asks: "Before this law, how can there be any inequality? ... How can a landlord be found guilty and a worker or a poor peasant not guilty after committing the same crime of murder? How can an ordinary person be found guilty and a cadre not guilty after committing the same crime of murder?"[152]

Indeed, that "no special privilege is allowed before the law" is specifically incorporated into the respective "equality" provisions of the current Organic Law of the Courts[153] and the Chinese CP,[154] in contrast to the 1954 relevant legal provisions that contained no such statement. This reflects the present leadership's concern about the abuse of power by Party and state officials without regard for the law. In an address delivered at the fifth NPC, Ye Jianying said:

> All citizens are equal before the law, whether or not they are Party members and whatever their rank, social position and social origin ... .
> All leading cadres, no matter how highly placed, are public servants of the people. They are under obligation to serve the people diligently and conscientiously and have no right whatsoever to place themselves above the law ... . While most of our leading cadres at all levels are good or fairly good, it is also true that there are a few who, by flouting the laws and institutions of the state or by taking advantage of certain imperfections in our legal system, have abused the power entrusted them by the people to seek personal gain. With regard to such bad practices as bureaucracy, the pursuit of privilege, "back-door dealings" and suppression of democratic rights, the Party and government must take resolute and effective measures to rectify them.[155]

Ye's view has been echoed by journal and press articles. The "equality before the law" is described as a sharp weapon against special privileges.[156] To think that one is above the law and cannot be restrained by law "reflects actually the mentality of the ruling feudal landlords in China thousands of years ago."[157] The socialist legal system, on the other hand, is said to be "applicable to all men."

> Whoever breaks the law and commits a crime, no matter how high his seniority, how important his office and how great his contributions, shall not be shielded but shall be punished according to the law. Otherwise, the principles of the socialist legal system will be undermined, the Party's prestige impaired, and the authority of judicial organs defied.[158]

Concrete cases have been used by the press to show the actual application of the "equality" principle in China today. Three rapists of a gang of seven, for instance, were sentenced to death in June 1980 by the intermediate people's court in Changchun, Jilin, with the chief culprit being the son of a leading cadre at the municipal level. In a commentary, the *China Youth News* said: "Gone are the days when Lin Biao and the Gang of Four lorded it over the people. In the eighties of socialist China, no one who breaks the law can escape the arms of justice."[159] The Beijing intermediate people's court also sentenced on August 9, 1980, four young men, three of whom were the sons of high-ranking officials, to imprisonment for illegal detention and extortion. This case has been the talk of the town and cited as yet another example of upholding the principle of "equality before the law."[160] A dramatic demonstration that no one is above the law was the punishment of top officials responsible for the offshore drilling rig disaster in Bohai Bay that claimed seventy-two lives on November 25, 1979. Not only was the Minister of Petroleum Industry removed from office by the State Council, but four oil industry supervisors were also given prison sentences for criminal negligence by the intermediate people's court of Tianjin on September 2, 1980.[161] Radio Beijing praised the verdicts as giving expression to the sanctity of the socialist legal system and upholding the principle of "equality before the law."[162]

On January 25, 1981, China's special court concluded the well-publicized trial of ten leaders of the Cultural Revolution with guilty judgments against the defendants. Jian Qing and Zhang Chunqiao, former Vice Premier, received death sentences suspended for two years, while eight others got sentences ranging from sixteen years to life in prison. In an editorial entitled, "The Just Court Verdicts," the *People's Daily* called the trial a great victory for the socialist legal system and for the principle that all are equal before the law.[163] Also in an editorial, the *Red Flag* said that the trial

> swept away the long standing pernicious influence of feudalism and shattered the decadent idea that 'penalties are not imposed upon officials.' All ten principal defendants occupied top leadership positions in the Party, government, or Army. Throughout the trial they were not given special consideration or protection because of their former high positions or previous merits. The court stood firm in protecting the people's interests and pronouncing the appropriate judgments according to the law.[164]

Official statements notwithstanding, the trial of the Gang of Four and others appears to be a poor case to show off Chinese legality. Most foreign observers regard the trial as primarily political.[165] Even a Chinese writer in a Hong Kong-based pro-PRC journal criticizes the political interference in the trial. He wonders how it is possible for the Chinese authorities to reconcile their commitment to the principle of "equality before the law" with the fact that they have routinely executed embezzlers and rapists while sparing the life of Jiang Qing who persecuted thousands of people and caused the death of many of them during the Cultural Revolution.[166] As regards the handling of the oil rig disasters two NPC deputies, speaking at a panel discussion in September 1980, stated that they and many of their colleagues were not fully satisfied. In their view, "we have attacked just flies but not tigers" and only by discontinuing the "feudal" practice favoring the privileged "can we truly succeed in having everyone equal before the law."[167]

V Appeal and review

Under the two-trial system as stipulated in Article 12 of the Organic Law of the People's Courts, a judgment or ruling of the court of first instance may be appealed to the court of the next higher level. An appeal may be initiated by the dependent or the procuracy. In the past, the fear of incurring heavier punishment seriously deterred the Chinese from exercising their right of appeal.[168] To remedy the situation, Article 137 of the Criminal Procedure Law specifically provides that in its judgment of a case based on appeal by the accused or his advocate, the court of a second instance is not allowed to aggravate the original punishment.[169] With this protection, more people have now sought redress through appellate proceedings. In his report to the NPC on September 2, 1980, Jiang Hua said that the courts at all levels "have in the past two years and more handled over 290,000 appeals of court decisions on criminal cases tried before and after the Cultural Revolution."[170]

A legally effective judgment in the PRC is also subject to a form of review called judicial supervision if some definite error in the determination of facts or application of law is found. Article 149 of the Chinese CP provides the following procedure of judicial supervision for such a situation:[171] (1) The court which gave the judgment in question may refer it to the judicial committee for disposal; (2) the Supreme People's Court or an upper court may review the case themselves or direct the lower court to conduct a retrial; (3) the procuratorates may lodge a protest against the given judgment in accordance with judicial procedure. This system of review, says one authoritative publication, insures that erroneous or unjust judgments are to be corrected and that criminal offenders are to be duly punished.[172]

In fact, the post-Mao leadership has taken vigorous steps to reverse unjust and wrong verdicts of the past. As reported by Jiang Hua, by the end of June 1980, the people's courts had reviewed over one million criminal conviction cases handled during the Cultural Revolution and had rectified more than 251,000 cases of injustice involving over 267,000 persons.[173] The guiding principle has been to "seek truth from facts and correct mistakes whenever discovered."[174]

It should be noted here that besides the appeal procedure, there are special review procedures for death penalty cases. Article 43 of the Criminal Law stipulates that except for those imposed by the Supreme People's Court, all other death sentences should be submitted to the Supreme People's Court for examination and approval.[175] According to Articles 15–17 of the Chinese CP, the court of first instance for capital crime cases is the intermediate people's court or above.[176] Part III, chapter IV of the same Law provides detailed review procedures for death sentences. Whether appealed or not and whether passed or imposed by a higher people's court, a death sentence has to be ratified by the Supreme People's Court.[177] As to death sentences with a two-year reprieve handed down by the intermediate people's court, only the approval of the higher people's court is required.[178]

Chinese officials and jurists generally agree that it is necessary to retain capital punishment in China because of its deterrent value in dealing with major counterrevolutionary crimes and other most heinous offenses that seriously endanger society or incur great popular indignation.[179] Nevertheless, they contend that the underlying principle of China's criminal legislation is to reduce and restrict the use of the death penalty and to combine punishment with leniency in the spirit of revolutionary humanism. As evidence, they cite the special review procedures provided for death penalty cases, the two years' reprieve of death sentences for the convicted to reform, and the exemption from capital punishment of young people committing crimes while under eighteen years of age and of women found to be pregnant during trial.[180]

Undoubtedly, the legal provisions mentioned above reflect the current Chinese leadership's policy to employ capital punishment with care and to avoid the past abuses in mass trials and "exemplary" public executions. There is, however, still a tendency on the part of the PRC to use harsh measures and to depart from legal requirements on occasions of political and social tensions. Chinese authorities, for instance, were reported to have increased the use of executions in 1970–80 against a wave of violent crimes. A check of official press and courthouse notices revealed that at least 198 persons had been executed for crimes ranging from murder to gold speculation in the year ending June 30, 1980.[181] An embezzler named Wang Shouxin was executed in February 1980 for taking about $350,000 from the fuel company where she was manager. According to a western observer, what may have proved fatal was that she seemed to have been a protégé of the radical Maoist clique purged in 1976.[182]

In several of the reported mass sentencing meetings, requirements for the Supreme People's Court's review of death sentences appear to have been ignored. The most well-publicized case was the trial of the Hangzhou rape gang and the execution of Xiong Ziping, leader of the gang. On November 14, 1979, the intermediate court of Hangzhou convened a mass sentencing meeting, attended by some 6,000 people, to announce the sentencing of Xiong Ziping to death. The condemned was immediately executed and later the whole proceedings were shown in a four-minute report on China's television news.[183] There was no mention of approval of the death sentence by the Supreme People's Court. While it is true that the Chinese CL and Chinese CP did not enter into force until January 1, 1980, the fact remains that as early as July 1957 the National People's Congress adopted a resolution requiring all death sentences of the lower court to be submitted to the Supreme People's Court for approval.[184]

In a latest move to mete out swift punishment to criminals who seriously endanger the social order, the NPC Standing Committee adopted a resolution on June 10, 1981, granting for the period of 1981–83 the right to approve death sentences on murderers, robbers, rapists, bomb throwers, arsonists and saboteurs to the higher people's courts of the provinces, autonomous regions and municipalities directly under the central authorities. Approval of Supreme People's Court shall continue to be required for death sentences passed on counterrevolutionaries and embezzlers.[185]

VI Conclusion

In the few years since coming into power, the PRC's present elite has clearly made conscientious and determined efforts to elevate the jural model of law and to institute a more stable and equitable system of criminal justice. To be sure, by Western standards there are still many deficiencies in the current Chinese legal order. Moreover, the major codes governing the criminal justice system only became effective on January 1, 1980, and the full implementation of the Chinese CP has been particularly hampered by technical and practical difficulties. Nonetheless, even at this stage of its development, the criminal process in the PRC today is already a substantial improvement over the Maoist system of justice in the protection of the individual against the arbitrary power of the state. Certainly, the presence of legal codes, the stress on evidence rather than confessions and the de-emphasis of class justice all appear to give the accused in a criminal case a more meaningful opportunity to defend himself now more than before in the history of the People's Republic.

On the other hand, thirty years of political uncertainty and policy shifts have instilled a sense of cynicism in the people of the PRC about the durability of the current regime's commitment to the rule of law. Their confidence has not been enhanced by the trials of Wei Jingsheng and Fu Yeuhua and the administrative sanctions applied against other political dissidents. On November 29, 1979, the Standing Committee of the National People's Congress adopted a resolution to revive a 1957 State Council decision on "Reeducation and Rehabilitation through Labor," permitting administrative agencies to confine without trial a wide range of offenders to labor camps for a period of one to four years.[186] Reports indicate that Chinese authorities have used this administrative measure to detain in rural labor camps thousands of people from dissidents to vagrants to those merely unemployed.[187]

Recently, in an effort to counter incidents of social and political unrest, Beijing has tightened controls over political and cultural life and threatened to crush antigovernment demonstrations and other "illegal" activities.[188] Given this situation, many Chinese understandably often wonder whether the pendulum of Chinese politics may again swing to the left, bending the law to the political wind and to the dictates of a major mass campaign as in the past.[189]

Another troubling question is the relationship between the Party and the judicial organs. Despite the prescription of official spokesmen that Party leadership over the judiciary should be exercised in areas of guidelines and policies and not in the handling of individual cases, some Party cadres have continued to intervene in the administration of justice. Furthermore, there are cases where Party discipline has replaced state law in applying sanctions against criminal offenders.

A serious incident at a construction site in Shanghai resulted in loss of lives. The two persons in charge were only given disciplinary demerits and were not prosecuted according to Article 114 of the Chinese CL.[190] A Party official in Xiyang County, Shanxi, allegedly committed many crimes, including rape and extortion. Again, he was reported to have been subjected to Party disciplinary sanctions and not legal punishment.[191] These and other similar occurrences have prompted critical comments in the press and legal journals. The consensus is that Party discipline and state law are two different things and that one cannot be used to substitute the other. In order to consolidate the socialist legal system, judicial cadres are urged to resist any power or pressure to uphold the principle that "Law must be enforced strictly and all lawbreakers must be punished."[192]

The fact that these criticisms and others cited elsewhere in this article can be freely voiced in China today is itself an encouraging sign. Undoubtedly, the bitter experience of the negative past and the pressing demands of the four modernizations have provided the post-Mao leadership with some vested interest in instituting a regular and stable legal order. For all its shortcomings, the current system of criminal justice in China has a good foundation on which to build and develop. Much remains to be done for Beijing to expand legal education, to train more lawyers and competent judicial cadres, and to cultivate a more positive attitude toward the law among the bureaucracy and the population alike.

As in the case of the Soviet Union, China can and must give its courts and procuracy sufficient and functional independence to administer justice within the broad framework of serving socialism under Party leadership. Special efforts also ought to be made to implement fully the penal codes, both substantively and procedurally, and to reduce, if not to eliminate, the use of extrajudicial measures in dealing with political dissidents. Only through such development can the credibility of the Chinese leadership and socialist legality be enhanced and legal rights of the accused in criminal justice be genuinely protected. This, of course, is a big order but may not be outside the realm of possibility.

Notes

1 *See, e.g., The Just Court Verdicts*, Renmin Ribao (People's Daily), Jan., 26, 1981, at 1. The cover of 23 BEIJING REV. (No. 48, 1980) has the pictures of the accused: Jiang Qing, Zhang Chunqiao, Yao Wenyuan, Wang Hongwen, Chen Boda, Hung Yongsheng, Wu Faxian, Li Zuopeng, Qiu Huizuo and Jiang Tengjiao.

2 *See, e.g.,* Bonavia, *Give Them Rice and Circuses,* FAR EASTERN ECONOMIC REV., Dec. 5–11, 1980, at 12; Butterfield, *Revenge Seems to Outweigh Justice at Chinese Trial,* N.Y. Times, Dec. 6, 1980, at 2; Ching, *Robes of Justice Sit Uneasily on Gang of Four Judges,* Asian Wall St. J., Nov. 18, 1980, at 4; *Peking's Trial, and Error,* N.Y. Times, Jan. 5, 1981, at A14. Professor Jerome A. Cohen, however, considers the trial as China's effort to bring a political case under the legal process. He also would compare

the trial to the Nuremburg war crime trials following World War II. Associated Press, Beijing, Dec. 6, 1980.

3 Texts of the Counterrevolutionaries Act and the Corruption Act are in ZHONGHUA RENMIN ZHENGFU FALING HUIBIAN (COLLECTION OF LAWS AND DECREES OF THE CENTRAL PEOPLE'S GOVERNMENT) Vol. II (1953), at 3–5, and Vol. III (1954), at 25–28, respectively [hereinafter cited as FLHB], and the texts of the SAPA and Arrest Act are in ZHONGHUA RENMIN GONGHEGUO FAGUI HUIBIAN (COLLECTION OF LAWS AND REGULATIONS OF THE PEOPLE'S REPUBLIC OF CHINA) Vol. I, at 239–42 (1956) and Vol. VI, at 245–61 (1957), respectively [hereinafter cited as FGHB].

4 For a discussion of Mao's impact on Chinese legal development, see Leng, *The Role of Law in the People's Republic of China As Reflecting Mao Tse-tung's Influence*, 68 J. CRIM. L. & C. 356 (1977).

5 The PRC's judicial development before the Cultural Revolution is examined in J. COHEN, THE CRIMINAL PROCESS IN THE PEOPLE'S REPUBLIC OF CHINA 1949–1963 (1968) and S. LENG, JUSTICE IN COMMUNIST CHINA (1967).

6 *See, e.g., China's Socialist Legal System*, 22 BEIJING REV. 25, 26–27 (No. 2 1979); *Trial of Lin-Jian Cliques: Indictment of the Special Procuratorate*, 23 BEIJING REV. 9, 18–23 (No. 48, 1980).

7 CONST. OF THE PEOPLE'S REPUBLIC OF CHINA, art. 41 (1978) [hereinafter cited as PRC CONST.]. English text of the 1978 constitution is in 21 BEIJING REV. 5, 5–14 (1978). A comprehensive analysis of it is available in Cohen, *China's Changing Constitution*, 1978 CHINA Q. 794.

8 PRC CONST., arts. 45, 47. SHAO-CHUAN LENG, *Human Rights in Chinese Political Culture*, in THE MORAL IMPERATIVES OF HUMAN RIGHTS: A WORLD SURVEY 89 (K. Thompson ed. 1980).

9 *New Minister of Justice Interviewed*, 22 BEIJING REV. 3 (No. 42, 1979).

10 *China is Said to Free 110,000 in Detention Since '57 Crackdown*, N.Y. Times, June 6, 1978, at 1.

11 *Policy Towards Descendents of Landlords and Rich Peasants*, 22 BEIJING REV. 8 (No. 4, 1979).

12 Foreign Broadcast Information Service, Daily Report: People's Republic of China [hereinafter cited as FBIS-CHI], Sept. 23, 1980 (Supplement), at 42.

13 CRIMINAL LAW OF THE PEOPLE'S REPUBLIC OF CHINA (1979) [hereinafter cited as CHINESE CL]. The English translation of the Chinese CL is printed at pp. 138–70 *supra*.

14 CRIMINAL PROCEDURE LAW OF THE PEOPLE'S REPUBLIC OF CHINA (1979) [hereinafter cited as CHINESE CP]. The English translation of the CHINESE CP is printed at pp. 171–203 *supra*.

15 ORGANIC LAW OF LOCAL PEOPLE'S GOVERNMENTS (1979) [hereinafter cited as ORG. L. LOCAL PEOPLE'S CONG. AND LOCAL PEOPLE'S GOV'TS].

16 ORGANIC LAW OF PEOPLE'S COURTS (1979) [hereinafter cited as ORG. L. PEOPLE'S CTS.].

17 ORGANIC LAW OF PEOPLE'S PROCURATORATES (1979) [hereinafter cited as ORG. L. PEOPLE'S PROCURATORATES].

18 FBIS-CHI, Sept. 23, 1980 (Supplement), at 34–35.

19 Renmin Ribao, Nov. 30, 1979, at 1. Peng Zhen estimated that over 1,500 state laws, decrees and administrative regulations were promulgated in the 17 years between 1949–1966.

20 Zhao Yusi, *Legal Education Should be Greatly Expanded*, Renmin Ribao, Oct. 10, 1980, at 5.

21 *Supreme People's Court Meets*, 22 BEIJING REV. 4 (1979); FBIS-CHI June 11, 1980, at L5.

22 FAXUE YANJIU is published by the Legal Research Institute of the Chinese Academy of Social Sciences; MINZHU YU FAZHI is published jointly by the East China Institute of

Politics and Law and the Shanghai Legal Society. Many legal books have been published by the Legal Research Institute of the Chinese Academy of Social Sciences and other research institutes and groups in legal affairs.

23 Renmin Ribao, Aug. 1, 1980, at 1.

24 Arts. 4–12. English text of the new ORG. L. PEOPLE'S CTS. is in FBIS-CHI, July 27, 1979 (Supplement), at 20–27. Text of the 1954 ORG. L. PEOPLE'S CTS. is in 1 FGHB 123–32.

25 ORG. L. PEOPLE'S CTS., arts. 35, 36 (1979).

26 ORG. L. PEOPLE'S CTS., art. 32 (1954).

27 PRC CONST., art. 25 (1978).

28 ORG. L. PEOPLE'S CTS., arts. 32, 33 (1979).

29 RESOLUTION OF THE FOUTH SESSION OF THE FIRST NATIONAL PEOPLE'S CONGRESS OF THE PEOPLE'S REPUBLIC OF CHINA TO THE EFFECT THAT DEATH PENALTY CASES SHOULD BE DECIDED OR APPROVED BY THE SUPREME PEOPLE'S COURT (adopted July 15, 1957), in 6 FGHB 296 (1958).

30 ORG. L. PEOPLE'S PROCURATORATES, art 2. English text of the law in FBIS-CHI, July 27, 1979 (Supplement), at 27–33. Text of the 1954 Organic Law is in 1 FGHB 133–38.

31 For a discussion of the Soviet Procuracy, see H. BERMAN, JUSTICE IN THE U.S.S.R., 238–47 (1963). In an interview with the author in Beijing in November 1979, Mr. Sun, Deputy Chief of the Legal Research Bureau of the Supreme People's Procuratorate, said that rather than follow the Soviet model, China had to make some changes regarding the procuracy in order to meet her specific conditions and needs.

32 For past attacks against the tendency to free the procuracy from local Party cadres' interference, see S. LENG, *supra* note 5, at 114–19.

33 ORG. L. PEOPLE'S PROCURATORATES, art. 10 (1979).

34 *Id.*, arts. 21–24.

35 ORG. L. PEOPLE'S PROCURATORATES, arts. 3, 4, 8, 19 (1954).

36 *Id.*, arts. 5–6 (1979).

37 Peng Zhen, *Explanation on Seven Laws*, 22 BEIJING REV. 8, 14 (No. 28, 1979).

38 ORG. L. PEOPLE'S PROCURATORATES, art. 1 (1979).

39 *Id.*, art. 5.

40 *Id.*, art. 9.

41 For comparison, Article 6 of the 1954 Law reads: "The Local People's procuratorates are independent in the exercise of their authority and are not subject to interference by local state organs."

42 CHINESE CL, art. 2. Consult the LEGAL RESEARCH INSTITUTE OF THE CHINESE ACADEMY OF SOCIAL SCIENCES, XINGFA JIANGHUA (LECTURES ON CRIMINAL LAW) (1979).

43 CHINESE CL, arts. 27–56.

44 *Id.*, arts. 90–192.

45 *Id.*, arts. 90–102.

46 *Id.*, art. 103. It should be noted that the penalty predominantly listed in the PRC's 1951 REGULATIONS FOR PUNISHMENT OF COUNTERREVOLUTION was capital punishment. *See* REGULATIONS in 2 FLHB 3–5.

47 CHINESE CL, arts. 106, 110, 132, 139, 150, 155.

48 *Id.*, art. 43.

49 *Id.* For discussions of the PRC's past policy regarding the death penalty and its two year reprieve, see AMNESTY INT'L, POLITICAL IMPRISONMENT IN THE PEOPLE'S REPUBLIC OF CHINA 61–69 (1978); S. LENG, *supra* note 5, at 166–68; Cohen, *Reflections on the Criminal Process in China*, 68 J. CRIM. L. & C. 323, 342–43 (1977).

50 Beating, smashing and looting were done by the Red Guards during the Cultural Revolution. CHINESE CL, arts. 136–37.

51 *Id.*, arts. 138, 143, 144.

52 *Id.*, art. 145.

53 J. COHEN, *supra* note 5, at 336–41, 348–553; S. LENG, *supra* note 5, at 159–61.

54 CHINESE CL, art. 9.

55 *Id.*, art. 79.

56 *See, e.g.*, Hungdah Chiu, *China's New Legal System*, CURRENT HISTORY 31 (Sept. 1980). This issue was discussed when the author had a meeting with President Hu Guang and a score of faculty members of the Southwest Institute of Politics and Law (Chongquing) in December 1979. According to the two criminal law professors who participated in drafting the PRC's Criminal Law, China has just begun the codification process and has no time to provide detailed regulations in her criminal legislation; consequently, it is necessary to permit the use of analogy in a "very restrictive" manner to meet practical needs and plug the loopholes in the current law. They expect, however, that in the future China will move to adopt the principle that an actor is held criminally responsible only when his act is punishable according to the provisions of the law in force at the time of its commission.

57 *See* Jerome A. Cohen's comment as reported in Butterfield, *Definition of Crime Clarified by Peking*, N.Y. Times, July 10, 1979, at A11.

58 As one Western jurist comments, the mere promulgation of the law is already an act of courage on the part of the present government. Meijar, *The New Criminal Law of the People's Republic of China*, 6 REV. SOCIALIST L. 138 (1980).

59 *See* sections III-V *infra*.

60 In his report on the current situation and tasks to a cadre conference on January 16, 1980, Deng Xiaoping even conceded that "we are at least 1 million short — I think it is 2 million in the number of cadres who can act as judges and lawyers, who have studied law and understand it and who can also enforce the law in a fair and impartial way." FBIS-CHI, March 11, 1980 (Supplement), at 20. Text of Deng's Report first appeared in 1980 CHENG MING (CONTENDING), at 11–23 (No. 29). *Cheng Ming* is a Hong Kong-published magazine sympathetic to the PRC. For more discussion of China's shortage of legal personnel, see Lin Shaodang, *Great Expansion of Political-Legal Education is Our Current Urgent Need*, 1979 MINZHU YU FAZHI 17 (No. 2).

61 New China News Agency (NCNA), Apr. 6, 1980.

62 CHINESE CP, art. 3. Text of the Law of Criminal Procedure is in Guangming Ribao (Enlightenment Daily), July 8, 1979, at 1–3.

63 CHINESE CP, art. 4.

64 *Id.*, art. 5.

65 Text of the revised Regulations is in Renmin Ribao, Feb. 25, 1979, at 1. Text of the 1954 Regulations, ignored in the past, is in 1 FGHB 239–42.

66 *See* CHINESE CP, arts. 38–52; REGULATIONS GOVERNING ARREST AND DETENTION, arts. 2–8. The difference between "detention" and "arrest" is clearly described in a 1968 study as follows: detention is the emergency apprehension and confinement of a suspect without an arrest warrant for the purpose of investigating whether there is sufficient evidence to justify his arrest while arrest is the apprehension and confinement or the continuing confinement, of a suspect on the basis of an arrest warrant for the purpose of investigating whether there is sufficient evidence to justify prosecution. J. COHEN, *supra* note 5, at 28.

67 CHINESE CP, art. 32.

68 *Id.*, art. 81.

69 *Id.*, art. 92. As explained by a Chinese jurist, the three month period before the trial is needed because China is so vast in size and transportation is difficult. Keith, *Transcript of Discussions With Wu Daying and Zhang Zhonglin Concerning Legal Change and Civil Rights*, 1980 CHINA Q. 112, 120.

70 CHINESE CP, art. 97.

71 Zeng Longyao, *Upholding the Principle of Mutual Coordination and Restriction by the Public Security Organs, Procuratorial Organs, and People's Courts*, 1979 FAXUE YANJIU 44–45 (No. 1).

72 Luo Ping, *The Principle of Measuring Penalty in China's Criminal Law*, HONGQI (RED FLAG), No. 9, 1979, at 71–72; TEACHING AND RESEARCH OFFICE OF BEIJING INSTITUTE OF POLITICS AND LAW, ZHONGHUA RENMIN GONGHEQUO XINSHI SUSONG FA JIANGHUA (LECTURES ON THE CRIMINAL PRODEDURAL LAW OF THE PEOPLE'S REPUBLIC OF CHINA) 74 (1979).

73 Qin Huaihe, *Need to Ensure People's Power to Direct State Affairs*, CHENG MING 82 (Nov. 1980).

74 *See, e.g.*, Butterfield, *Four Arrested in China at Democracy Wall*, N.Y. Times, Nov. 12, 1979, at A7; Laduguie, *The Human Rights Movement*, 9 INDEX ON CENSORSHIP 18–26 (No. 1, 1980). According to the report of the underground publication *Dadi* (*Great Earth*) on Nov. 4, 1979, when Wei Jingsheng was arrested on March 27, 1979, he demanded that the public security personnel show him their arrest warrant, but was told "we want to arrest you, why do we need an arrest warrant!" A week later, the arrest warrant was issued by a people's court. Chiu, *supra* note 56, at 32.

75 LECTURES ON THE CRIMINAL PROCEDURE LAW, *supra* note 72, at 52, 63–64.

76 Wang Shunhua, *Why Is It Necessary to Strictly Ban Torture in Extracting Confessions*," Guangming Ribao, Mar. 19, 1980, at 3.

77 Butterfield, *Chinese Said to Torture African Student in Sex Inquiry*, N.Y. Times, May 31, 1980, at 3.

78 1980 MINZHU YU FAZHI 31 (No. 8).

79 NCNA, Oct. 1, 1980.

80 FBIS-CHI, Nov. 21, 1980, at L3.

81 CHINESE CP, art. 100.

82 LECTURES ON THE CRIMINAL PROCEDURE LAW, *supra* note 72, at 87.

83 CHINESE CP, ch. II.

84 *Id.*, art. 105.

85 *Id.*, art. 111. One Chinese writer maintains that "public trial" not only serves educational purposes but also puts adjudication under the people's supervision. Liao Zengyun, *On Public Trial*, 1980 FAXUE YANJIU 35–38 (No. 5).

86 NCNA, Sept. 15, 1980.

87 Ching, *Justice Must be Seen to be Done to Gang of Four*, Asian Wall St. J., Oct. 3, 1980, at. 6.

88 Renmin Ribao, Nov. 22, 1980, at 4. A similar view was expressed by Wang Hanbin, Vice-chairman of the Commission for Legal Affairs of the NPC Standing Committee, when interviewed by a New China News Agency reporter. Renmin Ribao, Dec. 12, 1980, at 4.

89 PRC CONST., arts. 26–27.

90 *Id.*, art. 28.

91 *Id.*, art. 29.

92 Gelatt, *Resurrecting China's Legal Institutions*, Asian Wall St. J., Mar. 29, 1980, at 4.

93 NCNA, Nov. 4, 1980; Li Yunchang, *The Role of Chinese Lawyers*, 23 BEIJING REV. 24 (No. 46, 1980).

94 The 21-article Regulations became effective on January 1, 1982. Its full text is in Renmin Ribao, Aug. 27, 1980, at 4.

95 According to the First Vice Minister of Justice, all those who aspire for lawyer certificates shall be subjected to a strict process of scrutiny and evaluation, which may include a formal examination. Le Yunchang, *Several Points of Explanation Concerning the Provisional Regulations on Lawyers of the People's Republic of China*, Renmin Ribao, Aug. 29, 1980, at 4. The 1956 regulations made no reference to any examination and had even more flexible standards for lawyers than the current regulations. *See* S. LENG, *supra* note 5, at 137–39.

96 Provisional Regulations on Lawyers, art. 3.

97 *Id.*

98 *Id.*, art. 19. By comparison, the Lawyers Associations in the 1950s appeared to have more control over Chinese lawyers. As in the past, lawyers are paid by the state, but it is not clear whether a close relation between a lawyer's salary and his performance established by the 1956 Provisional Rules for Lawyers' Fees will be followed. Text of the Rules is in 4 FGHB, 235–38.

99 S. LENG, *supra* note 5, at 144.

100 1979 MINZHU YU FAZHI 36 (No. 2).

101 FBIS-CHI, Sept. 24, 1980, at L14.

102 1980 MINZHU YU FAZHI 10–11 (No. 4).

103 Xiao Yang, *We Should Correctly Treat Lawyers' Work, id.* at 14–15.

104 *China's Lawyers*, 23 BEIJING REV. 26 (No. 23, 1980).

105 Renmin Ribao, Aug. 29, 1980, at 4.

106 Gelatt, *supra* note 92, at 4.

107 CHINESE CP, arts. 115, 117.

108 Butterfield, *Peking Criminal Trial, in Bank Robbery Case, Opened to Foreigners*, N.Y. Times, June 18, 1980, at A3.

109 Jiang Qing initially wanted lawyers to represent her but failed to reach an agreement with the three lawyers recommended by the court. Guangming Ribao, Nov. 11, 1980, at 1.

110 Butterfield, *Revenge Seems to Outweigh Justice at Chinese Trial*, N.Y. Times, Dec. 6, 1980, at 2; Rodenick, *Gang of Four: Baffling Trial in China*, AP, Dec. 6, 1980.

111 *See*FBIS-CHI, Dec. 29, 1980, at L11–12; Dec. 22, 1980, at L6; Dec. 19, 1980, at L2, L4–5; Dec. 2, 1980, at L2–3. Shorter summaries are in 23 BEIJING REV. 20 (No. 50, 1980) and *id.* at 18–21 (No. 52, 1980).

112 FBIS-CHI, Dec. 29, 1980, at L11.

113 *Id.*, Dec. 19, 1980, at L2.

114 *Id.*, Dec. 22, 1980, at L6.

115 GENEVA INT'L COMM'N OF JURISTS, THE RULE OF LAW IN A FREE SOCIETY: A REPORT ON THE INTERNATIONAL CONGRESS OF JURISTS 249 (1979).

116 J. COHEN, *supra* note 5, at 49–50; S. LENG, *supra* note 5, at 164–65; Luo Ping, *supra* note 72, at 71–72.

117 CHINESE CP, art. 32.

118 *Id.*, art. 35.

119 *See, e.g.*, Gelatt, *The People's Republic of China and the Presumption of Innocence*, 73 J. CRIM L. & C. 259 (1982).

120 S. LENG, *supra* note 5, at 63,165.

121 Chen Guangzhong, *The Principle of Presumption of Innocence Should Be Critically Assimilated*, 1980 FAXUE YANJIU 34–36 (No. 4); Liao Zengyun, *View on the Principle of Presumption of Innocence, id.* at 32–34 (No. 5).

122 Wang Bingxin, *Exploration on the Principle of Presumption of Innocence*, 1979 XINAN ZHENGFA XUEYUAN XUEBAO (J. SW. INST. POL. & L.) 10–15 (No. 1); Wang Xizohua & Ma Qingguo, *Argue for the "Presumption of Innocence"*, 1980 FAXUE YANJIU 63–64 (No.1); Zhao Hong & Don Jixiang, *Comprehension on the Principle of Presumption of Innocence*, 1979 FAXUE YANJIU 47–48 (No. 3).

123 LECTURES ON THE CRIMINAL PROCEDURE LAW, *supra* note 44, at 55; Wang Zhaosheng & Wei Ruoping, *A View on the Principle of Presumption of Innocence*, 1979 FAXUE YANJIU 47–48 (No. 2); Yu Zhi, *Presumption of Innocence Cannot Serve as a Guiding Concept in Criminal Procedure*, 1980 MINZHU YU FAZHI 10–21 (No. 3); Zhang Zipei, *Analysis of the Principle of "Presumption of Innocence"*, 1980 FAXUE YANJIU 30–33 (No. 3).

124 Yi Xiaozhong, *Principle of "Presumption of Innocence" is Poles Apart From Our Country's Regulations on Arrest and Detention*, 1980 FAXUE YANJIU 63 (No. 1); Zhang Zipei, *supra* note 123, at 32.

125 *See, e.g.*, Yang Guanda, *A Concrete Analysis Should be Made of "Presumption of Innocence"*, 1980 FAXUE YANJIU 63 (No. 1).

126 FBIS-CHI, Nov. 20, 1980, at L2; *see also* Renmin Ribao, Nov. 22, 1980, at 4.

127 Article 4 of both the 1954 LAW and the 1979 LAW. For reference to the two legal texts, see note 24 *supra*.

128 J. COHEN, *supra* note 5, at 483–506; S. LENG, *supra* note 5, at 61–63, 98–101.

129 Liao Junchang, *Independent Adjudication and Approval of Cases by the Secretary*, 1979 XIAN ZHENGFA XUEYUAN XUEBAO 6–9 (No. 1).

130 *Id.* at 7–9; Chiu Min & Wang Liming, *Strengthen Party Leadership; Adjudicate Independently According to the Law*, 1979 MINZHU YU FAZHI 13 (No. 2); Special Group Assisting the Handling of Cases from the Southwest Institute of Politics and Law, *Looking at Some Problems Existing in Judicial Work from the Practice of Handling Cases*, 1979 XIAN ZHENGFA XUEYUAN XUEBAO 26–27 (No. 1).

131 Yu Haocheng, *Party Committees Should Not Continue Examining and Approving Cases*, Beijing Ribao, Jan. 23, 1981, at 3.

132 Renmin Ribao, Aug. 25, 1980, at 1.

133 Liu Guangming, *The People's Courts Administer Justice Independently*, 1979 FAXUE YANJIU 31–32 (No. 3).

134 Chen Shouyi, *A Review of New China's Research in Law During the Past Thirty Years*, 1980 FAXUE YANJIU 6 (No. 1).

135 Chang Gong, *A Fine Statute on the People's Judicature*, 1979 FAXUE YANJIU 35–36 (No. 4).

136 Peng Zhen, *Several Questions on the Socialist Legal System*, HONGQI, No. 11, 1979, at 7.

137 NCNA, Sept. 15, 1980. For similar complaints on the legal system by other deputies, see Renmin Ribao, Sept. 16, 1980, at 3 and Sept. 18, 1980, at 3.

138 *Strengthen Theoretical Study: Promote Institutional Reform: Excerpts of Comments from the Theoreticians Forum Held in the National Capital, I*, Guangming Ribao, Oct. 10, 1980, at 2.

139 Yu Haocheng, *Party Committees Should Not Continue Examining and Approving Cases*, Beijing Ribao, Jan. 23, 1981, at 3. The first example Yu cited apparently refers to an episode that occurred in Fuding County of Fujian Province. Ji Zhili, secretary of the county Party committee, came into conflict with Zhou Zongshuang, chief procurator of the county, over the disposal of a case. Ji questioned Zhou "which is superior, the law or the Party committee secretary?" and had Zhou dismissed on the pretext of his "resistance to Party leadership." This was reported in Beijing's ZHONGGUO FAZHI BAO (CHINESE LAW WEEKLY) and also in Hong Kong's 1980 CHENG MING 87 (No. 35). Because of the wide publicity of the incident, Zhou has since been reinstated to his post as chief procurator and Ji has been under investigation. For a comment on this episode, see Mao Rongjii, *Which is Superior, the 'Official' or the Law?* Renmin Ribao, July 29, 1981, at 5.

140 *Speeding the Work on Law Making*, 22 BEIJING REV. 3 (No. 9, 1979); FBIS-CHI, Sept, 23, 1980 (Supplement), at 44.

141 *Strange Injustice of Taihang*, Guangming Ribao, Sept. 20, 1980, at 3; Renmin Ribao, Sept. 21, 1980, at 3.

142 1980 MINZHU YU FAZHI 24–25 (No. 6).

143 *Id.* at 25 (No. 3).

144 CHINESE CP, art. 4; ORG. L. PEOPLE'S CTS., art. 5 (1979).

145 PRC CONST., art. 85 (1954).

146 ORG. L. PEOPLE'S CTS, art. 5. (1954).

147 Leng, *supra* note 4, at 365.

148 AMNESTY INT'L, *supra* note 49, at 7–13; Cohen, *supra* note 49, at 335–37; Leng, *supra* note 4, at 363–65.

149 *Policy Toward Descendants of Landlords and Rich Peasants*, 22 BEIJING REV. 8 (No. 4, 1979).

150 Chang Gong, *supra* note 135, at 36.

151 Luo Ping, *The Principle of Measuring Penalty in China's Criminal Law*, HONGQI, No. 9, 1979, at 75. A similar stand is taken in He Bingsong, *On the Democratic Principle of Our Country's Criminal Law*, 1980 FAXUE YANJIU 26 (No. 4).

152 Peng Zhen, *1980 Several Questions on the Socialist Legal System*, HONGQI, No. 11, 1979, at 5.

153 ORG. L. PEOPLE'S CTS., art. 5. (1979).

154 CHINESE CP, art. 4.

155 Ye Jianying, *Closing Address*, in MAIN DOCUMENTS OF THE SECOND SESSION OF THE FIFTH NATIONAL PEOPLE'S CONGRESS OF THE PEOPLE'S REPUBLIC OF CHINA 225–26 (1979).

156 Yuan Xiaofan, *On the Equality of the Application of Law*, 1980 FAXUE YANJIU 26 (No. 2).

157 Pan Nianzhi & Qi Naikuan, *On "Everyone is Equal Before the Law"*, Guangming Ribao, Feb. 9, 1980, at 3.

158 Cui Min, *How Should We Interpret "Everyone is Equal Before the Law"*, Renmin Ribao, July 24, 1979, at 3.

159 FBIS-CHI, July 2, 1980, at L6.

160 For this case, Beijing Ribao on August 9 carried a commentator's article entitled *Warn Those Cadres Children and Younger Brothers Who Violate the Law and Commit Crimes, cited in* Renmin Ribao, Aug. 9, 1980, at 4. *See also High Officials' Sons Punished*, 23 BEIJING REV. 7–8 (No. 35, 1980).

161 NCNA, Sept. 2, 1980; *Oil Rig Accident Sternly Dealt With*, 23 BEIJING REV. 7–8 (No. 36, 1980).

162 FBIS-CHI, Sept. 4, 1980, at L23.

163 Renmin Ribao, Jan. 26, 1981, at 1, 4.

164 *Advance in the Direction of Strengthening Socialist Democracy and the Legal System*, HONGQI, No. 3, 1981, at 15.

165 The delay in the Court's sentencing of the radicals, for instance, was reported to have been caused by the split of the Chinese leadership over the fate of Jiang Qing, and the final judgments were said to have been a compromise approved by the CCP's Politburo. *See* Sterba, *Former Chinese Leaders Given Long Prison Terms*, N.Y. Times, Jan. 26, 1981, at A1; *China's Leaders Said to be Split on the Sentencing of Jiang Qing, id.*, Jan. 11, 1981, at 7.

166 Li Mingfa, *The Chinese Leadership's Dispute Over the Sentencing of Jiang Qing*, 1981 CHENG MING 23 (No. 40).

167 *See* remarks made by Deputy Yang from Yiangxi and Deputy Zhang from Sichuan in Renmin Ribao, Sept. 18, 1980, at 3.

168 J. COHEN, *supra* note 5, at 556–63; S. LENG, *supra* note 5, at 151–53.

169 CHINESE CP, art. 137. This stipulation is interpreted as important to the removal of defendants' fear to appeal and to the protection of innocent people against unjust and wrong verdicts. Tao Mao & Li Baoyue, *The Principle of "Not Increasing Sentences on Appeal" Should Not be Negated*, 1980 MINZHU YU FAZHI 25–26 (No. 2).

170 FBIS-CHI, Sept. 23, 1980 (Supplement), at 42.

171 CHINESE CP, art. 149.

172 LECTURES ON THE CRIMINAL PROCEDURE LAW, *supra* note 72, at 118.

173 *See* note 170 *supra*.

174 *Continue to Reverse Unjust and Erroneous Verdicts Based on False Charges*, Guangming Ribao, June 28, 1979, at 1.

175 CHINESE CL, art. 43.

176 CHINESE CP, arts. 15–17.

177 *Id.*, art. 145.

178 *Id.*, art. 146. This provision is described as a design to simplify procedures and to reduce the work load of the Supreme People's Court. The decision on this arrangement was first made by the Supreme People's Court in 1958 and is now confirmed by this article. LECTURES ON THE CRIMINAL PROCEDURE LAW, *supra* note 72, at 112.

179 *See* Ge Ping & Wang Honggu, *On Capital Punishment*, FAXUE YANJI 29–32, 44 (No. 1, 1980); Zhao Canbi, *Strengthen the Concept of the Legal System and Act According to the Law*, HONGQI, No. 8, 1979, at 42–43; Chen Yiyun & Kong Qingyun, *On Capital Punishment*, Renmin Ribao, Feb. 25, 1980, at 3.

180 The provision concerning the underage youth and pregnant women is in CHINESE CL, art. 44. CHINESE CP, art. 154 also provides that execution will be stayed if the condemned is found to be pregnant and the case will be submitted to the Supreme People's Court for resentencing according to law.

181 Mathews, *Plagued by Crime, Chinese Increase Use of the Executions*, Washington Post, Aug. 5, 1980, at A13.

182 *Id.* This case was well publicized in China. For the Chinese account, see *Embezzler Sentenced to Death*, 22 BEIJING REV. 7 (No. 45, 1979).

183 FBIS-CHI, Dec. 6, 1979, at L9–10.

184 LECTURES ON THE CRIMINAL PROCEDURE LAW, *supra* note 72, at 108; J. COHEN, *supra* note 5, at 541–42.

185 Renmin Ribao, June 11, 1981, at 1.

186 For the NPC Standing Committee's resolution ratifying the State Council's Supplementary Regulation concerning Reeducation and Rehabilitation Through Labor, see Renmin Ribao, Nov. 30, 1979, at 1. The text of the original decision of August 1957 is in VI FGHB 243–44 (1957).

187 Butterfield, *Hundreds of Thousands Toil in Chinese Labor Camps*, N.Y. Times, Jan. 3, 1981, at 1, 4; Johnson, *China Dissidents Fall Through Cracks in New Legal Code*, Christian Science Monitor, June 18, 1980, at 4; Mathews, *China Revives Labor Camp System*, Washington Post, June 1, 1980, at A1.

188 Weisskopf, *China Ends a Fling at Free Thinking*, Washington Post, Mar. 13, 1981, at A1, A10. Bomb explosions in Beijing and Shanghai were interpreted by Chinese police as counterrevolutionary activities. For reactions to the explosion in the Beijing Railroad Station, see *Resolutely Strike at Criminal Elements*, Renmin Ribao, Nov. 11, 1980, at 1. For Agence France Presse (AFP) Reports on the possibility of clampdown in the face of growing social unrest, see FBIS-CHI Mar. 3, 1981, at R1 and Mar. 4, 1981, at L8.

189 For instance, several writers in their communications to Democracy and the Legal System agree that to maintain the dignity of the law, it should never again be dictated by the "requirements of circumstances" or be "blown in the direction of the wind." 1980 MINGHU YU FAZHI 38 (No. 2); *id.* at 48 (No. 1).

190 *Party Discipline Should Not Replace State Law*, Jiefang Ribao (Liberation Daily), Oct. 7, 1980, at 3. *See* CHINESE CP, art. 114.

191 Renmin Ribao, Oct. 4, 1980, at 3.

192 Jiefang Ribao, Oct. 7, 1980, at 2; Chiu Min, *Insist That Lawbreakers Must be Punished*, Renmin Ribao, Oct. 3, 1980, at 5; Wu Yaohui, *Stress on Mandatory Punishment for All Lawbreakers*, 1981 MINZHU XU FAZHI 24 (No. 2).

32

CHINA'S MAJOR REFORM IN CRIMINAL LAW

Cai Dingjian

Source: *Columbia Journal of Asian Law* 11:1 (1997): 213–218.

On March 14, 1997, the Fifth Session of the Eighth National People's Congress approved the Reform Bill on Criminal Law, which will produce significant changes to criminal law in China. China's existing criminal law statute was formulated in 1979 shortly after the Cultural Revolution. It was one of the first of seven groups of laws formulated. Triggered by the lessons learned from the Cultural Revolution, this series of statutory drafting reflected the importance China attributed to the rule of law at that time. A country with a history of a weak legal system, China had little experience in dealing with legal theories. Therefore, the resulting statute focused largely on principles and was comprised of definitions that were unduly formalistic as well as containing many loopholes. In 1982, the Standing Committee of the National People's Congress began its research on the reform of criminal law, which continued for fifteen years. During this period, the National People's Congress adopted 22 ordinances and decisions that amended or supplemented the criminal statute. In addition, it adopted 130 articles regarding criminal liabilities in context of civil, economic, and administrative law. The Reform Bill on Criminal Law was formulated out of the accumulated experiences from the enactment of criminal laws over the past 17 years, the research conducted on criminal laws of various foreign countries, and the studies made on modern criminal legislation and developmental trends.

The Reform Bill on Criminal Law is a significant one. Under the bill, the existing criminal statute will be expanded from 192 articles to 449 articles; all criminal ordinances and decisions will be assimilated to produce a unified criminal code. The reform encompasses the following areas.

1 Clarifications of three fundamental principles of criminal law

First, the reformed criminal code defines the legal elements of each criminal offense and abandons the principle of application by analogy. Article 79 of the existing criminal statute provides that, if a defendant's act is not explicitly proscribed by statute, the defendant can be convicted and sentenced based on the most analogous provision, as long as permission from the People's Supreme Court is obtained. Article 3 of the new criminal code provides that "if a defendant's act is proscribed by law explicitly, the defendant should be sentenced according to the provisions; if a defendant's act is not proscribed by law explicitly, the defendant should not be convicted or sentenced."

Second, the reformed criminal code follows the principle of equality before the law. Article 4 of the new criminal code states that "the applicable law for every defendant of the same offense should be identical; no person has the privilege of surpassing the law."

Third, the reformed criminal code clearly defines the principle of proportionate sanction. Article 5 of the new criminal code provides that "the applicable sanctions should be proportional to the crime committed by and the criminal responsibilities of the defendant."

These new provisions represent large improvements in Chinese criminal law.

2 Abolishment of counter-revolutionary crimes

Most offenses characterized in the counter-revolutionary chapter are redefined as offenses of endangering national security. Other articles are redefined as offenses endangering public safety or offenses interfering with the administration of public order. The new code increases the sanctions for offenses endangering national security when the act involves conspiracy with "foreign organizations, associations, and individuals." Most changes concerning counter-revolutionary crimes, however, are linguistic; few substantive changes have been made. For example, Article 102 of the existing criminal statute defines the offense of counter-revolutionary propaganda as "the use of counter-revolutionary slogans, leaflets, or other methods that provoke overthrowing the 'classless totalitarian government and socialist system." This offense is converted to that of solicitations to overthrow the government, an offense consisting of "the use of slander, libel, or other methods to provoke the overthrow of the government and destruction of the socialist system"; the offense of counter-revolutionary propaganda is thus discarded. The change reflects the end of the revolutionary period in which legal concepts focused mainly on struggles between the social classes.

3 Clarifications of the two "Pocket Offenses" in the existing criminal statute

"Pocket Offenses" proscribe conduct that endangers society. Their definitions focus on theoretical principles; thus, making identification of an offense as ambiguous as locating an item in a big pocket. There are two "pocket offenses." The first involves taking chances in a planned economy in an abusive manner. The offense punishes conduct that violates the administrative rules governing financial, currency exchange, monetary, and commercial areas. The boundaries of the offense are blurry, and the conduct proscribed is potentially very broad. Prosecutors thus have broad discretion in enforcing the statute. In the past, many were convicted of the offense because of improper conduct in the business areas of sales, trading, and agency. The offense has been abolished pursuant to the needs of a socialist market economy. Conduct previously proscribed is now analyzed and redrawn into narrower categories, such as the offense of manufacture and sale of fake commercial products, the offense of disrupting discipline in financial management, the offense of contractual fraud, the offense of dealing in licensed or patented products, and the offense of trading import and export permits.

The second "pocket offense" arises from the creation of public nuisance. Article 160 of the existing criminal statute defines the offense as any conduct that disrupts public order in a serious manner such as group fights, provoking trouble, and harassing females. In practice, judges have broad discretion in drawing the line of the offense and much improper conduct can potentially fall under the offense of creating public nuisance. The reformed criminal code divides the offense into four separate offenses: harassment and molestation of females, organized sexual activities, group fights, and provocation of trouble.

4 Strengthening of prosecution for breach of official duties

The existing criminal statute contains a chapter on breach of official duties, which address specific offenses committed by state officials, such as corruption and bribery and negligence of official duties. Recently, the number of cases involving corruption in public office has increased. A significant minority of state officials are corrupt, abusive, and gravely irresponsible, thus endangering the welfare of the state and the public. Some law enforcement officials, prosecutorial officials in particular, are biased in their implementation of the law, and they seriously tarnish the image of the legal system. The reformed criminal code contains additional, more concrete, and more stringent provisions targeted toward state officers. It contains one full chapter on bribery and corruption and expands the chapter on breach of official duties from 7 to 23 articles, thus greatly enhancing the sanctions imposed on state officers who breach their official duties. Breach of official duties includes abuse of power in approving the illegal formation and registration of corporations, the illegal issuance of equities and bonds, negligent execution of fraudulent contractual provisions causing heavy losses to the state, failure to collect tax revenues in full or in part, fraud or bias in the management of stock issuance, withholding of taxes, and administration of export refunds, illegal issuance of permits for timber harvesting, irresponsibilities that result in heavy environmental pollution, illegal issuance of permits for land use and permits for land possession, sale of land use rights of state property at a low price, trafficking, and falsification of inspection reports.

5 More stringent provisions on sentence reduction and probation

The existing criminal statute provides that sentence reduction and probation can be granted to criminals who have truly repented. The definition of "truly repented," is however blurry in practice. Consequently, a large degree of discretion is reserved for enforcement officials. Because there has been a serious corruption problem among enforcement officials in recent years, some criminals who have been sentenced heavily or sentenced to life without parole are imprisoned only for a short time in practice; by bribing enforcement officers, these criminals are either granted a reduction in their sentence or released on probation. The reformed criminal code sets forth the limits and conditions under which a reduction in sentence or probation can be granted. For example, violent sex offenders are not entitled to any reduction in sentence or probation at all. Under the new criminal code, an enforcement unit no longer has the power to decide whether a criminal is entitled to sentence reduction or probation. The unit must now submit a recommendation to an intermediary court or a court at a higher level. Consideration is then made by the judicial commission of the court.

6 New offenses that meet the needs of societal development and market economy

The main offenses created include participating in triad activities, terrorism, inciting racial hatred and disrupting racial harmony, money squandering, fraud in stock-related activities, destroying environmental sources, infringing trade secrets, tarnishing construction quality, kidnapping and detaining ransoms for debt collection, limiting individual freedom for labor work, attacking witnesses for revenge and endangering national security interests.

The reformed criminal code also contains articles governing breach of official duties by military personnel.

The reform bill is a big step in China's construction of a legal system. It unifies and outlines criminal law in China. By changing the existing scattered and chaotic criminal law statutes, ordinances, and rules, the reformed code facilitates the enforcement of criminal law. The new criminal code provides for principles of substantive due process, equality before the law, and proportionate sanctions. It increases the rights enjoyed by the public and criminal defendants. In addition, this reform raises the standard of criminal law. Criminal enforcement is facilitated as some provisions have been made more elaborate and concrete, hence greatly limiting the discretionary power of judges and reducing the chances of corruption.

Nevertheless, some legal scholars are not completely satisfied with the reform because little progress has been made in reducing the scope of capital punishment. Heavy criminal sanctions have been favored throughout Chinese history. In 1979, when the existing criminal statute was formulated, there were 28 capital offenses. Since 1982, there has been an increasingly strong societal sentiment against this broad classification. Supplemental ordinances of the criminal statute have greatly expanded the scope of capital punishment, increasing the number of capital offenses to 66. During the reform process, some legal scholars advocated reducing the scope of capital punishment, referring to the trends of criminal laws in other countries and the features of a modern legal system. Public safety, however, is highly emphasized in Chinese society today. At present, the country is focusing heavily on efforts directed against criminal activities. Under this climate, the police and the prosecutorial office believe that the death penalty should be used more frequently. The public also supports heavy punishment of criminals. Accordingly, this is not the best time to advocate a reduction in the scope of capital punishment. In view of the different opinions given by lawyers, police, and prosecutorial officers, the scope of capital punishment has neither been increased nor decreased. For criminals below the age of 18, however, the most severe punishment has been changed from the death penalty to life without parole.

Furthermore, one important reform was not instituted due to strong opposition from representatives of the People's National Congress. Recently, crimes involving heavy firearms have dramatically increased. To protect the safety of on-duty police officers, the police department proposed an amendment to the self-defense provision of the existing criminal statute. Under the proposal, the scope of self-defense by the police would have been overly broad: "if a police officer is forcefully attacked or is fearful of his or her personal safety during any legal interrogation, detainment, arrest, pursuit of fleeing suspects, and coup against illegal activities, the officer will be not criminally liable for the injuries or death of anyone because of the use of excessive force in self-defense, as long as the officer uses the weapon or firearm in a legally appropriate manner." When the bill was revised in the National People's Congress, many representatives believed that the provision would confer excessive power on the police as the degree of "forceful attacks" might vary. They argued that the lack of a strict limitation on the use of weapons would likely result in their excessive use by certain police officers, considering that the excessive use of firearms and weapons often occurred in practice. In view of these representatives' opinions, this provision in the original bill was deleted. The reformed criminal code retains the self-defense provision of the existing criminal statute. Self-defense must be reasonable in scope; the actor will be criminally liable otherwise.

33

CRIMINAL DEFENCE IN CHINA

The possible impact of the 1996 Criminal Procedure Law reform*

Hualing Fu

Source: *China Quarterly* 153 (1998): 31–48.

Criminal procedure in China had been governed by the 1979 Criminal Procedure Law (CPL 1979).[1] This was amended in 1996 (the Amendment).[2] In many aspects, the Amendment introduces important changes to the previous procedures and significantly redistributes the existing division of powers within the criminal justice system. It restricts police power and the prosecution's discretion. It enhances the position of the court and differentiates the role of judges.[3] It also offers more protection for the rights of the accused and enhances the position of defence lawyers in the criminal process in substantive and procedural aspects. Consequently criminal lawyers are expected to play a more active and meaningful role in criminal defence.

Justice demands that individuals accused of criminal activity have the right to defend themselves before the law, and this principle is contained in the Chinese Constitution 1982, which states that "the accused has the right to defence."[4] This principle is also provided in Article 26 of the CPL 1979. Although the accused may invoke the constitutional right to counsel, this right had been substantially limited and grossly distorted by subordinate laws, government regulations and administrative discretion. According to Zhang Sihan[5] from the Supreme People's Court, on average, only 20 to 30 per cent of defendants have been represented by lawyers during the trial; even in cases of serious criminal offences, only 40 per cent of defendants retained lawyers. Furthermore, the CPL 1979 structured China's criminal process in such a way that, in law and in practice, a criminal trial and the role of defence attorneys were mere formalities.

Will the 1996 Amendment make any practical difference in improving the accused's right to counsel? The Lawyers Committee for Human Rights cautions that: "Since the revisions are intended to change ingrained patterns of behaviour by law enforcement officials, it seems likely that the gap between the law and the practice of criminal justice in China will actually grow wider, at least in the short term."[6] But, on the other hand, without the Amendment itself, no change at all is likely. This article examines the fundamental flaws in the criminal defence provided in the CPL 1979, and discusses how criminal defence may be improved under the Amendment and what the limitations are in protecting the rights of the accused.

The role of defence lawyers under the CPL 1979

Once the procuratorate initiated proceedings against an accused and transferred the case to court, the court formed a collegial panel, composed of judges and people's assessors, to try the case.[7] Before the trial, the panel held meetings to discuss the case and to make a decision on the nature of the offence as well as on the sentence. In serious cases, decisions were made by the Judicial Committee, which was the leading body of any court.[8] Where a case was complicated or important, the opinion of the superior court or even the Supreme People's Court might also be sought. It was normal practice in China that a case was decided before a trial and that those who tried the case might not have the power to make the decision.

The court had to try the case unless there was not "clear and sufficient evidence" to support the prosecution, in which even the court would remand the case to the procuratorate for supplementary investigation. The court might ask the prosecution to withdraw its case if no criminal punishment was necessary.[9] When clarification was necessary, a people's court might initiate its own inquests, examination, search, seizure and expert evaluation. The fundamental characteristic of Chinese criminal trials under the CPL 1979 was that, through the pre-trial investigation, the judges decided on the facts and on the law involved. As a matter of law, no court would open a court session if the collegial panel was not certain about the facts, the offence and the sentence.[10]

Judges' involvement in the pre-trial investigation seriously diminished the role of defence lawyers. The trial judges would necessarily have prejudiced views on the case after they had read through the files and verified the evidence. They had difficulty in accepting alternative views from the parties, especially the defence. A challenge to the charge was not so much a challenge to the prosecution's case as a direct attack on the court's credibility. Unless there was strong new evidence, an open trial could not render any assistance to a defendant.[11]

Political interference in criminal defence was certainly the most serious problem facing any attempt to reform the system. When criminal defence was re-introduced into China's criminal justice system in the early 1980s,[12] the reaction from many governmental departments, including the courts, was hostile. In 1981, there were reports that court regarded defence lawyers as "troublemakers," "burdens" and "hindrances," the procuratorate called them "experts in picking bones from eggs" who would use loopholes to destroy the prosecution's case.[13] Defence lawyers complained that the "lawyers' function is not correctly understood and otherwise lawful defences are blatantly interfered with and limited."[14]

The most blatant interference took place in 1983 when the government launched its campaign on crime in China. The Ministry of Justice issued a Notice which severely limited the right of the defence and eventually made the defence part of the prosecution team.[15]

This Notice required that once the court appointed a defence lawyer to defend an accused, the lawyer was obliged to accept the task. Where there were no defence lawyers, Party and government officers could be seconded temporarily to serve the purpose. Defence lawyers were told that they should not direct their minds to "trivial matters and technicalities" where the main facts were clear; they should not even raise the issue of mitigation if there were not apparent mitigating factors. Furthermore, if defence lawyers found that the main facts of the case were not clear or the application of law was mistaken, they should communicate this to the court or procuratorate before a trial. In cases in which the death penalty could be imposed, defence lawyers should first convey their objections, if any, to the local Party committee via the local Bureau of Justice.[16]

Even though the Notice was issued specifically to serve the 1983 nation-wide war on crime, it continued to have an impact. Jiang[17] commented on incidents involving interference with lawyers' work and harassment of defence lawyers:

A few cadres blame defence attorneys for ignoring the larger social interests and blindly following the law during a trial; some departments in charge of lawyers even impose numerous restrictions on the defence. They may forbid lawyers to conduct a serious defence, they may even disallow a not guilty plea. In extreme cases, they even treat lawyers as co-conspirators of the defendants because of their defence, and the lawyers' liberty cannot be protected.

For some firms, a reporting system was created to ensure political control over the work of criminal defence. In Nanjing city, for example, "collective decision making is required in serious and complicated cases; for cases where a not guilty plea is proposed or no consensus can be reached in the firm, they will be referred to the Bureau of Justice for a decision."[18]

There has been less political interference in lawyers' defence work in criminal trials during the 1990s. The legal profession in general is gradually becoming more independent, essentially a private business which cannot be tightly controlled by the government.[19] One indication of such a development is the frequent use of a not guilty plea. In sensitive cases, such as that of Xi Yang, a Hong Kong-based reporter accused of unlawful disclosure of state secrets,[20] and those against Wang Dan, Wei Jingsheng and other dissidents for sedition and subversion,[21] not guilty pleas were seriously argued by the defence. The court, on the other hand, is often unsatisfied by the prosecution's case and, although this happens rarely, may give a not guilty verdict to assert its independence.

A defendant's right to counsel

Article 110 of the CPL 1979 states:

> After a people's court has decided to open a court session, it shall proceed with the following work: ... (2) to deliver to the defendant a copy of the bill of prosecution of the people's procuratorate no later than seven days before the opening of the court session and inform the defendant that he may appoint a defender or, when necessary, designate a defender for himself.

This seven-day rule effectively prevented any involvement by a defence lawyer at the investigation and prosecution stages of a criminal case. In other words, a defence lawyer had no right in law to enter the police station and the procurator's office to obtain information or meet and correspond with the accused. Practically, no legal representation was allowed until a week before the trial.[22]

In the vast majority of cases there were only one or two days available for a lawyer to prepare a defence. In a complicated case there might be hundreds of pages of documents and it would be impossible for a lawyer to review all the main facts.[23] The defence lawyer for a dissident after the 1989 "Tiananmen incident" was only given four days to examine a thousand pages of documents filed by the prosecution.[24] In 30 per cent of instances, cases were already at trial when the lawyer received the notice.[25] Without legal representation during the investigation and prosecution stages, the police and procurators might, as happened frequently, force or falsify confessions, or record only those statements favourable to the prosecution's case.[26]

The lack of time to prepare a defence had been recognized officially. A Joint Notice provided that where a case was complicated and time was not sufficient for preparing a defence, the defence lawyer might ask the court to delay the trial, and "the court should consider the application if the delay would not affect the trial of the case within the limit provided by law."[27] In practice, however, such extensions were rarely granted.[28] Even this limited protection was later abolished for some offences. According to the 1983 Decisions of the Standing Committee of the National People's Congress, the seven-day time limit "may be overstepped" for defendants "who cause explosions or commit murder, rape, robbery or other crimes seriously endangering public security, and who are punishable by death, where the main facts of the crimes are clear, the evidence is conclusive and the popular indignation is exceedingly great."[29]

In addition to the time constraints, defence lawyers' right of access to files and to the accused was limited. At the pre-trial stage, defence lawyers had the right to "consult the file record of the current case, acquaint themselves with the circumstances of the case, and meet and correspond with the defendant in custody."[30] According to the Joint Notice, lawyers might review the files in court and the court had the duty to provide necessary assistance, such as providing a room and allowing lawyers to make extracts from the files.

However, there were two limitations on lawyers' review of court files. First, the minutes of the Judicial Committee and the collegial panel could not be reviewed. This was a serious limitation given the fact that the Judicial Committee and collegial panel normally made a determination as to the offence and punishment prior to a trial. A Supreme People's Court document even classifies these minutes as "state secrets."[31] Secondly, courts could not provide satisfactory facilities for the defence. One study[32] of ten courts and seven law firms in China shed light on the reality of defence rights in reviewing court documents. Fang Deming investigated 22 criminal trials of the first instance, and found that lawyers did not have access to the full files in eight cases (36 per cent). Two sets of chairs and tables were provided in one court, but the other nine did not provide any facilities for lawyers to read and extract material from the files. The main problem, according to the author, was that most of the courts regarded legal representation as a mere formality. The common practice was that a defence lawyer would be given only what he specifically requested and any other documents would not be voluntarily offered by the court. Judges were especially reluctant to share evidence uncovered through their own investigation. They tended to produce that evidence only in court.

Interviewing an accused in police custody was a difficult matter for lawyers. Police concern over security hindered frank communication between lawyers and their clients.[33] The Joint Notice required a detention centre to provide necessary assistance for lawyers to interview their clients, including the provision of proper premises. It also asked the police to strike a balance between security and right to counsel. Though it did not require the guards to be absent during the interview, it required them to be wary that their presence did not make defendants afraid of talking to their defence attorneys. After the interview, the guards should not question defendants about the content of their interview. A similar requirement was made by the Ministry of Justice and the Ministry of Public Security in a 1956 Joint Notice.[34]

Pre-trial disclosure

No exchange of information was required between the defence and the procuratorate at the pre-trial stage and the two sides made their first contact in the court room. According to the CPL 1979, the procuratorate had to deliver the files of a case, together with the evidence collected, to the court. The defence had the right to review these files and evidence. In many cases, the family members of the accused retained a lawyer immediately after the detention or arrest, and the lawyer conducted an informal investigation of the case, even though he did not have the right to do so in law. Such an informal investigation might produce new evidence which might not be known to the procuratorate and the court. The defence could use such evidence to launch a surprise attack on both the court and the prosecution's case at the trial. However, the defence might not want a showdown in a courtroom. If the lawyer disagreed with the procurator, it was usually better to convey his disagreement before the trial started, convincing the procuratorate and the court to change their minds and thus avoiding any serious conflict with the procurators and the judges.

An informal pre-trial conference procedure had developed in China to increase understanding among the parties. Initially used as a measure to expedite criminal trials during the campaign on crime in the early 1980s, it received positive responses.[35] First, it had been argued, especially by defence lawyers, that a pre-trial conference was useful in narrowing down the issues of the case, so that the parties could focus on differences during the trial stage. Secondly, defence lawyers were only provided a brief time in court to put forward their defence, and as a result their case might not be clearly understood or accepted by the court and procuratorate. If they could discuss with the judges and procurator beforehand, they had more time to explain their defence. This also allowed time for judges to digest the defence argument.[36]

Finally, and perhaps most importantly, court-room debate was a final showdown, a battle fought in public. A lawyer's defence was perceived to be a direct challenge to the authority of the court and the procuratorate. The court especially would not be ready to accept such an open challenge, even if they knew they were wrong. As one lawyer commented: "Sometimes a correct defence in court may put the procuratorate and court in an embarrassing position and thus damage their dignity."[37] Another lawyer from Jiangxi province suggested that: "Once a case is transferred to the court, the case would basically be decided. A public trial is a mere formality. It would be really difficult to ask the judicial organs to withdraw a wrong decision."[38] Given the fact that a successful defence to a large extent depended upon the goodwill of the procuratorate and judges, it was essential to persuade the court to listen to the defence. A pre-trial meeting gave defence attorneys an opportunity to persuade the judges and procuratorate to alter their decision without embarrassing them in court.[39]

There had been strong objections to the pre-trial conference among Chinese lawyers. As a principle, it was said, defence lawyers should be independent from the court and procuratorate. If they had to share everything with the procurators, it would give the public an impression that the lawyers "wear the same pants and sing the same song."[40] The pre-trial conference had never become systematic and its existence always depended upon a lawyer's initiative. When properly conducted, it could compensate for a lawyers' disadvantages by providing an informal opportunity for them to communicate with the judges and procurators.

The rights of a lawyer during the trial

The CPL 1979 set out a clear scenario of the manner in which the criminal trial should proceed. Throughout the trial, the judge was the dominant figure. The presiding judge opened the session by announcing the subject-matter of the case and introducing the participants.[41] The public procurator then read out the Bill of Prosecution, which included the facts of the case, the law violated and the punishment sought. The judges then started to question the defendant, and the public prosecutor might also question the defendant with the permission of the court.[42] Next, the judges and prosecutors started to question witnesses, present the records of testimony of witnesses who were not present in court, and read out the conclusions of expert witness and documentary evidence.[43]

At this stage, the defence might raise questions. According to Article 115, CPL 1979: "The parties and the defenders may request the presiding judge to question the witnesses or expert witnesses, or ask the presiding judge's permission to put their own questions directly." But the court might stop to questioning of the defence if it considered it irrelevant.

During the trial, the defence might also call new witnesses and enter new evidence. But the court had discretion in granting such requests.[44] For instance, they did not allow expert witnesses produced by the defence because there was no provision allowing such witnesses in the CPL 1979.[45]

When the judicial inquisition was over, the procurator was allowed to make a speech to conclude his case; the accused was also allowed to make a statement. Afterwards, the defence was given an opportunity to make their case. A "debate" among the participants followed. When the judge regarded the issues of law and fact to have been fully debated, he might declare the conclusion of the debate and allow the defence to present a final statement.[46]

The dynamic of the court proceeding

Given the fact that a case was decided before the trial, the trial could only be ritual, with the parties knowing that any input would be too little and too late. This was not to say that there was nothing a lawyer could say in court. There were occasionally tense debates, and sometime names were called and insults were exchanged between procurators and lawyers. As early as 1983, defence lawyers were criticized for using the court room as "a forum of free speech."[47]

A major difficulty facing defence lawyers was that they could rarely question the prosecution witnesses and thus could only argue in the abstract. Defence lawyers were normally allowed to raise questions of any prosecution witness who testified, but the problem was that most of the witnesses did not testify in court but only provided a written statement which would be read out.

Another difficulty was that the court seldom treated the lawyers' arguments seriously. Most defence lawyers worked in state-owned firms as government employees. Compared with judges and procurators (also government employees but with higher administrative ranks), the status of lawyers was very low. Judges and procurators represented the state; lawyers were associated with "criminals." Lawyers were normally overwhelmed in court.[48] Some judges openly discouraged defendants from hiring lawyers and some regarded using a lawyer as a waste of money – "better to spend the money on some good meals."[49]

The court treats lawyers' defence arguments as they please. They can simply disregard their opinions. You say whatever you prefer, I decide whatever I want ... Some judges openly ask the defendants: what is the use of hiring a lawyer? Don't waste your money. Some even claim that: "The punishment will be lenient without a lawyer, and will be severe with a lawyer."[50]

The abuse of defence lawyers in criminal hearings was so prevalent that the Supreme People's Court, the Supreme people's procuratorate, the Ministry of Public Security and the Ministry of Justice found it necessary to issue a Supplementary Notice to address the problem. This stipulated that courts should respect a defence lawyer's basic rights:

- Courts should take defence arguments seriously. Written evidence provided by the defence and the statement of defence should be included in the court's files; other materials related to the case should also be included if necessary.
- Courts should consider the evidence presented by the defence. The court shall verify the evidence provided by the defence or ask the procuratorate to verify such evidence, so that it can be presented during the trial.
- Courts should not issue a summons to order a defence lawyer to defend an accused in court.
- Courts should pay due respect to defence lawyers in court and should not expel them from court rooms at will.[51]

The process of reform

The reform of China's criminal procedural law formally started in early 1995. There had been a consensus among the key players in the criminal justice system that defence lawyers should be available to an accused at an earlier stage. But opinions differed as to how early it should be, and, coloured by their different institutional interests, the police, procuratorate and court had different proposals.

The Supreme People's Court held the most liberal view, proposing that defence lawyers might intervene at the earliest stage of investigation. Through the early intervention of lawyers, any unlawful and deleterious activities of investigators would be brought to the court's attention. More importantly, the court's role in supervising the police and procuratorate would also be improved. The court's control had been limited mainly to the scrutiny of law and fact on the record prepared by the police and procurators. Most unlawful and prejudicial activities committed by the police and procuratorate did not appear on record and were not evident to the court. The early involvement of defence lawyers might protect the procedural rights of the accused.[52]

The Ministry of Justice, which regulates the legal profession in the country, held a similar view. Its officials proposed that whenever compulsory measures, such as detention and arrest, were imposed on a suspect, or whenever a suspect was summoned, he should be allowed to have legal representation. Earlier legal representation is the international standard which China should follow; and, through earlier involvement, defence lawyers could supervise the procedural fairness of the investigation.[53]

The Supreme People's Procuratorate agreed with earlier involvement of the defence at the prosecution stage in principle, but argued that the scope of such involvement should be different at different stages of an investigation. In addition, the right and duty of defence lawyers should be clearly stipulated. In particular, a defence lawyer's involvement should not be allowed to "interfere with the normal investigation."[54]

The Ministry of Public Security strongly opposed defence lawyers' involvement in the investigation stage. It argued that this was a stage in which the police sought to clarify the facts of the case, to collect evidence and to prove crimes. The investigation would be hampered by defence lawyers. Thus before the police were clear about a case, there should be no legal representation. Furthermore, crime would continue to increase and become more complex in the future, it argued. Given that the police bore tremendous responsibilities in criminal investigation, involvement of defence lawyers at the investigation stage would be detrimental to police work.[55]

While the key players in the criminal justice system were negotiating the redistribution of powers among themselves and making compromises on the rights of defendants and their legal representatives, the issue was also debated in public as part of the academic campaign for the reform of China's criminal process. There was a massive literature written by government officials and academics, published in law review journals, newspapers and magazines, largely supportive of liberalizing the criminal justice system and offering more protection of rights.[56]

It was openly admitted by an official from the Ministry of Justice[57] that criminal defence under the CPL 1979 was "inconsistent with Article 125 of the Constitution." Many looked at criminal defence in common law jurisdictions to study how the rights of an accused could be better protected. In a draft CPL prepared by a law school in Beijing at the invitation of the National People's Congress, it was proposed that, where a suspect is detained or arrested, he should be allowed to contact a lawyer immediately or within 48 hours after his detention or arrest.[58]

Attempts to make lawyers accessible during the investigation stage were also made in some local jurisdictions. In the draft Lawyers Regulations in the Shenzhen Special Economic Zone, for instance, it was provided that in criminal cases, lawyers "may be entrusted to provide legal services for citizens or suspects on whom are imposed compulsory measures by the public security organs or the procuratorate, or who are summoned by the public security organs or procuratorate for the first time."[59] But when the draft regulations were passed by the local legislature, these provisions were deleted.[60]

It was commonly held by academics and many decision makers in China that increasing the role of lawyers would not be sufficient to protect the rights of defendants unless the procedure of the criminal trial was changed. It was pointed out that the pro-active role of the judge and the inquisitorial style of trial were sources of real difficulty. The thrust of the criticism was that when trial judges became investigators, they could not be fair and neutral in conducting the trial. It was argued that the inquisitorial system was no longer suitable in China and that a more adversarial system needed to be put in place. The Supreme People's Court supported this notion and proposed that while the presiding judge would continue to play the leading role in criminal trials, the evidence should be produced directly by prosecution and defence. More importantly, witnesses must testify in court and may be cross-examined.

According to the Supreme People's Court, a more adversarial system would have three advantages.[61] First, the procurator and defence lawyer would be more responsible when each was made to bear the burden of presenting evidence. There had been mounting complaints about the deterioration in the quality of criminal trials in China and a more adversarial model was expected to improve the situation. Secondly, judges would not pre-determine a case and would become neutral adjudicators. A more adversarial system would rectify the phenomenon of "convicting before a trial." Thirdly, evidence, when it was presented by the witness directly in court, could be verified according to law.

The main objection to the proposal came from the Supreme People's Procuratorate which insisted that, although there were some problems in criminal trials, the present system was satisfactory. China should find its own way to reform trial procedures, instead of blindly following the "Western style."[62] The procuratorate objected to reform mainly from a fear that a more adversarial system would diminish its status. Under the CPL 1979, the procuratorate played the double role of prosecuting a criminal offence and supervising the court during the trial.[63] Under the proposal, the role of supervision would be substantially diminished, if not abolished. Under a more adversarial system, the prosecution would be a party on the same footing, legally, as the defence, arguing a case to the court.[64]

The procuratorate's objections were shared by others. Many judges expressed their concern that a more adversarial system meant that all the witnesses would have to testify in court, a goal which could not be easily achieved in China. The current arrangement, where the majority of witnesses did not testify in court but presented a written statement, was difficult as many of the witnesses simply refused to sign their names on the statement. To demand that witnesses testify in an open court would further aggravate the problems. The lack of civic consciousness, hostility towards and fear of testifying in court and the financial burden of a prolonged trial all meant that a more adversarial system would face tremendous practical difficulties in implementation.[65]

Legal representation under the 1996 Amendment

The 1996 Amendment enhances the position of the court in criminal proceedings and thus allows the defence counsel to play a more active and meaningful role. The prosecution bears the burden of proof. Where it decides to institute a prosecution, it will no longer transfer the evidence with the files to the court. The court will try a case where there is Bill of Prosecution which includes the alleged criminal facts, and has attached a list of evidence, names of witnesses and photocopies or photographs of primary evidence.[66]

The courts will no longer conduct or participate in any pre-trial investigation. In the Amendment, two important articles from the CPL 1979 have been repealed: Article 108 which authorized a court to remand a case to the procuratorate for supplementary investigation, and Article 109 which authorized the court to conduct its own pre-trial fact-finding.

These changes shift the burden of leading evidence from the court to the procuratorate. Accordingly, the procuratorate alone will be responsible for the validity of the evidence, and the court will no longer examine the evidence prepared by the procuratorate before trial. If this procedural reform is faithfully executed, judges may become neutral arbitrators, who decide a case according to whatever evidence is given in court.

The Amendment increases the powers of the collegial panel. Article 149 states that a collegial panel has the right and duty to render its decision after trial. If the panel is unable to make a decision on a complex and important case after a trial, it should submit the case to the Judicial Committee for consideration and decision.[67] There are two important changes. First, the collegial panel itself, not the President of the court, is to initiate the process of referring a case to the Judicial Committee for decision; secondly, such a referral occurs only after a trial is completed.

The reform of trial procedures will improve the quality of legal representation before and during a trial. Right to counsel is extended to the investigative stage. The Amendment divides legal representation in criminal procedure into two stages. At the investigative stage, an accused may retain a lawyer to provide legal consultancy. At the prosecution and trial stages, a defendant may retain a lawyer for criminal defence. A lawyer's rights differ at the two stages.

At the investigative stage, a lawyer has the right:

(1) to provide legal consultation, to represent the suspect or to lodge a complaint or accusation either from the first time a suspect is interrogated or from the day he is put under any restrictive measures by an investigative body; and
(2) to apply for bail on behalf of a suspect upon arrest.[68]

At the prosecution or trial stage, a lawyer has the right to read and copy case files, interview witnesses and the victim.

It is possible that a defence lawyer could make a difference in criminal trials in the future. The introduction of some adversary elements into criminal proceedings means, if anything, that the procurators have the burden of proving the guilt and leading evidence under a relatively neutral panel of judges. The defence should then have a real opportunity to challenge the prosecution's allegations.

The limits of the law reform

The Amendment introduces elements of procedural justice into China's criminal justice system. There are high expectations that it will better protect the rights of a suspect. The substantial improvements in the law and the symbolic values embodied in it should provide an opportunity for such an improvement. But can the 1996 Amendment meet these expectations?

Some of the rights in the Amendment are qualified by other articles in it. Article 96 states that if a case involves state secrets, the suspect may not retain a lawyer without the permission of an investigative body, and where the lawyer is allowed, he may not meet or correspond with his client without further permission of the investigative body. In addition, investigators of a case may be present during the interview between a lawyer and his client "according to the circumstances of the case and necessity."[69] While the Amendment clearly authorizes the lawyers to interfere at an earlier stage, it also equally explicitly authorizes the police to monitor and control the substance of the lawyers' service.

Article 38 is the most intimidating. It makes it a criminal offence for a defence lawyer to "help the suspect of a crime or defendant to conceal, destroy, or fabricate evidence; collude with each other; threaten or induce witnesses to alter their testimony, provide false evidence, or engage in other activities to interfere with the litigation procedure of the judicial organs."[70] As the terms "collude," "threaten" and "induce" are not defined, the Article could have the chilling effect of stopping any assertive legal practice. In fact, many lawyers are saying that the Amendment as a whole may be a regression from the CPL 1979 in criminal defence. Until this Article is clarified, many lawyers would be reluctant to continue their criminal law practice for fear of prosecution.[71]

The promotion of rights in the Amendment may well have been incidental to the reform process. The Chinese criminal process relies upon the checks and balances among the three systems, each jealously guarding its power. Once one's power is in danger, such as when the police power of detention outside criminal procedures was challenged, it will directly challenge the others and aim to have the others' power adjusted, thus reaching a new balance. This domino effect creates room for rights to develop. The recognition of rights of an accused may well be incidental to the conflict, negotiation and compromise among the powerful institutes in China. The rights of defence lawyers are often swept aside as the Ministry of Justice has been in a weak position compared with the other players.

Some of the rights created in the Amendment are ambiguous, general and abstract. They cannot really be enforced. This makes them illusory and theoretical: a type of window dressing. They are not capable of having serious legal consequence. Although the Amendment may have recognized the presumption of innocence, for example, it provides no remedies on this principle. The court has no right to exclude evidence unlawfully obtained. Where an appellant finds that procedural justice has been grossly violated by a trial court, the only remedy available is to remand the case for a retrial.[72] The court is not to quash a conviction simply because a court made a mistake, regardless of how serious it is.

While a defence lawyer may interview a client in police custody, the lawyer cannot obtain any assistance from the police except to be informed of "the name of the offence" the client is suspected to have committed.[73] The prevailing cynical view is that the lawyer's earlier intervention is more superficial than substantial. In addition, while the lawyer's role may have been enhanced, real enhancement of defence possibilities is undermined by the absence of any improvement in legal aid. Without a strong commitment from the government to finance legal aid, most of the suspects will not benefit from the newly implemented legal rights.[74]

The abstract rights are subject to government interpretation. In Chinese practice, a law passed by the National People's Congress cannot operate by itself but has to be put into operation by implementation regulations passed by the executive government. The regulation can expand the government's power and limit rights of citizens. There are no principles that a law protecting rights has to be construed broadly and interpreted in favour of rights; that subsidiary legislation has to be consistent with parent legislation[75]; or that national legislation cannot be inconsistent with the Constitution. All the rights are subject to redefinition and once the implementation regulations are passed, the rights may vanish or diminish.

The interpretation of "residential surveillance" in Wang Dan's case provides a good example. Police admitted they were holding Wang on 2 June 1995, but he was not indicted until 13 October 1996. It was not known when he was arrested and his family was not informed about it as they should have been under the CPL 1979. It appeared that the police detained Wang unlawfully but that such abuse (as prevalent as it was) would come to an end when the Amendment becomes effective. However, the police argued that the holding of Wang Dan was lawful because he was not detained at all. Instead he was put under residential surveillance. This was a novel interpretation of the law, to say the least. As resdential surveillance is retained in the Amendment it can be used by an investigative authority in the future, it seems, to hold a person in a unknown place for more than one year despite these recent changes in the law.[76]

The defendant's right to counsel, however it may have been enlarged by the 1996 Amendment, may be subjected to continued diminution in practice by the police. The Ministry of Public Security has proposed restrictions in its draft Implementation Rules so that a lawyer can only visit his client once during police investigation of a case for a limited period of time.[77]

Even if the government intends to implement the Amendment faithfully, there will be tremendous enforcement problems. The law is effective already, but so far the change is very slow, if there has been any at all. It will be enforced by the same police, procurators and judges. The Supreme People's Court and the Supreme People's Procuratorate have been circulating guidance to prepare for the enforcement of the new law. Yet they still disagree on several important issues, especially on the rules of evidence, which they have to develop from scratch.

Given the substantial changes made in the Amendment, one cannot help being cynical that the law in practice will definitely be different from the law in the book. How can it be possible for the police to accept genuine external review of arrest after near 50 years' practice of unsupervised arbitrary detention? How can a Chinese judge become accustomed to adversarial proceedings overnight after being an investigator/inquisitor throughout his career as a judge?

Conclusion

The key concept of the right to counsel is novel to Chinese legal culture. In the CPL 1979, there were few procedural requirements within the criminal process, and few protective measures to defend the rights of an accused. The CPL 1979 encouraged the police, the prosecutors and the judges to ascertain what they held to be the true facts of an offence with little regard to procedural rectitude. The rights of defendants were routinely ignored in the interests of crime control. The defendants and their defenders were marginalized within the criminal justice system. The constitutional right to counsel was severely restricted in form and substance.

The 1996 Amendment introduces an element of procedural justice into China's criminal justice system. There are high expectations that the Amendment will better protect the rights of a suspect. The substantial improvement in the law and the symbolic values embodied in it are expected to provide an opportunity for such an improvement. However, given the ingrained pattern of practice in China's criminal justice system, the practical impact of the Amendment in protecting the right to counsel will be limited. Efforts to amend the law will not alone guarantee the protection of rights. Amending the CPL will not make the rights real unless they can be effectively enforced. While the Amendment may have laid a foundation for improvement, there is little likelihood that the legislation will bring about meaningful change in the practice of criminal defence in the near future.

Notes

* An earlier version of this article was read at the Conference on Market Economy and Law in China, City University of Hong Kong, October 1995, and the Conference on the Right to Fair Trial, Hong Kong University, November 1996. The author would like to thank Dr Richard Cullen for his suggestions and helpful comments on the initial draft.
1 For studies of the CPL 1979 in English language, see Albert H. Y. Chen, *An Introduction to the Legal System of the People's Republic of China* (Singapore: Butterworths,

1992), ch.9; Lawyers Committee for Human Rights, *Criminal Justice with Chinese Characteristics* (New York: Lawyers Committee for Human Rights, 1993); Shaochuan Leng and Hungdah Chiu, *Criminal Justice in Post-Mao China: Analysis and Documents* (Albany: State University of New York Press, 1985).

2 The new law became effective on 1 January 1997. For commentaries on the Amendment, see H. L. Fu "Criminal Procedure Law," in Wang Chengguan and Zhang Xianchu (eds.), *Introduction to Chinese Law* (Hong Kong: Sweet & Maxwell Asia, 1997); and Lawyers Committee for Human Rights, *Opening to Reform? An Analysis of China's Revised Criminal Procedure Law* (New York: Lawyers Committee for Human Rights, 1996).

3 Art. 12 of the Amendment expressly states that: "No one is guilty of a crime without a people's court rendering a judgment according to law."

4 Art. 125, *Constitution of the People's Republic of China.*

5 Zhang Sihan, "Several proposals on the reform of the model of trial," *Zhongguo faxue* (*Chinese Legal Studies*), No. 5 (1994), p. 47.

6 Lawyers Committee for Human Rights, *Opening to Reform?* p. 1.

7 Except for "minor criminal cases and cases otherwise provided for by law" which can be tried by a single judge. Article 10, Organic Law of People's Court 1983 (OLPC).

8 Art. 11 of the OLPC states that the members of the judicial committee are appointed and removed by the Standing Committee of the People's Congresses at the corresponding levels, upon the recommendation of the presidents of these courts. The task of the judicial committee is to "practise democratic centralism," including summing up judicial experience and discussing important or difficult cases. As a practice, a judicial committee includes the president of a court, the vice-presidents and judges in charge of the different divisions (criminal law, administrative law, etc.).

9 Art. 108, CPL 1979.

10 Art. 109.

11 In rare cases, a lawyer may be able to persuade the court to change its pre-determined verdict. In a recent trial, a trial court was persuaded to accept a not guilty defence after "repeated studies and with permission." It is important to note that the defence lawyer in that case is a well-known criminal law professor and his personal influence had an effect. Zhao Binzhi, "Correctly distinguish a violation of financial disciplines and the offence of embezzlement," *Zhongguo lüshi* (*China Lawyer*), No. 3 (1995), p. 5 (interview with Professor Zhao Binzhi, July 1995). It is openly conceded by judges and lawyers interviewed by the author that a "well connected" lawyer will be useful for an accused. This article is partially based upon the author's informal and open-ended interviews with five judges, three prosecutors and 11 defence lawyers since 1995.

12 The system of criminal defence was formally set up in the People's Republic of China in January 1956. The system was met with hostility and abolished in late 1957. See Xu Jincun, *Lüshi xue* (*Studies on Lawyers*) (Chengdu: Sichuan People's Press, 1994).

13 Zhao Ying, "The position of defence lawyers in criminal litigation," in Ministry of Justice (ed.), *Zhongguo sifa xingzheng de lilun yu shijian* (*Theory and Practice of Judicial Administration in China*) (Beijing: Ministry of Justice, 1992), p. 1361. This book includes the abridged version of more than 1,000 published articles and conference papers related to the work of the Ministry.

14 Jiang Daijing "Protecting lawyers' rights in criminal litigation," in Ministry of Justice, *Theory and Practice*, p. 1367.

15 Ministry of Justice, "Notice on making full use of lawyers in severely striking down on crimes (14 October 1983)," *Zhonghua renmin gongheguo falü guifanxing jieshi jicheng* (*Compilation of Normative Interpretations of Law of the People's Republic of China*) (Changchun: Jilin People's Press, 1990), pp. 1730–31 (hereinafter *Compilation of Normative Interpretations*).

16 *Ibid.*
17 Jiang Daijing, "Protecting lawyers' rights."
18 Tan Zhen, "On pre-trial communication," in Ministry of Justice, *Theory and Practice*, p. 1380.
19 Zhen Dong, "Lawyers no longer officials," *China Law*, No. 1 (1994), p. 30.
20 See H. L. Fu and Richard Cullen, *Media Law in the PRC* (Hong Kong: Asia Law and Practice, 1996), ch. 6. Carlos Wing-Hung Lo, "Criminal justice reform in post-crisis China: a human rights perspective," *Hong Kong Law Journal*, No. 27 (1997), p. 90.
21 *Ibid.* H. L. Fu, "Sedition and political dissidence: towards legitimate dissidence in China?" *Hong Kong Law Journal*, No. 26 (1996), p. 210; Human Rights Watch, *Slamming the Door On Dissent: Wang Dan's Trial* (New York: Human Rights Watch, 1996).
22 Even this seven-day rule is violated by provincial legislation. In the Rules on Lawyers in Guangdong province and Anhui province, the notification period is shortened to three days. Art. 12, *Several Provisions of Anhui Province on the Performance of Duties of Lawyers* (1988); Art. 8, *Several Provisions of Guangdong Province on the Performance of Duties of Lawyers* (1987). *Difangxing fagui xuanban* (*Selections of Local Regulations*), p. 1651 and p. 2558 respectively.
23 Legislative Affairs Commission (LAC), National People's Congress Standing Committee, Submission of the Ministry of Justice on the Amendment of CPL 1996. The LAC held several consultation meetings with interested parties. The participants' submissions were summarized and distributed by the LAC. The nature of these documents is not clear. They are not publicized and their distribution is restricted to related government departments. But they are not formally classified as state secrets or internal materials. For a study of confidential information in China, see Fu and Cullen, *Media Law*, and Huai Yan and Suisheng Zhao, "Notes on China's confidential documents," *The Journal of Contemporary China*, No. 4 (1993), p. 75.
24 Lawyers Committee for Human Rights, *Criminal Justice with Chinese Characteristics*, p. 32.
25 LAC, Submission of the Ministry of Justice on the Amendment of CPL 1996.
26 LAC, Submission of Supreme People's Court on the Amendment of CPL 1996.
27 The Supreme People's Court, Supreme People's Procuratorate, Ministry of Public Security and Ministry of Justice, "Joint notice on several concrete provisions on lawyers' participation in litigation (27 April 1981)," in *Compilation of Normative Interpretations*, pp. 1727–28 (hereinafter Joint Notice).
28 Zhou Guojun, "Discussion on the time when lawyers' intervention is allowed," *Zhongguo lüshi* (*China Lawyer*), (1994), p. 32.
29 National People's Congress Standing Committee, *Decisions Regarding the Procedure for Prompt Adjudication of Cases Involving Criminals Who Seriously Endanger Public Order* (1983).
30 Art. 29, CPL 1979.
31 Supreme People's Court and the State Administration of Protecting Secrets, *Regulations on the State Secrets Involving the Work of the People's Courts and the Classification* (1989). See Fu and Cullen, *Media Law*.
32 Fang Deming, "Defence lawyers' right and duty in reviewing files," in Ministry of Justice, *Theory and Practice*, p. 1365.
33 Lawyers Committee for Human Rights, *Criminal Justice with Chinese Characteristics*.
34 Ministry of Justice and Ministry of Public Security, "Joint notice on the problem of lawyers meeting the defendants in custody (13 November 1956)," in *Compilation of Normative Interpretations*, pp. 1748–49. The Notice required a detention station to provide a separate room, if possible, for a lawyer to interview his client, so that the defendant "would not feel worried."

35 Wu Jieming, "Preliminary discussion on pre-trial communication among lawyers, judges and procurators," in Ministry of Justice, *Theory and Practice*, p. 1376.
36 *Ibid.*
37 *Ibid.*
38 Zhang Zhanlin, "Lawyer's early involvement prevents a wrong conviction," *Zhongguo lüshi* (*China Lawyer*), No. 9 (1994), p. 6.
39 "A lawyer suspected that a defendant in a murder case was a psychiatric patient. He raised the defence of insanity in the pre-trial meeting, but was rejected by the judge. Then the lawyer invited experts to explain the case to the judges. After a pre-trial psychiatric examination participated in by the judge, procurator and lawyer, the procuratorate withdrew its charge." Zhao Zhongqing, "The necessity of exchanging information between lawyers and judicial personnel at pre-trial stage," in Ministry of Justice, *Theory and Practice*, p. 1376.
40 Guo Zhongwu, "The position of defence lawyers in criminal litigation," in Ministry of Justice, *Theory and Practice*, p. 1359.
41 Art. 113, CPL 1979.
42 Art. 114.
43 Art. 116.
44 Art. 117.
45 Yang Yinche, "Defence lawyers should have right to produce expert witness," *Zhongguo lüshi* (*China Lawyer*), No. 11 (1994), p. 8.
46 Art. 118, CPL 1979.
47 Xiao Shanren, "A person without legal qualification may not be a defender," in Ministry of Justice, *Theory and Practice*, p. 1319.
48 Qiao Bin and Sun Qikang, "A preliminary study of the psychology of the criminal lawyers," in Ministry of Justice, *Theory and Practice*, p. 1404.
49 Tan Zhen, "On pre-trial communication," p. 1380.
50 Qiao Bin and Sun Qikang, "A preliminary study,"
51 Supreme People's Court, Supreme People's Procuratorate, Ministry of Public Security and Ministry of Justice, "Joint notice on several supplementary provisions on lawyers' participation in litigation (26 June 1986)," in *Compilation of Normative Interpretations*, p. 1736.
52 LAC, Submission of Supreme People's Court on the Amendment of CPL 1996.
53 LAC, Submission of Ministry of Justice on the Amendment of CPL 1996.
54 LAC, Submission of Supreme People's Procuratorate on the Amendment of CPL 1996.
55 LAC, Submission of Ministry of Public Security on the Amendment of CPL 1996.
56 Lawyers Committee for Human Rights, *Opening to Reform?*
57 Zhang Wei, "Several questions in lawyers' participation in criminal litigation," *Zhongguo faxue* (*Chinese Legal Studies*), No. 5 (1994), p. 40.
58 Li Baoyue, "On the question of lawyers' participation in criminal litigation," *Zhengfa luntan* (*Forum of Politics and Law*), No. 4 (1994), p. 72; and Li Baoyue, "On the time when lawyers can participate in criminal litigation," *Zhongguo faxue* (*Chinese Legal Studies*), No. 4 (1994), p. 98.
59 Art. 26, *Lawyers' Regulations of Shenzhen Special Economic Region* (draft). On file with the author.
60 Shenzhen Special Economic Zone, *Lawyers' Regulations of Shenzhen Special Economic Zone* (1995). On file with the author.
61 LAC, Submission of Supreme People's Court on the Amendment of CPL 1996.
62 Lu Fei, "Reforming the model of trials," *Zhongguo faxue* (*Chinese Legal Studies*), No. 5 (1994), p. 48.
63 Art, 15 of the Organic Law of People's Procuratorate (1983) provides: "In legal proceedings instituted by a people's procuratorate, the chief procurator or a procurator

shall attend the court session, in the capacity of state prosecutor, to support the prosecution and exercise supervision over the court proceedings, and to determine whether they conform to the law." According to Lu Fei (*ibid.*) from the Supreme People's Procuratorate, the procuratorate has the power to supervise the trial by raising objections whenever "there is something unlawful during the trial." But the objection raised is often ignored by the court. Judges in Zhuhai admit that the procuratorate's supervision is not very useful.

64 Lu Fei, "Reforming the model of trials," pp. 47–49.
65 LAC, Submission of Supreme People's Procuratorate on the Amendment of CPL 1996.
66 Art. 150, CPL 1996.
67 Art. 149.
68 Art. 96.
69 *Ibid.*
70 Art. 38.
71 Interviews with lawyers from Beijing, January and February, 1997. See Lawyers Committee for Human Rights, *Opening to Reform?* p. 58.
72 A case shall be remanded for retrial in following circumstances: (1) the requirement for public trial is violated; (2) the requirement for withdrawal is violated; (3) the parties' lawful rights in litigation are deprived or unlawfully limited, and such deprivation and limitation may have prejudiced a fair trial; (4) the trial organs are not lawfully set up; or (5) there are violations of other rules regarding litigation procedures, and the violation may have affected a fair trial.
73 Art. 66, CPL 1996.
74 The Ministry of Justice is now formulating plans for legal aid in China. Pilot projects have been set up in Beijing and Guangdong. According to Shen Bailu, Head of the Department of Lawyers in the Ministry, China's legal aid will follow international experience and at the same time consider China's actual circumstances. The purpose of the proposed plan is to demonstrate the fairness and justice of the legal profession and force the legal profession to consider not only the economic effect of their profession but also the social impact. Thus the plan is both to serve those unable to afford lawyers and to enhance lawyers' public conscience and civic responsibility. *Fazhi ribao,* 22 February 1995.
75 For a study of the inconsistency between China's National Security Law and the Implementing Rules for the National Security Law, see H. L. Fu and Richard Cullen, "National security law in China," *Columbia Journal of Transnational Law,* No. 34 (1996), p. 149.
76 Zhang Waiguo, "The abuse of 'residential supervision' in Beijing," *Mingbao,* 31 October 1996. Such practices are said to be popular now. In the Shenzhen Special Economic Zone, for example, the police have built at least one hotel-style detention centre, where a suspect is detained for a prolonged period of time under the name of "residential surveillance." The suspect has to pay for the accommodation (interviews with lawyers from Shenzhen, May 1997).
77 Interview with three lawyers from Beijing, March 1997. They all predicted that the police proposal would meet strong resistance from the Chinese Bar.

Part 13

THE GENERAL PRINCIPLES OF CIVIL LAW

34

THE GENERAL PRINCIPLES OF CIVIL LAW OF THE PRC

Its birth, characteristics, and role

Tong Rou

Source: Jonathan K. Ocko (trans.), *Law and Contemporary Problems* 52:2 (1989): 151–175.

I Introduction

Civil law[1] is the basic (*jiben*) law used to regulate relations in a commodity economy. In the legal system of the People's Republic of China ("PRC") civil law occupies a critical position. Chinese law is divided into three levels: fundamental (*genben*) law, basic (*jiben*) law, and specifically enacted (*danxing*) law. The fundamental law is the Constitution, which has the greatest legal effect in the legal system; basic law is law which regulates certain aspects of social relations, and its effect is subordinate to that of the Constitution but superior to special law. Civil law is a basic law which regulates the property and personal relations between equal subjects and assumes the leading role toward the various sorts of special enactments (*danxing fagui*) and economic regulations (*jingji fagui*) in the economic sector.

On April 12, 1986, the Fourth Session of the Sixth National People's Congress passed the *General Principles of Civil Law of the Chinese People's Republic*. This not only legislatively established the central position of civil law in the Chinese legal system, but it also symbolized that the construction of Chinese law and democracy had entered a new stage. This article is an exposition of the emergence, characteristics, and role of the *General Principles of Civil Law* in the PRC.

II The birth of the *General Principles*

The *General Principles* is the fruit of thirty years of civil legislation in China. China's civil legislation, like China's economic development, has followed a tortuous path. This process of the development of the *General Principles* can essentially be divided into three stages.

A Stage one: from the early period of the establishment of the country to the completion of the first five-year plan (1949–1956)

After the establishment, in October 1949, of the PRC, the country was faced with the arduous tasks of restoration of the national economy, socialist reform, and the initiation of large-scale economic construction. In response to these needs, the nation employed civil law methods to regulate social economic relations. The People's Government formulated and disseminated a set of civil enactments. For instance, to affirm and protect the right of property ownership, it promulgated and put into force the Land Reform Law of the PRC and the Method for Handling Debts in New District Villages; to embody the nation's policy toward the use, control, and reform of the private capitalist economy, the government issued the Temporary Regulations for Privately Managed Enterprises. Legal forms were used to confirm the legality of various types of privately managed enterprises. In order to regulate property relations, appropriate civil law standards were promulgated for: purchase and sale of goods and materials, supply and marketing, processing contracts, basic construction contracting, circulation of technology, building rental, transport of goods and passengers, storage, consignment, property and personal insurance, credit, settling accounts, savings, etc.

Moreover, on April 30, 1950, another law that also belongs within the scope of civil legislation was published, the Marriage Law. Its promulgation marked the replacement of several thousand years of a feudal marriage system with the new system of the people's democracy. It clearly propounded the abandonment of the feudal customs of coercive arranged marriages, gender inequality, and disdain for the interests of women and children. All of this important civil legislation played a vital role in terms of regulating civil relationships, in protecting the lawful rights of citizens, and in stabilizing the socioeconomic order.

At this stage, in order to complete the socialist reformation of agriculture, handicraft industry, and capitalist industry and commerce, and to realize the profound transformation of the means of production from private ownership to collective ownership, there was a demand not only for the formulation of many special civil law enactments but also for the formulation of a civil code that could reflect the socialist economics, thought, culture, and morality of the new China. Therefore, in the winter of 1954 the Standing Committee of the National People's Congress organized a civil law drafting group and charged it with drafting a civil code. Based on an integration of the borrowed experiences of the Soviet Union's construction of a legal system and our own experience in China, the completed first draft was made up of four parts: general principles, ownership, obligation, and inheritance. Subsequent political movements, however, interrupted this work.

B Second stage: from the beginning of the construction of socialism to the smashing of "The Gang of Four" (1956–1976)

After the socialist transformation was basically completed, China began to shift into full-scale socialism. As was pointed out when the Eighth Congress of the

Chinese Communist Party convened in September 1956, the chief task was for the people to concentrate their strength to develop society's productivity, to realize the country's industrialization, and to steadily satisfy their material and cultural demands, all of which were increasing daily. But, beginning in 1958, because objective economic laws, especially the law of prices, were overlooked, the "Great Leap Forward" and the rural "People's Communes" movements were rashly initiated, thereby causing rampant and still extant leftist mistakes in the socialist economy.[2] In the midst of economic construction, this exaggerated communism and the accompanying confused and arbitrary directions caused collective property and the legitimate property rights of individual citizens to be violated as the rule of no compensation replaced the principles of equal value and mutual benefit that should characterize economic contact between civil subjects. Under the influence of the ideological trend of legal nihilism, civil legislation fell into desuetude. In 1960 the party and the state began to correct the errors of this "left" tendency and resolved in regard to the national economy to carry out the principles of "regulation (*tiaozheng*), consolidation (*gonggu*), strengthening (*chongshi*), and enhancement (*tigao*)." In these circumstances, the Party and state formulated a series of civil policies and enactments such as Work Regulations for Rural People's Communes (Draft), Work Rules for State-Run Industrial Enterprises (Draft), Temporary Regulations for the Protection and Administration of Cultural Artifacts, Provisional Method for the Management of the Registration of Industrial and Commercial Enterprises, Trademark Administration Regulations, and Rules for Rewards for Technical Improvements. This series of civil enactments and regulations, which were formulated and put into effect in the midst of the correction of the national economy, played a vital role in expunging the harm that the radical policies of the "left" had created in the economic sector, in overcoming the economic difficulties of that time, and in recovering and developing the national economy.

Following the recuperation and development of the national economy, the work of drafting the Civil Code began once again. In the latter half of 1962, the Standing Committee of the National People's Congress ("NPC") organized anew the drafting work, and in 1964 formally put forward the Provisional Draft of the Civil Code of the PRC. This draft tried to escape from the premises of the Soviet legislative style and integrate the experience of China's economic construction and judicial practice in order to formulate a civil code with Chinese characteristics. But because of the limitations of the economic situation, the drafting work at that time was still influenced by the ideological trend of the "left." Using beneficial foreign legislative experience as a reference was overlooked, so that when completed the Provisional Draft lacked the force of normative law. Subsequently, following the beginning of the Cultural Revolution, the work of drafting a civil code was again forcibly halted, and in the ten years of chaos which followed, not only was civil legislation placed in a suspended state, it also suffered serious injury.

C Stage three: from the smashing of the "Gang of Four"[3] to the promulgation of the general principles (1976–1986)

After the "Gang of Four" was smashed in October 1976, the PRC entered a new period of historical development. In particular, after the Third Plenum of the Eleventh Central Committee was convened, and after the shift in the emphasis of the country's goals to socialist modernization and construction, and together with the formulation and implementation of the policies of reform, the opening of the PRC to the outside and the invigorated renewal of socialist legal construction was emphasized and China's civil legislation entered a new period of development. Large numbers of civil enactments were continuously issued and put into effect such as those promulgated by the standing committee of the NPC: the Economic Contract Law, the Inheritance Law, the Mineral Resource Law, the Foreign Economic Contract Law, the Joint Venture Law, the Trademark Law, and the Patent Law. The State Council also promulgated special enactments: sales contract regulations for industrial and mineral products, sales contract regulations for agricultural side-line production, loan contract regulations, contract regulations for contract processing, regulations for the control of urban private housing, regulations for property insurance contracts, architectural engineering responsibility contracts, regulations for invention rewards, regulations for rewards for work in natural sciences, and so forth.

In the process of invigorating the domestic scene and opening to the outside, the formulation of an appropriate civil code was an urgent need. So, in October 1979, the Law Committee of the Standing Committee of the NPC specially organized the civil code small drafting group to begin the work of drafting a civil code for the third time. After three years of diligent labor, the group produced a fourth draft of the Civil Code in 1982. Because of the breadth of the civil law's scope and the complexity of its contents, and also because the economic reforms were still new and concrete social experience was relatively meager, conditions for working out a complete civil code were not yet ripe. Under these circumstances, the NPC Standing Committee resolved, on the basis of what was needed and what was possible, first to take from the Civil Code those parts that were more urgent and relatively more mature and make them separate laws. So through several years of hard work, the PRC continued to formulate certain key, independent civil legislation, such as the aforementioned Economic Contract Law, Foreign Economic Contract Law, Patent Law, Trademark Law, and Inheritance Law. These were of great use in perfecting civil legislation and regulating relevant civil relations. Still there were a number of fundamental questions, such as the object (*duixiang*) of civil law's regulation, the basic principles of civil law, the position in civil law of the citizen and the legal person, civil juristic acts, the rights of civil agency, obligations, and periods of limitation, that still lacked legal enactment and caused civil activities and civil judicial work to lack the necessary legal basis.

During these last several years, China's legislative and judicial practice and the reform of the urban economic structure have both accumulated rich experience. It is not only necessary but also possible for the state's legislative organs to make a number of enactments to deal with common problems in civil activities. But considering that the urban economic system's reform has just begun and that agricultural economic reform is deepening, there are many questions that are still unclear. Therefore, the moment to enact a complete civil code is still not propitious. In light of the above, the legal working committee of the NPC's Standing Committee, together with the Supreme People's Court and other specialists, summed up the practical experience of reform, opening, and invigoration, along with the practical experience of the courts in handling civil matters and economic cases on the basis of the draft of the civil law. The Standing Committee broadly solicited opinions and made repeated revisions, before it finally brought before the NPC for debate and passage a document with clearly Chinese characteristics, the *General Principles of the Civil Law.*

The resolution concerning reform of the economic system which was passed in October 1984 at the Third Plenum of the Twelfth Party Central Committee pointed out that the PRC's economy is a planned socialist commodity economy with socialist public ownership as its base. Responding to this need, our country has quickened the pace of economic reform with the city as the key. The *General Principles'* promulgation and implementation indubitably provide a legal standard and guarantor for the quickening of this pace. But because economic life and social relations are so richly varied and the *General Principles* is insufficient, we still need to formulate several supplementary enactments. Accordingly in the seventh five-year plan a series of discrete civil enactments will be promulgated: the Technology Contract Law, the Maritime Law, the Company Law, and a Law on Negotiable Instruments. One may predict that during the seventh five-year plan, a large quantity of civil law adapted to reform, opening, and invigoration will appear.

III Chief characteristics of the *General Principles*

Produced on the foundation of a summation of the more than thirty years of practical experience acquired in civil legislation and civil adjudication since the founding of the PRC, and produced in response to the needs of the reform of China's economic system and the development of its socialist commodities economy, the *General Principles* contains clear-cut Chinese characteristics. Four of the chief ones are discussed below.

A The object of the civil law's regulation and the style of legislation

Civil legislation is intimately tied to a society's commodity relations. That is, the civil law reflects social commodities relations. The norms of the civil law are the expression in legal form of the conditions of a society's economic life. As Chinese socialist civil legislation, the *General Principles* reflects the demands of socialist commodities relations. Speaking in terms of its characteristic essence and leading aspect, the object of regulation is socialist commodity relations or, in other words, horizontal property and economic relations. Article 2 of the *General Principles* stipulates: "The civil law of the People's Republic of China regulates property relations and personal relations between subjects of equal status—between citizens, between legal persons, and between citizens and legal persons." This stipulation is an objective reflection of our socialist commodities relations, and it is a stipulation that has not come easily.

Since 1949, in order to repair the war damage inflicted on the national economy and to transform the semi-colonial and semi-feudal economic system, and in order to smash imperialism's economic blockade of our country, the Party and the state, in addition to implementing a series of revolutionary reforms in the ownership of the means of production, had to adopt administrative methods of centralized management to direct the economy so that the national economy would develop rapidly, thereby creating the preconditions necessary for large-scale socialist economic construction. However, owing to our insufficient knowledge about a highly developed commodities economy, a stage of development that cannot be skipped in the progression toward an ideal state, we went so far as to mistake many of the measures necessary in the development of a socialist commodities economy for capitalism. Consequently not only was there no correction of the problem of centralization, but gradual development also became a sort of ossified form not suited to the development demands of socialist productivity. In a management system that overlooked the commodities economy and the law of value, the role of civil law in the economy was of course sharply weakened.

After the Third Plenum of the Eleventh Central Committee (October 1978) affirmed the policy of opening to the outside and invigorating the domestic economy, the villages implemented a system of contracting management responsibility. Many sorts of management forms appeared, and the villages gradually made the transition from self-sufficiency or half self-sufficiency toward a commodities economy. In the cities, with the simplification of administration and the devolution of authority as the heart of the reform, initial results have been achieved. At the Third Plenum of the Twelfth Central Committee, a resolution concerning reform of the economic system was passed which clearly pointed out that our socialist economy is "a planned commodities economy on a foundation of public ownership." Moreover, it pointed out the need to accelerate the reform of the economic system with the city as the key, the duty to vigorously develop the socialist commodity economy, and, in accord with these two points, the need to rapidly complete the legal system that would regulate the activities of the commodity economy. This last in turn became the urgent task of the legislative bodies.

Practice has proven that civil enactment is an important condition for stabilizing and developing commodity relations. It is a key standard for regulating the planned commodity relations that are taking shape on the foundation of the system of public ownership. Only with assistance from a civil law characterized by equality and equal value can we establish order in the socialist commodity economy, effectively prevent the defects that appear in commodity economies in capitalist societies, and cause the commodities economy to develop smoothly under the plan along the path of socialism. Article 2 of the *General Principles* provides for property relations between equal subjects. Speaking in terms of its essence, the relationship between ownership and the flow of commodities, the civil law is the legislative embodiment of the situation and summation of our commodities economy.

Article 2's stipulation considered the actual state of the development of horizontal economic ties, summed up the new circumstances of reform, opening, and invigoration as well as new problems and experiences, and embodied two prime characteristics of the civil law: First, a significant part of the civil law reflects in legal form the relationships between the commodities economy and the equality of the status and rights of participants in the exchange of commodities, and the quality of the legal status and rights of participants in civil affairs; second, the civil law chiefly regulates the property relations of equal subjects, that is horizontal property and economic relations. Relations that are not between equal subjects do not belong to the regulatory scope of the civil law. In accord with these two principles, the *General Principles* stipulated what constitute the core subjects of civil law: ownership, obligations, and contract. It also coordinates these three systems and plays the main role in the systems of legal acts, object, agency, and periods of limitation. Besides this, in order to protect the personal relations of citizens and legal persons, it also stipulates the right of citizens to name, reputation, their personal likeness, their right of life and health, and the legal person's right to name, reputation, and so forth. Considered from the legislative viewpoint, the scope of civil legislation also encompasses the systems of marriage, inheritance, and the results of intellectual effort.

The legislative style of the *General Principles* also possesses distinctly Chinese characteristics. Legislative style means the forms by which civil legal norms are compiled. Looking at it in terms of the rest of the world, England, the United States, and other common law countries do not have a written civil code. Civil law norms are dispersed in a mass of separate law and a vast sea of case law. Countries with the Continental system often establish a written civil code. Socialist countries also have enacted their own civil codes. In terms of civil code style, these codes generally include two parts: a general principles (*tongze*) section and a section of specific provisions (*fenze*). The general principles are concerned with provisions applied commonly to various sorts of civil relations such as the subject of civil relations, juristic acts, agency, periods of limitation, and so forth. The specific provisions regulate various sorts of concrete civil relations such as ownership, obligations, inheritance, and compensation for injury. Yet, since the conditions are not yet ripe for us to establish a complete civil code and since we have recently promulgated a series of important independent civil enactments, we have adopted the general principles (*tongze*) form in our civil legislation. This form contains not only general provisions but also some specific ones. It has not been limited by the traditional civil law legislative style of general and specific provisions. Moreover, its stipulations apply to those prior separate civil laws which continue to have force. Therefore, the legislative style of the *General Principles* is an innovation in the history of civil legislation, a product of the unique historical circumstances of the reform of our economic system and also suitable to China's situation.

B *The* General Principles' *establishment of a regulatory system of economic law*

Economic law's regulatory system refers to the regulation of economic relations by the adoption of various legal forms, thereby achieving the goal of establishing and protecting an economic order that is beneficial to the ruling class. In a country with public ownership, there exist two dissimilar structures of economic regulation. One adopts a regulatory system of "departmental (*bumen*) economic law," takes public ownership as the base with the plan as the core, and uses the centralized economic part of the law to adjust economic relations between socialist organizations. This type of system of regulation by economic law, found in post-war Czechoslovakia and East Germany, requires the intervention of the state plan and either denies or deprecates the status of the enterprise legal person. Therefore it is adapted to centralized forms of economic control. The second type, represented by post-war Hungary and Poland, adopts a regulatory structure of "civil law-economic law." This type of structure recognizes the status of the enterprise legal person and insists on the independent rights, duties, and responsibilities of the enterprise in civil activities and is therefore adapted to a structure of control which combines both concentration and dispersion.

The PRC has adopted a structure of legal regulation that is better suited to the needs of our economic life and new economic structure. Article 2 of the *General Principles* concerning the regulation of personal and property relations between equal subjects scientifically resolves this question. According to the stipulations of this provision, and according to the statement "Concerning the Draft of the *General Principles*" by Wang Hanbin, Secretary of the Standing Committee of the NPC and Chair of the Legal Work Committee of the NPC Standing Committee, the salient characteristic of the Civil Code is its reflection in legal forms of the demands of the relations of the commodity economy. It principally regulates horizontal property and economic relations between equal subjects. As for the state's control of the economy, because vertical economic relations or administrative control relations between the state and enterprises and between parts of an enterprise are characterized by administrative subordination, relations with the state are chiefly regulated by economic administrative law. Therefore, the *General Principles* establishes the fundamentals of a regulatory system of economic law: Civil law regulates horizontal economic relations between equal subjects; economic law (also known as economic administrative law) regulates vertical economic relations in the process of economic management. The two are complementary and perform the regulatory role in the society's economic relations.

Once the regulatory system of "civil law-economic administrative law" is established, the regulatory network for China's commodity economic relations will be constituted. Regardless of what concrete form these commodity economic relations may take, they must all come under the regulatory scope of the civil law; none can violate equality or the principles of voluntariness, fairness, exchange of equivalent values, and good faith that are derived from the foundation of equality. But because we are a socialist country with public ownership as the base, the state must shoulder the responsibility of supervising, administering, and controlling civil activities. This requires the state to employ methods of economic administrative law to strengthen its administration of civil activities and to prevent the appearance within civil activities of actions that will destroy the national plan or disrupt the socialist economic order. The external integrated regulatory structure of "civil law-economic administrative law" puts socialist commodity economic relations into an ordered system.

After the establishment of our regulatory structure of economic law, neither administrative interventionist methods nor other legal regulation of a coercive character can be applied to economic relations between equal subjects. Methods of civil law must be used. Some people consider that relations formed by contracts that conform closely to the mandatory plan are not produced on a basis of equal voluntariness and exchange of equivalent values and therefore cannot belong to the regulatory scope of the civil law. Under the conditions of socialism, the use of the state plan means that certain contracts are directly based on the mandatory plan and that the ordered plan's targets become the subject matter and amount of the contract. The contract's subject matter and price are also fixed on the basis of the state plan's prices. But these circumstances cannot change the civil character of these contracts. Because these contracts still occur between two equal civil subjects, and because their contents are still a reflection of the relations of commodity exchange, they still are regulated by the civil law.

C The fundamental principles of civil activities established by the General Principles

In order to give full play to the civil legislation's guarantee of the citizen's and legal person's lawful civil rights, and to correctly regulate civil relations, the *General Principles* stipulates that various civil acts must adhere to certain fundamental principles. These fundamental principles are the starting point and basis for the formulation, explanation, implementation, and research of our civil law norms. They are also the concentrated manifestation in the *General Principles* of China's socialist essence.

1 *The Principle of the Equal Status of Parties.* The third article of the *General Principles* states: "In civil activities, the positions of the parties are equal." The

principle of the equal status in law of all parties to civil activities is an inevitable reflection in China's civil legislation of horizontal economic relations. What the civil law regulates are the property and personal relations between equal subjects, that is, horizontal social relations. It is fixed that in civil legal relations, the legal position of the parties is uniformly equal.

The concept of the equal position of the parties contains four principal ideas. First, regardless of whether the parties' units are large or small, their position high or low, their economic power great or weak, and regardless of whether their economic character is state, collective, or individual, they occupy an equal legal status in their civil acts and are independent, equal subjects with civil rights and duties. No subject may use its own staff position, duties, or administrative influence and power to cause itself to be put in the position of a privileged civil subject. Second, civil subjects in concrete civil activities enjoy civil rights and undertake democratic duties equally. They are not permitted only to enjoy civil rights and not to undertake democratic duties or to undertake democratic duties and not to enjoy civil rights. It is not permitted for any civil subject in concrete legal relations to have special rights in excess of the law. Third, the law's protection of the civil rights of the parties is equal. Fourth, any citizen, regardless of nationality, sex, age, belief, or difference in cultural level, regardless of whether or not there has been participation in any sort of organization or undertaking of leadership responsibilities, and regardless of whether or not he is mentally healthy or has the ability to understand his own acts, has equal rights and abilities.

It is especially important to note that the principle of equality in civil activities is of particular significance in opposing bureaucratism and special individual privilege. Bureaucratism and special individual privilege are the remnants of feudalism and feudal ideology. Civil law is of the "innate equality school" and does not recognize any special rights. As soon as one enters into the kingdom of civil relations, that person is equal.

2 *Principles of Voluntariness, Fairness, Exchange of Equivalent Values, Honesty, and Good Faith.* Article 4 of the *General Principles* states that civil activities should conform to the principles of voluntariness, fairness, exchange of equivalent values, honesty, and good faith.

Voluntariness means that when equal subjects establish, revise, or terminate civil legal relations, both parties must of their own true will express their willingness. This is because any concrete civil legal relationship occurs between two equal subjects who enjoy independent property and personal rights. Whether or not they want to establish between them some sort of a relationship of civil rights and duties, how they should establish it, and with whom they should establish it should not only accord with legal stipulations but should also be voluntarily determined by the parties. Therefore, at the time parties carry out civil activities based on the law, other organizations and people cannot interfere with the desire of the parties or force one civil subject into committing or not committing a certain civil act. Of course, civil subjects must respect the desires of the other party at the time they exercise their civil rights and cannot damage the interests of the public or other people. To use fraud or coercion, to take advantage of another's peril, or to threaten someone's life is a violation of the principle of voluntariness; and any civil acts resulting therefrom would be without effect.

Fairness means the equality of civil subjects' opportunity to engage in civil activities, and reciprocity in the enjoyment of civil rights and the undertaking of civil duties. Each party is exposed to civil liability and consequential damages proportionate to the degree of legal violation. The principle of fairness is manifested by the economic interests between equal subjects. In judging whether a civil act is fair or not, one ought to take people's general sense of social value, concept of morality, and concept of interests as a basis. Courts have the right to void a patently unfair civil act. Nullified civil acts are without effect from the inception of the act; but if they are partially without effect, it does not influence another part which still has effect.

The so-called exchange of equivalent values means that in obtaining the other party's property or services one must provide the opposite party with an equivalent value unless otherwise provided by law or contract agreement. This principle is a legal reflection of horizontal economic relations. Commodities economic relations in essence manifest the benefit relations between equal subjects. If one side wants to realize its own interests it must abide by the law of exchange of equivalent values and give to the opposite party a commensurate benefit or recompense. To violate the rule of exchange of equivalent values can be harmful to ordinary civil law relations and violates the objective law of development of a commodities economy. In this matter we learned an exceedingly painful lesson during the time of the people's communes. Then, in order to achieve greater size and higher levels of collective ownership, we engaged in "reallocation without compensation." Not only did this brutally trample the principle of exchange of equivalent values, it also created an odious legacy for socialist economic development. Presently, as we uphold this principle in the midst of the economic reform, we must oppose and resist such illegal acts as the uncompensated transfer and allocation of state and collective enterprises' property, the concoction of various pretexts to impose assessments on collective and individual property, the monopolization of markets by deception, and the driving up of prices.

Honesty and good faith mean that in civil activities the subjects of civil rights ought to say what they mean, be particular about reputation, scrupulously abide by promises, not practice trickery, not pass off second-rate goods as first quality, not damage the lawful interests of the state, collectives, or individuals, and, according to the provisions of the law or contract, fulfill their civil duties. The principle of honesty and good faith also demands that at the time they carry out civil activities, parties respect habits and customs and society's public good, not evade the law, not deliberately misinterpret contracts, not misuse rights, and not engage in improper competition. Upholding the principle of honesty and good faith is both the embodiment and requirement of our socialist spiritual civilization in civil activities.

3 *The Principle of Protecting Lawful Civil Rights and Interests.* Article 5 of the *General Principles* states: "The lawful civil rights and interests of citizens and legal persons are protected by the law; no organization or individual may violate those rights and interests."

Protecting the lawful civil rights and interests of citizens and legal persons is the chief duty of our civil law. The extensive rights of property and persons granted by our Constitution in politics, economics, culture, family, and other areas can be implemented only through the civil and other categories of law. In the civil law, all the civil rights and duties that may be enjoyed by citizens and legal persons as stipulated by law are within the scope of lawful civil rights and duties. These rights and duties are rather extensive, such as the right of property ownership, the right of obligation, the right of intellectual property, the right of person, the right of inheritance, the right to use state property, the right to inherit management, the right of mining, the right to manage state enterprises, and so forth. All of these are safeguarded by the law; when illegally infringed, remedy may be sought by accusation in the people's courts. No social group, including Party and state organs, enterprise, business, legal person, or social organization, can rely on its special position to violate, either directly or indirectly, the lawful civil rights and duties of another person. This basic principle of the civil law thoroughly and abundantly reflects the socialist essence of China's civil law, the legal embodiment of the political position of the people as masters of their own house.

4 *The Principle of Abiding by the Nation's Laws and Policies.* Article 6 states: "Civil activities must be in conformity with the law; where there is no provision of law, activities must be in conformity with state policy." The laws and policies formulated by the nation are the highest manifestation of the will of China's people and are the basic guideline to which all acts of every citizen and legal person must conform. Only under conditions in which every civil activity of all citizens and legal persons follows the country's laws and policies can these actions be recognized and protected, and produce the result anticipated by the parties under civil law.

In saying that civil activities ought to abide by the law, we mean not only the *General Principles* but also the Economic Contract Law, the Inheritance Law, the Marriage Law, the Trademark Law, the Patent Law, and other discrete civil enactments, as well as the Constitution and other laws, such as the Criminal Law and the Code of Civil Procedure. The legality of behavior is a basic demand that the law places on civil activities. If one does not respect the law, then a civil activity cannot normally be carried out; and the interests and rights of other people are damaged.

Because of the breadth and complexity of civil activities, the stipulations of the law cannot be without omissions. Moreover, the reform of our urban economic system is ongoing, and for many problems provisions cannot be produced immediately. In these circumstances we must follow national policies. If civil activities violate the law or national policy, then one must bear the burden of either civil or other legal responsibility.

5 *Civil Activities Must Observe Social Morality, and Must Not Damage the Collective Interests of Society, Wreck the State Economic Plan, or Disrupt Social Economic Order.* To respect social morality and abjure from injuring society's collective interests are the common criteria with which all activities in a socialist society must comply as well as the ideal to which all civil activities must conform. Our economy is a planned commodity economy based on public ownership, and this determines that civil activities cannot wreck the state economic plan or disturb the economic order of society. In particular, economic contracts between legal persons cannot disregard or violate the state's mandatory plan. Otherwise they are without effect.

4 *The General Rule Concerning Commodity Economy Activities Established by the* General Principles. The commodities economy is an economic stage that succeeds the natural economy and that cannot be skipped. A civil law that regulates the relations of a commodities economy is from beginning to end an accompaniment and adaptation to the commodities economy. Thus, the entire history of the civil law is the history of the development of the commodities economy, and civil law norms are nothing more than a reflection of the internal demands of the commodities economy. Engels has stated that civil law principles are but the expression in legal form of the conditions of economic life in a society. The *General Principles* elevates the internal laws of the socialist commodities economy to the level of legal norms, thereby establishing a common rule of conduct to be observed in activities of the commodities economy.

First, the *General Principles* affirms the equal legal position of the subjects of commodities exchange. As Marx pointed out in *Das Kapital*, commodities are things without will and cannot take themselves to the market to be exchanged.[4] If one wants to have reciprocal relations occur between commodities, it must occur through the expression of one's desire to the guardian or owner of these commodities. In civil law the commodities' guardian or owner is the subject of civil rights. The establishment of the system of subject makes it feasible to protect the legal interests of the producer and manager of commodities, and to stablize the order of routine exchange. Commodities exchange is a sort of free transaction between parties of independent will. "The circulation of commodities differs from the direct exchange of products (barter), not only in form, but in substance."[5] Consequently, civil law rejects administrative compulsion and demands that no distinction be made between organizations and individuals, between ministries and regions. The subjects of civil rights are equal in civil legal relations. Article 3 of the *General Principles* provides: "In civil activities, the positions of the parties are equal." This then is not only a rejection of the system under the old structure in which a system of direct control was implemented by administrative interference in commodities exchange but also an advocacy and protection under the new structures of the development of economic ties between equals. The current process of moving from the old to the new system is fraught with contradictions and clashing explanations. But without legal protection of equality, we cannot have mutually beneficial and voluntary associations. Horizontal economic linkages cannot reach their proper development. Thus the equality of the subjects of civil rights is a general requirement for carrying out commodities exchange.

Next, the *General Principles* affirms the ownership or management rights of commodities production. The core duty of our urban economic reform is to increase enterprise vitality and to develop the socialist commodities economy. This duty requires of the law that it supply a powerful guarantee of the realization of this central duty. The key is that it must affirm the right of ownership or management of commodities production. In regard to the state enterprise, ownership is to be separated from management. The measure of the ownership right that is the management right is to be served and given to the enterprise, thereby transforming the enterprise from an administrative creature into a relatively independent commodities producer, one which of its own will can free itself from bureaucratic and territorial restraints and rapidly develop horizontal economic ties. Adapting to this need of the economic structure, article 82 states: "The right enjoyed by a state-owned enterprise to operate according to law state property that has been given to it to operate and manage is protected by law." Thus, the state enterprise has a legally defined scope of rights to possess, to use, to benefit from, and to dispose of the property entrusted to its management and control by the state. Unless provided for in law, no unit or individual may interfere. The ownership right or management right is the precondition for the enterprise to devote itself to commodities exchange. The free use of this sort of right under conditions in which the interests of neither society nor other persons are harmed is a general rule of commodities exchange.

Third, the *General Principles* establishes the legal form of commodities exchange—namely the contract system. In its present form, China's socialist system of public ownership is expressed in two basic shapes, ownership by the whole and collective ownership. In addition, the individual economy still exists as a necessary supplement to the collective economy. Whether between units of different or identical ownership forms, economic linkages must be carried out in the form of contracts with consideration. Under the traditional economic system, because forms of ownership other than state ownership were deprecated, the independent interests of enterprises as commodities producers were seized and redistributed without compensation. The administrative plan displaced the contract system. With the economic reform all forms of ownership have developed abundantly, and the material interests of units of the same ownership system have also been respected. Therefore, commodities transfer is substituted for commodities exchange and the contract system begins to play a role. Article 85

142

of the *General Principles* states: "A contract is an agreement whereby parties establish, modify, or terminate civil legal relations. Contracts formed in accord with law are protected by law." Thus, the contract system has been adopted to supply effective legal protection to the process of developing horizontal economic ties in our country.

IV The role of the *General Principles* in the reform of the economic system

What strikes the world about China's reform of the economic system is that its essence is the development of a socialist commodities economy. A commodities economy is the unification of commodities production and commodities exchange. Commodities exchange is a system of never-ending circulation and uninterrupted development. Various forms of exchange perdure while new ones arise, inevitably demanding the protection of a civil law characterized by equality and equal value. Indeed as Marx noted, "Whenever industrial and commercial development produce new forms of exchange, the law cannot but recognize them as a new type of property."[6] Following the reform of our economic system and the development of the commodities economy, we must extend the scope of our civil law and stress the position and role of the civil law in regulating all aspects of commodities relations in the sector of circulation. The chief uses of the civil law in China's economic reform will be discussed below.

A The civil law affirms and safeguards various rights of economic organizations and citizens

Historically, the civil law norm adopted vigorous methods to confirm and safeguard existing economic ties. The *General Principles* also does this. However, the *General Principles* is not a summation of the discrete experimental results of economic reform, but is rather an abstraction of the rules of inevitability and inherent limitation of cause and effect that exist beneath the surface of the economic reform. Therefore it already is not an idea concerned with the general confusion, but a rich totality possessed of numerous definitions and relations. This sort of ideal in the *General Principles* is reflected in the civil rights of its subjects. It recognizes and protects the civil rights of the numerous and various exchangers of commodities described below.

1 *The Legal Person.* The legal person is an important form in traditional civil law. Since the German civil law first established this type of economic organizational form, every country's civil law has subsequently followed suit. China's stipulations on the legal person have certainly borrowed from the enactments of foreign countries, but the Chinese character is still perfectly clear.[7] First, it makes the enterprise legal person a sort of independent legal person, and in this way breaks the discrete categories found in foreign civil legislation between the

public and private legal person, between the social group legal person and the financial group legal person, and between the state legal person and the collective legal person, and provides clear direction for the organizational reform of our companies' administrative character. Second, it stipulates the property scope for which the ownership-by-the-whole enterprise legal person undertakes responsibility, namely the property entrusted to its operation and management by the state, thereby legislatively affirming the independent property rights and responsibilities of the ownership-by-the-whole enterprise legal person. Third, on the basis of the first principle, it affirms the phenomenon of bankruptcy. Bankruptcy is the inevitable consequence of fierce competition in a commodities society, though nations with collective systems of ownership often do not want to face up to this fact. In responding to the needs of advancing economic reform, the *General Principles* clearly stipulates that the enterprise legal person can be terminated through the declaration of bankruptcy. In the civil legislative history of public ownership in this country, this is an innovative stipulation.

2 *Joint Operation.* Joint operation is when two or more than two economic organizations organize a horizontal economic association in order to obtain a common economic goal. It can be a union between similar forms of ownership, or it can be a mutual infiltration by different forms of ownership. Joint operation is something of vitality that has emerged from our economic reform. It is one of the essential forms in the development of our commodities economy, of benefit in destroying localism, improving the circulation of commodities, expanding the exchange of economic technology, and promoting the rationalization of enterprise organization.

In order to protect and encourage its development, the *General Principles* made special provisions for joint operation, which, based on the degree of tightness of joint operation, may be divided into three situations. First, all newly organized economic entities that possess the conditions for a legal person may obtain the qualification of a legal person and independently assume civil liabilities. Second, all joint operations that do not possess the conditions for a legal person may, either on the basis of the proportion of capital invested by each of the joint operators, or, through agreement, with each side's own property, undertake civil liability; but if the law or the agreement so provides, joint operations must undertake joint and several liability. Third, if according to contractual agreement each operates independently, then each assumes its own civil liability. At present, in the midst of the process of encouraging and developing horizontal economic associations, regardless of which of the three forms is adopted, parties to the association must abide by the principles of equality, mutual benefit, and voluntariness. Supervising units cannot give orders like a parent or run things by themselves without consulting the parties. At the same time, the shape of each parties' rights, duties, and liabilities must be clarified, the regular order of the circulation of commodities safeguarded, and the legal rights and interests of creditors and both parties to the association protected.

3 *Rural Contract Management Households, and Individual Commercial and Industrial Households.* Throughout rural areas, after the widespread implementation of two types of family linked production contract responsibility systems— output responsibility (*baochan*) and full responsibility—the position and role of the rural management household in the economic activities of society have received special attention. The party and the state have already established and perfected the systems of production responsibility and full responsibility. The encouragement and support of rural households' development of commodities production is a long-term policy. But in the past the question of whether or not the rural household becomes a subject with rights and duties in civil law had not been resolved. Article 27 of the *General Principles* provides: "Members of rural collective economic organizations who in accordance with the provisions of a contract conduct business with respect to goods within the scope permitted by the law are rural contract operation households." This fundamentally resolves the legal position of households which undertake operational responsibility. It makes them a subject with rights in civil affairs. The household with contracts for operation can, on the basis of the law, undertake production management activities, and the law protects its lawful rights and interests against violation. Concerning the individual industrial and commercial household, article 26 of the *General Principles* provides: "Citizens who, upon approval and registration in accordance with law, conduct industrial or commercial business within the scope permitted by law are private industrial/commercial households. A private industrial/commercial household may have its own trade name."

4 *Individual Partnerships.* Partnerships are a form of economic organization in a commodity economy. Since the Third Plenum of the Eleventh Party Congress, an array of economic organizations with partnership characteristics has appeared throughout our cities and villages. In this sort of organization, property is under the unified control and use of the partners. There is collective management, collective labor, and division of the returns and liabilities. But because there were previously no legal provisions for a partnership system, the legal status of partnership was unclear, as were the internal and external responsibilities of partners, so that conflicts were relatively common. Our *General Principles* made special provisions in regard to individual partnerships and moreover insisted that unless the law provides otherwise, partners must undertake joint (and several) liability for debts.

5 *Citizens.* To be a citizen who is a civil subject is to enjoy rights in civil affairs and to undertake the duties in civil affairs of a natural person. Based on the provisions of the *General Principles*, our citizens enjoy broad rights in civil affairs. In respect to property rights, citizens enjoy the right of individual ownership, the right to administer and use collective property, the right to be recompensed for labor, the right to inherit property, the right of patent, the right to trademark, and others. In terms of the rights of the person, citizens enjoy the right to life and

health, the right to one's name, the right to one's likeness, the right to one's reputation, the right of free marriage, the right of authorship, the right of discovery, and so forth. The civil rights of our citizens are uniformly equal, and cannot, except by law, be restricted or eliminated. Anytime a citizen's rights are infringed, the citizen can seek protection from the people's courts. In China, rights and duties are united, so that citizens must undertake appropriate civil duties at the same time they enjoy civil rights. It is impermissible to damage the interests of the state, the collective, or of other individuals in carrying out one's rights.

B The General Principles' *affirmation of the system of ownership and system of the enterprise legal person is an effective method of properly maintaining the balance between the state and the enterprise and of strengthening the vigor of the enterprise*

A survey of the world's modern civil codes shows that the systems of ownership and legal person are the core of their contents. The system of right of ownership is the legal reflection of ownership relations and is the inner link with commodity relations. The process of the exchange of commodities demands of law that it clarify in whom property is vested because the essence of commodities exchange is the yielding of the right of ownership. The right of ownership is the prerequisite for and the result of the production and exchange of commodities. Whoever enjoys the right of ownership is the person who enjoys the legally established right to possess that property. Article 71 of the *General Principles* stipulates: "Ownership means an owner's right in accordance with law to possess, use, benefit from, and dispose of his own property." This reveals from a legal point of view the connotation and character of the right of property ownership.

In China's *General Principles*, the right of property ownership is one of the most vital rights in civil affairs. Because China's socialist collective system is expressed in the two basic forms of ownership, ownership by the whole and collective ownership, the *General Principles* appropriately affirms these two systems of ownership.

Article 73 of the *General Principles* states: "State property belongs to all the people." In the present circumstances, property owned by the whole means that the representative of all the people—the state—occupies the property and exercises the right of ownership over it. Therefore property owned by the whole can also be called state property. In our country the right of ownership by the whole has the following features:

1 *Ownership by the Whole is Exclusive and Unified.* The exclusive character refers to the fact that the subject of the ownership right is only one person, that is, the state. Other than the state, no organization or individual can become the subject of the right of ownership by the whole or with the state jointly become the subject of the right of ownership by the whole. The unified character refers

146

to the fact that legally the state unites the control and exercise of the right of ownership by the whole. But this does not signify that all property owned by the whole can be directly administered and operated only by the state or government organizations. The state can, through law or direct authorization, convey operation and administration of property of the whole to enterprise and business units.

The object of ownership by the whole is of unlimited breadth. That is, any property can become the object of ownership by the whole. Based on the provisions of the *General Principles*, some property can be owned only by the whole, such as minerals, water, cultural artifacts beneath the soil, historical relics, wild animals, and so forth. Some enterprises, businesses, and installations of vital relation to the national well-being, such as the postal service, military industries, military installations, railways, airline facilities, etc., are also owned solely by the state. In addition, the state also may, based on society's collective interests and needs, from time to time by law or orders proclaim that certain property belongs to all the people, such as the twenty-two nature preserves established by the plan, or the establishment of national parks.

The law provides strong protection for ownership by all the people. Article 73, section 2, of the *General Principles* stipulates: "State property is sacred and inviolable: It is forbidden for any organization or individual to interfere with possession or to loot, secretly divide up, divert for personal use, or destroy [it]." Any conduct that violates ownership by all the people must be punished by the law.

Article 74 of the *General Principles* provides: "The property of collective organizations of the working masses belongs to the working mass collective."

a *Ownership by the working mass collective is another Chinese form of collective ownership.* Those working mass collective organizations that are legal persons include urban collective economic organizations, village peasant collective economic organizations, and township collective economic organizations. All of these organizations are independent subjects of rights in civil affairs which independently exercise the right of property ownership on their own authority and may possess, use, benefit from, and dispose of property, without the illegal interference of or violation by any organization or individual.

b *The object of working mass collective ownership is fairly broad.* It includes that land legally stipulated as collectively owned: land and forests, mountains, grasslands, wasteland, shoreline, and so on; the property of collective economic organizations; collectively owned buildings, reservoirs, agricultural irrigation facilities, and educational, scientific, cultural, health, and sports facilities, as well as all other collectively owned property. Beyond this, the *General Principles* stipulates that collectively owned land belongs according to law to the village collective and is operated and managed by agricultural collective economic organizations such as village agricultural production cooperatives or the village committee. Land already owned by the township peasant collective economic organizations can belong to the township peasant collective.

147

c *Working mass collective ownership is strictly protected by law.* Article 74, section 3, provides: "Collective property is protected by law. It is forbidden for any group or individual to interfere with possession, or to loot, secretly divide up, destroy, or illegally impound, sequester, freeze, or confiscate it."

The ownership system provided by the *General Principles* not only affirms the status of the state and the collective as, respectively, subjects of the systems of property ownership by all the people and by the working mass collective, it also provides forceful legal protection. Furthermore, in the course of reform of the economic system it balances state and enterprise relations and gives direction for the invigoration of enterprises that is part of the reform of the economic system.

The enterprise legal person is an extremely important subject of civil rights. Under our socialist conditions, the system of enterprise legal person is an efficacious organizational form that takes an enterprise which is engaged in the activities of a commodities economy and sets it on a course of legality; it concentrates capital to initiate large-scale economic construction and develop science and technology. Article 36 states: "Legal persons are organizations that have civil capacity, are competent to perform civil acts, and according to law independently enjoy civil rights and assume civil duties." Articles 41 to 49 contain various concrete provisions on the enterprise legal person. Thus the forms of the *General Principles* formally establish the legal status of the enterprise legal person. These provisions in the *General Principles* are responses to the need to strengthen enterprise vitality in the course of economic reform and in turn provide the legal guarantee for the invigoration of the enterprise.

The Third Plenum of the Twelfth Party Congress pointed out: "To strengthen enterprise vitality, to strengthen large- and medium-scale enterprises owned by all the people is the key link in the reform of the urban economic structure." But if we are fully to invigorate enterprises, then it is essential to cause them truly to become relatively independent objects, to achieve self-control, and to become socialist commodities producers and operators that take responsibility for gains and losses, that is, in the final analysis to become legal persons that have fixed rights and duties. This point is something that was truly overlooked before reform.

Before reform, our urban economic system's defect was in its emphasis on implementing the plan's control over enterprises and in ignoring the enterprises' relatively independent position, as if the state's control over enterprises meant the deader the better. In this sort of situation, state ownership could not be separated from the right of operational control and led to the state using administrative methods to interfere willfully in the enterprises' horizontal economic activities, substituting the desires of senior officials or administrative orders for the law of value in commodities exchange. Not recognizing that each enterprise had its own material interests and not recognizing that the means of production are a commodity meant that the production responsibility of enterprises owned by the whole were transmitted downward by the state, goods were distributed by the state, personnel were assigned by the higher levels, equipment was allocated by the state, all profit was sent upward to the state, and losses were the responsibility of the state. In this way, enterprises became nothing more than branch organizations of this large enterprise, the state, and possessed none of the qualifications of an independent legal person. Within, they lacked vitality. Without, they lacked force. They were bereft of the life that an economic organization ought to have.

The system of enterprise legal person creates an appropriate separation of ownership and operation/management, an excellent organizational form for stimulating the invigoration of the enterprise. Article 82 of the *General Principles* states: "The right enjoyed by a state-owned enterprise to operate, according to law, state property that has been given to it to operate and manage is protected by law." This is the first legislative confirmation of the separation of the enterprise legal person form of ownership and of the separation of ownership and operation rights. The subject of the enterprise property ownership right is the state; the subject of the right of operation is the enterprise. In Chinese socialism, the right of operation is the core of the system of economic management. The vesting of the right of operation is the most important indicator of the direct expression of the nature of the system of economic management. Only if the divorce of state ownership from enterprise operation is effected can the enterprise truly be granted the status of a legal person.

The operational right of the legal person is a new type of right that is assigned from and is separated from the body of the state's ownership rights. In terms of its nature, it is a sort of independent "real right," or right over things, and includes the various civil rights that commodities producers and operators ought to enjoy. Not only can it, based on law, resist any person, including the owner, but through the exchange of commodities there may also occur the acquisition and transfer of the right of ownership of state property. Because the enterprise possesses the operational right, it enjoys the right to possess, use, receive benefit from, and dispose of property according to law.

In horizontal relations of exchange, the transfer of property between enterprises is conducted through forms of commodity exchange. Protective methods may be used to protect ownership rights against unlawful violations and compensation demanded. In administrative regulation of vertical and horizontal relations, the operational rights of the enterprise are strictly safeguarded and cannot be subjected to any extra-legal interference. If because of administrative supervisory organizations' mistakes, the enterprise operation suffers a loss, the administrative organization must undertake the appropriate liability. In sum, the *General Principles*' establishment of the enterprise legal person's operational rights is of help in stimulating the enterprise to win over various benefits in the course of operational management and of help in making clear that the enterprise is liable for bankruptcy if its operational management is poor and its losses accumulate to a certain level. Therefore, the enterprise legal person plays an extremely important role in motivating and invigorating the enterprise, which is the heart of the reform of the urban economic structure.

2 *The* General Principles' *Provision of a Contract System is the Fundamental Link in the Establishment of a Unified Socialist Market System.* According to Marx's theory of labor value, the value of commodities set by socially necessary labor-time and measured in commodity-currency relations is expressed as price. Under the influence of supply and demand, price revolves around the fluctuations of value, thereby leading to a generalized competition between operators. This sort of competition demands the removal of all obstacles to competition, so that it becomes a unified market system. If there is no unified market, it can become only a sort of stunted commodity economy. To become a smoothly functional unified market, it is necessary to assist the reflection of the law of commodity economy, and to carry out administration and adjustment through forceful rules. The contract system is precisely this sort of rule in legal form of commodities exchange in a unified market, and also becomes an essential legal guarantee of the unified socialist market. In this regard, article 85 states: "A contract is an agreement whereby parties establish, modify, or terminate civil relations. Contracts formed in accordance with law are protected by law."

A system of unified socialist markets includes a commodities market, a labor market, a capital market, and a technology market. Regardless of the type of market, the principal subject of the circulation is the enterprise; regardless of the type of market, the buying and selling of objects must conform to the law of value and be conducted in accordance with the principles of exchange of equal value and mutual equality. The general concept of contract established in the *General Principles* and the concrete provisions in the Economic Contract Law regarding these four types of market are a high level ideal and generalization of the law of circulation. They provided the legal standing and requirements of the enterprise as the subject of market circulation at the time it signed agreements, stipulated the subject matter and price of the contract, and defined certain conditions for a contract to have effect. Experience proves that an enterprise can avoid being forced into contractual relationships by administrative fiat only if it voluntarily selects partners with whom to deal, can agree on mutually acceptable contract terms achieved through negotiation, willingly accepts contract terms as binding and enforceable, and accepts the fundamental principle of equal exchange. By emphasizing the relatively independent interests of the enterprise, the localism and departmentalism of the past which severed horizontal linkages within the economy can be changed and suitable cooperative relations of division labor can be established.

Using the contract system to establish and regulate a unified socialist market system, we must adhere to the following principles.

a *Equality of mutual benefit, and exchange of equal value.* As the subject of market circulation, relations between enterprises must be relations between equal subjects. Thus, despite belonging to different administrative spheres or having different ownership regimes, once they enter the marketplace, all enterprises are in an equal legal position. They ought to regard their opposite as an equal owner or exchanger of commodities, and in obtaining the opposite's commodities, labor, capital, or technology must pay the actual value in money or in other forms of compensation permitted by law. (This principle has already been discussed so the remarks here are brief.)

b *Abiding by the principle of protecting the enterprise's independent interests.* The enterprise is an economic organization characterized by profit, which has its own material interests. The source of the enterprise's interest is in its independent management, and it may freely allocate and dispose of its property within a fixed scope. Its interests are the source of the enterprise's impetus. In the marketplace, the enterprise has the right to protect its own lawful interests, and other subjects have the duty to respect and not to violate the enterprise's interests. Thus can we objectively encourage the stability and prosperity of the unified socialist market. On the other hand, we can further stimulate the interest motive of the enterprise, thereby invigorating its operational management. First, the enterprise acts as the independent subject intended by law; in order to protect its own "character" and reputation in the market, it must demand that all of its members strengthen the sense of being master of their own affairs, continuously advance industrial technology, improve product quality, create high-grade products and first-class trademarks, and compete successfully against foreign goods. Second, the enterprise participates in economic circulation with its own property or with that which it operates and manages, thereby fostering its focus on market news, strengthening its ability to meet an emergency and reduce or avoid economic loss. Third, in order to protect its own economic interests in the market, the enterprise must completely fulfill its duties under the state plan and continuously improve its operational and management level and economic benefit, independent accounting, and responsibility for profit or loss. It must also emphasize contract, receive credit, and exercise its right to resist and file suit against all violations of its interests. In this way, the prosperous development of the socialist unified market is objectively encouraged and its good working order safeguarded.

c *Uphold the principle of the enterprise independently assuming responsibility for property.* Since the enterprise manages itself and takes sole responsibility for profit and loss, it possesses independent economic interests and property. Thus, at the time of market movement, it ought to undertake property obligations independently. This obligation includes consciousness of violation or failure to implement contracts and concurrent responsibility for compensation. It also includes accepting the consequences that bankruptcy carries with it. In this regard, article 48 states clearly: "A state owned enterprise legal person bears civil liability to the extent of the property the state has given it to operate and manage. A collective enterprise bears civil liability to the extent of the property the enterprise owns. Civil liabilities of a collective enterprise shall be satisfied from the assets the enterprise owns. Sino-foreign joint venture enterprise legal persons, Sino-foreign contractual joint venture enterprise legal persons, and wholly foreign-owned enterprise legal persons bear civil liability to the extent of the property the enterprise owns, unless the law provides otherwise." This provision is the first clear differentiation of the scope of property for which the enterprise undertakes civil liability. Consequently, for the enterprise, especially the state enterprise, it means an end to the psychology of the Cultural Revolution period. No longer can enterprises ignore whether or not a task is completed or performed well. No longer can they simply relegate losses and debts to the state. Elsewhere, the civil law also stipulates that the enterprise can be ended because it has been declared bankrupt. In 1986 the NPC passed the Bankruptcy Law, which became effective in 1988. This further clarified the property obligations of the enterprise in market exchange. Owing to the role of the law of value in market exchange, inevitably some enterprises profit while others suffer losses. When the losses reach a fixed proportion of the net worth of that enterprise's property, it can become bankrupt. Legally speaking, bankruptcy occurs when the debtor's entire property is insufficient to meet its obligations and the creditor is forced to employ procedures of litigation determined by law to obtain full payment. Bankruptcy is the elimination by competition of the less advanced and less efficient, an effective mechanism for motivation, and of enormous use as a spur to the enterprise legal person. Therefore, to uphold the principles of the enterprise independently assuming debt and the consequence of bankruptcy is advantageous to the encouragement of fair competition in a flourishing socialist market.

Notes

1 Throughout this article, civil law refers generally to those legal norms that regulate property and personal non-property relationships. *See* definition of *minfa* (civil law) in FAXUE CIDIAN (LAW DICTIONARY) 204 (1989). *See also* TONG ROU ET AL., MINFA GAILUN (GENERAL DISCUSSION OF CIVIL LAW) 1–20 (1982).

2 Special Editor's note: The Great Leap Forward of 1958 to 1960, of which the rural People's Communes movement was a part, sought to achieve an economic breakthrough and political mobilization which would allow China not only to leap beyond the industrial levels of Western European nations but also to leap from its just completed socialist revolution directly into communism. The People's Communes were created by aggregating smaller agricultural producers' cooperatives into larger units which had a more collective character and combined political and economic administration. The guiding policies of this period, many of which resurfaced during the Cultural Revolution (1966–1976), have been subsequently labelled "leftist." They included mass mobilization, preference for large-scale social organizations as closer to true communism, persistence of the language of class struggle, emphasis on "redness" or correct ideology over expertise, and insistence on the ability of the human will to overcome objective circumstances. *See* M. MEISNER, MAO'S CHINA 204–54 (1977), for a general discussion, and R. MAC FARQUHAR, THE ORIGINS OF THE CULTURAL REVOLUTION: 2: THE GREAT LEAP FORWARD 1–4, 326–36. For an early criticism by Lenin of "leap" thinking see A. CHAN ET AL., CHEN VILLAGE 169–85 (1984).

3 Special Editor's note: The Gang of Four was composed of Mao Zedong's wife, Jiang Qing, and three of her minions—Wang Hongwen, Zhang Chunqiao, and Yao Wenyuan—previously lower-level political operatives who rose to national power under her aegis and helped shape the direction of the Cultural Revolution (1966–

1976). Upon Mao's death in September 1976, the Four were arrested by Mao's successor in an action that is called "the smashing of the Gang of Four." On the Cultural Revolution, see M. MEISNER, *supra* note 2, at 309–81, and H. LEE, THE POLITICS OF THE CULTURAL REVOLUTION (1978).

4 Special Editor's note: 1 K. MARX, CAPITAL 84 (1967).

5 Special Editor's note: *Id.* at 112.

6 Special Editor's note: *See The German Ideology*, in R. TUCKER, THE MARX-ENGELS READER 188 (2d ed. 1987).

7 Special Editor's note: *But cf.* Epstein, *The Theoretical System of Property Rights in China's General Principles of Civil Law*, LAW & CONTEMP. PROBS., Spring 1989, at 177, 178.

35

SOME QUESTIONS REGARDING THE SIGNIFICANCE OF THE GENERAL PROVISIONS OF CIVIL LAW OF THE PEOPLE'S REPUBLIC OF CHINA

William C. Jones

Source: *Harvard International Law Journal* 28:2 (1987): 309–331.

In 1949, the new Chinese government repealed all of the laws of the Nationalists, including the civil code.[1] Ever since then, it has been trying to draft a replacement. In 1982, the government abandoned the idea of publishing a comprehensive code, and decided to draft a general collection of basic principles.[2] This general part, the General Provisions of Civil Law of the People's Republic of China (General Provisions), was enacted in April 1986, and went into effect in January 1987.[3] Despite the fanfare with which the General Provisions was passed,[4] it is written in such broad abstract terms that it cannot be used directly to resolve any legal problems, except perhaps for the appointment of a guardian for an infant or a person of limited mental capacity and a few similar matters.[5] Thus, the General Provisions may not be the "milestone in Chinese legal history" some have thought it to be.[6]

What is this law? In form, it is a general part of a civil code constructed on the German or pandectist model.[7] Such codes are the product of a belief that the study of law is a science whose aim is to find the basic elements of law in a way corresponding to physical scientists' search for the basic elements of matter. When the juridical scientists completed their work, they arranged concepts in hierarchies from the most general down to the most particular. In civil law, the central group of concepts they formulated consists of a person (an abstraction meaning a rights-bearer or subject of rights, not necessarily a human being)[8] who, by means of a declaration of intent, executes a juristic act. Juristic acts include contracts, deeds and wills, but are all subject to provisions on capacity, fraud, conditions, good faith, etc.

The general part of a civil code is followed by special parts (obligations, property, family law, and succession in the German Code)[9]. A special part may in turn be divided into a general part and special parts. For example, in the obligation part of the German Code, the general part includes such matters as good faith, impossibility, effect of obligee's default, discharge of obligations, etc., while the special parts include the various types of contracts such as sale, hire, loan for consumption, lease, etc. as well as restitution and torts.[10] The particular rules, the nature of seller's warranty,[11] for example, will be found in the special parts as well.

The Chinese General Provisions follows the German model exactly.[12] While most of the provisions are broad, there are some more specific provisions on substantive areas: property, including intellectual property, contracts and civil responsibility (breach of contract and torts). These provisions are of the type that would normally be expanded in the special parts. It is unusual to find torts or intellectual property in a civil code's general part,[13] but there is no reason they should not be there. The problem with the General Provisions is that there are no special parts.

The chairman of the drafting committee, Wang Hanbin, in presenting the draft to the National People's Congress, stated that the lack of special parts would be compensated for to a certain extent by other statutes that dealt with civil law matters such as the Economic Contracts Law, the Foreign Economic Contracts Law, the Trademark Law, the Patent Law, the Marriage Law, and the Succession Law. Any gaps would just have to remain for a time.[14]

The difficulty with this is the extent of the gaps. There is almost nothing on property except for the two types of intellectual property. The question of how authorized interests in land are to be conveyed, is not treated. Nor is there any provision on the transfer of chattels (movables). Indeed movables and immovables are not even defined or differentiated. The Economic Contracts Law is fairly complete, but it does not apply to noneconomic contracts,[15] and it would require considerable work to factor out the general principles of contract law from it (formation, for instance).[16] The provisions on juristic persons in the General Provisions make constant reference to laws that do not yet exist.[17]

The result is that it will not be possible to use this act as it stands. It can only be used by means of supplementary statutes, regulations, and treatises, or, of course, precedents if they are available.[18] In other words, the enactment of this statute did not change Chinese civil law much.

That is, prior to the promulgation of the General Provisions, to apply law of the type that is embodied in it (civil law of the German-Japanese type) one had to refer to treatises on civil law, and, of course, to any other relevant statutes in force. There is some evidence that there were such treatises, and that they existed as a source of civil law of a sort in China from the time of the repeal of the Nationalist codes.[19] They were used to teach civil law whenever law schools or legal institutes were open. Civil law was taught as if it existed, despite the lack of a code.[20] Hence, in a very real sense, these treatises *were* the civil law of China so far as legal scholarship was concerned. It is not clear that the law was ever applied to real cases, but it occupied a place in the minds of the Chinese academics. It is what they thought of when they thought of civil law.

The civil code of 1929 and following, very much in the German–Japanese tradition, existed primarily in the academy as well. It was probably not used much except in large cities.[21] The Nationalists did not control all of China in 1929 or subsequently, and had neither the time nor the resources, nor perhaps even the desire, to do the extensive preparatory work that would have been required to make the largely illiterate Chinese peasants willing to make use of the translated fruit of the *Pandektwissenschaft* that a gracious government had put at their disposal. The most important business disputes would normally be decided (if they came to court) in the extraterritorial foreign courts in the cities. Thus German-style civil law has always been almost entirely an academic or foreign law in China. This law in the books has been treated as if it were the law of China, but this was almost certainly not the case. Hence the repeal of the code in 1949 could not affect the only life the code had ever had: being taught out of a treatise at a university. The closing of the universities was, of course, another matter.[22]

To say that codified civil law was not used does not mean that it was unimportant. Over the years, tens of thousands of students learned that this was what law was. As there are not many college graduates in China, these law graduates have occupied very important positions in Chinese life. Still, one cannot say exactly what its influence has been, since it was not the law in fact. What was?

I Law in fact[23]

A The formal legal system

Because legal institutionalization has been less extensive than China's history and size would predict, it often seems to be assumed today, both in China and outside, that China had no law prior to July 1, 1979, or whatever post-Mao date one picks.[24] Clearly, even without clear formal legal institutions, the normal functions that law serves are accomplished in a given society. After all, law is an aspect of organized society by definition.

In fact and in practice, China's central government policies and decisions have performed the function of civil law; thus, it is the centralized policies which comprise the "formal" legal system in China.

What role does civil law play in society? What tasks does it fulfill? How are these matters handled in China?

While the outlines of civil law are not clearly defined, it has always been concerned with such matters as status, the ownership of land, and the transfer of movables.[25] All of these are matters of great concern in China, and everyone who has studied post-Liberation China is more or less familiar with the way they were handled.

China during the Mao years was unusual relative to the West in the prominent role accorded to personal status. No subject was more important to the average person than his class designation. A landlord, meaning a former landlord or the descendant of one, was the object of discrimination in every aspect of life—from housing to schooling. On the other hand, for a worker or poor peasant, many doors were opened, at least in theory.[26] The process of categorizing people began before Liberation, and was done in accordance with a statute. In north China, for instance, in the late 1940's, there was a document from the Central Committee of the Communist Party that set out the criteria for land reform.[27] These criteria were definitions of classes. Those classified as landowners and rich peasants were to lose land, while poor peasants would gain it.[28] The statute also set up the procedure by which the determinations of classes were to be made and land redistributed.[29] Essentially, poor peasants' leagues were to be established at the village level. These would decide the class and rights to land of every inhabitant of the village. But the statute is less clear on the way this whole process would be organized by the Communist Party.[30] The process constituted a campaign, and the technique of mobilizing a campaign was standardized into a regular procedure.[31] In this particular campaign, both status and land ownership were determined. In other words, the land reform campaign was a significant legal activity by which legal rights were determined.[32]

This process was repeated throughout the Mao years. That is, land ownership was changed from individual proprietorship, through cooperatives to collective ownership, usually by means of a campaign. Now it is being changed back to individual ownership. Further changes may be in store.[33] Formerly, status was always being redetermined.[34] Now it is said not to matter.[35]

The same pattern can be observed in commerce. In a poor, overpopulated country like China that is always one or two bad harvests away from starvation, the most important item of commerce is, of course, grain. Supervision of the planting, procurement, and marketing of grain was and is one of the principal activities of the government of China. The techniques of exercising control have varied. After the collectivization of farmland, the basic production unit was not the individual farmer but the production team, which planned production subject to the supervision (sometimes considerable) of the commune and the production brigade. "Distribution [of the yield] takes place on the basis of work norms which are fixed by the production team and converted into work points for the individual."[36] The production teams had to meet certain quotas and pay taxes. The entire process took place within a general plan that was prepared by the central government.

Recently, of course, this scheme has been changed. Now, the basic unit is usually the household, which is free to grow whatever it wishes after satisfying a state quota of grain at a fixed price. But this does not mean that the central government lacks ultimate control.[37] It is conceivable that even less direct control may be exercised over agricultural activities in the future so long as the results are consonant with state goals.[38] Nevertheless, the ultimate decision maker is still Beijing. Hence the functions that civil law performs in our society are being exercised by administrative law, or planning, or however one wishes to characterize it, in China.

This kind of control was not limited to status, land, or commerce in grain. Every aspect of human life was potentially subject to government control. For instance, in the first half of 1957,[39] statutes were promulgated that regulated, inter alia, surplus inventory, the use of bamboo in reinforced concrete,[40] rural-urban migration,[41] profits of state enterprises,[42] the collection of used flour sacks,[43] the cost of moving construction and installation enterprises,[44] the organization of the principal tasks of the administrative departments of industry and commerce,[45] the 1957 supply of cotton cloth,[46] spring plowing,[47] apprenticeship,[48] the use of enterprise award funds by state motion picture theatres,[49] the release of banned operas,[50] the quota system in connection with teachers' workload,[51] and the elimination of schistosomiasis.[52] The ideal technique of control was not to give orders, although orders were certainly given, but to induce the persons concerned to decide correctly, that is, in accordance with government policy. Thus all of the fanfare that we associate with political campaigns, as well as the other persuasion techniques that we associate with Maoist China, are very much part of the Chinese equivalent of civil law and procedure.[53]

This basic situation has not changed. At about the time the General Provisions was enacted, a land-use statute was also promulgated to bring all land in China under central control. Each level of government is authorized to issue land use permits for large plots from one fifth of a hectare at the county level to 67 hectares and above at the province level. The largest projects require State Council Approval.[54] Obviously, this statute makes many of the decisions about property that are left to persons by a civil code. Nor have campaigns and techniques of persuasion disappeared, whatever may be said to the contrary. One has only to consider the birth-control program.[55] It is difficult to conceive of a more private matter than the decision to have children. The matter is particularly acute in China. The production of a male heir is, in some respects, the principal aim of marriage, but about half the population are being told that they cannot have sons. This is obviously not a short-lived campaign, since it must continue so long as population growth is regarded as a problem. Hence it is not as flamboyant as the campaigns of the Cultural Revolution or even the campaigns of the 1950's. But it is very intensive and is employing the same techniques.

In sum, the basic functions that we look to civil law to perform are accomplished in China primarily by decisions of the central government which are implemented in a variety of ways at the local level. One central feature of this system has been the induced decision. That is, the persuasion by various means of individuals to get them to think and decide in accord with government plans. This whole process may be characterized as the formal legal system of the People's Republic of China.

B The nonformal legal system

But the process just described is not, of course, the only legal system operating in China. Every large country has more or less informal legal systems that function apart from the formal legal system.[56]

In China, there is also a large area of life in which individuals and governmental units are able to engage in activities and settle disputes without coming into contact with the formal legal system. Evidence of this activity can be seen in the reports of decisions of courts that have been collected by various legal offices to be used in teaching.[57] The courts are not the formal legal system in China, at least in civil matters. They deal with fringe activities and only in an erratic way.[58] That is, litigation in a court or formal arbitration tribunal of what we would call civil matters is not a normal way of handling such problems. Still, litigation of a sort does occur from time to time. This litigation indicates the existence of an informal legal system that is removed from plans and campaigns. While one cannot read cases to find out much about legal developments, they do reveal a lot about life in China and show the existence of what one might call an underground legal system.

One selection of cases in civil law prepared in 1982 by the former Beijing Institute of Politics and Law has been translated, and seems to give fairly typical examples of ordinary behavior in China.[59] These cases show, for example, that there has been continuously a significant amount of private property that has been transferred by sale,[60] inheritance,[61] or lease.[62] The cases also show that public entities act independently at times, and deal with each other.[63] People injure others and compensation is demanded.[64] One person will ask another to carry out some task for him, that is, use mandate or agency.[65] In other words, people carry on activities which give rise to disputes settled through the Chinese "informal" legal system, which in the American system, would be dealt with through formal civil law. Of course, there are serious limits to these activities. Only those property interests—particularly in land—whose transfer is authorized can be transferred.[66] Still, the model universe of a Western civil code exists in China—discrete entities forming relationships with each other, transferring products, planning joint activities, and so on.

The cases chosen for the Beijing anthology were probably not meant to illustrate any particular area of substantive law such as contract. The volume is arranged in accordance with the categories of a German-style civil code,[67] but these categories have little to do with the individual cases. Thus a case is labelled agency or representation because an agent is involved, although an American lawyer would say the issue is conversion.[68] But the cases are revealing of the kind of activities that go on in China, and the sorts of matters that are litigated. The best way of getting some idea of them is just to list a few at random. The first ten in the translated version[69] are as follows:

1   A foodstuffs company sued a railroad bureau for pulling down a building. The railroad bureau claimed to own or control the land. It won.[70]
2   A credit cooperative sued an individual for a debt incurred by his father. It won.[71]
3   A hospital sued individual for the bill for his aunt's hospital expenses. It won.[72]

4   A production brigade sued an individual to get back possession of two rooms in a house that it owned or controlled. It won. (The real parties in interest seem to have been persons from whom the rooms had been confiscated during the Cultural Revolution and to whom they were to be restored under current government policy.)[73]

5   A niece sued her uncle for a share of the compensation he had received for having been forced to move out of his house during the Cultural Revolution on the ground that she owned a share in the house which had belonged to her grandfather. It was held that she had no claim to the house, which was rented (presumably by her grandfather originally).[74]

6   The natural mother of an adopted child, to whom the child had been returned, brought an action to force the adopting parents to retake the child. The defendants claimed that the child was sick and wished to cancel the adoption. They had had the child physically examined before they adopted her. They lost.[75]

7   The Baoshan steel mill ordered a large quantity of steel from Nippon Steel. Most of it was below standard, but timely inspection and objection were not made as to the majority of the steel. As to the small quantity that was inspected on time, the buyer steel company had an inspection made and obtained a price adjustment. There was no law suit.[76]

8   A hardware store sold to a hydraulic-cell company lacquer and other things and received two bad checks in payment. The seller sued for payment. The defendant did not appear, so the court ordered the sum to be paid from its bank account.[77]

9   A building-management office sued a tenant for back rent which had not been paid. The nonpayment was part of a rent strike (the tenants on the top floor felt they should pay less than those on the bottom floor). The striker was educated to discover the error of his ways; he paid.[78]

10 Action by a production brigade against an electrical contractor—an "electrical installation team"—for a refund of a portion of an advance payment made for work that was not completed. The money had been owing for ten years. The direction of the original contractor had been changed many times. Nevertheless, the defendant had to pay. (It took a good deal of education to get it to do so.)[79]

The problems with which these first ten cases deal are almost all normally found under the heading of civil law. Thus, the nonproperty cases include an action for money owed on a debt,[80] an action for goods had and received[81] and services rendered,[82] an action for rent,[83] and one for breach of warranty in the sale of goods.[84] A Chinese and a foreign enterprise were parties to this last action though the matter was never litigated. There was an action to cancel an adoption for fraud.[85] The fact situations in these cases could exist anywhere. And there are actions in tort in the same book,[86] and even one for medical malpractice.[87] The property cases are, to be sure, a little different. There are clearly property interests that give rise to private disputes, but they exist only to the extent and in the manner allowed by the government (and the term "government" includes local governing units). It is difficult to know just what property interests are, because, so far as I know, there is no clear analysis of property rights in China. It is not clear what can be owned and by whom and how.[88] But the important point is that there are rights and powers that the Chinese recognize and exercise, and that are in turn recognized by courts.

There are other problems. For example, the entire field of juristic persons is unclear in China. It is not only that there is no company law. There is no clear differentiation of the legal status of the many kinds of entities that exist in Chinese society and engage in some kinds of activities more or less on their own. The cases do nothing to clarify this. They simply indicate the diversity of the entities that obviously have some sort of legal capacity.

But the greatest difference between Chinese law, as shown in these cases, and our law does not lie in the substantive law, but in the procedural. Our system is prepared to consider changes in the nature of substantive-law rights with ease so long as the remedies and devices to enforce them remain the same. We can go from no action against a manufacturer unless there is privity to no-fault liability, for instance, and not feel that the legal "system" has been changed or even affected because the procedure remains the same. The actuality of Chinese civil procedure as shown in these cases is radically different from ours, and this difference in turn affects the substantive rights. This should occasion no surprise to jurists whose substantive law is said to have "the look of being gradually secreted in the interstices of procedure."[89]

The principal difference is the rarity of the clear-cut decision. In China the parties more often than not do not get a clear victory or defeat. In many if not a majority of the cases, the court works out a purported compromise. Even if it grants the plaintiff's main request it may turn down some subsidiary request.[90]

The reported cases seem to me to be typical. They are not simply compromises. The Chinese courts are apparently quite capable of recognizing the validity or invalidity of a claim and granting a request for relief or denying it. But they are more likely to try to work out a settlement that will really end the dispute in the minds of the parties and that will cause the one who has done wrong to understand his errors. The Chinese courts are also very conscious of the possible implications for society of particular behavior and of the way it is handled by the courts. In other words, the work of the court is an aspect of the work of government in achieving its purposes. It is not just settling a private dispute.

This attitude is consistent with the theory that government and its institutions are a temporary expedient used by the Communist Party to help prepare society for the establishment of communism. This is not a fashionable way of talking about China at the present time either inside or outside China. Inside, the only slogan is the Four Modernizations.[91] Outside, China is said now to be in the hands of "pragmatists."[92] "Pragmatism" seems to be a code word for "having given up faith in Marxism." This may or may not be an accurate description of

161

the state of mind of the present rulers of China,[93] but the decisions of Chinese courts in the early 1980's are quite consistent with a philosophy that regards law as an aspect of the superstructure reflecting the attitudes and needs of the ruling class. As the tactics for advancing particular phases of the revolution change, the law—and hence "rights"—changes too. This has notably been the case with housing. What was taken away in the Cultural Revolution is being given back in the counter-Cultural Revolution. To the extent that this attitude persists in the judiciary, it affects the nature of the rights.

Of course, it is not clear that ordinary citizens have the same perception as the courts do either of their rights or of those of their units. They seem to be living their lives independently of government plans to the extent they can. They seem to require a good deal of "education" to realize the truth of the government's current position. Still, they are educable. At least, those whose cases are reported seem to be.

In short, ordinary Chinese seem to perceive the universe as being in many ways similar to the model universe of a Western civil code. They have interests in land and other property that can be transferred in various ways. They recognize that debts and other obligations have to be satisfied. Capacity and its consequences are recognized. Collectivities are treated like human beings. They can own property, sue and be sued. It would not be going too far to say that the Chinese seem to have the concept of rights. This nonformal law is, in one sense a sort of *Gemeinrecht* or common law.[94] But it is unsystematized. So far as one can determine from the cases, it does not seem to have the regularity or certainty that one expects of established custom either in China or the West.[95] The courts recognize these institutions; they enforce or deny claims. But they often do so with the aim of advancing government policy.

The formal system of law in China—the central government's plans and its mechanisms for carrying them out—allows for a considerable degree of activity that is, in fact, uncontrolled, so long as certain boundaries are not overstepped. These two types of activity in my view, constitute the civil law in fact in China. Until the enactment of the General Provisions, there was also the civil law in the books. How does the General Provisions fit into or affect this situation?

II The effect of the General Provisions

The General Provisions does not, as previously indicated, make much difference in a situation where someone—a lawyer or judge for instance—wishes to apply German-style law. Prior to the promulgation of the General Provisions, those who understood this kind of law looked to general treatises—Chinese (from both the People's Republic of China and Taiwan)[96] and non-Chinese—to find discussions and analyses of legal problems. There seems to be no question that civil law was thought to exist in China. It was apparently also a sort of *Gemeinrecht* or common law that consisted of the general ideas current in civil law circles throughout the world, though organized in the German way. Since the General

Provisions is constructed like a general part, it cannot be used alone to settle cases, but must be supplemented. Normally this supplementation is by statute—the special parts in a code and other statutes outside it. Where there are no such statutes, then the supplementation comes through doctrine—through the writings of commentators. That is the case now in China. The primary materials that have to be used to solve problems are treatises. Where there are statutes, as in the case of economic contracts, the statutes will continue to be used. Previously, they had to be supplemented by treatises because they lacked some of the general rules. Now the treatises may have been supplented to a degree by the General Provisions but there is no reason to expect that there will be any change in result. The General Provisions could be described as being for the most part a codification of the general provisions in the treatises. The situation is, in other words, essentially unchanged. Problems that had to be decided by treatise still must be so decided. Where special statutes existed, as in the case of patents and economic contracts, they will still be used. The promulgation of the General Provisions is, in terms of its practical utility, something of a nonevent.

A The general provisions as a political statement

It seems likely that those who drafted and pushed enactment of this law are aware of these facts, although it may be that the principal political figures who do not have legal training, and who would have had to back the legislation in order for it be enacted, were not. But if the draftsmen knew what they were doing, what did they hope to accomplish? It is difficult to know what anyone in a responsible position in China actually thinks. But there is a strong possibility that the General Provisions were meant primarily as a political statement.[97] This aim was to confirm, in as permanent a form as possible, the new economic organization of the country, including the individual responsibility system in the countryside and the decentralization of decision-making power in industry. This is shown in two ways. In the first place, it is shown by the use of provisions that expressly recognize the existence of these new arrangements, and, in the second, by the overall approach of the General Provisions, which is implicitly antagonistic to the legal philosophy that has existed up to now.

The explicit provisions are contained in the portion devoted to "persons." In the Article entitled "Citizens (Natural Persons)," after dealing with the problems of birth, death, infancy, mental incapacity and the like, the statute provides:

Part 4

Individual Industrial and Commercial Households; Rural Contract Management Households

sec. 26. Citizens who, within the scope allowed by law, having been checked and approved and registered, carry on an industrial and commercial enterprise, are individual industrial and commercial households.

Individual industrial and commercial households may use a commercial name.

Sec. 27. Members of agricultural collective organizations who, within the scope permitted by law, according to an output responsibility contract, carry on commodity management, are rural contract management households.

sec. 28. The lawful rights of individual commercial and industrial households and rural contract management households are protected by law.

sec. 29. When individual industrial and commercial households and rural contract management households are managed by individual[s], the property of the individual[s] is liable for their obligations. Where they are managed by the household, the property of the household is liable.

Those sections refer to the new kinds of individual enterprises that are being encouraged—those Orville Schell referred to in his book, *To Get Rich Is Glorious*.[98] That is, the devices through which farm land is being decollectivized in fact, though not in theory. Through these devices, peasants are now permitted to keep most of the proceeds from what they grow and may carry on small businesses.

It is difficult to see the significance of these provisions for civil law. The legal positions of those involved are not affected. The provisions do not create a legal entity separate from natural persons. There is no limitation of liability.[99] The statement that the household assets are liable for the obligations of the enterprise if the household operates it, probably says little more than that individual family members with capacity can carry on separate economic activities while living at home. This would seem to be the normal result that would have been reached without a code. When people act together in an enterprise, they are jointly liable for its obligations.[100]

But though these provisions do not seem to have much significance in affecting civil-law relations, they are an affirmation that these economic activities are recognized and entitled to legal protection. It is a much more final and permanent statement about their validity than anything that might appear in Party Congress speeches, Five Year Plans and the like, or even in the Constitution, since the civil code may be expected to endure longer than any of those.[101]

This policy, if that is what it is, is continued in section 80 of the General Provisions, in which the rights of parties to output contracts "are protected by law." Obviously these contracts are already protected by law; otherwise they could not exist. In fact they were created by law.[102] Such contracts represent the principal economic policy of the government; they are not spontaneous activities of the peasants outside the legal system. But government policy can be easily changed. These provisions try to give the contracts a more durable status by placing them in the most permanent available setting.

164

A similar set of provisions exists for juristic persons, and, for that matter, for joint ventures, including foreign joint ventures. After some general provisions, the first part of the Article on juristic persons begins with "Enterprise Juristic Persons." These sections are obviously designed to be the general provisions for a company law, since they provide for the existence as a juristic person of enterprises that have been properly approved and registered.[103] They leave to other statutes the task of providing what proper investigation and registration might consist of. Once an enterprise has been properly organized and registered, it has legal capacity to hold and exercise rights. The concept of the enterprise juristic person is not defined very clearly, but it seems to be basically the Chinese equivalent of a profit-making corporation.[104] The Chinese equivalents of not-for-profit corporations—associations of artists, hospitals, research organizations and the like—are also recognized as being juristic persons.[105]

These provisions again do not accomplish very much except possibly to give foreign investors a slightly increased sense of security as to their protection from creditors because of the limited liability of enterprise juristic persons. But the elements of the concept of the juristic person have existed since the beginning of the People's Republic of China. That is, the various units of government have been recognized as being capable of carrying on fairly independent activities.[106] Since the provisions on juristic persons do not prescribe the conditions for being recognized or registered, or for having the status without being registered, it seems likely that things will go on much as they have. Units that have been operating as fairly independent entities will continue to do so. Now perhaps they will be juristic persons, unbeknownst to themselves. Those that have not been operating in that way will not be so recognized.

But the statement in a law passed by the National People's Congress that a great number of units in China have a discrete existence—that they have rights and property, can deal with one another and make their own decisions—may have quite a lot of meaning. It suggests that the highest officials in China, presumably including the Party, have decided to accept a model of society in which discrete entities—persons—make decisions. There is control, potential and actual, by the government, but most of the activity in society is controlled by independent decision makers, some of which are collectivities—juristic persons. This is the model of modern civil-law systems in France and Germany. It is also the model of classical or market economics. It is a complete rejection of the Maoist model.

It is very difficult to know whether the draftsmen saw all the implications of such a statute. For one thing, it is possible to point to the Soviet Union, which has had a German-style code since its early days.[107] That code has certainly not prevented the development of a highly centralized economy, and indeed, society, where individual initiative is very limited. There are differences, however. The principal one is that the civil codes in the U.S.S.R. were promulgated during the New Economic Program (NEP), when private property was allowed.[108] They were complete civil codes, not just the general parts. They were promulgated in a European country where the law that they codified was familiar. They were not simply statements of general principles with little practical application. Their scope might be limited, but courts with legally trained judges could decide such matters as personal contracts.

But it is at least possible that some of the draftsmen of the Chinese code appreciated the significance of giving legislative recognition to what is perhaps the most distinctive feature of the German Civil Code: the concept of the juristic act. It does not exist in other systems. If one adopts a German code understandingly, then one must intend to adopt the approach to law which this concept implies. Perhaps the concept is basic enough to the code so that if one adopts the code, the concept will influence one's thinking about law as one works with the code, even if the concept was not understood at first. At any rate, the basic principle underlying the juristic act is freedom of will—self-determination. As a standard German text states: "The concept of the juristic act corresponds to the principle of self-determination."[109] Consciously or unconsciously, is this the concept of those who drafted the General Provisions? The vehemence with which a recent writer on this subject rejects the notion makes one think there may be something to it.[110] However, even if it were in the minds of the draftsmen, will it affect society at all?

B The General Provisions as law

On the other hand, it may be that the draftsmen did not really understand what they were doing. The draftsmen are probably professors or researchers in the field of civil law. They have been working with civil law for decades as a completely academic pursuit. It was never used in fact. Everyone who knows anything about law in China accepts the institution of codes as normal. Once law is regarded very positively, as it is at present, a civil code is an obvious requirement. The appropriate committee is told to draft a civil code, and does so. They follow the old Nationalist or Soviet models, or both. They try to incorporate as many current institutions as they can. Since property law is in a state of great disarray, and is, moreover, extremely sensitive politically because of the question of private ownership of the means of production, they decide just to draft a general part and to say what they can about property, which is not very much. Since they have never been involved with a system of law that existed anywhere except in books, the problem of practical application does not concern them.

It is hard enough to get American law teachers to deal with law in fact despite decades of legal realism. It would not be surprising if Chinese law teachers who were trained in a system of abstract foreign law did not worry very much about its actual application. Almost none of the rulers of China has had any legal training or any experience of living and working in a country that had a western legal system. "Rule of law" has become a motto, but it is not clear that those who prescribe it have any idea what it means. Lawyers are trained. Laws are passed. So long as nothing offensive is said—as might be the case with property law—no one cares much what the laws provide, nor if any are used. Enactment is enough.

Of course, both attitudes may be present. Some may see the General Provisions as a civil code like any other, without considering its utility, and others may hope to use the General Provisions to make a political statement. Regardless of the attitude of the draftsmen, it is hard to see how a German-style civil code could become a critical part of Chinese formal law even if it were complete. Such a code requires quite a lot of academic training in order to be understood and applied. Few judges or lawyers have such training. Even if the average Chinese somehow became accustomed to using the legal process to get disputes settled, or to going to lawyers for advice, if he wished to sue or get documents drafted, it would be impossible for him to do so. The number of legally trailed persons is simply too small in comparison to the whole population, and it will remain very small.[111]

The formal legal system as it is characterized here has operated without serious interruption since 1949. Even during the most violent period of the Cultural Revolution, 1966–71, grain continued to be produced, procured, and marketed, fuel got to factories and public utilities, electricity was produced, trains, ships and planes functioned, and factories continued to operate. They required raw materials and product distribution. And this meant that there was government direction going on. The informal system also operated. People got married, died, left property to favorite nephews, arranged to buy materials for manufacture, etc.[112] Those two aspects of Chinese law have both existed without anybody paying much attention to the Western law that is embodied in the General Provisions and taught in the law schools. No doubt they will continue to do so. But the promulgation may give more prestige to Western law. If present policies continue, there will be a continually increased supply of persons trained in varying degrees in Western law. Many existing judges will attend short legal courses, and the law-department graduates will begin to occupy positions of responsibility. At the same time, there will be more scope for civil law because the formal system is making more use of indirect controls in many areas. Enterprises may have a lot more independence, and commercial contracts may play a much more important role in commerce.

If all of this goes on for a significant period of time, Western law, and hence the General Provisions, will probably become an aspect of the law in fact in China. But it will certainly not be all there is to law in China. The real legal system in China will be quite complex and will continue to include the formal and informal systems mentioned here, and perhaps other unknown elements, as well as Western law. Given this likelihood, one would hope that the Chinese would make some effort to take all of these elements into account in studying and describing their system. They would have free access to the materials on the basis of which such a study could be made; it is doubtful that outsiders ever will. In the meantime, we shall have to do the best we can with the materials we have. We cannot expect much help from the Chinese, who seem to be limiting themselves to a very academic approach,[113] probably for nonacademic, that is, political, reasons.

Notes

1 Common Program of the People's Consultation Conference of China, adopted on September 29, 1949, at the First People's Political Conference of China, Art. 17.

2 *See* Wang Hanbin, *Explanation on 'General Principles of the Civil Code (draft)*, Summary of World Broadcasts-Far East (SWB-FE) C1/10 (Apr. 22, 1986). *See also* Jiang Ping, *Min Fa Tongze de Shiyong Fanwei ji qi Xiaoli (The Scope and Effectiveness of the Use of the General Provisions of Civil Law)*, 3 FAXUE YANJIU (LEGAL RESEARCH) 1 (1986).

3 The official text of the General Provisions is published in *Zhonghua Renmin Gongheguo Guowuyuan Gongbao (Bulletin of the State Council of the People's Republic of China)*, no. 13, May 20, 1986. A translation appears in SWB FE LCI/1 (Apr. 22, 1986).

4 See, e.g., *Civil Rights: Essence of New Law*, China Daily, Apr. 21, 1986, at 4, where comments from three Chinese language newspapers are printed.

5 This may be unfair. The provisions on torts in the General Provisions, §§ 106, 110, 117–33, are fairly complete as civil codes go. The French code has only four sections on torts after all (§§ 1382–1386). Though there are problems with the treatment in the General Provisions, i.e. the basic principle in § 106 is liability for fault, and there is non-fault liability if the law so provides. The law so provides in the case of, *inter alia*, product liability (where there is apparently no privity requirement) (§ 122), and extra-hazardous activities (§ 123). But no distinction is made between intentional and negligent acts although there is a provision for reducing liability if the injured party is also at fault (§ 131), and for dividing the responsibility when no one is at fault (§ 132). Negligence would seem a natural concept in such a context. I have gone into torts in somewhat more detail in Jones, *The New General Rules: A Realistic Perspective on Chinese Civil Law*, 8 E. ASIAN EXEC. REP., Sept. 15, 1986, at 9. The choice of law rules are fairly clear (§§ 142–50), but in § 15 a distinction is made between residence and domicile (without much definition of domicile). However, in the choice-of-law provisions nothing depends on domicile, except the law governing the inheritance of immovables (§ 149).

6 *The Law Leaps Ahead*, FAR E. ECON. REV. 52 (Apr. 12, 1986).

7 It is natural that this should be so since the civil code of the Republic of China, still in force in Taiwan, follows this pattern. The Germanic background of that code is described in J. ESCARRA, LE DROIT CHINOIS 152 n.2, 157, 238–41 (Browne trans. 1961). The Japanese influence is very important, and that too is mostly Germanic. *See* NODA, INTRODUCTION TO JAPANESE LAW 48–52 (Angelo trans. 1976).

The Soviet civil codes may have been influential also, particularly in the 1950's. But they are also very Germanic. *See* O. Ioffe, *Civil Law*, in ENCYCLOPEDIA OF SOVIET LAW 114, 115–16 (2d rev. ed., F. Feldbrugge, G. van den Berg, W. Simons eds. 1985) [hereinafter *Ioffe*]. Professor Ioffe uses the word "pandectist" rather than "Germanic." "Pandects" is another term for the Digest of Justinian. The pandectists were the German scholars—particularly of the nineteenth century—who developed the theories of law that governed the drafting of the German civil code. *See infra* text accompanying note 8.

8 That is, it includes the juristic person as well as the natural person. The juristic person is defined in § 36 of the General Provisions. The term "person" standing alone is rarely used in the General Provisions; instead, the word "citizen" is employed. However, in Article II, "natural persons" is inserted in parentheses immediately after the word "citizens." Section 8 provides that the provisions of the act that apply to persons will normally be applied to foreign and stateless persons. Hence, the total effect is probably the same as in other civil codes that use the word "person."

9 The German Civil Code—Bürgerliches Gesetzbuch—is normally cited by its initials, BGB, and that course will be followed here. Obligation Law is contained in BGB §§

241–853; property, *id.* §§ 854–1296; family law, *id.* §§ 1297–1971; succession, *id.* §§ 1923–2386.

10 Good faith, *id.* § 242; impossibility, *id.* §306; effect of obligee's fault, *id.* §§ 293–304; discharge of obligations, *id.* §§ 362–71; sale, *id.* §§ 453–514; hire, *id.* §§ 631–51; loan for consumption, *id.* §§ 607–10; lease *id.* §§ 535–97; restitution and torts, *id.* §§ 812–53.

11 Seller's warranty, *id.* § 463.

12 The table of contents is as follows:

I   Basic Principles
II   Citizens (Natural Persons)
    1   Capacity to Hold Rights [Rechtsfahigkeit] and Capacity to Engage in Civil Law Actions [Geschaftsfahigkeit]
    2   Guardians
    3   Declaration That a Person is Missing or Dead
    4   Individual Industrial and Commercial Households; Rural Output Management Households
III   Juristic Persons
IV   Civil Law Juristic Acts and Representation
V   Civil Law Rights (Property, Obligations, Intellectual Property, and Personal Rights)
VI   Civil Responsibility
VII   Prescription
VIII   The Application of Law In Foreign Civil Law Relations
IX   Other Provisions

13 Intellectual property is not included in the BGB at all, for no apparent reason except tradition. *See* F.H. LAWSON, A COMMON LAWYER LOOKS AT THE CIVIL LAW 59, 60 (1953).

14 Wang, *supra* note 2, at C1/11.

15 Section 2, Economic Contracts Law of the People's Republic of China, adopted at the Fourth Session of the Fifth National People's Congress on Dec. 13, 1981, *reprinted in* CHINA INTERNATIONAL ECONOMIC CONSULTANTS, INC., THE CHINA INVESTMENT GUIDE 1984/85 574–83 (1984). See also section 54 of the Economic Contracts Law, which states that the act is applicable to contracts between self-employed individuals and legal persons.

16 Formation is governed by section 8, which provides: "Once both parties in accordance with the law go through consultation and reach agreement on the principal terms of an economic contract, the economic contract is formed." There are also provisions on agency (§ 10), use of writings (§ 3), and compliance with the law (§ 4), but the traditional problems—offer and acceptance, for instance—are not dealt with.

17 Section 36, the basic provision, states: "Juristic persons are organizations that have the capacity to have civil law rights and the capacity to engage in civil law actions, and which, *according to law*, independently enjoy civil law rights and assume civil law obligations." (emphasis supplied) The question comes to mind, what law? Section 38 treats the one who, "according to rules of law," represents a juristic person as its statutory representative. Section 42 provides that enterprise juristic persons, upon proper "investigation, approval and registration," will have the status of juristic persons, but there is no indication as to just what might compose this procedure. What one might call (though the Chinese do not) nonenterprise juristic persons—institutions such as hospitals, professional associations and the like—"which according to law do not have to be registered as juristic persons, have the status of juristic persons from the day they are formed." § 50. Again, what law, what requirements?

18 Reports of cases obviously exist somewhere. One can see this in the collections that appear from time to time. *See infra* note 35. And some reports of the Supreme

People's Court are published. But in general, case reports are not available to foreigners, and their use, if any, in China is unclear.

19 The principal evidence is the little book, *Basic Problems in the Civil Law of the People's Republic of China, prepared by the Institute of Civil Law, Central Political-Judicial Cadres School, Beijing 1957*, translated in U.S. Joint Publications and Research Service (JPRS), no. 4879 (Aug, 15, 1961) [hereinafter *Basic Problems*]. The original is also available in the United States. Civil law was taught in the law schools and legal institutes in the period prior to the Cultural Revolution. Hence, some kinds of texts must have been available. *Basic Problems* is very much in the Germanic tradition, though possibly by way of the Soviet Union.

20 My only evidence for this statement is conversations with Chinese professors and students who were in law departments in the 1950's, *Basic Problems, id.*, and extrapolations back to that period from lectures on civil law I heard in China during 1982–83.

21 I cannot prove this. Civil law teachers to whom I have talked in Taiwan do not like to admit it, and those in China do not talk too much about pre-Liberation matters. However, all I have heard about conditions in rural China, pre-1949, make it inconceivable to me that a European legal system had any place in life in the countryside, and the countryside is most of China.

22 I simply do not know what happened to the study of civil law between, say, 1960 and 1978. In at least some of the universities, the books were available to no one.

23 The phrase is taken, more or less, from Roscoe Pound, *Law in Books and Law in Action*, 4 AM. L. REV. 12 (1910), though Pound was more concerned with the difference between the way the formal legal system worked in fact as opposed to theory rather than to alternative legal systems inside one society.

24 Seven important statutes were enacted on July 1, 1979: the Joint Venture Law, the Code of Criminal Procedure, the Penal Code, the Organic Law of the National People's Congresses and Local People's Congresses, the Election Law for the National People's Congress and Local People's Congresses, the Organic Law of the People's Courts, and the Organic Law of the People's Procuratorate.

25 One has only to look at the tables of contents for the German (BGB, *supra* note 9) and French civil codes and their many followers. The French civil code is divided into three books: I. Persons; II. Goods and the different types of property; III. The different ways in which property is acquired (including succession, gifts inter vivos and wills, contracts in general, quasi-contracts and delicts, specific contracts, liens and mortgages, creditors rights, prescription).

26 *See* Jones, *An Approach to Chinese Law,* 4 REV. SOC. L. 13–14 (1978) and authorities cited.

27 Basic Program on Chinese Agrarian Law Promulgated by the Central Committee of the Chinese Party, 1947 [hereinafter Basic Program]. It can be found in W. HINTON, FANSHEN 615–18 (1966); Supplementary Measures for Carrying Out the Basic Program on Agrarian Law (Draft promulgated by Hopei-Honan-Shanshi-Shantong Border Region Government on Dec. 28, 1947), *id.* at 619–22.

28 *Basic Program,* §§ 2, 6, 87, 10A.

29 *Id.* at §§ 5–8. See also the rules for determining class status that were developed in the Jiangxi Soviet period in 1933, and repromulgated in 1950 as *Decisions Concerning the Differentiation of Class Status in the Countryside*, reproduced in A. BLAUSTEIN, FUNDAMENTAL LEGAL DOCUMENTS OF COMMUNIST CHINA 291 (1962).

30 This process is vividly described in William Hinton's book, *supra* note 27.

31 *See* G. BENNETT, YUNDONG: MASS CAMPAIGNS IN CHINESE COMMUNIST LEADERSHIP (1976).

32 *See* M. MEISNER, MAO'S CHINA 101–11, 140–57 (1977).

33 *See* Kueh, *The Economics of the Second Land Reform in China,* 101 CHINA Q. 122 (1985). *See also Meanwhile Back on the Farm,* CHINA NEWS ANALYSIS (Jan. 2, 1984).

34 See, for examples during the Cultural Revolution and its aftermath, A. CHAN, R. MADSEN, & J. UNGER, CHEN VILLAGE 141–85 (1984).

35 See, e.g., the case of *Wang v. Xu* in Wang Xu, *Collection of Cases on General Principles of the Civil Law*, 18 CHINESE LAW AND GOVERNMENT 49 (No. 3–4, 1985–86) [hereinafter *Cases*]. There was a dispute over the ownership of a common wall. One party said the other's grandfather was of rich peasant origin. "He was the one from whom the property was taken. I was the one to whom it was awarded. The common wall has to be my property." *Id.* at 49. The court decided the wall was common property. The editors' note stated "Article 9 of the Constitution provides that the citizen has the right to the materials of his livelihood regardless of his origin or class [*cheng fen*]." *Id.* at 50. This attitude was a significant change, and obviously a shock to Wang; who thought a "good" class background would prevail. Article 9 of the 1978 Constitution protects the rights to livelihood of all citizens, but says nothing about class.

36 *See* J. DOMES, SOCIALISM IN THE CHINESE COUNTRYSIDE 55–60 (1980); D. PERKINS & S. YUSUF, RURAL DEVELOPMENT IN CHINA 83–87 (1984).

37 Kueh, *supra* note 33.

38 There seems to be some sentiment for further changes, perhaps in the direction of larger individual farms or some sort of corporate farming since small plots are said to be inefficient. *See China's Agriculture and Reforms: Part 2 ... Excerpts from an Article on China's Agriculture and Rural Industry by Liu Wenpu from the Institute of Rural Development of the Chinese Academy of Social Sciences,* China Daily, May 24, 1986, at 4.

39 This period was selected since it was a time of relative quiet and prosperity. The references are to statutes published in 5 LAWS AND REGULATIONS OF THE PEOPLE'S REPUBLIC OF CHINA (Jan.–June 1957) [hereinafter *Laws and Regulations*]. The tables of contents have been published in T.T. HSIA, GUIDE TO SELECTED LEGAL SOURCES OF THE PEOPLE'S REPUBLIC OF CHINA (1967). The statutes are numbered consecutively throughout all the volumes of the collected statutes. The statute on inventory is no. 942, *Laws and Regulations*, at 172.

40 Laws and Regulations, supra note 39, no. 944, at 173.

41 *Id.* no. 946.

42 *Id.* no. 951.

43 *Id.* no. 975a, at 175.

44 *Id.* no. 967.

45 *Id.* no. 992, at 177.

46 *Id.* no. 981, at 176.

47 *Id.* no. 996, at 177.

48 *Id.* no. 1009, at 179.

49 *Id.* no. 1012.

50 *Id.* no. 1013.

51 *Id.* no. 1023, at 180.

52 *Id.* no. 1030, at 181.

53 *See* Jones, *supra* note 26, at 3; Jones, *On the Campaign Trail in China,* 5 REV. SOCIALIST L. 457 (1979). The former article discusses the types of statutes mentioned here. The latter discusses the campaign as a type of legal procedure by way of a book review.

54 *See New Law Aims to Halt Land Waste,* China Daily, July 4, 1986, at 4.

55 For a report on current progress and an indication that it will go on, see *Family Planning Improves,* 29 BEIJING REV. 4 (July 14, 1986). For a more sensational account, see S. MOSHER, BROKEN EARTH 224–61 (1983).

56 In our country there are many informal legal systems. Commercial matters are often dealt with by custom and extrajudicial dispute-settling mechanisms. Indeed, the

commercial law of our formal system was originally created by merchants acting among themselves, and was called the law merchant. *See* Jones, *An Inquiry into the History of the Adjudication of Mercantile Disputes in Great Britain and the United States*, 25 U. CHI. L. REV. 445 (1958). There are probably more determinations of the validity of marriages, legitimacy of children and the like within the administrative agencies that deal with pensions and survivors' benefits, such as the Veterans Administration and the Social Security Administration, than the courts ever see. In theory these decisions are subject to judicial review, but such review is so rare as to be insignificant. Hence a whole extrajudicial legal system has developed.

57 *Cases* is one such book. *Supra* note 35. It was published by what used to be the Beijing Institute of Politics and Law, now the Chinese University of Political Science and Law.

58 The principal subject for civil jurisdiction is divorce. See *Divorces Come Out Top in Civil Cases*, China Daily, July 9, 1986, at 4, where it is said that divorce has constituted 30–40 per cent of the total. Chinese law students who have spent their fourth year practicum in civil courts have told me that the great majority of the cases involve divorce and succession.

59 *Cases, supra* note 35.

60 *Id.* case no. 72, at 138 ("defendant sold one-and-one-half rooms").

61 *Id.* ("Tong Lian X inherited the two rooms that were handed down"). See also *id.* case no. 19, at 56, a succession case in which a number of relatives argued over the distribution of an estate.

62 *Id.* case no. 46, at 111 ("He XX bought a private residence with two rooms.... Fu XX had rented one of the rooms prior to purchase").

63 *Id.* case no. 53, at 122. A light industry company sold a set of tools to an engineering construction company.

64 *Id.* case no. 35A, at 90. Minor children caused physical injury. Their parents were held liable.

65 *Id.* case no. 68, at 132. A farm asked an automobile-parts factory to buy iron plates for it, and gave a check to be filled in by the agent.

66 *See, e.g., id.* case no. 97, at 151. The defendant owned a house which she had given to the government during the Cultural Revolution (presumably because she was forced to). A portion had been rented out before being transferred to the state, and the state continued to rent it to the same tenant. When he moved out, having exchanged it with one Deng, the defendant occupied it—relying on policies for returning property seized during the Cultural Revolution to its former owners. See also *id.* case no. 5, at 29, where the court held that there could be no inheritance right to rented property. See also *id.* case no. 50, at 118, 119, where the editors comment, "The privately constructed [house] is an object that cannot be transferred in civil law, therefore the sale has no effect."

67 *See* table of contents, *id.* at 1.

68 *Id.* case no. 62, at 129.

69 One of the first ten cases in the original is omitted from the translation.

70 *Id.* case no. 1, at 24.

71 *Id.* case no. 2, at 26.

72 *Id.* case no. 3, at 27.

73 *Id.* case no. 4, at 28.

74 *Id.* case no. 5, at 29.

75 *Id.* case no. 6, at 30.

76 *Id.* case no. 7, at 32.

77 *Id.* case no. 8, at 33.

78 *Id.* case no. 10, at 34.

79 *Id.* case no. 11, at 37.

80 *Id.* case no. 12, at 26.

81 *Id.* case no. 7, at 33.

82 *Id.* case no. 3, at 27.

83 *Id.* case no. 10, at 34.

84 *Id.* case no. 7, at 32.

85 *Id.* case no. 6, at 30.

86 *Id.* case no. 35A, at 90.

87 *Id.* case no. 15, at 46.

88 To be sure, the Constitution states that there are three kinds of property: state and collective, Art. 6, and private, Art. 13. The Constitution also provides that the land in cities is owned by the state. Art. 100. This is confirmed in case no. 41, *Cases, supra* note 35, at 104, 109. But if one accepts the statement in the Restatement that property consists of "legal relations between persons with respect to a thing," RESTATEMENT OF PROPERTY, introductory note, then it is clear that private persons and collectives can have rights of some sort to land, to say nothing of chattels. These are evidently quite complex, and as yet unanalyzed.

89 H.S. MAINE, EARLY LAW AND CUSTOM 389 (1883).

90 Thus, in the ten cases, there were the following results: in the first case of a dispute over trespass to land where the owner, defendant, pulled down a building constructed by the plaintiff, the defendant was recognized as owner of the land but had to let plaintiff use it until defendant needed it. Meantime defendant had to rebuild the building. The result was reached after much work to change the attitudes of the parties. In the second case, the demand for payment of a loan, the facts of the loan were proved, the evidence of defenses was no good and the creditor prevailed. In the third case, the claim for hospital expenses, the court made out a repayment schedule. In the action of a landlord production brigade against an individual to recover possession of rooms, which the defendant had occupied during the Cultural Revolution, the plaintiff won. Defendant was ordered to deliver possession. The claim of the niece who sought to obtain part of the compensation her uncle had received for being forced to vacate her grandfather's rented housing during the Cultural Revolution was rejected without any reasons being given by the trial court. The appellate court stated that her suit was unjustified since she had no property interest in the premises, but the matter should have been decided by the trial court. In an action to force the adopting parents to keep the adopted child, mediation was tried and failed. The court decided that the adoption was valid, but the natural mother had made a contribution to the child's support which seemed to be important. The quality (breach-of-warranty) dispute between Nippon Steel and Baoshan Steel was worked out by agreement. When the drawer of bad checks refused to appear in court to answer a claim by the payee, the court ordered the sum to be charged against its account. In the case where the building sued for back rent withheld in a rent strike, the main purpose of bringing the action—and particularly of having it tried publicly—was stated to be to eliminate the causes of the situation. Intensive "education" was carried on against the striker and his family to make them see the error of their ways. The striker made a self-criticism in open court "and the masses all said this was an excellent handling of the case... . Among the households that occupied the top floors of buildings 35 and 36, there is not one that owes back rent." In the case of the bill that had been overdue for ten years, the "Economic Chamber, on the basis of investigating the facts clearly, first worked on the thinking of the leadership of the defendant unit." It granted the plaintiff's basic request, but denied the claim for expenses incurred in trying to collect the debt.

91 This is the theme of the Constitution. The Preamble declares that "The basic task of the nation in the years to come is to concentrate its effort on socialist modernization," utilizing "a broad patriotic united front." "The exploiting classes as such have been eliminated," although the class struggle will continue to exist within certain limits.

92 *See* Pye, *On Chinese Pragmatism in the 1980's*, 106 CHINA Q. 208 (1986).

93 *Id.* at 210, 211.

94 Prior to the effective date of the BGB on January 1, 1900, in many parts of Germany there was no general codification. Courts, in consequence, applied "Roman private law—in the form in which it had obtained formal recognition as the common law [Gemeinrecht] of Germany." R. SOHM, THE INSTITUTES 5 (3d ed. Ledlie trans. 1907). This consisted of the original Roman law texts, canon law, legal treatises and usage. *Id.* at 3. *See also* LAWSON, *supra* note 13, at 40–41 (1953).

95 The principal collection of Chinese customs with which I am acquainted is the *Min-shang Shi Xigukan Diaocha Baogao Lu* (Report on Investigation of Civil and Commercial Customs) published in 1930 in Nanking. The original is not available to me now, although I have seen it. It is partially translated in German in E.J.M. KROKER, DIE AMTLICHE SAMLUNG CHINE-SISCHER RECHTSGEWOHNHEITEN (1965). These customs are very precise, and contain detailed rules on such matters as sale. Thus, in the prefecture of Qing-yuan in Zhili province, in the case of a sale there was the rule "In the case of lease three, sale, four." This meant delivery of the property had to be made within three months of the conclusion of a lease contract, and within four months of a sale contract. *Id.* vol. 1, at 103. In English law, one has only to think of gavelkind. Peasants in Kent knew exactly who took when the old man died.

96 The Taiwanese treatises are available in PRC libraries.

97 There is some confirmation for this in the statements made at the time of the adoption of the General Provisions. For example, a newspaper editorial states: "Civil law rules and regulations have crystallized many of the preliminary achievements of these reforms [apparently economic reforms]. By elaborating their philosophies in legal terms, China is in fact preparing for even greater reforms." China Daily, May 3, 1986, at 4.

98 O. SCHELL, TO GET RICH IS GLORIOUS (1984).

99 Both of these elements are present in the rules on juristic persons. Section 36 provides for the legal personality of organizations. General Provisions, *supra* note 3. Section 48 provides, in effect, for liability limited to the assets of the juristic person.

100 This is recognized for partnerships. *Id.* § 35. It is also recognized for joint ventures, which are not juristic persons and which "by the provision of law or agreement, assume joint liability." *Id.* § 52.

101 The 1982 constitution is the fifth since 1949, if one counts the Common Program as a constitution.

102 *See* Kueh, *supra* note 35. They are, furthermore, implicitly recognized by the Constitution, Art. 11. It provides: "The state protects the lawful interests of the individual economy."

103 *See supra* note 29.

104 The term translated "enterprise" seems to have the connotation of an organization that engages in what we would term business.

105 The examples in the text are those given to me by Chinese as representative of institutions that would be included in § 56. General Provisions, *supra* note 3.

106 Indeed, case no. 43, *Cases, supra* note 35, at 105, discusses some nuances of the concept of juristic person. A party organization may engage in limited civil law acts such as "buying commercial products," but the production brigade is a juristic person. As to the status as a juristic person of a state administrative office (a civil defense office), see *id.* case no. 41, at 104.

107 *See* Ioffe, *supra* note 7, at 114, 115.

108 *Id.*

109 W. FLUME, DAS RECHTSGESCHAFT 23 (1965).

110 *See* Jiang Ping, *supra* note 2. Professor Jiang writes, "The principle of self-determination of the will of capitalist law is shown in agreements between the

parties are law" [presumably a reference to French Civil Code § 1134]. He states "that what this means is that many rules, especially in contracts, are determined by the volition of the parties." He goes on, "Our country's General Provisions of Civil Law is compulsory," and hence is not the same at all as systems based on voluntariness. *Id.* at 6. The entire tone of the article seems to betoken a lot of opposition from "leftists" whom the author is trying to get around.

111 It is said there were about 20,000 lawyers in China in 1986. Leung, *The Emergence of the Legal Profession in the People's Republic of China* 6 N.Y.L. SCH. J. INT'L & COMP. L. 275, 285 (1985). Twelve thousand lawyers are employed full-time. I think these figures may be inflated.

112 Several of the cases involve fact situations that go back to the Cultural Revolution. Case no. 83 involves a 1966 boundary dispute that was mediated at that time. *Cases, supra* note 37, at 143. One party applied to build on the land in 1968. In Case no. 81, there is mention of rent received from 1967 to 1972. *Id.* at 140, 142. In Case no. 32, there is reference to a 1969 marriage. *Id.* at 121. The privately built house in Case no. 50 was built in 1968. *Id.* at 118. A house was sold in 1969 in Case no. 49. *Id.* at 117. The transaction that gave rise to the bill overdue for ten years cited in the text as case number ten arose in 1969. Case no. 11, *id.* at 37.

113 For example, neither the official introduction of the General Provisions to the National People's Congress, *supra* note 2, nor the article by Professor Jiang, *supra* note 2, deals with the way the code will be used in fact. Neither mentions the obvious foreign derivation. Yet all the Chinese jurists I have talked to are perfectly aware of the German influence and cheerfully admit to making use of Taiwanese materials.

36

FROM PUBLIC TO PRIVATE

The newly enacted Chinese property law and the protection of property rights in China

Mo Zhang*

Source: *Berkeley Business Law Journal* 5:2 (2008): 317–363.

Abstract

Protection of Property Rights has become a pressing issue in China since the country strived to move from a planned economy to a market economy in late 1970s. The passage of the Property Law of China on March 16, 2007 marked an historic change in the country from public to private with respect to property rights. Effective on October 1, 2007, the Property Law for the first time in Chinese history grants an equal protection to both public and private properties, breaking up the orthodox ideology in favor of public ownership against private ownership and individual liberty.

With a notable civil law tradition, the Property Law is intended to set forth comprehensive rules regulating creation, alteration, alienation as well as termination of property rights, and protecting private property rights in China, a country where the public or state ownership is still playing a leading role in the nation's economy. Many aspects of the Property Law, which are different from those in other countries, particularly common law countries, are unique not only in their content but also in their application. The land use rights typically reflect a Chinese reality, in that the ownership of land is separated from the possession and use of it.

Adoption of the Property Law in China is a substantial step toward protection of private property rights in the nation. The greatest challenge facing the country, however, is how to enforce the law so that the private property rights are effectively protected, especially in situations where public ownership is involved. The "Nail House" syndrome that has spread across the country indeed raises the serious issue of compensation in cases of government takings. Whether or not compensation for takings will be just and reasonable remains to be answered.

I Introduction

The *Book of Songs* (also translated as the *Book of Poetry* or *Book of Odes*), a collection of Chinese folk songs describing part of China's history during the period of West Zhou (1100 to 770 BC),[1] contains a song named "*Bei Shan*" (North Mountain). The song includes a very famous verse: "All land under the heaven belongs to the King, and all people on the earth are the subjects of the King."[2] The verse was widely cited in later history and even today because it stated the view that a ruler is not only the governor of the people, but also the sole owner of the land of the country.[3]

Indeed, for over two thousand years in China, it was well-established that the emperor had the right to determine the ultimate fate of all kinds of property in the country. With regard to an individual person, an axiom from the governing Confucian rites held that if the ruler wanted a subject to die, the subject must die.[4] Thus, the emperor was in control of both property and the very lives of his citizens. Since Confucianism was adopted as the orthodox state ideology during the Han Dynasty (206 BC to 220 AD),[5] the Confucian rites have become the highest moral standard and fundamental legislative principles in China.[6] Until the fall of the Qing Dynasty (1644–1911), there had been a strong belief that everything was at the mercy of the emperor.[7] Chinese history books have commonly portrayed the reality that when an official is removed from office, the government may conduct a thorough search of his residence without notice and may confiscate his property without a hearing. .[8]

The history of China reveals that the concept of private property was never really developed in the country's past, as private ownership scarcely reached the level of being properly respected and legally protected. Even after the Republic of China—a government structured to a great extent under the ideas of western democracy and liberty—was established in 1911, the concept of private property continued to receive little attention or legislative protection due to chaotic battles amongst Chinese warlords. Under Chiang Kai-shek (1887–1975), who reigned from 1927 to 1949, a civil code was adopted in 1930. The 1930 Civil Code consisted of five parts, with Part III dealing with "Rights over Things" (a civil law concept for "Property").[9] Unfortunately, the 1930 Civil Code was not applied due to Japanese occupation, followed by China's eight-year war against Japan and then its three-year civil war. In 1949, when the Communist party came into power, the 1930 Civil Code along with five other codes were entirely annulled.[10]

From 1949 to 1976, China experienced a painful period of internal class struggle in Chairman Mao's era.[11] Driven by the former Soviet Union model and socialist ideology, Mao pushed very hard for a system that would diminish both private ownership and individualism. As a result, private interests and private property rights became synonymous with capitalism and the bourgeoisie—both enemies of socialism. During this period, people were trained to follow the lead of the proletariat (meaning the class of people with no assets or property) and do whatever the Communist party commanded. This made it impossible for Chinese citizens to make any claims of property rights against the government since the government could take away all private property, even at the whim of a low-level officer. The ten-year Cultural Revolution stripped the people of China still further, if not completely, of any private property and property rights.[12]

After 1978, when the country adopted its famous "Opening-Door" policy and undertook vast economic reforms, China entered into a stage of lining up with the rest of the world and shifting from its rigid planned economy to a market economy. Ever since, the shift has dramatically changed the way people think about public interest *vis-à-vis* private interest. A striking consequence is that the concepts of freedom and individual liberty are no longer taboo in the country. For nearly three decades, people in China began to regain consciousness of their private property rights and sought further protection of these rights. Private property gradually gained its independence from public property.

On March 16, 2007, the long awaited and highly debated Property Law of China passed the National People Congress (NPC) after a fourteen-year legislative marathon.[13] Effective since October 1, 2007, the Property Law has been widely hailed in the country as a milestone of modern Chinese history, granting legal protection to private property rights.[14] Indeed, the Property Law is a significant piece of legislation in China because it fills in the country's "legal blank" with regard to private property and property in general. Furthermore, it helps enhance the legal infrastructure of the country by establishing a framework that is badly needed for the regulation and protection of property rights. Perhaps more importantly, the Property Law reinforces the inviolable nature of private property in China, a concept that was constantly denied in the country until 2004, when the 1982 Constitution was amended for the fourth time.[15]

The Property Law is intended to be comprehensive legislation on property. It contains five parts and nineteen chapters consisting of 247 articles in total. The five parts include "General Provisions," "Ownership," "Usufructuary Right," "Right of Security Interest," and "Possession." The "General Provisions" cover basic principles as well as creation, alteration, alienation, termination, and protection of property rights. "Ownership" covers state ownership, collective and private ownership, partitioned ownership of buildings, neighbor relationships, and common ownership. "Usufructuary Right" deals with rights related to contracted management of land, land use for construction, and land use for housing and easements. The "Right of Security Interest" concerns the rights involving mortgages, pledges, and liens. "Possession" has to do with contractual possession, remedies for property damage, the right to accrued interests, and restitution.

However, it is important to note that in China, as in many other civil law countries, the term "*res*" (things) is commonly used to refer to property and as such the property rights are normally phrased as "real rights" (*jura in re*). One possible reason for this is that the term "property" is considered overly broad, as it could potentially include anything of value.[16] Meanwhile, "things" generally has a narrower definition, referring to tangibles and intangibles of certain economic value.[17] In this context, a more restrictive definition limits the thing to tangibles or corporeal *res*.[18] Although some argue that the use of the term "things" rather than "property" is merely a matter of Chinese tradition,[19] it is important to note that under the definition of "thing," creditor rights would not be regarded as a "thing "or *res*," but such rights may be deemed a kind of "property."[20]

Under the civil law tradition, the law regulating civil matters has two major components: one dealing with "things" and the other dealing with "obligations." Thus, the law of "things" is meant to protect the rights over property against any other person, while the law of obligations has a function of safeguarding the right of a creditor against a debtor. In common law countries, no such line seems to exist as to the laws regulating property and obligations. Despite the difference, however, it is without question that "things" are property and "real rights" are property rights. In this context, and also to avoid confusion, this Article uses the term "property law" instead of "real rights law," as commonly used in China.

The objective of this Article is to offer an analytical review of Chinese property law, with the central theme focused on the protection of private property rights. Part II of the Article discusses how the concept of private property emerged and evolved recently in China along with the economic reform of the country, as well as the ideological change in the nation toward the value of private interest and personal liberty. Part III provides an analysis on the equal protection issue relating to private property as opposed to the state and collective property. Part IV examines key property principles embedded in the Property Law and the significance of these principles in their application to property rights, including some comparisons to American property law. In addition, the Chinese reality with regard to property rights and the right to use the land in contrast to the ownership will be addressed. Part V takes a special look at the "Nail House" phenomenon arising from the disputes over the taking of private property, discussing compensation and other remaining issues facing the Property Law.

This Article does not attempt to simply browse or describe provisions of the Property Law, but rather it focuses on certain important principles and rules that typically reflect the unique characteristics of the Property Law, while analyzing how such principles and rules are to be applied and what impacts they may have on the development of a property system in China. In conclusion, Part VI of the Article suggests that the adoption of the Property Law of China (at least in its text) brings an end to the ignorance of private property rights in the country and represents a significant move from public to private in property rights protection. The most important point is that the Property Law places private property on equal footing with public property. One issue that lies ahead, however, is the debate over how to implement the Property Law in a manner that properly respects and protects private property and private property rights.

II Liberty v. government control: recognition of private property rights

In the Western world, property is a concept more closely associated with individual entitlement[21] or private assets that are individually owned.[22] In the United States, for example, the concept of property denotes a citizen's right to possess, use, and dispose of his property.[23] Property rights are generally understood as held by individuals, making the concept of ownership by a social collective virtually unknown.[24] In the Anglo-Saxon legal tradition, the right of property, the right of life, and the right of liberty are all deemed fundamental.[25]

This is certainly not the case in China. Historically, China was a country where the "imperial power" or the "power of emperor" was the supreme authority of the land. Pursuant to Confucianism, to rule a country is like ruling a family. The father has absolute power to decide everything for the family, and each individual member in the family must subordinate his or her own interest to the family interest. This was imperative to holding the family together, and all individuals within the family were subject to the paternal power. Thus, in a society structured on the stratification order of familism or kinship,[26] the individual's way of life, rights, and obligations were not decided in the way best to benefit the individual. Instead, rights and obligations were determined by the need of the rulers or the government.[27]

Since the Qin Dynasty (221–206 BC), each Chinese dynasty followed a pattern of having a highly-centralized state power with an easy reach over every corner of the country and ultimate control of the people. Even after the dethronement of the last emperor in 1911, many revolutionaries, including Dr. Sun Yat-sen and his followers, still believed that it was necessary to establish a government with an "all-purpose" function, with each individual under government power, ready to sacrifice personal interests in order to preserve such power.[28] Although Dr. Sun Yat-sen based his idea of revolution on nationalism, democracy, and equalization, he actually tried to promote a so-called "guided democracy," because he believed that people in China were not ready yet to exercise democracy.[29]

After the founding of the People's Republic of China in 1949, socialism became the dominant force in the nation. In Chairman Mao's theory, the core of socialism was public ownership. One idea that was widely upheld is a concept translated from one of Lenin's books that became a creed in China for many years: "We do not recognize anything private."[30] Under Mao's guidance, a movement called the "socialist transformation" took place in the country during the mid-1950s. All private properties were either confiscated or transformed into pubic use, and all private ownerships were replaced by public ownerships.[31]

Therefore in Chinese history, a system or institution of private property never developed, and the right of property never became a fundamental right of individuals. For decades after the birth of People's Republic of China, the country was structured both politically and economically for the sole promotion of public ownership, because it was believed that only public ownership could keep China on the socialist track. Maintenance of government control and Communist party leadership was deemed of paramount importance over individual rights.[32] Concepts such as individual liberty, freedom, or democracy were considered capitalist and evil, and everyone from an early age was educated to be prepared to give their lives for the cause of Communism, despite the fact that few people really understood what Communism was. Thus, during that period, people barely had anything that could be claimed and recognized as privately owned.

As noted, not until 1978 when the economic reform took place in China did private ownership become a subject of discussion. But it still took another twenty-six years for the country to finally recognize private property rights in 2004. There are various reasons for this slow pace of recognition, but perhaps the most significant is the clash between the drives for socialism and the concerns about capitalism. More specifically, there had always been heavy debates in the country among scholars and legislators over private rights, individual liberty, and private property. At the c enter of the debate is how to keep the socialist ideology untarnished while maintaining the stability of state control and public ownership.

A Private rights v. socialist ideology

China is known as a socialist country. By definition, the term "socialism" originally referred to the ideology aimed at improving society through collective and egalitarian action.[33] Applied in China, however, socialism seemed to be more closely associated with political endeavor than social needs, and at most times was ill-defined. Under Mao's interpretation, the very purpose of socialism was to eliminate all capitalist elements and abolish all exploitation systems.[34] Affected by the strong belief that "only socialism may save China," Mao adopted a policy in early 1949 of "leaning to one side" for the country as a commitment to the Socialist bloc let by the former Soviet Union.[35]

Thus, Chinese socialism was basically Soviet-style. China had a centrally planned economy, and the state owned all of the means of production. Marxism-Leninism became the ruling ideology of the country and was regarded as universal truth. Strikingly, through a "socialist transformation," all industries were nationalized and agriculture was collectivized for the purpose of establishing public ownership throughout the nation at an accelerated pace during the country's First Five-Year Plan (1953–1957).[36] As a result, private enterprise was virtually extinguished and private ownership was rooted out.[37]

Ideologically, the socialist pursuit was uniformly imposed upon everyone by the coercive power of the government. At that time, a popular social norm was that no individual could claim private rights other than to make selfless dedication to the common good. All personal interests were subordinated to the public or state need. The illusion that everyone would be better off without pursuing private interests was promulgated among the general public. A classic model was the one of "being the first to bear hardship but the last to enjoy life"—supporting the idea of giving up anything individual for the endeavor of socialist construction. Hence, individual rights were deemed to be at odds with socialism, as private property was considered as an element dangerous to public ownership.

Therefore, public ownership was the sole ownership in China for many years, including collective and state ownership. In the meantime, an extremely strong bias against individual rights and private ownership developed, as people were led to believe that individual rights and socialist ideology were mutually exclusive. Moreover, under Mao's revolutionary doctrine, people were divided by "class": whoever followed the Communist party's leadership and stayed with socialist public ownership was a "revolutionary." All others were deemed "counter-revolutionary." Such classification was further radicalized during the ten-year mess of the Cultural Revolution (1966–1976), which was meant to get rid of all "capitalist roaders."[38] One of the charges against such capitalist roaders was their sympathy towards individual rights and private ownership.[39]

After 1978, when the economic reform began in the country, people started to question Mao's socialist theory and wonder whether private rights should be respected in the course of development of socialism in China—particularly during the nationwide discussion in the late 1970s about "Practice as the Sole Criterion for Testing the Truth," a theme advanced to reevaluate Mao and his legacy.[40] The country finally woke up from blind worship of Mao and the superstition of Maoism, as people were liberalized from a long period of ideological confinement. Finally, they felt free to explore different thoughts. This led to a restoration of the public faith in private rights.

Unfortunately, the discussion on the criterion of truth was used more often to help the victims of Mao's purge regain their power than to promote liberal ideas in the nation. Concerned about the official ideology of the country[41] and the leadership of the party, Deng Xiaoping, though determined to carry on the economy reform, attempted to unify the country politically by setting forth the so-called "the Four Cardinal Principles" as the core value of the nation.[42] Because of their stubborn nature and vague content, the Four Cardinal Principles actually became an obstacle to further liberalizing people's thinking, creating fear among the public of being labeled "anti-socialist."[43] With this in mind, the Chinese people remained uncomfortable using the term "private" when discussing ownership. A major concern was that using the word "private" might be interpreted as capitalism.

Nevertheless, the economic reform changed China in an unprecedented manner. One significant change was that the reform brought an end to the single public ownership structure of the country and generated public rethinking about socialism. As part of the reform, the country was repositioned at the "preliminary stage of socialism" in the early 1980s, meaning an underdeveloped commodity economy.[44] A notable result was the country's move from planned economy to market economy and from pure public ownership to co-existence of multi-ownerships. In 1992, the ultimate goal of economic reform was reset to the establishment of a system of a socialist market economy.[45] Although the term "socialist market economy" did not seem to be clearly defined, the market economy was not the symbol of capitalism anymore in China.

A direct impact of the economic reform is the ideological change of the country. The infusion of the market concept ignited social desire for materialism or getting rich,[46] and the existence of non-public ownership gave rise to the need to respect private rights.[47] In 1986, China adopted the General Principles of Civil Law of China (the Civil Code), whose stated purpose was protection of lawful civil rights and the interests of citizens.[48] Despite the fact that the Civil Code still shied away from using the term "private rights" at the time of its enactment, a common belief that has developed ever since is that private rights ought to be protected no matter what the socialist ideology is about.

It should be noted that with its reform endeavor, China is now on course to develop a so-called "socialism with Chinese characteristics." What the "Chinese characteristics" exactly mean is ambiguous, but they obviously serve a two-fold goal. First, China needs to show to the world that the country has actually departed from the Mao socialist ideology and has become more rational in respecting private rights, while maintaining state ownership in a dominant position. Secondly, the Communist party has a profound interest in keeping its authority unchallenged and wants to be able to hold the reins of the country in its own way.

B Individual liberty v. state power

Closely related to, but different from, private rights is the concept of individual or personal liberty. They are related because without rights there would be no liberty—and vice versa.[49] On many occasions, the two together are simply termed "liberty rights."[50] However, they differ in that private rights primarily deal with what people may own or have as individuals, while personal liberty is more concerned with how much people may own or how far their private rights may reach.[51] In the United States, liberty is generally defined as freedom from all restraints except those that are justly imposed by law.[52] This includes the right to be free of arbitrary physical restraint or servitude and the right of citizens to be free to use their facilities in all lawful ways; to live and work where they will; to earn their livelihood by any lawful calling; and to pursue any livelihood or vocation.[53]

In Western jurisprudence, liberty and property are related to each other so intimately that "you can't give up one without losing the other."[54] It is believed that property rights are the cornerstone of liberty because the right to own and use private property is among the most essential human rights and is the essential basis for economic growth.[55] A popular dictum by Daniel Webster is that no other rights are safe where property is not safe.[56] Thus, in the context of property, liberty explicitly means two things: right to private property and freedom against arbitrary interference by government.[57] Although the scope of property rights is allocated and defined by law, which means that government power is necessary to the creation of property rights,[58] the rights are so fundamental to individuals that no government may interfere with them without due process of law.[59]

Individual liberty and private property rights unfortunately had a different fate in China. Although Mencius (372–289 BC), the Chinese philosopher, understood that people would not have a persistent life if their private property was not secure,[60] his words were never taken seriously because of the country's historical structure based on a highly centralized government and a self-sufficient natural economy where people heavily relied on the benevolence of government. In other words, in its thousands of years of history, China never reached the point of becoming such a civil society as the one developed in the West to uphold individual liberty and democracy.[61] As a result, people in China seldom saw the rise of private property, while state control remained the center of attention.

A conceptual difference between China and the West is the basic view of rights in general. In China, few inalienable rights exist for individuals. Whatever rights are recognized are considered to be given or granted. In the West, it is widely accepted as self-evident that people are endowed with inherent and inalienable rights—including life, liberty, and the pursuit of happiness.[62] The substantial difference is that when the rights are deemed to be given or granted, they may be taken away at the pleasure of government, but if the rights are considered inherent, they may not be alienated or deprived of without a compelling reason and a just process.

For a long time after the Communist party took power in China in 1949, maintenance of state ownership and the leadership of the Communist party was China's top priority. In an effort to carry out the "class struggle" against capitalism and the bourgeoisie, China was led into a course of construction of socialism to which all citizens must devote. Thus, during that period, individual liberty was regarded as a bourgeois pursuit, and democracy was labeled a capitalist idea. A typical misconception created among the public was that to seek individual liberty was to attempt to diminish the state control or to reverse the socialist path of the country—an act considered completely intolerable.[63]

However, there were two occasions after 1949 during which China was considered to be at the edge of moving toward individual liberty and democracy. The first occurred during 1956 to 1957, when the country was called upon to help the Communist party with the "party rectification," and people were encouraged to freely and openly express their view on the Communist party's policies and the role of government. Inspired by the slogan, "Let a hundred flowers blossom and a hundred schools of thought contend," (or the "Double Hundred Policy"), intellectuals took the lead in criticizing the party and government for their lack of respect toward individual liberty and private interests and excessive state control. Many strongly advocated a liberalized political climate and the restoration of freedom.[64]

This widespread intellectual criticism, however, was soon viewed as an attempt to undermine the Communist party leadership and to invite capitalism into China. Consequently, a nationwide crackdown known as the Anti-Rightist Campaign was launched to suppress all divergent thoughts. Many critics were jailed or sent to labor camps. Suddenly, the rising voice for individual liberty was silenced, and the emerging democratic atmosphere vanished. Although the

Double Hundred Policy may have produced a certain sobering effect on the leadership,[65] a significant drawback of the Anti-Rightist Campaign was that the Communist party's exclusive control was reinforced[66] and Mao's socialism was firmly reestablished as the country's orthodox ideology.[67]

The second occasion was the student movement in the late 1980s. Motivated by the liberal ideas of then-ousted leader and reformer Hu Yaobang (1915–1989),[68] and outrage over ever-spiraling government corruption, university students held open demonstrations in Beijing and many other cities, calling for political reform. The strongest themes of the demonstrations were liberty and democracy—concepts students apparently learned from the West during the decade of economic reform. Unfortunately, the demonstrations ended with bloodshed in June 1989, followed by a countrywide cleanup of the "idea of bourgeois liberalization"—a term used to refer to any attempt to depart from the Four Cardinal Principles.

However, a major difference between the 1950s Anti-Rightist Campaign and the 1980s repression of student demonstration was that the former actually sent the country into a dark period in which the desire for individual liberty was frozen, while the latter never had the effect of preventing people from thinking differently. As a matter of fact, the ongoing economic reform not only increased the public desire for change, but also pushed the Communist leadership to become more tolerant toward ideas prevalent in the West. Even Deng Xiaoping, who played a decisive role in the crackdown of the 1980s student demonstration, asked for an end to the debate over whether China was headed in a socialist or capitalist direction, to help clear up ambiguity over the reforms.[69]

The most obvious change in China to come out of this reform has been the acceptance of a market economy based on private ownership and free enterprise.[70] To maintain its socialist image, however, China termed it a "socialist market economy," attempting to tie public ownership to a market economy. Nevertheless, the terminology is not nearly as relevant as the actual introduction of a market economy in China. As a result, China began to recognize individual liberty and private ownership, even imposing certain restraints on governmental power when private interests were concerned.[71]

Behind these changes stands a rethinking of socialist ideology. Many concepts that had been linked to capitalism have been reclassified as necessary elements to the preliminary stage of socialism. The notions of liberty, democracy, and human rights are now considered values consistently pursued by human beings throughout history, instead of the unique characteristics of capitalism alone.[72] This allows China to remain socialist, while embracing individual liberty and private property rights.

C Recognition of private property rights

Legally speaking, private property rights were not officially recognized in China until 2004 when the 1982 Constitution was amended. Since 1949, China has had four constitutions. The first was adopted in 1954,[73] followed by new versions in 1975 and 1978.[74] The current Constitution was adopted in 1982,[75] although it has since been amended four times (in 1988, 1993, 1999, and 2004).[76] Because of their transitional nature, both the 1975 and 1978 Constitutions only existed briefly and therefore are not considered as important as the other two.[77]

The 1954 Constitution was important in China for a number of reasons. It was the first socialist Constitution in China and was meant to hold the country together as it entered into a peaceful period of construction and development after eight years of war against the Japanese and three years of civil war. Secondly, the 1954 Constitution was based on the blueprint of the Common Program—a principal legal document jointly drafted in early 1949 by the Communist party and other parties to serve as an interim or provisional constitution for the new China.[78] One important characteristic of the Common Program was its theme of promoting democracy by granting the citizen ample freedoms, including freedom of speech and freedom of religion.[79] Thirdly, the 1954 Constitution was adopted at a time when China was believed to be on a path, though limited, to building a democratic country, and many provisions in the Constitution reflected to a certain extent democratic ideals.[80] Even Mao himself admitted that it was necessary to have "a broad people's democratic united front composed of all democratic classes, democratic parties and groups, and people's organizations."[81]

As laid out in the 1954 Constitution, China's economic system consisted of four different forms of ownership: state ownership, collective ownership, individual working people ownership, and capitalist ownership.[82] Under the 1954 Constitution, with the state ownership as the core, the other three forms of ownership (particularly the two private ownerships—individual working people ownership and capitalist ownership) were legally recognized and protected, although each faced the possibility of being transformed into state ownership. In this context, the 1954 Constitution was acclaimed by many Chinese constitutional scholars as a socialist constitution with Chinese reality in allowing private ownership to coexist with public forms of ownership.[83]

Unfortunately, but not surprisingly, the 1954 Constitution was never really enforced as intended and died a few years after its passage.[84] This was partly due to inherent flaws in the 1954 Constitution, as whatever forms of democracy were provided in the constitution were to be strictly within the iron framework of the Communist monopoly of power.[85] More significantly, the unlimited controlling force of the Communist party made it ultimately possible for Mao to take the country into a period of lawlessness[86] in which the people's democracy was replaced with Mao's "democratic centralism."[87] The law became merely a weapon used to eliminate capitalism and other counter-revolutionists.[88] Economically, the multi-ownership structure set forth in the 1954 Constitution was abruptly destroyed, leaving public ownership the only form of ownership in the country.[89]

After the death of the 1954 Constitution, private ownership completely disappeared from the country's economy, and no private property rights were recognized. Not until 1988 when China was redefined at the preliminary stage of socialism did private ownership return as a topic of discussion. to allow non-public forms of ownership to exist in order to revive the country, China amended its 1982 Constitution in 1988 to legalize private ownership and to protect private property rights. The 1988 Amendment permitted "the private sector of the economy to exist and develop within the limits prescribed by law,"[90] recognized the private sector of economy as "a supplement to the socialist public economy,"[91] and protected "the lawful rights and interests of the private sector of the economy."[92] In addition, the 1988 Amendment provided for transfer of the right to the use of land among individuals,[93] creating a concept of a transferable property interest that could be privately owned.[94]

The tone of the 1988 Amendment with regard to private property rights was very cautious. It did not use the terms "private property" or "private ownership," but rather the vague term "private economy." In addition, it made the private sector merely a supplement to the country's public economy. Moreover, it granted the state the power to exercise "guidance, supervision and control over the private sector of the economy."[95] At the time the 1982 Constitution was initially amended, China was determined to keep the country on the track of economic reform, but was skeptical of moving away from the road of socialism. Nevertheless, the 1988 Amendment was regarded as a legal watershed for the overall economic reform in China in the sense of legalizing private ownership.[96]

Eleven years later, the 1982 Constitution was further amended in 1999. One significant change in the 1999 Amendment was to treat the "individual, private and other non-public economics" as "major components of the socialist market economy,"[97] a highly notable step forward in granting legal status to a private economy. The latest amendment to the 1982 Constitution was made in 2004. The 2004 Amendment holds that the state "protects the lawful rights and interests of the non-public sectors of the economy such as individual and private sectors of the economy" and "encourages, supports and guides the development of the non-public sectors of the economy,"[98] but also emphasizes that the "citizen's lawful private property is inviolable."[99]

With regard to private property rights, the 2004 Amendment was historical. It was the first time in Chinese history that private property was clearly stated in the country's constitution.[100] More importantly, it was the first time in China that private property was deemed constitutionally inviolable. It is true that the effective protection of the private property rights is dependent upon the mechanism of enforcement of the constitution, but to the extent that "it is the fundamental law of the State and has supreme legal authority,"[101] the constitution indeed provides a safeguard for private property and private property rights. Pursuant to the constitution, the Property Law was adopted to specifically define and protect private property and the rights of private property holders.[102]

Under Article 64 of the Property Law, private property includes lawful income, housing, livelihood goods, production instruments, raw materials, and other moveable and immovable property.[103] This provision is said to be based on

Article 75 of the 1986 Civil Code, where the personal property of a citizen is defined to consist of lawful income, housing, savings, livelihood goods, cultural relics, book materials, woods, livestock, and production materials permitted by law to be owned by the citizen as well as other lawful properties.[104] A big difference between Article 64 of the Property Law and Article 75 of the 1986 Civil Code is that the Property Law explicitly uses the term "private property" while the Civil Code is limited to "personal property" in order to avoid using the term "private." Another difference is that the Property Law adopts the legal term "private person," instead of the political term "citizen," because "private person" includes both citizens and non-citizens. Still, it is necessary to consider the inclusion of the word "lawful." Although "lawful" is used to exclude any unlawfully gained income or property, the word indeed provides leeway for the government to define what is lawful and what is not.

III Private property v. public property: an outcry for equal protection

Under the Chinese Legislation Law, the enactment of a law at the national level requires three readings by the Standing Committee of the NPC before the drafting of the law is submitted to the general meeting of the NPC for a vote by all delegates attending the meeting.[105] With regard to the Property Law, there were eight readings in the Standing Committee before the NPC passed it in March 2007.[106] The delay and debate were not only because the Property Law is vitally important to both the general public and the nation, but also because many issues involved at the time of drafting were so controversial that hardly any consensus could be reached.

One of the most controversial issues was the legal status of private property. At the heart of the issue was whether private and public property should be treated and protected equally. Underlying this question is the debate over the conception of "public" and "private." A significant impact of the economic reform is that it broke up the monopoly of public ownership and brought into China's economic system the coexistence of multiple forms of ownership. But views differed sharply with respect to the legal treatment of private property and private property rights, though nobody challenged the legality of the existence of private ownership anymore.

A Supremacy of public ownership

It has been observed that socialist economies were all centered on public ownership,[107] but the dominance of public ownership was unrealistically overstated for decades in China so that the entire country was dragged into efforts to maintain and defend public ownership against any non-public ownership—even at the cost of nearly driving the nation to bankruptcy.[108] This practice had the effect of convincing the Chinese people that public ownership is superior to all other forms of ownership, even if non-public forms of ownership are allowed to coexist with public ownership.[109]

From a legal perspective, the superiority of public ownership was first stressed in the 1954 Constitution. Under Article 6 of the 1954 Constitution, ownership by the whole people, represented by the state-run economy, was "the leading force in the national economy and the material foundation of the socialist transformation." The state was determined to ensure "the priority of the development of the State-run economy."[110] The 1975 Constitution not only emphasized the leading force of the state-run economy, but also added the principle that "socialist public property is inviolable."[111] This principle was then carried over verbatim into the 1978 Constitution.[112]

The 1982 Constitution further emphasizes this principle by adding the word "sacredly," making it read: "socialist public property is sacredly inviolable." Although the reason for the change was not given in the official report on the draft revision of the 1982 Constitution, it is clearly an indication of a more serious stance toward the protection of public property. This stance can also be seen in the 2004 Amendment, in which protection of private property becomes a constitutional mandate. While Article 12 of the 1982 Constitution (as amended in 2004) holds socialist public property as "sacredly inviolable,"[113] Article 13 holds lawful private property of citizens as merely "inviolable."[114] While these two articles differ by only one word, it is clear that public property is more stringently protected than private property in China.[115]

Protection of public property has long been an issue of national concern. Instead of determining whether or not to protect public property, however, China has been debating the best method to protect public property. Behind the issue is concern about the possible erosion of state ownership, particularly when the matter of private property is involved. Since 1979, for example, China has witnessed through its period of economic reform three nationwide major debates, all of which involved the socialist nature of the country and the supremacy of public ownership.[116]

The first debate occurred during 1981 to 1984, when the concept of a socialist commodity economy was introduced and the idea of "relying mainly on the planned economy but using market force as a secondary regulator" was promoted.[117] The center of the debate was whether the public ownership-based planned economy could be regulated by market force.[118] Opponents of market force insisted that a planned economy is not a commodity economy and that the market force is an element of a capitalist economy.[119] The underlying argument was that promotion of a commodity economy would undermine socialist plans and public ownership.[120] The debate ended with the issuance of the Communist Party Central Committee's "Decision on the Reform of Economic Structure" in October 1984,[121] confirming the socialist economy of China to be a "planned commodity economy."[122]

The second debate began in 1989 and lasted until 1992. This debate was triggered by the attempt to lead China into a market economy and centered over whether a market economy would help maintain public ownership and serve the socialist economy. A prevalent view in the past was that a market economy is tied to capitalism, while socialism stands entirely separate from the free market.[123] In order to pave the way for further reform, Den Xiaoping made his famous "Southern Tour,"[124] where he made it clear that a "planned economy is not equivalent to socialism because there is planning under capitalism too; a market economy is not capitalism, because there are markets under socialism too."[125] The crux of Deng's remarks was that a market economy is not an indicator of capitalism. Thanks to Deng, who brought the second debate to an end, the reform entered into the phase of building socialism on a market economy.[126]

The third debate started in 2004 with an argument about the restructuring of state-owned enterprises. The focus of the argument was whether the restructuring would necessarily lead to the draining of the state assets—the backbone of public ownership. The argument then went into a broader question about the nature of the last two decades of economic reform. Concerned about the possible loss of dominance of public ownership, some questioned the legitimacy of the reform and argued that the past reform was *de facto* led by mainstream Western neo-liberalism[127]—in other words, free enterprise and privatization.[128] On this ground, detractors strongly opposed the state's encouragement of developing non-public forms of ownership.[129] In 2006, the Communist Party Central Committee announced its "Decisions on Several Major Issues related to the Building of Socialist Harmonious Society." The "Decisions," which assured the continuing reform in China in the way that some more harmonized measures would be taken,[130] marked a conclusion of the third debate.

Still, these debates between public and private ownership never truly ended. During the drafting of the Property Law, one of the most contentious issues was the treatment and protection of private ownership. Many advocated equal protection, but met resistance from those who strongly held the supremacy of socialist public ownership over all other forms of ownership.[131] Some even cited constitutional language, arguing that protection of private property equal to protection of public property is unconstitutional.[132]

B Constitutionality of equal protection for private property

The constitutionality of providing equal protection to public and private property was openly raised by a professor at the Beijing University Law School. This professor became a prominent opponent of equal protection after writing an "Open Letter" to challenge the constitutionality of granting the private property an equal protection.[133] The Open Letter, which was sent to the Chairman and the Standing Committee of the NPC on August 12, 2005, generated more than a year of legal turmoil with regard to private property protection. It was also believed that the because of the Open Letter, the draft of the Property Law was taken out of the agenda of the 2006 General Meeting of NPC, thus delaying the passage of the Property Law by one year.[134] Although the validity of this belief seems to be questionable, the Open Letter did catch the attention of many Chinese legislators.

The main assertion of the Open Letter was that the draft of the Property Law violated the Constitution and was against basic socialist principles.[135] Trained at a law school in the former Yugoslavia, the author of the Open Letter contended that the draft of the Property Law was unconstitutional because it failed to state that socialist public property is sacredly inviolable and it intended to place both private property and public property on an equal footing.[136] According to the Open Letter, public ownership is the most important difference between socialism and capitalism. It also noted that public ownership and state property are the most important and fundamental bases of safeguarding the property rights of individual people.[137] The Open Letter concluded that the draft of the Property Law was totally contradictory to the socialist tradition and to the concept of the Soviet civil code, as it catered to the falsehoods of Western neo-liberalism.[138]

The Open Letter premised its arguments entirely on Article 12 of 1982 Constitution and Article 73 of the 1986 Civil Code. As discussed above, both of the articles include the principle that "the public property is sacredly inviolable."[139] In the published draft of the Property Law, it was provided that state, collective, and individual ownership are protected by law and any encroachment upon or damage to any of these entities is prohibited.[140] This provision did not single out public property to make it sacredly inviolable, but rather listed public property together with private property to provide them equal legal protection.

The Open Letter denounced the draft for having actually abolished Article 12 of the 1982 Constitution and Article 73 of the 1986 Civil Code, insisting that private property should not be protected to the same extent as public property.[141] One of the major points of the Open Letter was that the privatization in the Property Law would lead to a disparity between rich and poor and would become a source of social instability, eventually destroying the Communist party leadership.[142] The Open Letter did not tie the supposed constitutionality of equal protection to the Constitution itself, instead focusing on socialist orthodoxy and Communist party leadership.

Nevertheless, a vast majority of the Chinese disagreed.[143] Many believed that equal protection would not be unconstitutional if the law did not use the same words or phrases as the Constitution. They believed that granting protection to private protection does not necessarily constitute a denial of protection to public property.[144] In addition, the 1982 Constitution contains a provision encouraging, supporting, and promoting the development of non-public forms of ownership, as the draft of the Property Law actually followed a constitutional spirit.[145] It was further argued that the draft actually highlighted the superior position of public property by emphasizing the special status of state property.[146]

C Equal footing and equal protection: a civil principle

Under general jurisprudence, law can be classified into public law and private law. The public law is the law that regulates the relationship between individuals and the state, while private law is the law that primarily governs the relationships among individuals and entities—or, to use a more generic term, civil relationships.[147] There is no doubt that the Property Law is private law. Despite its being affected one way or the other by the public law, such as the Constitution, the Property Law remains in the domain of private law due to its civil nature, and it is subject to principles that are embodied in private law.

A significant characteristic of private law is that the relationship governed by the law is horizontal. In other words, parties in the relationship maintain a civil status of equal footing and should be dealt equally. Thus, what has become a rudimental principle in private law is that all players in civil matters are equal. Applied to property rights, this principle requires that owners of property shall be equally protected, regardless of the form of ownership. Equal protection is vitally important in China because of the country's long existing bias against private ownership and its government's overreaching power, especially when public property is involved. Many in China believe that without equal protection, public confidence in creating social wealth would be dampened and the very purpose of enacting the Property Law would be frustrated.[148]

Scholars calling for equal protection argue that as an important civil principle, equal protection is unequivocally stated in the 1986 Civil Code and should be embodied in the Property Law. Under Article 3 of the 1986 Civil Code, all parties in civil activities have equal status.[149] The gist of Article 3 is that parties to civil matters should be treated equally.[150] Many addressed equal protection from a constitutional ground and pointed out that equal protection is a constitutional principle in China, because under the Constitution, all people are equal before the law.[151] Without equal protection in property, there would be no value of the equality and individual rights and personal liberty would not be realized.[152]

A popular argument in favor of equal protection rests with the idea of promoting a market economy in China. It is believed that equal protection is essential to the market-based economic system.[153] Therefore, since China is determined to stay with the socialist market economy, it must follow the market rules.[154] One such rule is to grant equal protection to market players, enabling them to enjoy equal rights and assume corresponding responsibilities.[155] This argument was well-received among legislators during their review of the draft of the Property Law. They believed that a market economy demanded equal protection of different property owners and that without equal protection the market economy would fail.[156]

The Property Law follows the majority view and makes equal protection a basic principle of the law of property. Under Article 4 of the Property Law, the property rights of the state, collective, individual, or any other right-holder shall be protected by law and shall not be infringed by any entity or individual.[157] Obviously, Article 4 grants no special status to public property—state or collective. Further, private property is protected in the same manner as public property pursuant to Article 4. Article 4 is clear that a violation of property rights is prohibited, regardless of the type of property owner.

For the purposes of Article 4, equal protection contains at least three elements. The first element is the equal status of property owners. With regard to property rights, nobody shall be discriminated against on the basis of the nature of ownership.[158] This notion is also underscored in Article 3 of the Property Law, which provides that the state protects the equal status and development rights of all market players.[159] The second element is an application of the same rules. It is important that if a dispute over property occurs between the state and an individual, each party has the same right of claim, the same access to legal redress, and is subject to the same rules.[160] The third element is equal liability. Whenever a property right is infringed, the infringer shall bear the same liability, no matter whether the infringer is the state or an individual.[161]

However, it should be noted that Article 4 equal protection may not be used to belittle public ownership. In fact, it is easily discernable that public ownership is placed in a uniquely prominent position. First, the Property Law does not take the single term approach to simply using "property rights" to cover all properties, but instead uses a separate term mechanism to differentiate the state or collective property right from individual or other holder's property rights. Second, the Property Law emphasizes the backbone role of public ownership in the Chinese economy by providing that the state upholds the principal role of public ownership in the nation's economy.[162] Third, there is a general consensus in China that equal protection does not necessarily mean an equal role for public property and that the leading force of public ownership must be maintained.[163]

Of course, it is highly commendable that the Property Law grants equal protection to private property rights. But whether or not private property rights will actually be protected equally to state property in practice is an important question going forward. Given the supremacy of public ownership and the increasing concern about the possible looting of state assets during the process of privatization (or, in less sensitive words, the course of "absorbing private investment"), it remains to be seen how private property rights are to be effectively protected, particularly when public property is at issue (e.g., the acquisition of assets or shares of a government-owned enterprise).

IV Statutory prescription of property rights: civil law tradition and Chinese reality

China is a country whose legal system bears a great deal of civil law tradition. This tradition is also reflected in the Property Law in that many provisions are rooted in the civil code of civil law countries, such as Germany and Japan.[164] Still, considerable references were taken from the practices of the common law system during the drafting of the Property Law.[165] Another aspect from which the civil law tradition is typically visible is that the Property Law, like all other major laws of China, contains "General Provisions" that provide basic principles and rules.

As a national law regulating property, the Property Law is defined to apply to the civil relationships arising from attribution and utilization of the *"res"* or things.[166] Under this definition, the Property Law is meant to govern civil relationships among people with regard to things. These civil relationships are limited to those incurred from attribution and utilization of things. To speak loosely, attribution means the ownership of things and utilization concerns the power over things. Again, it is important to keep in mind that a "civil relationship" denotes a horizontal relationship under which all related parties are equal.[167]

The "General Provisions" of the Property Law have three major parts. The first part states basic principles. The second provides rules concerning creation, alteration, alienation, and termination of property rights. The third part involves protection of property rights.[168] The "General Provisions" are important because the principles and rules prescribed therein not only serve as the grounds for other provisions to rely on, but also have practical significance for courts in applying the Property Law—especially when some provisions are ambiguous. Note, however, that there are certain approaches that are not implicated in the Property Law, though they were extensively discussed during the drafting. In practice, these approaches are likely to be taken into consideration.

A *The* Numerus Clausus *principle*

A well-known civil law principle that governs property is that property rights must be prescribed by law and may not be created by and between parties. This principle is widely stated in civil law countries as the "*Numerus Clausus*," a classic Roman concept meaning that "the number is closed."[169] As applied to property, the *Numerus Clausus* is aimed at excluding the autonomy of the property owner to invent any property interest that is not named or provided by the law.[170] It is considered a substantial limitation on the definition of property implicated in the code.[171] In common law systems, the concept of the *Numerus Clausus* is understood to mean that property rights must conform to certain standardized forms.[172]

The *Numerus Clausus* principle is also provided in the Property Law of China. Pursuant to Article 5 of the Property Law, the kinds and contents of property rights shall be prescribed by law. In other words, without statutory prescription, nothing may be deemed a property right or property interest, and the legal dimensions of property must be within the boundary clearly stated by law.[173] In this context, the provisions concerning property rights are generally compulsory and may not be varied by the conduct of any right owner.[174] But under Article 5 of the Property Law, the principle of *Numerus Clausus* applies only to the types and contents of property. One interpretation is that other aspects—such as the formality of change of ownership, the way to exercise the property right, the method of publicity, and the effect of property rights—need not be included in the *Numerus Clausus*, because they do not involve in the possible creation of property rights or interests.[175]

The idea underlying the *Numerus Clausus* is that a property right is an absolute right or a right against all others.[176] Unlike the contractual right that is related only to relevant parties, the property right is the right between the owner of the right and anyone else.[177] Thus, if an owner is allowed to create property rights or interests at will, the creation would affect all other people.[178] This notion is also accepted in common law to the extent that the *Numerus Clausus* serves to prevent situations in which too many individuals have a veto right over the use or disposition of a resource.[179] One of the positive reasons to have the *Numerus Clausus* is to ensure the safety of property transactions, as the principle has the effect of clearing title to the property.[180] Another reason is that the *Numerus Clausus* may help reduce measurement costs of property rights.[181]

During the drafting of the Property Law, there was a suggestion that it should adopt a limited *Numerus Clausus* to leave the door open for the kind of property rights that may come up in the future. For example, in one draft presented during the legislative hearing, it was suggested that the kinds and contents of property rights shall be provided by law, while rights that are not provided by law but meet the nature of property rights shall be deemed as property rights.[182] This suggestion was rejected by the majority of legislators due to a concern that the creation of property rights may become immeasurable.[183] On the other hand, it is believed that even if a new kind of property right emerges in the future, the gap could be easily filled in through a legislative interpretation of law.[184]

A question lingering over the *Numerus Clausus* principle is how to define the term "law" as used in Article 5 of the Property Law. More specifically, the issue is whether term includes administrative regulations, judicial interpretation, or customs with respect to application of the *Numerus Clausus*.[185] This is critical, because it directly affects the actual determination of legally prescribed property rights. Many in the judiciary believe that for the purposes of Article 5 of the Property Law, "law" shall only mean the statute passed by the national legislature—i.e., the NPC or its Standing Committee.[186] Still, a common understanding is that a violation of the *Numerus Clausus* principle may only result in voiding the property rights so claimed.[187]

B Registration: publicity mechanism

Given the "against all others" nature of property rights, a certain formality is required whenever there is a change of such rights, so that the change is made known to the public. This process is commonly called a system of publicity for property rights.[188] It is important to follow the required formality, because failure to do so may adversely affect the property acquired and the right of owners to their property. Another important aspect of the publicity lies with the safety of property transactions and the certainty of property ownership. But it should be noted that the publicity mostly deals with immovable property or land.

The most common publicity mechanism is registration, but countries differ in the effect granted to registration. In civil law countries, there are two major registration systems: one is known as "effective by registration" and the other one is termed "against third party." The "effective by registration" system can be found in countries such as Germany and Switzerland, where registration is a prerequisite to the acquisition of ownership in land.[189] Under the "effective by registration" system, the change of property rights in land does not take effect until registration is made. The system of "against third party" is employed in countries like Japan, where registration may not necessarily affect the change of property rights but may serve as a defense against a third party. Under the Japanese civil code, for example, acquisition, loss, or alteration of rights in immovable property may not be made against a third party without registration, which renders registration essential only to make the rights available against a third party.[190]

In common law countries, a widespread mechanism for land registration is called the "Torrens" system. Introduced by Sir Robert Torrens of Australia in 1858, the "Torrens" system established a legal procedure whereby property is transferred by registration instead of deeds and the state guarantees the owner's indefeasible title to the property registered.[191] In the U.S., a comparable system called "recording" is used instead of registration.[192] But in most states, recording is not required to validate the transfer of the property interest, although it is deemed "essential to both to provide an official record of the state of the title and to protect the buyers against any competing claim that may be created by the grantor in others."[193]

China seems to follow a combined civil law practice. At first, it makes registration a basic mechanism of publicity for the change of property rights. Under Article 9 of the Property Law, the creation, alteration, alienation, or termination of the rights to immovable property shall not become effective until registered. Unless otherwise provided by law, the change will have no effect without registration.[194] A careful reading of Article 9 leads to at least four points: (1) the change of property rights includes creation, alteration, alienation as well as termination; (2) no change becomes effective before registration; (3) registration only applies to immovable property; and (4) the registration is subject to exceptions.

On the other hand, the Property Law adopts a "delivery" approach for moveable property. According to Article 23 of the Property Law, the creation or alienation of property rights to moveable property shall come into effect upon delivery except when otherwise provided by law.[195] Thus, registration is not a condition for the effectiveness of change of property rights when moveable property is at issue. Note, however, that ships, aircraft, and vehicles are all classified as moveable property in China. However, with regard to a change of the property rights to those moveable properties, no claim may be made against a *bona fide* third party if the change is not registered.[196]

In addition, there are some exceptions to the registration requirement. The first concerns natural resources. Pursuant to Article 9 of the Property Law, no registration is needed for the ownership of national resources that belong to the state.[197] The second exception deals with certain situations in which the effectiveness of change of property rights is not dependent on registration. One situation is the change caused by a legal document issued by a court, arbitration body, or a government decision of expropriation.[198] Another situation is the acquisition of property rights by inheritance.[199] Also a situation is the change of property rights as a result of factual acts, such as construction and housing demolition that are lawfully undertaken.[200]

Under the Property Law, the exception to registration also applies to the change of rights to certain use of land. As will be discussed later, no individual in China may own the land—only the right to use land. Land use is divided into different categories, such as the right to the contracted management of land, the right to perform construction on land, and the right to use house sites. With regard to the right to contracted management of land or the right to the use of house sites, registration is not required for these rights to become effective,[201] although it may be necessary for the claim against a third party.[202] The same rule also covers such property interests as easements.[203]

As far as registration is concerned, the Property Law requires that property registration be handled by the registration agency of the place where the property is located and a unified registration system be employed nationwide.[204] It is prohibited under the Property Law for a registration agency to ask for an appraisal of real property, to register the property repeatedly in the name of annual inspection, or to conduct any activities beyond the scope of registration responsibilities.[205]

C "One thing, one right" doctrine

Among Chinese property law scholars, there is an ongoing debate about a civil law doctrine known in China as "one thing, one right." The doctrine emphasizes that property should be considered a "thing" with an exclusive right of ownership.[206] In other words, no two conflicting property rights may exist over any "one thing" and, as such, the subject of property rights must be specific and ascertainable.[207] The debate is on whether the "one thing, one right" doctrine should be made a principle of Chinese property law.

In civil law theory, property rights can be divided into two major categories: *plena in re potestas* (complete and absolute property rights) and *jura in re aliena* (certain property rights to the property owned by others).[208] It is commonly understood that the *plena in re potestas* basically denotes ownership or *dominium*, and the *jura in re aliena* mainly refers to other property rights such as usufructuary rights and rights on securities.[209] Given the difference between the *plena in re potestas* and the *jura in re aliena* in terms of the degree of exclusivity, it is debatable whether the "one thing, one right" doctrine applies narrowly to the issue of ownership or to property rights as a whole. This debate has also raised the issue of whether the "one thing, one right" doctrine is necessary at all.

Some Chinese scholars have argued that the "one thing, one right" doctrine is both the core and the very foundation of property rights in China and, therefore, the doctrine should be embraced in the country's legal property scheme.[210] The argument is based on the proposition that because property rights are absolute and exclusive, it is impossible to establish two ownerships on any given property. In addition, it is believed that the sole or unique nature of property rights gives rise to the necessity to have a singular right only to any one thing.[211] Some try to modify this argument by limiting the application of the "one thing, one right" doctrine to ownership in particular. They point out that "one thing" means "one ownership" because only ownership possesses both exclusivity and universality, which requires "one right," while other property rights such as usufructuary rights might not necessarily be exclusive.[212]

Those who oppose the "one thing, one right" doctrine argue that with the diversification of real rights, the doctrine has become obsolete because it is now common to see a "thing" with multiple real rights over it (e.g., multiple ownerships of a condominium building, especially the common areas).[213] Moreover, the "one thing, one right" doctrine was created with tangible things in mind, but the property in today's world contains many intangible things (e.g., intellectual property), and it is unrealistic to have property rights that govern only "one thing."[214]

A very practical matter facing the "one thing, one right" doctrine is the emerging conflict between the independent civil status of state-owned enterprises and state ownership. The conflict directly involves the attribution of property ownership over state-owned enterprises. As players in the market, state-owned enterprises must be able to act independently, including the ability to dispose of property they control. On the other hand, state-owned enterprises are not the actual owners of property and have no right to dispose of the property.[215] Many believe that the "one thing, one right" doctrine is clearly inapplicable in this situation. Some suggest the approach of "dual ownerships," under which the state owns the value of property, while state-owned enterprises own the value of the use of the property.[216]

The Property Law is evasive to the adoption of the "one thing, one right" doctrine. It does not directly endorse "one thing, one right," but defines property rights as the exclusive right of control over a specific thing.[217] Although some argue that the exclusive right to a specific thing actually means "one thing, one right,"[218] many argue that the Property Law only addresses the exclusivity of the property and does not necessarily lead to "one thing, one right."[219] Still, the Property Law does have a provision called "advanced registration," which is designed to prevent a "thing" from becoming subject to dual ownership.

Under Article 20 of the Property Law, parties entering into a purchase agreement for a house or other immovable property may apply for advanced registration to ensure their singular ownership in that property.[220] After advanced registration, no other person may dispose of the property without consent from the owner that registered in advance.[221] Note, however, that in the context of Article 20, the advanced registration essentially deals with rights of claim or a creditor's rights related to future rights of immoveable property.[222]

D *Priority of property rights over creditor rights*

In civil law systems, property rights and creditors' rights are regarded as two different, but closely related, classes of rights.[223] They are different in that the former is the right over a thing and the latter is the right arising from a contractual relationship. They are related because creditors' rights are often created by a property right. For example, when two parties enter into a contract in which party A agrees to transfer a piece of property to party B, which agrees to pay a certain amount of money in return, party B has a creditor's right over party A's property. If party A defaults in delivering the property, party B has a contractual claim against A and under some circumstances can assert its right over party A's property.[224]

Since a property right and a creditor's right can both attach to a piece of property, one of those rights must be superior to the other. Generally, there are two situations in which the priority between property rights and creditors' rights becomes an issue. One situation involves a sale of property to two buyers, one of which has possession of the property. The other situation concerns a security interest between a creditor and a debtor.[225]

During the drafting of the Property Law, some suggested that it should adopt a principle granting property rights priority over creditors' rights. In the first draft of the Property Law, there was a provision that if a specific immoveable or moveable property was subject to both a property right and a creditor's right, the property right should receive a priority unless otherwise provided by law.[226] A similar provision was provided in the second draft.[227]

Proponents of this priority scheme asserted that priority should be determined by the nature of the right, as property rights are exclusive, while creditors' rights are not. Thus, when a property right is in conflict with a creditor's right, the property right should generally have priority.[228] These proponents also argued that, pragmatically, priority of property rights would help identify the attribution of certain property in which multiple creditors' rights are involved.[229] Still, there are certain exceptions, one of which is in leased property. For example, when an owner sells his property during a valid leasing period, the lessee's interests should remain unharmed by the change of ownership.[230]

Opponents have argued that this priority scheme did not clearly address the nature of property rights and actually neglected essential elements of the law that provide for changes in property rights.[231] In addition, these opponents have challenged whether any workable definition about the term "priority" has developed to determine which property right has priority. Moreover, they believe that no such scheme exists in the property legislation of any other country and therefore China would be wise not to be the first.[232]

Due to this controversy over the priority doctrine and the concerns of some legislators regarding the confusion it may cause, the priority provision was taken out of later drafts of the Property Law. The major concern was that legislators did not know what effect such a priority scheme would produce if enacted.[233] In practice, however, it is highly likely that the courts will give more weight to property rights over creditors' rights in conflicts that arise between the two.[234]

E Property rights without land ownership

It is important to emphasize that property rights in China are not necessarily identical with the right to own a piece of land. Under the Chinese constitution, land in urban areas are owned by the state and land in the rural and suburban areas are owned by collectives, except for those that belong to the state according to law. No individual or organization may own land.[235] On this constitutional ground, Article 47 of the Property Law provides that urban land, and land in rural areas that belong to the state as provided by law are owned by the state.[236] Article 58 of the Property Law defines the collectively owned property as including land that belongs to collectives, under the provision of law.[237]

Thus, no private ownership of land exists in China. There is, however, a kind of "non-ownership" interest in land that is commonly called "the right to the use of the land" or "the land use right."[238] In the Property Law, the land use right is defined as a usufructuary right, namely the right to the property owned by others. As noted, the Property Law further divides the land use right into three categories: the right to the contracted management of land, the right to the use of construction land, and the right to the use of house sites. The common character of the right to the use of land is that the user of the land has the right to possess and use the land and the right to gain interest from the land, but has no right to dispose of or sell the land.[239] In addition, as a property interest, the right to the use of land is inheritable.

Therefore, the owner of a house in China is actually the holder of the right to use the respective land. In other words, ownership of a house may reach everything affixed to the house, but not the land on which it is built. Additionally, the right to use land is on a term basis, and acquisition of such a right has an economic value which is included in the purchase price of the house. Under the 1990 State Council Interim Provisions for the Granting and Transferring of Land Use Rights on State-owned Land in Cities and Towns, the maximum term for the use of land for a residential purpose is seventy years.[240] The term is renewable but a fee for the renewal may be levied.[241]

Pursuant to Article 40 of the 1990 Provisions, the state shall retain the land use right and ownership of other fixtures for free when the term of right to the use of land expires.[242] Thus, despite a commonly accepted principle that a request for renewal of land use rights may not be denied without a legitimate need for public interest,[243] there is a public concern about a possible loss of the right to the use of land during the renewal process, particularly for land that is used for residential buildings.[244]

In response to this public concern, the Property Law adopts an automatic renewal approach to land use rights for residential buildings. Under Article 149, the term of a right to use construction land for a dwelling house shall be automatically renewed.[245] This automatic renewal, however, does not apply to the right to use non-dwelling construction land. In accordance with Article 149 of the Property Law, the renewal of land use rights for non-dwelling construction land shall be determined by law. The attribution of the houses and other immoveable property on the land shall be made according to the contract between the related parties or relevant law if there is no contract or the provisions in the contract are unclear.[246]

Still, with automatic renewal for the term of use, the right to use land does not mean ownership of the land. The differences between the two are obvious. One of the most striking differences is that ownership of land contains the right to own everything on the land, under the land, and to a certain extent, above the land. The right to use land does not contain these additional rights. Furthermore, ownership of land embraces a right to the disposal of land, while the right to the use of the land does not.

V "Nail House" syndrome and unresolved issues

"Nail House" is a symbolic phrase used in China to refer to a household that defies the public notice or order of "demolishment and removal" by the government for real estate development in the area where the house is situated and sticks out like nails in an otherwise changed environment. The house is called a nail because it remains intact, no matter what has happened in the surrounding area. As to the owner of the household, the word "nail" conjures up the image of a stubborn owner who refuses to be hammered down.

In recent years, the "Nail House" syndrome seems to have become commonly caused by the direct conflict between household owners and real estate developers. Still, there are many cases in which the conflict is actually between households and the government. In the past, the "Nail House" syndrome in land development could not have existed in China, as no individual rights in property were recognized. After private property was officially recognized in the country, the "Nail House" phenomenon came to the fore when many urban areas in China became massive development zones. The issue of whether there should be fair treatment and just compensation in such situations then arose.

Perhaps the most notable "Nail House" incident attracting national attention occurred in early 2007 in the city of Chongqing. Reported in the media as the "strongest nail house in history,"[247] the incident involved a couple who lived in an old two-story house located at 17 Hexing Road, Jiu Nong Po District, Chongqing. In 2003, the district government sold the right to the use of the land to a private developer in order to make the area more business-oriented. Approximately 280 households were affected as development commenced in the summer of 2004.[248]

Unfortunately, after several attempts, the developer failed to reach an agreement with the couple on the replacement value of the house or relocation alternatives. The couple—husband Yang Wu and wife Wu Ping—responded by refusing to move out. By October 2004, the surrounding area was torn down, leaving the house standing alone. Since then, the house has been without water, electricity, or even a proper exit, because the developer dug a ditch more than ten meters deep around it.

After unsuccessful negotiations, the developer filed an administrative petition with the district housing management bureau ("district housing bureau"). On January 11, 2007, an administrative decision was issued against the couple, ordering them to voluntarily move out to a relocated place within fifteen days after the issuance of the decision. The couple disagreed with the district housing bureau and took no action to comply with the administrative order. On February 1, 2007, the district housing bureau filed an enforcement petition with the district people's court. After a hearing on March 19, the court ruled in favor of the district housing bureau, ordering the couple to comply on or before March 22, 2007.[249]

But, the couple refused to comply. On March 23, the case went into the process of forced enforcement of judgment. On March 29, a notice of forced enforcement was sent to the couple urging them to obey the court order. Facing continued resistance from the couple, on March 30, the court issued a public notice ordering the couple to voluntarily move out by April 10 or else face demolition of the house and relocation by court order.[250]

While battling in court, the couple tried to seek public support by talking to the media. On March 19, China Legal Daily first published an interview with Wu Ping about the case. Wu Ping and her "Nail House" became a national flashpoint immediately, allowing her to fight to protect her property. According to Wu, their demand was simple: to be given an apartment unit in the building that is to be built in the same area with comparable square-footage to the house she currently owns. This demand was refused by the developer, who claimed it was impossible to comply. In order to attract more public attention, the couple flew a Chinese national flag on the roof of the house, and met with reporters in front of it, holding a copy of the Chinese constitution in their hands.

Ironically, during the time when the district court ordered the couple to move out, the General Meeting of the NPC was held in Beijing to discuss the passage of the Property Law. Many regarded this case as a test of the protection of private property rights that the Property Law is supposed to promote.[251] Dealing with tremendous public pressure, the district court made additional efforts to try to bring the parties together for a settlement.[252] In the meantime, the chief officer of local government also met with Wu Ping in person to discuss her options for a settlement.[253] On April 2, an agreement was finally reached on a mutually compromised basis, under the auspices of the district court,[254] ending the three-year long standoff.

The most widely publicized "Nail House" has gone, but many legal issues remain. Aside from the merits of the dispute over compensation, the "Nail House" has become a microcosm of the status quo of private property rights in China. The rights in many cases are not well-respected or properly protected, although they have been constitutionally recognized.

One legal issue is the process of taking. In the United States, the Fifth Amendment of the Federal Constitution explicitly prohibits private property from being taken without just compensation.[255] In China, there was no such constitutional clause to govern government taking until the latest amendment to the 1982 Constitution was adopted in 2004. Under the 2004 Amendment, the state may, for the public interest and in accordance with law, expropriate or requisition private property of citizens for its use and make compensation for the property expropriated and requisitioned thereof.[256]

Obviously, the Chinese constitution does not seem to make proper compensation a prerequisite for a taking. Unlike the Fifth Amendment in the U.S., the Chinese constitutional provision does not have any effect of curbing government power over private property to the extent that proper compensation is guaranteed. In the United States, property rights are deemed to serve a dual role: to protect individual rights against other citizens and to safeguard against excessive government interference.[257] Unfortunately, the role of safeguarding against excessive inference from government appears to be considerably overshadowed by the overreaching authority possessed by government agencies at all levels in China.

The Property Law contains a more detailed provision with respect to government expropriation. Under Article 42 of the Property Law, private premises or other real property may be expropriated for the public interest under statutory discretion and procedure. In the case of expropriation, compensation shall be made for demolishment and relocation, and the lawful rights and interests of the owner of expropriated property shall be maintained. When a private house is expropriated, the living condition of the owner shall be ensured.[258]

However, much like the 1982 Constitution (as amended in 2004), the Property Law sets no standard or requirement to guarantee a fair and just process for the taking. Instead, the Property Law leaves the door open by using vague terms, such as "under the statutory discretion and procedure." It is understood in China that the legal authority referred to in the Property Law is the Law of Land Management of China and other relevant regulations, such as the Regulation of Administration of Demolishment and Relocation of Urban Houses (Urban Houses Regulation). The Land Management Law was first adopted in 1986 and was amended in 1988 and 1998,[259] basically dealing with land use and farmers' interests associated with land.

The most relevant and controversial law pertaining to the taking is the Urban Houses Regulation. Promulgated by the State Council in 2001, the Urban Houses Regulation is currently the major regulation that governs the demolishing and relocating of houses in urban development. Although there is disagreement among Chinese scholars as to whether demolishment and relocation in urban areas is equivalent to an expropriation, as ownership of land is not at issue, it is believed that the nature of demolishment and relocation indeed constitutes a taking,[260] for which a fair process shall be established and a reasonable compensation shall be made.

The problem, however, is that the Urban Houses Regulation has a focus on the advancement of urban development, and as such it does not make the fair process for takings a priority. On the contrary, it has a bias against owners of households. For example, under the Urban Houses Regulation, a developer may not undertake demolishment and relocation without obtaining a license from an administrative agency of local government, but the license may be issued without any knowledge of the owner of the household affected.[261] In addition, as soon as the license is issued, the owner of the household is obligated to enter into a contract with the developer for demolishment and relocation.[262] Moreover, if the owner and developer fail to reach an agreement, the developer may seek a decision by the local administrative agency.[263] If the house's owner disagrees with the administrative decision, the owner may file a lawsuit with a people's court. During the legal proceeding, execution of demolishment and relocation shall not be halted if money compensation is made or a relocation house is provided.[264] Finally, if the owner of the household refuses to move, a forced demolishment and relocation may be imposed.[265]

The second issue is the purpose of takings. Both the 1982 Constitution and the Property Law allow a taking to take place for public interest. The question then is what constitutes the public interest to justify a taking. During the drafting of the Property Law, many suggested the "public interest" should be well-defined in order to help prevent abuse, particularly when commercial development is involved.[266] Others preferred to have a generalized provision for various reasons, including, among others, that (a) it is impossible to make a complete list of public interests; (b) the public interests shall have a broad content in order to meet the different public needs in a constantly changing environment; and (c) the law in many other countries does not limit public interests within certain categories.[267]

Facing difficulty in defining public interest, the Property Law simply makes public interest a general criterion for the taking without bothering to specify what it means. Courts will have to determine what constitutes public interest on a case-by-case basis. Still, trying to differentiate public interests from commercial use in many cases is a thorny issue because the two are closely tangled. Thus, the Property Law has been criticized for failing to make any substantial improvement in protecting individual property interests in cases of taking.[268] Nevertheless, in order to help identify public interests, some scholars have proposed a factor-based approach under which the following factors would need to be considered to determine public interests: (a) scope of beneficiaries, (b) burdens on the general public, (c) priority of interests involved, and (d) availability of alternatives.[269]

The third issue is compensation. This issue is perhaps the primary attribute to the occurrence of nail houses. Interestingly, all laws in China in relation to takings provide for compensation, but none of the laws require compensation to be reasonable. As noted, for instance, under Article 13 of the 1982 Constitution (as amended 2004), the requirement for expropriation of private property is to "make compensation," yet no standard for the compensation is provided.[270] Although the Land Management Law for expropriation of land provides a calculation formula for compensation, reasonableness is not a criterion.[271] Since the compensation is not defined, it creates a situation that leaves the owner of private property far under-compensated in many cases.

In response to the public outrage at the inadequate compensation in cases of taking or expropriation, the Property Law tries to deal with this issue in a seemingly reasonable manner by specifying the nature of the subject expropriated with more detailed compensation means such as "compensate for demolition and reloca-tion," "protect the lawful rights and interests," and "guarantee the housing conditions."[272] Still, no requirement for a reasonable and just compensation is set out in the Property Law. Thus, as long as compensation is made, the level of the compensation in terms of reasonableness may become irrelevant, because the lawful rights and interests as well as the living condition as stated in the Property Law are too vague to be measurable.

In reality, the idea behind undefined compensation is that the compensation is a matter of local concern.[273] Thus, it is asserted that since the actual standard of compensation is provided by local government in consideration of local needs and development level, it is difficult to establish a general or uniform standard.[274] However, many scholars view this matter differently. They argue that it is neces-sary to provide a national standard or principle because without it there is no way to ensure adequacy of compensation and, as a matter of fact, the local gov-ernment always has a tendency to keep the compensation as low as possible in order to reduce development costs.[275] Many suggest that, as a common practice, the uniform standard for the compensation should be the reasonableness stand-ard, and reasonableness shall be determined by the court if a dispute occurs.[276]

VI Conclusion

If it is true that during the mid-1950s campaign of socialist transformation, China made a historical move from private to public in the means of production and property ownership, then it is equally true that the passage of the Property Law in 2007 legally reversed the course and posted a historical change in the property rights from public to private. In this context, the Property Law is a land-mark legislation bringing China into the mainstream global economy and laying down a foundation for the market economy that the country has been trying to pursue.

However, nothing in this Article is intended to suggest that the protection of property right in China is secure. On the contrary, several legitimate concerns remain regarding how the Property Law is to be implemented. Further, many provisions in the Property Law are either ambiguous or need to be further defined. To speak more explicitly, a big challenge facing China in the legal realm of property is changing the ideology of the supremacy of public property to really put a legal framework in place to guarantee an equal protection of both public and private property.

Perhaps the biggest challenge is limiting government power to interfere with individual liberty and private property rights. The interference in most cases originates from the government's strong appetite for control as well as its desire to try to maintain social stability. Surely, there is nothing wrong with the gov-ernment's maintaining social stability, but the issue is whether stability should be achieved at the cost of loss of property or rights of particular individuals, or if it should be maintained by preventing the misconduct of government. Unfortunately, the focus in China has been largely on the behavior of individuals rather than on government actions.[277] This is affected by the fact that lower level Chinese government officials care more about their job performance report than actual citizens dealing with these issues.[278]

Nevertheless, the Property Law represents significant progress in China for protecting private property rights. It is conceivable that many existing rules and regulations will be modified to be consistent with the Property Law, as some new rules and regulations will be adopted to help implement the Property Law. It is also highly expected that the Supreme People's Court of China will exercise its function of judicial interpretations from time to time to facilitate application and enforcement of the Property Law and, in the meantime, to help clarify certain ambiguities that are contained in the Property Law.

Notes

* The author would like to thank Professor Robert Reinstein, the Dean of Temple University Beasley School of Law for his guidance, and Professor Jane Baron of Temple University Beasley School of Law for her suggestions and advice.

1 In Chinese literature, there are five books known as the FIVE CLASSICS (*Wu Jing*): the BOOK OF SONGS (*Shi Jing*), the BOOK OF HISTORY (*Shu Jing*), the BOOK OF CHANGES (*Yi Jing*), the BOOK OF RITES (*Li Jing*), and the SPRING AND AUTUMN ANNALS (*Chun Qiu*). The BOOK OF SONGS contains folk poems, along with royal and ritual poems compiled by Confucius (551–479 BC). The FIVE CLASSICS together with four other books are commonly called FOUR BOOKS AND FIVE CLASSIC (*Shi Su Wu Jing*). The FOUR BOOKS are the GREAT LEARNING (*Da Xue*), the DOCTRINE OF THE MEAN (*Zhong Yong*), the ANALECTS OF CONFUCIUS (*Lun Yu*), and the MENCIUS (*Meng Zhi*).

2 *See Bei Shan, in* THE BOOK OF SONGS (SHI JING); for an English translation, see ARTHUR WALEY, THE BOOK OF SONGS: THE ANCIENT CHINESE CLASSIC OF POETRY (Grove Press 1996).

3 *See* ZHANG JINFAN, EVOLUTION OF CHINESE LEGAL CIVILIZATION 54 (China University of Politics and Law Press 1999).

4 The core of the Confucian rites consists of the so-called "three cardinal guides and five virtues" (*San Gang Wu Chang*). The three cardinal guides were "ruler over subject, father over son and husband over wife," and the five virtues included benevolence, righteousness, propriety, wisdom and fidelity. *See* ZHANG JIFAN, THE TRADITION AND MODERN TRANSITION OF CHINESE LAW 51, 82 (2d ed., Law Press 2005).

5 In the early Han Dynasty, Dong Zhongshu, who served as Prime Minister for Emperor Wu, put in place a state policy known as "Proscribing all other schools of thought and espousing the Confucian orthodoxy only." *See* WU SHUCHEN, HISTORY OF CHINESE LEGAL THOUGHTS 191 (Law Press 2004).

6 Even Han Feizhi, the leading opponent of Confucianism and founding father of legalism, acknowledged the importance of the three cardinal guides. According to Han, "Subject serves ruler, son serves father, and wife serves husband—if all of the three are followed, the country then would be in good shape; or if the three were violated, the country would be in chaos—these are the common sense on the earth." *See* HAN FEIZHI, LOYALTY AND FILIAL PIETY; 1 W.K. LIAO, THE COMPLETE WORKS OF HAN FEI TZU (Arthur Probsthain 1939).

7 *See* William Jones, *Trying to Understand the Current Chinese Legal System, in* UNDERSTANDING CHINA'S LEGAL SYSTEM 7, 9 (2003).

8 In some situations, the "Imperial Edict" from the emperor would be read on the spot. *See* ZHANG JINFAN, *supra* note 4, at 541–543.

9 The five parts in the 1930 Civil Code were: General Principles, Obligations, Rights of Things, Family and Succession. Part 1 was adopted on May 23, 1929, and took effect October 10, 1929; Parts II and III were promulgated in November 1920, and effective May 30, 1930; Parts IV and V were enacted in the end of 1930. *See* JOSEPH AN-PAO WANG, STUDIES IN CHINESE GOVERNMENT AND LAW, CIVIL CODE OF THE REPUBLIC OF CHINA (University Publications of America 1976) (1930).

10 The 1930 Civil Code and other five codes were known as the "Six Codes." In addition to the Civil Code, the Six Codes included the Constitution, Commercial Code, Criminal Law, Criminal Procedure and Civil Procedure. The Six Codes were repeated by the Communist party in February 1949. *See* RALPH H. FOLSOM ET AL., LAW AND POLITICS IN THE PEOPLE'S REPUBLIC OF CHINA: IN A NUT SHELL 25 (West 1992).

11 Mao divided people into different classes depending on the status of the people (e.g. working class, peasants, intellectuals, etc.). According to Mao, the human history is actually a history that one class of people struggles against other classes. *See* STANLEY LUBMAN, BIRD IN A CAGE, LEGAL REFORM IN CHINA AFTER MAO 41, 42 (Stanford University Press 1999).

12 As it has been observed, the Anglo-American conception of "rights" is basically associated with individuals and is often linked with defying state authority, while in China "rights" are more commonly related to the public or collectives. *See* NEIL DIAMANT, ENGAGING THE LAW IN CHINA, STATE, SOCIETY, AND POSSIBILITIES FOR JUSTICE 14 (Stanford University Press 2005).

13 The drafting of the Property Law started in 1993 and the draft was submitted in 2002 to the National People's Congress for the first reading. *See* WANG SHENMING, QUESTIONS AND ANSWERS TO THE STUDY OF THE PROPERTY LAW 2 (China Democracy and Legality Press 2007); *see also* Su Yongtong, *Road to Legislating China's Property Law: Never so Tortuous, Never so Resolute*, Mar. 23, 2007, *available at* http://www.sinofile.net/saiweng/sip_blog.nsf/d6plinks/YZHI-6ZKAZJ.

14 *See* Wang Zhaoguo, Vice-Chairman of the Standing Committee of the National People's Congress, *Explanation on China's Draft Property Law*, CHINA DAILY, Mar. 8, 2007, *available at* http://www.chinadaily.com.cn/china/2007–03/08/content_822719.htm.

15 XIAN FA art. 13 (1982) (P.R.C.) (The English translation is available at http://english.people.com.cn/constitution/constitution.html). The current Constitution of China was adopted in 1982, and was amended in 1988, 1993, 1999 and 2004. Under Article 13 of the Chinese constitution, as amended in 2004, citizens' lawful private property was declared "inviolable." It was the first time that the private property was written into Chinese constitution after 1949.

16 For example, in the United States, property may denote everything which is the subject of ownership. This can be objects that are corporeal or incorporeal, tangible or intangible, visible or invisible, real or personal, or that which has an exchangeable value or which goes to make up wealth or estate. BLACK'S LAW DICTIONARY 1216 (8th ed. 2004).

17 *See* JIANG PING, A COURSE IN CHINESE REAL RIGHTS LAW 1 (Intellectual Property Right Press 2007).

18 *See id.* at 2.

19 *See id.* at 60.

20 *See* WANG LIMING, STUDY ON CRUCIAL AND DIFFICULT PROBLEMS OF CHINESE CIVIL CODE 258, 259 (2006).

21 *See* JOSEPH W. SINGER, INTRODUCTION TO PROPERTY 2 (Aspen 2005).

22 *See* Lawrence M. Friedman, *The Law of the Living, the Law of the Dead: Property, Succession, and Society*, 1966 Wis. L. Rev. 341, 342 (1966).

23 *See* Cereghino v. State By and Through State Highway Comm'n, 370 P.2d 694, 697, 230 Or. 439, 445 (1962).

24 *See* Friedman, *supra* note 22, at 342.

25 *See* Bernard H. Siegan, Property Rights: from Magna Carta to the Fourteenth Amendment 2 (2001).

26 *See* Tung-Tsu Chu, Law and Society in Traditional China 9–10 (Rainbow Bridge Book Co. 1965).

27 *See* Xu Zhong Min & Ren Qiang, The Legal Spirits of China 414–415 (Guang Dong People's Press 2007).

28 *See id.* at 416–417.

29 *See* Richard Hooker, *Modern China, available at* http://www.wsu.edu:8080/~dee/MODCHINA/SUN.HTM.

30 *See* Jiang Ping, *supra* note 17, at 4–5.

31 From 1953 to 1956, a nationwide campaign labeled "Three Big Socialist Transformations" swept over China. Its only purpose was to turn agriculture, handicraft, and capitalist industry and commerce over to public ownership. By the end of 1956, state and collective ownership in China reached over 92.9 percent of the country's economy. *See* Meng Lingwei, *Standing in the Beginning of 21st Century to Look Back to the Three Transformations Campaign, available at* http://www.tecn.cn/data/detail.php?id=981.

32 *See* Jones, *supra* note 8, at 25. Since the movement of history is to finish the class struggle by establishing communism, there can be no such concept as an inviolable right in the traditional western sense. The only real "right" that existed at this stage of history was the right—and indeed the duty—of the proletariat and its instrument, the Communist party, to eliminate the domination of the bourgeoisie and establish the socialist system.

33 *See* Wikipedia, *Socialism*, http://en.wikipedia.org/wiki/socialism (last visited Feb. 25, 2008).

34 In Mao's view, capitalism is established on exploitation of man by man. For example, if a landlord hired a person to work on his land, the landlord would be deemed to have exploited the person by taking away the "surplus value" that the person created from his work. The "surplus value" is an idea from Marxist political economy. *See* Mao Zedong, *On the People's Democratic Dictatorship, in* Selected Works of Mao Zedong 4, 411–424 (Beijing Foreign Language Press 1969).

35 According to Mao, after World War II, the world was divided into capitalist and socialist blocs, and China belonged to the socialist bloc. *See id.*

36 *See* William C. Jones, *The Constitution of the People's Republic of China*, 63 Wash. U. L. Q. 707, 717–718 (1985); *see also* Meng Lingwei, *Standing in the Beginning of the 21st Century: The Movement "Three Transformations" Revisited*, http://zhidao.baidu.com/question/24579373.html? fr=qrl3.

37 *See* Zhang Qinfu & Han Dayuan, Studies on the 1954 Constitution 163 (2005).

38 Invented by Mao himself, the phrase was used to refer to those in power who were alleged to tend to lead the country in a capitalist direction, namely to turn public ownership of the means of production to private ownership. See Folsom et al., *supra* note 10, at 33.

39 A famous slogan spread all over China during the Cultural Revolution was "strike hard the word 'private' that flashes through one's mind," which meant nobody should even think about the word "private." *See* People's Daily Editorial, Oct. 6, 1967.

40 The discussion was initiated and advocated by Deng Xiaoping and his followers as an effective means to deal with "the ossified leftist view" that insisted in the faction of so-called "two whatevers": whatever Chairman Mao had said must be followed and

whatever Chairman has decided must be observed. *See* HONG YUNG LEE, FROM REVOLUTIONARY CADRES TO PARTY TECHNOCRATS IN SOCIALIST CHINA 318 (1990).

41 *See id.*

42 The Four Cardinal Principles were "to stick to Marxism-Leninism-Mao Zedong thought, to persist in the Socialist road, to uphold the People's Democratic Dictatorship, and to adhere to the leadership of Communist party. According to Deng Xiaoping, China must hold firmly to the four principles during the course of its modernization. *See id.*

43 *See id.* at 319:

> The specific contents of the principles, however, are so ambiguous that they have given party leaders the freedom to crack down on anything they deem unsocialistic." They were "effective as a control mechanism for the top leaders, but not as the basis for forming a new ideological consensus.

44 *See* FENG CHEN, ECONOMIC TRANSITION AND POLITICAL LEGITIMACY IN POST-MAO CHINA: IDEOLOGY AND REFORM 58–60 (State University of New York Press 1995).

45 On the 14th National Conference of the Communist Party, held October 1–18, 1992, establishing the socialist market economy system was officially prescribed as the ultimate goal of the economic reform. *See* Xin Hua News Agency Report on the Conference, *available at* http://news.xinhuanet.com/ziliao/2003–01/20/content_697129.htm.

46 According to Deng Xiaoping, the very purpose of socialism is to develop production force and achieve common wealth. To that end, the first step is to allow a group of people to get rich in the market economy. See PEOPLE'S DAILY, *Deng Xiaoping Wet with American Quests*, Oct. 24, 1985.

47 *See* JIANG PING, *supra* note 17, at 4–5.

48 *See* 1986 Civil Code art. 1, General Principles of the Civil Law of China, *available at* http://www.law-bridge.net/english/law/20065/1322572053247.html.

49 *See* Walter Dellinger, *The Indivisibility of Economic Rights and Personal Liberty*, CATO SUPREME COURT REVIEW (2003–2004).

50 *See* Charlie Savage, *Foes Cite Alito's Stance on Liberty*, BOSTON GLOBE, Dec. 27, 2005, *available at* http://www.boston.com/yourlife/health/women/articles/2005/12/27/foes_cite_alitos_stance_on_liberty/. In recent decades, the Supreme Court has invoked liberty rights to strike down laws forbidding contraception, abortion, interracial marriage, and gay sex between consenting adults; a zoning law that prevented extended families from living together; and a law that forced parents to let grandparents visit their children.

51 *See* SINGER, *supra* note 21, at 5. "Rights" are claims, enforceable by state power, that others act in certain manner in relation to the right holder. "Liberties" are permissions to act in a certain manner without being liable for damages to others and without others being able to summon state power to prevent those acts.

52 *See Liberty*, BLACK'S LAW DICTIONARY (8th ed. 2004).

53 16 AM. JUR., *Constitutional Law* §329 (1998).

54 *See* Leon Felkins, *Property and Liberty: You Can't Give Up One without Losing the Other* (Jan. 2, 1999), http://www.progress.org/leon01.htm; *see also* JAMES BOVARD, LOST RIGHTS: THE DESTRUCTION OF AMERICAN LIBERTY (Palgrave Macmillan 1995).

55 *See* TIMOTHY SANDEFUR, CORNERSTONE OF LIBERTY: PROPERTY RIGHTS IN 21ST CENTURY AMERICA (Cato Institute 2006).

56 *See* 3 DANIEL WEBSTER, SPEECHES IN THE CONVENTION TO AMEND THE CONSTITUTION OF THE STATE OF MASSACHUSETTS 15 (1890).

57 *See* Jeremy Paul, *The Hidden Structure of Takings Law*, 64 S. CAL. L. REV. 1093, 1402 (1991) (property rights serve "twin roles—as protector of individual rights against other citizens, and as safeguard against excessive government interference").

58 *See* SINGER, *supra* note 21, at 676.

59 In the United States, for example, the Constitution mandates that "no person shall ... be deprived of life, liberty or property, without due process of law." For more discussion about due process and protection of property rights, see SIEGAN, *supra* note 25, at 105–08.

60 *See* Meng Zhi, *Liang Hui Wang (Part 1)*. For an English Translation, see Charles Muller, *Mencius (Selections), available at* http://www.hm.tyg.jp/acmuller/contao/mencius.html. *See also Property Law Draft on the NPC's Table*, CHINA DAILY, *available at* http://english.people.com.cn/200703/09/eng20070309_355866.html.

61 The term "civil society" can be traced through the works of Cicero and other Romans to the Ancient Greek philosophers, but John Locke was deemed as one of the first to really articulate it, followed by George Hegel who developed a notion of civil society as a domain parallel to but separate from the state, and emphasized individual freedom. The idea was said to grow out of the mounting demand for liberty, as manifested in French resolution. For more discussion about civil society, see SUDIPTA KAVIRAJ & SUNIL KHILNANI, CIVIL SOCIETY: HISTORY AND POSSIBILITIES (Cambridge University Press 2001). *See also* HE JINGHUA ET AL., PURSUIT OF THE RULE OF LAW: COMPARISON OF IDEOLOGIES, PATHS AND MODELS 66–71 (Beijing University Press 2005).

62 *See* DECLARATION OF INDEPENDENCE [¶ 1] (1776).

63 ZHANG QINFU & HAN DAYUAN, *supra* note 37, at 276–289.

64 *See* LASZLO LANDANY, LAW AND LEGALITY IN CHINA: THE TESTAMENT OF A CHINA—WATCHER 67–70 (1992).

65 *See* Library of Congress Country Studies, *China, The Transition to Socialism* (1953–57), *available at* http://workmall.com/wfb2001/china/china_history_the_transition_to_socialism_1953_57.html.

66 In the early 1950s, as a gesture of forming a people's democratic government, a number of non-Communist members were appointed ministers in the country's cabinet. However, they were soon dismissed during the "anti-rightist" movement to ensure the supremacy of the communist party's leadership. See FOLSOM ET AL., *supra* note 10, at 29.

67 *See* Library of Congress Country Studies, *China, Policy Toward Intellectuals, available at* http://lcweb2.loc.gov/cgi-bin/query/r?frd/cstdy:@field(DOCID+cn0124).

68 Hu Yaobang became General Secretary of the Communist Party of China in 1980 and Party Chairman in 1981. He was dismissed in 1987 for being sympathetic about the student movement for politic reform. *See* Joseph Kahn, *China to Give Memorial Rite to Hu Yaobang. Purged Reformer*, N.Y. TIMES, Nov. 15, 2005.

69 Deng had a famous cat theory that "a cat is a good cat if it could catch a mouse no matter whether the cat is white or black in color." Analogizing the cat theory to his call to stop debating meant that either capitalism or socialism, whichever makes China prosperous, would be good. For general discussion about Deng's cat theory, see Suisheng Zhao, *Deng Xiaoping's Southern Tour: Elite Politics in Post-Tiananmen China*, Asian Survey, Vol. 33, No. 8, 739–756 (University of California Press 1993).

70 *See* Michael Watts, *What is a Market Economy?*, http://uninfo.state.gov/products/pubs/market (explaining that market economies may be practical, but they also rest upon the fundamental principle of individual freedom: freedom as a consumer to choose among competing products and services; freedom as a producer to start or expand a business and share its risks and rewards; freedom as a worker to choose a job or career, join a labor union, or change employers). The market economy is defined as "[a]n economic system in which economic decisions and the pricing of goods and services are guided solely by the aggregate interactions of a country's citizens and businesses and there is little government intervention or central planning." *See* Forbes, *Investopedia*, http://www.investopedia.com/terms/m /marketeconomy.asp.

71 *See, e.g.*, Administrative Procedure Law art. 2 (promulgated by the NPC, Apr. 4, 1989, effective Oct. 1, 1990), *translated at* http://www.cecc.gov/pages/newLaw/

adminLitigationENG.php (providing a legal vehicle for regular citizens to sue government agencies against their misconduct or abuse of power). *See also* State Compensation Law art. 2 (promulgated by the NPC May 12, 1994, effective Jan. 1 1995), *translated at* http://www.cecc.gov/pages/newLaws/stateCompensationENG. php (allowing the victims of State infringement actions upon the right of their person or property to sue the government for damages, although the standards of compensation are criticized as too low and basically compensatory rather than punitive).

72 *See* Wen Jiabao, *Speech on Several Questions about Historical Tasks of the Preliminary Stage of Socialism and the Foreign Policies of China* (Feb. 26, 2007), *available at* http://news.sina.com.cn/c/2007–02–26/160612374687.shtml.

73 The original version of the 1954 Constitution is available from the website of the National People's Congress of China at http://npc.gov.cn/zgrdw/common/zw. jsp?id=4264&1mfl. XIAN FA [Constitution] (1954) (P.R.C.).

74 XIAN FA [Constitution] (1975) (P.R.C.) (The English translation is available at http://chr.sagepub.com/cgi/reprint/11/1/52 and http://chr.sagepub.com/cgi/reprint/14/2/97); XIAN FA [Constitution] (1978) (P.R.C.) (The English translation is available at http://chr.sagepub.com/cgi /reprint/11/1/52 and http://chr.sagepub.com/cgi/reprint/14/2/97).

75 XIAN FA [Constitution] (1982), *supra* note 15.

76 The First Amendment to the 1982 Constitution was approved on April 12, 2988, the Second Amendment was approved on March 29, 1993, the Third Amendment was approved on March 15, 1999, and the Fourth Amendment was approved on March 14, 2004. *Id.*

77 Because the 1975 Constitution was adopted a year before the Cultural Revolution ended, it was considered to be full of fallacies from the Cultural Revolution. The 1978 Constitution was promulgated right before the adoption of the Opening Door Policy, and was regarded as falling behind the need of the Country's economic reform. *See* William Jones, *The Constitution of China, in* UNDERSTANDING CHINA'S LEGAL SYSTEM 712–13 (2003).

78 The Common Program was drafted and adopted by the Chinese People's Political Consultative Conference—a multi-partisan body containing all political parties of China. An English text of the Common Program is available at http://www.fordham. edu/halsal1/mod/1949-ccp-program.html.

79 Under Article 5 of the Common Program, the people of the People's Republic of China shall have freedom of thought, speech, publication, association, correspondence, person, domicile, change of domicile, religious belief and the freedom of holding processions and demonstrations. *See id.*

80 Despite the fact that the 1954 Constitution was intensively influenced by the 1936 Constitution of the former Soviet Union, it contained a list of individual rights that was deemed more impressive than the corresponding section of the 1936 Soviet Constitution. *See* Franklin Houn, *Communist China's New Constitution*, 8 W. POL. Q. 199, 203–204 (1955).

81 *See* Mao Zedong, *Speech at the Thirtieth Session of the Central People's Government Council* (June 14, 1954), *available at* http://www.marxists.org/reference/archive/mao/ selected-works/volume- 5/mswv5_37.htm.

82 1954 Constitution art. 5 (P.R.C.), *available at* http://npc.gov.cn/zgrdw/common/ zw.jsp? id=4264&lmfl.

83 *See* ZHANG QINFU & HAN DAYUAN, *supra* note 37, at 4–5.

84 *See id.* at 164–165.

85 *See* Houn, *supra* note 80, at 233. Whatever form of democracy the Constitution provides, it will probably operate strictly within the iron framework of the Communist monopoly of power. Thus, the Communist Party of China is always the controlling force behind the formal arrangement of government structure.

86 *See* LANDANY, *supra* note 64, at 52–78.

87 "Democratic Centralism" refers to the principles of internal organization used by Leninist political parties. The democratic aspect describes the freedom of members of the political party to discuss and debate matters of policy and direction, but once the decision of the party is made by majority vote, all members are expected to uphold that decision. This latter aspect represents the centralism. *See* Wikipedia, *Democratic Centralism*, http://en.wikipedia.org/viki/democratic_centralism. Under Lenin's description, democratic centralism consisted of "freedom of discussion, unity of action." Mao, however, used it to impose his will on the country. *Id.*; *see also* Frank Ching, *All Eyes on Future of "Inner Democracy" in China*, CHINA POST, Sept. 19, 2007, *available at* http://www.chinapost.com.tw/print/123161.htm.

88 *See* LANDANY, *supra* note 64, at 54–55.

89 *See* ZHANG QINFU & HAN DAYUAN, *supra* note 37, at 162–163.

90 *See* 1988 Amendment to the 1982 Constitution of China, *supra* note 15, at art. 1. Note that in China, "complement" was preferred to "supplement."

91 *See id.*

92 *See id.*

93 *See id.*

94 *See* Patrick Randolph, *Speech at the 2003 Congressional-Executive Commission on China Roundtable, Ownership with Chinese Characteristics: Private Property Rights and Land Reform in the People's Republic of China*, *available at* http://www.cecc. gov. In fact, before the 1988 Amendment, several places in China such as Shenzhen, Fuzhou, Guangzhou, Xiamen, and Shanghai had adopted local regulations experimenting with the transferability of land use rights. Scholars called it the phenomenon, which is true in China, that "the actuality of the concept preceded its technical validation." PATRICK RANDOLPH & LOU JIANBO, CHINESE REAL ESTATE LAW 19 (2000).

95 *See id.*

96 *See* Natalie Lichtenstein, *Law in China's Economic Development, An Essay from Afar, in* UNDERSTANDING CHINA'S LEGAL SYSTEM 279 (2003).

97 XIAN FA (1982), *supra* note 15, at art. 16.

98 *See id.* at art. 5.

99 *See id.* at art. 6.

100 In the past, private property only referred to inheritance. The 2004 Amendment changed Article 13 of the 1982 Constitution from "the State protects according to law the right of citizens to inherit private property" to "the State protects according to law the private property right and inheritance right of citizens." *See id.* at art. 13.

101 *See* Preamble of the 1982 Constitution of China (as amended in 2004), *supra* note 15.

102 Article 1 of the Property Law provides that:

> In accordance with the Constitution, the present Law is enacted with a view to maintaining the basic economic system of the state, protecting the socialist market economic order, clearly defining the attribution of the res, bringing into play the utilities of the res and safeguarding the real right of the right holder.

> *See* National People's Congress (China), Real Property Law (Mar. 16, 2007), *available at* http://www.bjreview.com.cn/document/txt/2007–07/26/content_70481.htm [hereinafter referred to as Property Law].

103 *See id.* at art. 64.

104 *See* 1986 Civil Code, *supra* note 48, at art. 75.

105 The Legislation Law of China (2000), Article 27, *available at* http://www.novexcn. com /legslat_law_00.html.

106 On July 10, 2005, the Draft Property Law was also published for a nationwide discussion. During July 10 and August 20, 2005, the Standing Committee received about 11,543 suggestions from the general public, and received comments from twenty-six provinces, fifteen large cities, forty-seven central government agencies,

sixteen big companies, and twenty-two law schools and institutes. *See* Legal Committee of the Standing Committee of the NPC, *Report on the Changes of the Draft Property Law of the People's Republic of China* (Oct. 19, 2005), *available at* http://www.law-lib.com/fzdt /newshtml/20/20051023173231.htm.

107 *See* Mario Ferrero, *A Rational Theory of Socialist Public Ownership, in* 16 RATIONALITY AND SOCIETY, No. 4, 371–72 (SAGE Publications 2004), *available at* http://ss.sagepub.com/cgi/content /abstract/16/4/371.

108 A typical example is the "Great Leap Forward" campaign from 1958–1960, aiming at eliminating all private elements in the countryside by bringing (if not forcing) millions of farmers into people's communes, the basic forms of public ownership, where the formers would not work for themselves but for the communes to ensure that everyone will follow the party's policy to "speedily run into communism." A direct result of the "Great Leap Forward" was the disaster of severe famine in the early 1960's that led millions of people die of starvation. *See* LUBMAN, *supra* note 12, at 80; *see also* JASPER BECKER, HUNGRY GHOST (Free Press 1997).

109 In China, public ownership includes state ownership and collective ownership. State ownership, also called the ownership by the whole people, controls both industry and commerce. Collective ownership used to mean the ownership held in the rural people's communes through a three-level structure including communes, the production brigade, and the basic level called the production team. XIAN FA (1975), *supra* note 74, at art. 7. Now it is referred to ownership held by rural collective economic organizations through the household-based output-related contracted responsibility system. XIAN FA (1982), *supra* note 15, at art. 7.

110 *See* XIAN FA (1954), *supra* note 73, at art. 6

111 XIAN FA (1975), *supra* note 74, at art. 8.

112 XIAN FA (1978), *supra* note 74, at art. 8.

113 XIAN FA (1982), *supra* note 15, at art. 12.

114 *Id.*

115 A carefully reading of these two constitution articles further reveals the difference: for "socialist public property," Article 12 uses the words "*shen sheng bu ke qin fan*" (is sacredly inviolable), while for "private property," Article 13 says "*bu shou qin fan*" (may not be infringed). *See* XIAN FA (1975), *supra* note 74, at art. 12, 13.

116 *See* Wu Jinglian, *Speech at 2006 Annul Meeting of China Economy Top 50 Person Forum, Rethinking Reform and Clarifying the Direction* (Feb. 11, 2006), 7 PHOENIX WEEK 212 (2006), *available at* http://www.wujinglian.net/Articles/articles0604_01.htm; *see also* MA GUOCHUAN, BIG CLASH, CHRONICS OF CHINA REFORM 240–243 (Xinhua Press 2006).

117 The main theme of the socialist commodity economy was to recognize the market force as a regulator of the economy. Although it is believed that a market economy is nothing but another version of commodity economy from the angle of the commodity circulation, the term "market economy" was still a taboo at that time. *See id.* at 180–184.

118 *See* WU JINGLIAN, SELF SELECTED WORKS OF WU JINGLIAN 66–70 (Shanxi Economic Press 2003); *see also* MA GUOCHUAN, *supra* note 116, at 176–179.

119 *See* WU JINGLIAN, *supra* note 118, at 66–67.

120 *See id.* at 67.

121 The "Decision" was announced on October 20, 1984. A full text of the "Decision" is available at http://www.china.org.cn/chinese/archive/131659.htm.

122 The "Decision" was adopted in response to the widespread household-based production units in the countryside as a result of the economic reform. By the end of 1983, more than 175 million households in the countryside became independent production units, accounting for over 94.5 percent of total households of farmers. In addition, the number of privately-owned small enterprises in rural areas reached 41,950 at the same time. *See* THE YEARBOOK OF CHINA ECONOMY 50–52 (Economic Management Press 1984).

123 *See* WU JINGLIAN, ECONOMIC REFORM OF MODERN CHINA 391–94 (Shanghai Far-East Press 2003).

124 It referred to his visit to the southern part of China, including Shenzhen, Zhuhai, Wuhan, and Shanghai during January 18 to February 21, 1992. *See* Suisheng Zhao, *supra* note 69, at 739–40.

125 3 DENG XIAOPING, SELECTED WORKS OF DENG XIAOPING 373 (1994), *available at* http://english.peopledaily.com.cn/dengxp/vol3/text/dl200.html.

126 After Deng's "Southern Tour," the "socialist market economy" became a new term in Chinese vocabulary. *See* MA GUOCHUAN, *supra* note 116, at 182.

127 *See* MA GUOCHUAN, *supra* note 116, at 101–105; *see also* Zhou Xincheng, *Neo-Liberalism Should Not Be Allowed to Mislead the Reform of State-Owned Enterprises*, 5 J. SHANXI UNIV. FIN. & ECON. (2004), *available at* http://www.kmeasy.net/qiyeguanli/guanlizhishi/qiyeguanli_2377.html.

128 Neo-liberalism is a set of economic policies that have become widespread in the west during the last twenty-five years or so. One of the main points of neo-liberalism is to liberate "free" enterprise or private enterprise from any bonds imposed by the government, no matter how much social damage this causes, and another main point is to privatize by selling state-owned enterprises to private investor. *See* Pierre Bourdieu, *The Essence of Neoliberalism, available at* http://www.analitica.com/bitblio /bourdieu/neoliberalism.asp; *see also* Wikipedia, *Neoliberalism, available at* http://en.wikipedia.org /wiki/neoliberalism.

129 The opposition was essentially the repetition of the 1989–1992 argument about whether the reform would keep China on the "socialist" rather than "capitalist" road. *See* MA GUOCHUAN, *supra* note 116, at 181–182.

130 The Decision was made on October 11, 2006, at the 6th general meeting of the 16th Central Committee of the Communist Party. A full text of the Decision is available at http://news.xinhuanet.com /politics/2006–10/18/content_5218639.htm.

131 *See* JIANG PING, *supra* note 17, at 172–177.

132 *See id.* at 175.

133 *See* Gong Xiantian, *An Open Letter to Chairman Wu Bangguo and the Standing Committee of the National People's Congress, available at* http://www.chinaelections.org/newsinfo.asp?newsid= 45986.

134 In early 2006, the Standing Committee decided not to review the draft Property Law and put the draft on hold because more time was needed to discuss major issues involving the Property Law. Eva Cheng, *Wrangle over Law to Legitimate China's Looted State Property*, INT'L NEWS, GREEN LEFT WKLY., Jan. 24, 2007, *available at* http://www.greenleft.org.au/2007/695/36092.

135 *See* Gong Xiantian, *supra* note 133.

136 *See id.*

137 *See id.*

138 *See id.*

139 Article 12 of the 1982 Constitution provides:

> Socialist public ownership is sacredly inviolable. The State protects socialist public property. Appropriation or damage of state or collective property by any organization or individual by whatever means is prohibited.

XIAN FA (1982), supra note 15, art. 12

Article 73 of the 1986 Civil Code provides:

> State property shall be owned by the whole people. State property is sacredly inviolable, and no organization or individual shall seize, encroach upon, privately divide, retain or destroy it.

1986 Civil Code, supra note 48

140 *See* Article 47 of the published Draft Property Law, *available at* http://www.lawlib. com/law/lfbj/lfbj_view.asp?id=10379.

141 *See* Gong Xiantian, *supra* note 133.

142 *See id.*

143 On February 25, 2006, a group of well-known civil law and constitutional law scholars and professors held a special roundtable discussion at People's University to respond to the "Open Letter." *See People University's Response to the "Open Letter,"* XINHUANET NEWS, Feb. 28, 2006, *available at* http://news.xinhuanet.com/ legal/2006–02/28/content_4236357.htm.

144 *See* JIANG PING, *supra* note 17, at 2.

145 *See id.*

146 According to Article 48 of the Draft Property Law, no entity or individual shall acquire ownership over movable and immovable that exclusively owned by the State. *See supra* note 140.

147 *See Public Law*, BLACK'S LAW DICTIONARY (8th ed. 2004); *see also Private Law*, BLACK'S LAW DICTIONARY (8th ed. 2004).

148 *See* WANG LIMING, *supra* note 20, at 247–250; *see also* HU KANGSHENG, EXPLANATIONS TO THE PROPERTY LAW OF THE PEOPLE'S REPUBLIC OF CHINA 7–9 (Law Press 2007) (Hu serves as the head of Legislative Affairs Committee of the Standing Committee of NPC).

149 *See* 1986 Civil Code, *supra* note 48, at art. 3.

150 Civil Law Office of the Legislative Affairs Committee of the Standing Committee of the National People's Congress (hereinafter Civil Law of Office of NPC), THE PROPERTY LAW OF THE PEOPLE'S REPUBLIC OF CHINA—PROVISION EXPLANATION, LEGISLATIVE REASONS AND RELATED RULES 5 (Beijing University Press 2007).

151 *See* JIANG PING, *supra* note 17, at 176. All citizens of the People's Republic of China are equal before the law. XIAN FA (1982), *supra* note 15, at art.33.

152 *See id.*

153 *See* HU KANGSHENG, *supra* note 148, at 29; *see also* HUANG SONGYOU, UNDERSTANDING AND APPLICATION OF THE PROVISIONS OF THE PROPERTY LAW OF THE PEOPLE'S REPUBLIC OF CHINA 54 (People's Court Press 2007) (Huang is the Vice President of the Supreme People's Court of China).

154 *See* HU KANGSHENG, *supra* note 148, at 29–30.

155 *See id.*; *see also* YAO HONG, DETAILED EXPLANATIONS TO THE PROPERTY LAW OF THE PEOPLE'S REPUBLIC OF CHINA 8 (People's Press 2007).

156 *See* JIANG PING, *supra* note 17, at 173; *see also* HU KANGSHENG, *supra* note 148, at 7–8.

157 *See* National People's Congress (China), Real Property Law 1 art. 4 (Mar. 16, 2007), *available at* http://www.bjreview.com.cn/document/txt/2007–07/26/content_70481. htm.

158 *See* WANG LIMING, *supra* note 20, at 245; *see also* HUANG SONGYOU, *supra* note 153, at 55.

159 *See* Property Law, *supra* note 102, at art. 3.

160 *See* WANG LIMING, *supra* note 20, at 246.

161 *See* HUANG SONGYOU, *supra* note 153, at 245.

162 *See* Property Law, *supra* note 102, at art. 3. In addition, Article 41 of the Property Law explicitly provides that no entity or individual may acquire ownership of real estate and chattel that exclusively belong to the sate as prescribed by law. Moreover, there are twenty-five articles (from Article 45 to Article 69) in the Property Law that specify state ownership, collective ownership, and private ownership.

163 *See* HU KANGSHENG, *supra* note 148, at 7, 28; *see also* YAO HONG, *supra* note 155, at 8.

164 *See* Civil Law Office of NPC, *supra* note 150, at 6–11. In its explanation to each provision of the Property Law, the book lists all relative provisions contained in

major foreign countries' civil codes to indicate source or origin. Many of the provisions are cited from German Civil Code as well as Japanese Civil Code.

165 For example, in real estate registration, the common law country's "Torrens System" (Registration System) was considered. *See* WANG LIMING, *supra* note 20, at 310. For "Torrens System," see SINGER, *supra* note 21, at 562.

166 *See* Property Law, *supra* note 102, at art. 2.

167 *See* HU KANGSHENG, *supra* note 148, at 24. The Property Law does not generally regulate all relationships concerning attribution and utilization of things. It only deals with property relationships among equal subjects arising from attribution and utilization of things.

168 *See* Property Law, *supra* note 102, at arts. 1–38.

169 *See* John Merryman, *Policy, Autonomy, and the Numerus Clausus in Italian and American Property Law*, 12 AM. J. COMP. L. 224 (1963).

170 *See id.*

171 *See* Thomas W. Merrill & Henry E. Smith, *Optimal Standardization in the Law of Property: The Numerus Clausus Principle*, 110 YALE. L.J. 1, 4 n.6 (2000).

172 *See id.* at 4. The article actually says that in contrast to civil law systems, where numerus clausus is recognized explicitly, "[i]n the common law, the principle that property rights must conform to certain standardized forms has no name." *Id.*

173 As described in an English case, "incidents of a novel kind cannot be devised and attached to property at the fancy or caprice of any owner." Keppell v. Baily (1834), 39 Eng. Rep. 1042, 1049 (Ch.).

174 *See* WANG LIMING, *supra* note 20, at 265.

175 *See* JIANG PING, *supra* note 17, at 126–128. Also, under the 1986 Civil Code, transfer of property rights on movables may be made in the way as agreed upon by the parties. *See* 1986 Civil Code, *supra* note 48, at art. 72. Unless the law stipulates otherwise or the parties concerned have agreed on other arrangements, the ownership of property obtained by contract or by other lawful means shall be transferred simultaneously with the property itself.

176 *See* HU KANGSHENG, *supra* note 148, at 30. A similar concept in U.S. property law is the "fee simple absolute," meaning that ownership lasts forever. *See* SINGER, *supra* note 21, at 308.

177 *See* WANG LIMING, *supra* note 20, at 266.

178 *See* JIANG PING, *supra* note 17, at 129.

179 *See* MERRILL & SMITH, *supra* note 171, at 6.

180 *See* WANG LIMING, *supra* note 20, at 266.

181 *See* MERRILL & SMITH, *supra* note 171, at 8. "When property rights are created, third parties must expend time and resources to determine the attributes of these rights, both to avoid violating them and to acquire them from present holders." *Id.*

182 *See* HUANG SONGYOU, *supra* note 153, at 60–61.

183 *See* HU KANGSHENG, *supra* note 148, at 31.

184 Under the Chinese Law of Legislation, the national legislative interpretation of law has the same effect as law in the nation. *See* Legislation Law of China, *supra* note 105, at art. 47.

185 Note that in China courts have no authority to interpret law but to interpret application of law. Thus, the interpretation of law is deemed as a legislative action, and the interpretation of application of law is a judicial function. See XIAN FA (1982), *supra* note 15, at art. 67 (The Standing Committee of National People's Congress exercises the following functions and powers: ... (4) to interpret laws); *see also* The Organic Law of People's Courts of China art. 33 (adopted on July 1, 1979, amended on Sept. 2, 1983 and Oct. 31, 2006), *available at* http://www.dffy.com/faguixiazai/xf/200611/200611001194362.htm.

186 *See* HUANG SONGYOU, *supra* note 153, at 61.

187 The voidance may not, for example, affect in any way the validity of contract involved. *See id.*

188 The term "publicity" is popular in China to refer to the formality for the change of property. *See* WANG LIMING, *supra* note 20, at 306.

189 Under section 891 of the German Civil Code, the registration of a property right in the land register is required for obtaining the ownership of the land. *See* MICHAEL WENDLER ET AL., KEY ASPECTS OF GERMAN BUSINESS LAW 121–130 (3d ed., Springer 2006). According to section 656 of Swiss Civil Code, the entry thereof in the land register is necessary to the acquisition of ownership in land. *See* THE SWISS CIVIL CODE 155 (Boston Book Company 1915).

190 *See* Kazuo Hatoyama, *The Civil Code of Japan Compared with the French Civil Code*, 11 YALE L.J. 354, 362 (1902).

191 *See* JESSE DUKEMINIER ET AL., PROPERTY 615–623 (6th ed. 2006).

192 Today, only a few states in the United States use registration for the title of land. *See id.* at 617.

193 *See* SINGER, *supra* note 21, at 545.

194 *See* Property Law, *supra* note 102, at art. 9.

195 *See id.* at art. 23. The easement shall be established at the time when the easement contract comes into effect. Where the related parties request to have the easement registered, they may apply to the registration agency for the registration. Without being registered, no easement shall be made against a *bona fide* third party.

196 *See id.* at art. 24.

197 *See id.* at art. 9.

198 *See id.* at art. 28.

199 *See id.* at art. 29.

200 *See id.*, art. 30

201 *See* Property Law, *supra* note 102, at arts. 127, 155.

202 *See id.* at art. 127

203 *See id.* at art. 158.

204 *See id.* at art. 10.

205 *See id.* at art. 13.

206 *See* JIANG PING, *supra* note 17, at 116.

207 *See* HUANG SONGYOU, *supra* note 153, at 43.

208 *See* LUIGI MIRAGLIA, COMPARATIVE LEGAL PHILOSOPHY APPLIED TO LEGAL INSTITUTIONS 523–524 (John Lisle trans., Boston Book Company 1912).

209 *See* WANG LIMING, *supra* note 20, at 264.

210 *See* XU DIYU, LECTURES ON HOT TOPICS OF PROPERTY LAW 30 (2007).

211 *See* JIANG PING, *supra* note 17, at 115–116.

212 *See* XU DIYU, *supra* note 210, at 27.

213 *See* JIANG PING, *supra* note 17, at 120–21.

214 *See id.* at 121.

215 Ownership is considered to comprise a bundle of rights, including right to possession, right to use, right to interest and right to disposition. Among those rights, the right to disposition is deemed as the most crucial one. *See* SINGER, *supra* note 21, at 2–3.

216 By analogy, State and a state-owned enterprise are deemed as shareholder and a company where a shareholder owns equity of the company but does no have the ownership to the value he contributed to the company, and company is the owner of the property of the company. *See* XU DIYU, *supra* note 210, at 32.

217 *See* Property Law, *supra* note 102, at art. 2.

218 JIANG PING, *supra* note 17, at 121–122.

219 *See* HOU SHUPING ET AL., ANALYSIS ON THE ISSUES OF PROPERTY LAW 93 (Law Press, China 2007).

220 See Property Law, *supra* note 102, at art. 20.

221 *See id.*

222 Pursuant to Article 20 of the Property Law, the advance registration will be vacated if after the advance registration the creditor right is extinguished or the registration is not applied within three months from the date when the immovable can be registered. *See id.*

223 *See* Xu Diyu, *supra* note 210, at 3; *see also* Cui Jianyuan & Shen Weixing, Study on the Thorny Issues of Property Law Legislation of China 111–134 (Tsinghua University Press 2005).

224 For instance, under Article 20 of the Property Law, where the parties concerned conclude a purchase agreement on a premise or other real property, they may apply to the registration organ for advance notice registration to guarantee the realization of the property right in the future. After the advance notice registration, any disposal of the real property without obtaining the consent of the holder of the advance notice registration shall produce no effect of property right. *See* Property Law, *supra* note 102.

225 *See* Yang Lixin, Property Law 35 (2007).

226 *See* Jiang Ping, *supra* note 17, at 166.

227 *See id.* If there were both property right and creditor right on a specific immoveable or moveable, the priority of protection shall be given to the property right, except for otherwise provided by law.

228 *See* Wang Liming, *Speech at the 22nd Legal Lecture of the Standing Committee of the National People's Congress, available at* http://www.law-lib.com/Lw/lw_view.asp?no-741.

229 *See* Jiang Ping, *supra* note 17, at 166–167.

230 In China, a lease is not regarded as a property interest, but as a contractual relationship. And as such the lease is provided in contract law other than in property law. *See* Contract Law of the People's Republic of China ch. 13 (adopted by NPC on March 1999, effective October 1, 1999), Contracts for Lease, *available at* http://www.cclaw.net/lawandregulations/chinese_contract_law.txt.

231 For example, a buyer of a house who has possession of the house may not have a valid claim against other buyers who also have signed contract with the seller because registration is the prerequisite to the effectiveness of the change of the property right. Even if a buyer of a house who has registered would take the house against all other buyers, it is not because of the priority of the property right, but because of the registration that enables him to own the house. *See* Jiang Ping, *supra* note 17, at 167.

232 *See id.* at 171.

233 *See id.*

234 *See* Wang Liming, *supra* note 228; *see also* Yang Lixin, *supra* note 225, at 35.

235 Xian Fa (1982), *supra* note 15, at art. 10.

236 *See* Property Law, *supra* note 102, at art. 47.

237 *See id.* at art. 58.

238 *See* Randolph & Jianbo, *supra* note 94, at 85.

239 Article 10 of the Chinese constitution explicitly prohibits organization or individual from appropriating, buying, selling, or in any other ways unlawfully transferring land. Xian Fa (1982), *supra* note 15, at art. 10.

240 The Provisions put the right to use of land into different categories and each category has a different term for the use. Under Article 12 of the Provisions, the maximum term for each category is as follows: Residential: seventy years; Industrial fifty years, Education, Science and Technology, Culture, Public Health, or Athletic Facilities: fifty years; Commercial, Tourist, or Recreation: forty years; Combined or other purposes: fifty years. A full text of the Provisions in Chinese is available at http://www.jincao.com/fa/law19.95.htm. Chengzhen guoyoutudi shiyongquan

churang he zhuanrang zhanxingtiaoli [Temporary regulation for transfer of the right to use the state owned land] Order No. 55 by St. Council of China. *See also* RANDOLPH & JIANBO, *supra* note 94, at 127–128.

241 *See id.* at art. 41 (Provisions).

242 *See id.* at art. 40 (Provisions).

243 *See* HUANG SONGYOU, *supra* note 153, at 447.

244 *See* Civil Law Office of NPC, *supra* note 150, at 274–275.

245 *See* Property Law, *supra* note 102, at art. 149.

246 *See id.*

247 *See Southern Weekends: Investigation of Inside Story About the Incident of Chong Qing "Nail House"*, YCWB NEWS, Mar. 29, 2007, *available at* http://www.ycwb.com/news/2007–03/29 /content_1431372.htm; *see also* Wu Qi, *Behind the Incident of Chong Qing "Nail House"*, LIFEWEEK, Apr. 12, 2007, *available at* http://www.lifeweek.com.cn/2007–04–12/005318208.shtml.

248 The development plan was actually made by the city in 1993, but for some reason the process of implementing the plan was delayed until 2003. *See id.*

249 *See* Press Release, Chongqing City Jiulongpo People's Ct., *Report of Enforcement on Yangwu's Property at Chongquing City Jiulongpo*, http://www.ycwb.com/news/2007–04/03/content_1436519.htm (last visited Feb. 25, 2008).

250 *See id.*

251 *See* DANWEI, *Property Rights: the Coolest Nail House History*, http://www.danwei.org/bbs /property_rights_the_coolest_na.php.

252 *See supra* note 249 (Court Statement).

253 *See id.*

254 *See id.*

255 *See* DUKEMINIER, *supra* note 191, at 941; *see also* SINGER, *supra* note 21, at 677.

256 XIAN FA (1982), *supra* note 15, at art. 13.

257 *See* Paul, *supra* note 57, at 1409–10.

258 *See* Property Law, *supra* note 103, at art. 42. The full text of Article 42 of the Property Law reads:

> In order to meet the demands of public interests, it is allowed to requisition lands owned collectively, premises owned by entities and individuals or other realties according to the statutory power limit and procedures.
>
> When requisitioning land owned collectively, it is required to, in accordance with law and in full amount, pay land compensation fees, placement subsidies, compensations for the above-ground fixtures of the lands and seedlings and other fees, arrange for social security fees for the farmers with land requisitioned, guarantee their livelihood and protect their lawful rights and interests.
>
> When requisitioning the premises owned by entities and individuals or other realties, it is required to compensate for demolishment and relocation in accordance with law and protect the lawful rights and interests of the owners of the requisitioned realties; when requisitioning the individuals' residential houses, it is required to guarantee the housing conditions of the owners of the requisitioned houses.
>
> The compensation fees for requisition and other fees may not be embezzled, misappropriated, privately shared, detained or delayed in the payment by any entity or individual.

259 Land Management Law of China (promulgated by the National People's Congress on June 25, 1986, amended on August 29, 1998 and August 28, 2004 respectively), *available at* http://news.xinhuanet.com/zhengfu/2004–08/30/content_1925451.htm.

260 *See* WANG LIMING, *supra* note 20, at 425.

261 *See* Regulation of Administration of Demolishment and Relocation of Urban Houses art. 6 (promulgated by the Standing Committee, National People's Congress, June 6, 2001, effective November 1, 2001) (P.R.C.), *available at* http://www.law-lib.com/law/law_view.asp?id=15353.

262 *See id.* at art. 13.

263 *See id.* at art. 16.

264 *See id.*

265 *See id.* at art. 17.

266 For example, one scholar proposed defining the public interest to include public roads and transportation, public health, disaster prevention and treatment, courses of science, culture, and education, environmental protection, preservation of cultural and historical relics and national scenery, protection of water sources and land for water channeling and draining, protection of forests, and other public interests as provided by law. *See* LIANG HUIXING, ARTICLES, EXPLANATIONS, RATIONING, AND LEGISLATIVE REFERENCES OF PROPOSED DRAFT PROPERTY LAW 191–192 (2000).

267 *See* HUANG SONGYOU, *supra* note 153, at 162–163.

268 *See* JIANG PING, *supra* note 17, at 287–288.

269 *See* WANG LIMING, *supra* note 20, at 420.

270 XIAN FA (1982), *supra* note 15, at art. 13.

271 *See* Land Management Law, *supra* note 259, at art. 47 (requiring that for expropriation of land, compensation be given in accordance with the original use of the expropriated land).

272 *See* Property Law, *supra* note 102, at art. 42.

273 *See* YAO HONG, *supra* note 155, at 71.

274 *See* HU KANGSHENG, *supra* note 148, at 102–103.

275 *See* WANG LIMING, *supra* note 20, at 427.

276 *See id.* at 429. During the drafting of the Property Law, four major standards were proposed: reasonable compensation, proper compensation, adequate compensation, and marker price compensation. But legislators chose to keep "compensation" undefined, leaving power to determine the standard for compensation to local governments and other central government agencies. *See* HU KANGSHENG, *supra* note 148, at 103.

277 For example, in a "Nail House" situation, the owner of the household is normally blamed for not respecting the government, and rarely were people led to think that there was something wrong with the government. *See* Su Sengxiang, *How Should We Treat "Nail House"?*, Mar. 22, 2007, *available at* http://news.xinhuanet.com/legal/2007–03/22/content_5879558.htm.

278 In China, many government officers are "position-oriented," not "service-oriented," meaning that they tend to do what they think their superior wants in order to keep their positions stable and have a chance at promotions, rather than listen to what the people they are supposed to serve would like. *See* Cai Huihong, *Cultural Shackles—On the Slow Pace of the State Owned Enterprises Reform of China*, *available at* http://www.myshow.com.cn/class/oBarticle 1.htm. In China, local, county, and provincial government overlords all have an interest in power, and were they to coincide, the power is going to come down very hard on the neck of the average citizen. *See* Randolph, *supra* note 94.

Part 14

ADMINISTRATIVE LAW AND ADMINISTRATIVE LITIGATION

37

ADMINISTRATIVE LAW

Lin Feng

Source: Wang Chenguang and Zhang Xianchu (eds), *Introduction to Chinese Law*, Hong Kong: Sweet & Maxwell Asia, 1997, pp. 75–106.

Introduction

Administrative law has been widely accepted in the last two decades as a fully-fledged law subject. Unlike the approach generally accepted in common law jurisdiction where, administrative law is almost equivalent to judicial review, the concept of administrative law in China is much wider. Various definitions have been provided.[1] Each of them approaches the subject from a difference angle. An examination of those definitions shall reveal that they all include three ingredients, namely administrative law theory, substantive and procedural administrative law. Most textbooks and monographs on administrative law deal with the historical development and general principles of administrative law, administrative legal relationships, administrative organs and their personnel, administrative activities, administrative supervision and so on. Some textbooks may also cover part of substantive administrative law, such as laws on military administration, external administration, civil affairs administration, public security administration, education and culture administration, land administration, national economic administration, judicial administration and so on. More frequently, substantive administrative legislation is dealt with in other law subjects such as economic law, land law, customs law and so on.

Apart from substantive administrative legislation, procedural administrative law has developed well over the last two decades. Different legal procedures have been established to address grievances against the administration or its personnel for any decisions undertaken in the process of administration, upon which this chapter will focus. This chapter first examines an important concept in procedural administrative law, *i.e.* administrative acts. It then analyses the procedure available within the administration for the handling of grievances, *i.e.* administrative reconsideration. Afterwards, the chapter moves to examine external procedures, for the handling of grievances against the administration by judiciary, *i.e.* judicial review. The next part of the chapter looks at the handling of compensation claims against the administration by the judiciary. The chapter concludes with a few comments on the development of the system for the control of the exercise of executive power.

223

Administrative acts

Administrative acts refer to any administrative activities undertaken by the administrative organs. They should be distinguished from legislative and judicial acts which are undertaken by the legislature and judiciary respectively. Administrative acts can be classified in different ways. These classifications are essential to the understanding of the scope of administrative reconsideration and judicial review.

Concrete administrative act versus abstract administrative act

The concept of the concrete administrative act is the most important one in Chinese procedural administrative law because only concrete administrative acts are subject to administrative reconsideration and judicial review. However, neither the *Regulation on Administrative Reconsideration* (RAR) nor the *Administrative Litigation Law* (ALL) provide any definition as to what will constitute a concrete administrative act. But section 1 of the Opinions of the Supreme People's Court on the Interpretation of the ALL states that:

> "A concrete administrative act is a unilateral act undertaken by an administrative organ or its personnel, legally authorized organization, or organization or individual entrusted by an administrative organ, in exercising administrative authority in the process of administration, targeting at a specific citizen, legal person or other organization with regard to his rights and obligations."

Concrete and abstract administrative acts are a set of concepts. An abstract administrative act refers to the activity of administrative organs to make administrative regulations, regulations, decisions and orders which have a general binding effect in a certain area. Compared with a concrete administrative act, the target and the scope to which an abstract administrative act is applicable are quite different, as an abstract administrative act aims at all kinds of citizens, legal persons or organizations instead of a specific one. To include abstract administrative acts under administrative reconsideration will make it difficult to converge with the existing legal system of supervision.[2] However, that does not mean that an abstract administrative act will not be subject to proper legal supervision. Instead, alternative means have been provided by laws to deal with the issues of their illegality and inappropriateness. The Constitution and *Organic Law of Local People's Congresses and Local People's Governments* provide that abstract administrative acts shall be subject to the supervision of legislature (at both national and local levels) and the administrative organ at the next higher level. Furthermore, the ALL has also provided certain means to deal with certain kinds of problems concerning abstract administrative acts.

Internal administrative act versus external administrative act

Internal administrative acts refer to various measures taken by administrative organs against their own personnel, including warning, recording a demerit, removal from position, probation, dismissal and any other disciplinary actions. Disputes with regard to these internal acts are expected to be resolved within the original administrative organ, the organ at the next higher level or supervisory organ. External administrative acts refer to actions taken by administrative organs towards citizens, legal persons or other organizations not within the same administrative organ. The scope of external administrative acts is quite wide and not all external administrative acts are subject to administrative reconsideration and judicial review.

Act of State

Acts of State are a unique kind of administrative act. They are those undertaken in the name of the State and are sovereign actions. In order to protect national interests, every state grants special status to the Acts of State. China is not an exception. There are mainly two common categories. One relates to national defence, such as war and military practice. The other relates to diplomatic relationships, such as relationships with other countries or international organizations, establishment, severance of diplomatic relationships with foreign countries, and conclusions of treaties. Besides, Acts of State also include other important acts relating to state interests, such as the imposition of curfew by the State Council in certain areas or regions. Complaints against Acts of State can be brought neither for administrative reconsideration nor for judicial review. Instead they can only be duly addressed through other means.

Administrative reconsideration

Administrative reconsideration is a procedure through which grievances against the decision of an administrative organ can be reconsidered by another administrative organ either at the same level or at the next higher level. Upon the application of the aggrieved party, the original concrete administrative act, with which a citizen, legal person or any other organization is not satisfied and appeals against, will be reconsidered by another administrative organ.

With the adoption of the ALL, the importance of administrative reconsideration has become even more obvious and the requirement of administrative reconsideration has been enhanced. One source has revealed that about 70% of administrative litigation cases have been through the stage of administrative reconsideration before their submission to the people's court.[3]

Administrative reconsideration was available well before the adoption of the RAR in 1990. However, many important issues regarding administrative reconsideration, such as the conditions for application, jurisdiction, scope of reconsideration, and procedures etc. were not stipulated in any other legislation. They are provided for in the RAR for the first time.

The legal sources of the RAR

The 1990 RAR is a secondary legislation enacted by the State Council. Its legal status is lower than primary legislation adopted by the National People's Congress or its Standing Committee. Section 1 of the RAR states that the Constitution and other pertinent laws are its legal source. Other pertinent laws include the 1989 ALL, the *Organic Law of the State Council of the People's Republic of China 1982*, the *Organic Law of the Local People's Congresses and Local People's Governments of the People's Republic of China 1986* and other laws which have incorporated provisions on administrative reconsideration. The *Land Administration Law of the People's Republic of China 1986* is one of them. After the promulgation of the 1982 Constitution and before the adoption of the 1990 RAR, the system of administrative reconsideration had already been provided in more than 100 laws and regulations. These legal provisions had contributed to the effective resolution of administrative disputes and the strengthening of supervision by administrative organs themselves.

The RAR has clarified those provisions in primary legislation. It has provided for the scope of administrative reconsideration and makes it unnecessary to stipulate the availability of administrative reconsideration in every primary or subsidiary legislation, apart from those not falling within the listed categories in the RAR.

The Administrative Reconsideration Law is at present under draft and is very likely to be enacted soon.

Its nature and function

The purpose of administrative reconsideration is to safeguard and supervise administrative organs in exercising their functions and powers, to prevent and rectify any malfeasant or improper concrete administrative acts, and to protect the lawful rights and interests of citizens, legal persons and other organizations.

In modern society, public administration is becoming more and more complicated and diversified. Administrative organs are involved in all sorts of activities. Whenever a decision is made by an administrative organ, it is bound to affect the interests of citizens, legal persons and other institutions in one way or another. In every country, especially a developing country like China, it is quite natural that certain administrative tortious activities may be committed. Furthermore, it will not be surprising that some administrative organs or their functionaries may, while exercising their authorities, misuse or even abuse their powers.

Therefore, the State should provide remedial measures for the aggrieved parties to redress their grievances and get compensation wherever it is appropriate. Administrative reconsideration is one such remedial measure. It is of an administrative nature as it is an administrative organ at the same level or the next higher level that will, through reconsidering the original decision, maintain, rescind or change an illegal or inappropriate concrete administrative act so as to effectively protect the legitimate interests of the aggrieved parties.

Another function of administrative reconsideration is to supervise the administrative organs in exercising their functions and powers. Through administrative reconsideration, administrative organs at the next higher level may examine the concrete administrative act undertaken by the organ at the lower level in order to see whether it is illegal or inappropriate. In so doing, the illegal or inappropriate concrete administrative act can be rectified within the system of administration. There are obvious advantages, such as the reduction of the workload on the people's courts, the increase of the grievance addressing speed and the increase of the efficiency of administration.

Administrative reconsideration has another equally important role to play, *i.e.* to protect and maintain administrative acts undertaken according to law. Administrative reconsideration is provided by legislation and it has to be conducted according to the conditions and procedures laid down by the RAR. The aggrieved party has to strictly follow those conditions and procedure. For example, section 5 of the RAR provides that administrative reconsideration shall usually apply a single-level system of reconsideration. It can prevent the aggrieved party from endlessly bothering an administrative organ and the legality of a concrete administrative act can be recognized in time and the efficiency of administration can be guaranteed.

Conditions for administrative reconsideration

In order to bring a case for administrative reconsideration, the aggrieved party must prove that the following conditions are satisfied. Firstly, the party at which the complaint is directed against must be an administrative organ, legal person or other organization which is authorized by laws or regulations to exercise administrative authority. This covers two situations. One is that the administrative organ is directly involved in disputes with the aggrieved party through exercising its administrative authority. The other is that the party at which the complaint is directed against is a non-governmental organ or other organization which is nevertheless authorized by laws or regulations to exercise administrative authority. For example, professional banks are authorized to exercise certain management authority. If an aggrieved party is not satisfied with their decisions, it can appeal to the people's bank at the same level for reconsideration.

Secondly, an aggrieved party can only apply for administrative reconsideration when it believes its own lawful rights or interests have been infringed upon by the concrete administrative act of an administrative organ or its functionary. This is a subjective test and there does not have to be a real infringement. It does not imply that the administrative organ involved has committed tortious action and the applicant is therefore entitled to compensation.

Thirdly, only concrete administrative acts can be reconsidered. For example, the refusal by a land administration bureau to grant land-use rights illegally or unreasonably. Excluded are abstract administrative acts and other acts. The latter includes actions of administrative organs in handling civil disputes as a third party or any civil activities conducted by the administrative organs themselves.

Sometimes relevant laws and regulations may also provide that the aggrieved party must fulfil the obligations imposed by the concrete administrative act before bringing a case against that decision. Taxation law provides a typical example.

Administrative reconsideration organs

The administrative reconsideration organs refer to those which accept applications for reconsideration, and shall, according to law, conduct reviews of the concrete administrative acts, and make decisions accordingly. Not all administrative organs will undertake the task of administrative reconsideration. For example, State Council, as the highest administrative organ, will not undertake administrative reconsideration. The purpose is to relieve it from becoming too involved in specific matters. Therefore, any complaints against provincial, autonomous regional, and autonomous municipal people's governments will be handled by themselves. Similarly any complaints against any Ministries will be dealt with by themselves. Any departments under county people's government, which do not have any further established institutions under their control, will not bear the responsibility of administrative reconsideration. For those departments which have further established institutions under their control, they will still not have the responsibility if the further established institutions do not perform the concrete administrative acts in their own names. The responsibility remains in the hands of county people's government. Township people's governments do not have the responsibility because they are at grassroots level and do not have any working departments under their control.

It is not those administrative organs that actually reconsider the original concrete administrative acts. Instead, there are reconsideration offices which are set up within the administrative reconsideration organs who are responsible for this. Such offices are internal components of administrative organs and do not have the status of independent legal persons. They cannot therefore make any decisions in their own names. All decisions have to be made in the name of the administrative organs to which they belong.

Grounds for administrative reconsideration

There are two main grounds for administrative reconsideration. One is illegality and the other is inappropriateness. The administrative reconsideration organ can review whether or not a concrete administrative act is legal or appropriate. Legality covers three different aspects. The first one is whether or not the administrative organ undertaking the concrete administrative act has exceeded its legal authority; the second is whether the administrative act complies with the provisions of the relevant laws and regulations; the third is whether the administrative organ undertaking the concrete administrative act has followed the proper legal procedure. Moreover, a concrete administrative act undertaken without sufficient evidence, with abuse of power or *ultra vires* elements are also regarded as illegal acts. It is therefore not difficult to see that the concept of illegality in China's administrative reconsideration is much wider than its counterpart in common law.

The other ground is inappropriateness of a concrete administrative act. It is impossible for laws and regulations to make detailed provisions in every aspect. There are bound to be discretions left in the hands of administrative organs. If an administrative organ exercises its discretionary power within its limits, the concrete administrative act undertaken will be lawful. But it may not be appropriate or reasonable. That is how the issue of inappropriateness arises. The RAR grants the authority to the administrative reconsideration organ to review the appropriateness of a concrete administrative act. If a concrete administrative act is inappropriate or unreasonable, then the administrative reconsideration organ may alter or change that act partially or completely, depending on the necessity. As an inappropriate act is lawful, review of inappropriateness will only take place after the review of the legality of the act. It is at the secondary level.

Scope of administrative reconsideration

The scope of administrative reconsideration deals with the kinds of concrete administrative acts which are reviewable by the administrative reconsideration organ. It determines the breadth and depth of administrative supervision and remedy. Chapter two of the RAR has listed the categories of concrete administrative acts subject to and not subject to reconsideration.

The first category is administrative sanction, including detention, fine, rescission of a permit or a licence, or order to suspend production or business operations or confiscation of property, which a citizen, legal person or other organization refuses to accept. Administrative sanction is imposed by administrative organs or other organizations authorized by laws or regulations to punish any citizens, legal persons or other organizations for violation of laws, regulations or rules. These are just a few main forms of administrative sanction. They are by no means the only ones subject to administrative reconsideration. In fact, there are many other kinds of administrative sanctions, such as the circulation of a notice of criticism, warning, order of destruction of food products which are prohibited to be produced, confiscation of illegal income and fake medicines and so on. They are all subject to administrative reconsideration.

The second category is compulsory administrative measures, including restriction of personal freedom or the sealing up, distraint, or freezing of property, which one refuses to accept. This category has two components. One is compulsory measures taken against personal freedom, which include the following main measures. Education through labour is a compulsory educational reform measure. The duration is between one to three years and can be extended for another year if necessary. Education has duel functions, *i.e.* both in terms of education and punishment. It is not an administrative sanction and should be distinguished from reform through labour which is targeted at criminals and executed by prison or labour reform teams. Detention is a compulsory administrative measure to restrict personal freedom. For example, under *Customs Law*, suspected smugglers can, after the approval of the head of the Customs office, be detained for 24 hours which can be extended to 48 hours under special circumstances, if the Customs office intends to transfer the case to the judicial organs. There are also other kinds of compulsory administrative measures such as segregation, which can also be brought to administrative organ for reconsideration.

The second component is restriction on property, including the sealing up, distraint and freezing of property in order to prevent its owner from disposition. The property concerned is sealed at its location and will not be transferred to the administrative organ. The seal cannot be removed by the property owner without the permission of the administrative organ. Restraint is a measure to take movable property under the control of the administrative organ either for the purpose of collecting evidence or preventing the party concerned removing the property. Freezing is a measure to freeze the bank account of the party concerned by the bank in order to prevent the party from disposing of the money in its account.

The third category is infringement upon a managerial decision-making authority, which is held to have been perpetrated by an administrative organ. This provision aims to protect the managerial decision-making authorities of all kinds of enterprises. Managerial autonomy, including the right to possess, to use, and to dispose of property, is essential to the success of any enterprise. Various legislation has now been passed to separate ownership from managerial authority. Any unlawful or inappropriate infringements of such autonomy may be challenged through administrative reconsideration.

The fourth category is refusal by an administrative organ to issue a permit or licence, which one holds oneself legally qualified to obtain, or a failure to respond to an application. Whether or not a certain kind of activity needs a licence or permit is governed by legislation. Currently, licence or permit systems are widely used in many areas, such as in the protection and maintenance of important resources and the ecological environment, the protection of public safety and health, the maintenance of normal economic order, the management of cultural activities and so on. There are several conditions which have to be satisfied by an applicant in order to obtain a licence, *e.g.* the relevant administrative organ must have the authority to grant the licence, the applicant must apply within the law and so on.

The fifth category is refusal by an administrative organ to perform its statutory duties with regard to protecting one's personal or propriatory rights, as one has applied for, or its failure to respond to the application. Only those organs which have the legal responsibility to protect personal and propriatory rights can be complained against under this provision.

What has been discussed above is one aspect of the authority enjoyed by administrative organs, *i.e.* the authority to grant or deprive the party concerned of its rights. The next category is about the other aspect, namely the authority to impose upon or relieve someone from an obligation. It is where an administrative organ is held to have illegally demanded the performance of duties. All duties to be imposed should have clear legal basis. However, this is not the case in practice. Reports are often heard about unlawful collection of fees and imposition of other duties. The parties concerned can not only refuse to pay but also apply for administrative reconsideration. However, it is claimed that no application for administrative reconsideration is allowed if the administrative organ concerned requests the citizens, legal persons or other organizations to pay in terms of a donation provided that no administrative authority is used. This is not logical. When an administrative organ is involved, it is quite natural that the people will believe that administrative authority will be invoked if they do not pay the so-called donation. It is better to prohibit administrative organs from requesting donations. Moreover, section 9(8) provides that all kinds of concrete administrative acts are subject to administrative reconsideration if they have infringed upon either other personal rights or other proprietary rights which are not covered in the above categories.

Section 9(9) further broadens the scope of administrative reconsideration by providing that application for administrative reconsideration can be lodged against any other concrete administrative acts against which, according to the laws and regulations, an administrative lawsuit or an application for reconsideration may be instituted. One kind of application which could be lodged under section 9(9) is complaints against infringement upon rights other than personal or proprietary rights, such as civil and political rights. Election right is one example. As the RAR was enacted after the promulgation of the ALL, it is obvious that the intention of the State Council is to bring the RAR in line with the ALL. Certain concrete administrative acts which are not judicially reviewable may also be subject to administrative reconsideration as long as a specific law or regulation so provides. It is reasonable that remedial measures should be provided as long as the rights or interests of the party concerned are infringed upon. The *1989 Law of the People's Republic of China on Assemblies, Processions and Demonstrations is* one such example where judicial review is not allowed but administrative reconsideration is nevertheless allowed. *Regulations on Registration and Management of Social Organizations* is another one. In this sense administrative reconsideration can be said to be complementary to judicial review.

There are four kinds of administrative acts which are not subject to administrative reconsideration. They are abstract administrative acts, internal administrative acts, Acts of State and arbitration, conciliation or other dispositions of civil disputes. However, any decisions made by administrative organs concerning the ownership of or the right to use land, mineral resources, forests and so on are subject to administrative reconsideration.

Applicable legislation

The concept of legislation in its broad sense covers the laws enacted by the NPC, the administrative regulations adopted by the State Council, local regulations promulgated by local legislatures, regulations, decisions and orders with a general binding force formulated and promulgated by administrative organs at higher levels according to law, and the regulations passed by autonomous regions. The legal effects of these normative documents are different. The issue is whether they can all be applied by the administrative reconsideration organ in handling cases. There is no argument with regard to the applicability of laws, administrative regulations, and local regulations. Controversy focuses mainly on the applicability of regulations, decisions and orders with a general binding force formulated and promulgated by administrative organs at higher levels according to law.

As far as regulations are concerned, the Constitution and *Organic Law on Local People's Congresses and Local People's Governments* provide that certain administrative organs have the authority to make universally binding regulations. They include various Ministries and Commission of the State Council, Provinces, Autonomous Regions and Municipalities under direct control of the Central Government. These regulations will normally work out the details of the laws and administrative regulations and they therefore play an essential role in the implementation of the laws and administrative regulations in social life and in the enhancement of administrative efficiency. Practice also reveals that a large quantity of concrete administrative acts are undertaken by relying on various regulations. In certain areas more than 70% of applicable normative documents are these regulations and given this fact, administrative reconsideration must apply those regulations. Otherwise, people will doubt the legal effect of regulations, especially when concrete administrative acts are undertaken according to these regulations. Therefore the RAR provides that regulations should also be applied by the administrative reconsideration organ. One pre-condition is of course that the regulations must be made according to laws and are therefore lawful and effective regulations.

The next issue to look at are decisions and orders. These play an important role in filling the vacuum left by laws, administrative regulations and regulations, especially in cities which do not have the authority to make local regulations. However, existing decisions and orders from different departments or governmental organs sometimes contradict each other and no sound system has been developed to improve on the making of decisions and orders. The RAR has provided that decisions and orders should be relied upon in administrative reconsideration cases. In theory this means that the lower administrative organs should obey the decisions and orders from higher administrative organs, as opposed to concrete legal decisions.

Concern has been expressed about the different provisions in this aspect between administrative reconsideration and judicial review. The ALL provides that laws and administrative regulations are to be relied on whereas regulations can only be referred to. The issue then arises of applications of different standards in dealing with the same case. If the decisions or orders relied upon by the administrative reconsideration organ are themselves lawful or effective, then those decisions or orders are consistent with the laws and administrative regulations, and so reliance upon the decisions and orders will make it easier to resolve the case in dispute.

What is left is a more complicated issue. That is what the administrative reconsideration organ is supposed to do if it finds that the regulations, or decisions or orders with a general binding force, which serve as the basis for a concrete administrative act, are in conflict with the laws, administrative regulations or other regulations?

It is clear that no application for reconsideration can be lodged against any decisions or orders with a general binding force because they are abstract administrative acts. Even worse, they need to be relied upon by the administrative reconsideration organ. Neither is it possible to bring a case for judicial review against these decisions or orders. However, procedures do exist to redress such problems. The first is an administrative procedure, based on the supervisory role played by a higher administrative organ or people's government over a lower administrative organ or people's government. If the decisions or orders fall within the scope of functions and powers of the competent administrative reconsideration organ, it can then decide to nullify or change the decisions or orders.

The administrative reconsideration organ, will not have the power to handle the matter and has to report to the administrative organ at the next higher level if the regulations, decisions, or orders with a general binding force, which serve as the basis for a concrete administrative act, are made by an administrative organ or people's government enjoying a higher status than itself. If the administrative organ at the next higher level does not have the power to handle the case either, the case shall be submitted to an organ which does have the power. Once the inconsistency between the normative documents is resolved by the administrative organ with authority, the administrative reconsideration organ may resume the hearing of the case.

Remedies

As far as a concrete administrative act is concerned, if the application of laws, administrative regulations, regulations as well as the decisions and orders with a general binding force are correct, the facts are clearly ascertained, and the statutory limits of authority and procedures are duly complied with, then the applicant shall not have a case for administrative reconsideration. The concrete administrative act, which has been challenged, will be sustained. On the other hand, if the applicant has got a case, there are various kinds of remedies available through administrative reconsideration. The defending party may be required to rectify procedural inadequacies, or a fixed time may be set for the defending party to perform the duty, or the concrete administrative act may be annulled or changed. Even a specific performance can be required of the defending party.

Judicial review

Administrative litigation (judicial review) refers to the litigation activity under which a citizen, legal person or other organization, believing that his legitimate rights or interests have been infringed by a concrete administrative act of an administrative organ or its personnel, applies to the people's court for judicial protection. The court will then exercise its power of review of the administrative act concerned and adjudicate upon it. This is a kind of judicial control over the exercise of administrative power by the executive branch of the government. Different countries have different constitutional structures due to their different historical, political and cultural backgrounds. The relationship between the three main branches of the government, *i.e.* legislature, executive and judiciary, differs from one country to another. Judicial control of executive power is concerned with the relationship between the judiciary and the executive. It is quite natural that the organs responsible for judicial review, the scope, grounds and remedies for judicial review may differ from one country to another. The main legislation in China governing judicial review is the 1990 ALL.

The objective of the ALL

The ALL intends to achieve two kinds of objectives namely the procedural and substantive objectives. The direct (procedural) objective of the ALL is to ensure the correct and prompt handling of administrative cases by the people's courts. The ALL lays down the procedural requirements as to how a litigation against the administration should be conducted. It has not only defined the authority of the courts in adjudicating administrative cases, but also laid down certain restrictions on the judicial control of administration. These procedural requirements are enacted to achieve correctness and accuracy of adjudication in administrative cases.

However, procedural legislation is to ensure the proper application and implementation of substantive legislation. The ALL has two substantive objectives to achieve. One is to protect the lawful rights and interests of citizens, legal persons and other organizations. The other is to safeguard and supervise the exercise of administrative powers by administrative organs. Through the adjudication of specific administrative cases, the people's courts will examine the legality of administrative acts undertaken by the administrative organs. If the acts undertaken are illegal, the courts have the responsibility to rectify them and exercise their authority accordingly and issue an order of rectification or nullification.

The two substantive objectives of the ALL are in theory not contradictory, but they have a different emphasis and in practice it is very difficult to achieve the balance between the two. Judicial practice has shown that the proper exercise of authority by the administration has often been over-emphasized.

Sources of judicial review

As China adopts a continental legal system, the jurisdiction of the courts over lawsuits against administration has to be prescribed by legislation.

The constitutional source of judicial review in China is section 41, which has to be brought into operation by other legislation. The direct source of judicial review has therefore to be provided for by specific laws or administrative regulations. Section 2 of the ALL provides that:

"If a citizen, a legal person or any other organization considers that his or its lawful rights and interests have been infringed upon by a specific administrative act of an administrative organ or its personnel, he or it shall have the right to bring a suit before a people's court in accordance with this Law."

This provision has provided for the three essential conditions for a case to qualify as an administrative case. Firstly, the plaintiff must be one who believes that his lawful rights or interests have been infringed upon by administrative activities. Secondly, the defendant must be an administrative organ or its functionary which or who is authorized to exercise administrative authority. None of the people's courts, legislative organs, Party's branches and military organs can be sued as defendants. Thirdly, the administrative activities to be sued against must be concrete administrative acts.

Scope of jurisdiction

Section 2 of the ALL only provides for the general condition under which a person may bring a case to the people's court for judicial review. However, not all concrete administrative acts are judicially reviewable by the people's courts. The concept of scope of jurisdiction is concerned with the categories of administrative acts which are, and are not, subject to judicial review.

Chapter two of the ALL lays down the categories of administrative acts which are reviewable and non-reviewable. The Opinions of the Supreme People's Court on the Implementation of the ALL provide more detailed provisions with regard to the scope of jurisdiction. The general principle is that the people's courts can only accept lawsuits against those concrete administrative acts which are reviewable according to legislation. If a concrete administrative act is not specifically mentioned by any legislation as reviewable, then it is not subject to judicial review. Section 11 of the ALL lists eight categories of concrete administrative acts which are reviewable. They are exactly the same as those categories for administrative reconsideration.

Section 12 of the ALL lists four kinds of matters which are not subject to judicial review. The first three that are excluded, are also excluded from administrative reconsideration. If a person is not satisfied with arbitration awards or any other disposition of civil disputes, he cannot bring a case for judicial review either. Instead, he can bring the matter to the relevant people's court as a civil case. If any concrete administrative acts shall, as provided by law, be finally decided by an administrative organ, they shall not be subject to judicial review.

Grounds for judicial review

Grounds for judicial review refer to the legal basis upon which a concrete administrative act may be lawfully challenged. They are the legal grounds upon which the judiciary may review a concrete administrative act. There are altogether seven specific grounds for judicial review.

Illegality

Section 5 of the ALL lays down the principle of legality, *i.e.* the people's courts shall examine the legality of a concrete administrative act. That means the people's courts shall normally only review whether or not an administrative organ has breached any legislation in undertaking a concrete administrative act. But the scope of illegality seems to be very wide. It covers insufficiency of evidence, inaccuracy in the application of legislation, failure to comply with legal procedure, and *ultra vires*. In principle, the people's courts will not review a concrete administrative act falling within administrative discretion. Any complaints against the appropriateness of the exercise of discretionary powers should usually be handled through administrative reconsideration. But this does not mean that the courts can never review inappropriate administrative decisions. In fact, the people's courts have been granted certain jurisdiction to scrutinize the improper exercise of discretionary power, based on the grounds of abuse of power, and delay or failure in the performance of statutory duty, obvious unfairness, which will be discussed in the section on judicial control of discretionary power.

LACK OF EVIDENCE

It must first be established whether the evidence is accurate and sufficient, which is the pre-condition and basis for the legality of a concrete administrative act. Deviation from this basis and precondition will make it impossible for the application of legislation to be correct.

Evidence can be classified as ordinary and essential evidence. The former refers to all kinds of materials and methods as provided under the ALL to be used to prove the facts of the case. The latter must satisfy three requirements. Firstly, it must be objective. Secondly, it must be relevant. The people's courts will examine the submitted evidence to see whether or not it is directly related to the case and therefore essential to the adjudication of the case. Thirdly, the evidence must be lawfully obtained. If the methods adopted to obtain the evidence are unlawful, then the evidence, even though essential to the case, cannot be used as evidence for the adjudication.[4]

In order to ensure that the concrete administrative act is lawful, the facts relied on by the administrative decision-maker must be accurate, reliable, sufficient and conclusive. Failure in this respect may make the decision unlawful.

Sufficiency and conclusiveness are closely related. Sufficiency of evidence means that there must be enough evidence to prove all the material facts of the case. If any of the material facts do not have any evidence, this will be regarded as insufficient evidence. All the evidence used must be coherent and must point to one conclusion. We are only concerned with key evidence which is essential for the undertaking of the concrete administrative act. Conclusiveness of evidence refers to the importance of evidence, upon which the people's court can review whether or not the decision undertaken by the administrative organ is lawful.

Section 32 of the ALL provides that the defendant shall bear the burden of proof for the concrete administrative act he has undertaken and shall provide the evidence and regulatory documents in accordance with which the act has been undertaken. If the defendant cannot provide the court with the key evidence or the normative documents before the completion of the trial at the first instance, then the people's court may annual the concrete administrative act. If the defendant fails to provide evidence or the evidence provided does not include key evidence, then the people's court can rule against the defendant. If the defendant only submits evidence which is to his own advantage, then the plaintiff can rebut by providing his own evidence. There is one issue worthy of discussion, *i.e.* when the defendant is supposed to discharge his burden of proof and whether late submission of evidence should be accepted. Section 43 of the ALL states that the defendant shall provide the people's court with the documents on the basis of which a concrete administrative act has been undertaken and file defence pleadings within ten days of receiving the copy of the plantiff's pleadings. It is made very clear that the defendant is required to submit his defence before the actual hearing. However, section 30 of the Opinions allows the defendant to submit evidence at any time before the completion of the trial at the first instance. That provides a contradiction between two different sources of law. According to the hierarchy of legislation, the provision in the ALL should prevail over the Opinions issued by the Supreme People's Court.

ERRORS IN THE APPLICATION OF LEGISLATION

The exact meaning of inaccuracy in the application of legislation is not explained either in the Opinions or the ALL. One scholar suggests that application of legislation should refer to the application of both substantive and procedural legislation.[5] The people's courts should review not only the errors in the application of substantive legislation but also errors in the application of procedural legislation. It is correct to say that legislation includes both substantive and procedural ones. It seems better to restrict the erroneous application of legislation to substantive legislation. In other words, the inclusion of both substantive and procedural legislation under 52(2)(b) would make the provision of 52(2)(c) redundant.

Errors in the application of legislation may be caused by various factors. Firstly, China adopts a unilateral legal system and there are different levels of legislation. Central legislature (the NPC), local legislature, central government, local government, and various governmental organs have respective authorities to promulgate legislation (law, administrative regulations, regulations, and other normative documents). It happens sometimes that two pieces of legislation are contradictory. If that is the case, the administrative organ concerned has to choose one, which is often a difficult task especially if the two pieces are at the same level of the legal hierarchy.

Secondly, Chinese legislation is, compared with legislation in the United Kingdom or Hong Kong, very general and the provisions in the legislation only lay down the principles in the areas concerned and normally lack detailed provisions. This has something to do with the tradition of the continental legal system which normally emphasizes the importance of legal principles. Furthermore, China has, since 1978, started to develop from a planned economy to a market economy and therefore many former legislations are no longer suitable for the growing needs of economic development. During a transitional period, it is not surprising to find gaps in legislation. It is therefore almost unavoidable that errors will occur in the process of application of legislation.

Thirdly, the quality of law enforcement officers is also essential to the accurate application of legislation because any legislation must be implemented by people.

Errors in the application of legislation can be classified into different categories.

a   Application of a Wrong Piece of Legislation
    Application of a wrong piece of legislation may be caused by several different factors. The first could be that the administrative act undertaken is according to legislation A while the applicable legislation should be legislation B. This may occur when several pieces of legislation govern the same kind of administrative activities, or one legislation grants different authorities to more than one administrative organ or several authorities to the same administrative organ. Therefore it often happens that one kind of activity is governed by several pieces of legislation, or several administrative organs. The second factor could be that the administrative organ has applied a legislation which has not come into force yet. The third possibility is that the administrative organ has, in undertaking the concrete administrative act,

applied a legislation which has already lost its legal effect. The fourth possibility is that the administrative organ has applied a legislation which it does not have the authority to apply. Normally, every piece of legislation stipulates its law enforcement organ to exercise administrative authority. That organ is empowered to apply the relevant legislation within the scope defined by the legislation. If an administrative organ has applied a legislation which it is not authorized to apply, then it will be deemed to have committed an error in the application of legislation. For example, if a municipal planning Administrative division handles the violation of municipal planning by a resident according to Land Administration Law, not City Planning Law, that decision may be set aside by the court. The fifth possibility is that the administrative organ intentionally avoids the application of an appropriate piece of applicable legislation. This may occur when there are several pieces of legislation. The administrative organ will choose the legislation that is to its advantage. Another possibility is that the administrative organ is supposed to apply special legislation, but it applies ordinary legislation.

b   Application of Wrong Provisions of Correct Legislation
There are two possibilities. One is that the administrative organ should apply one section or sub-section, but it actually applies another section or sub-section. The second possibility is that the administrative organ should apply several sections in the legislation, but it only applies one of them.

c   Application of Correct Legislation to Wrong Subject
This refers to situations under which the administrative organ either grants rights to, or imposes administrative penalties upon, those who are not entitled to receive such rights or penalties. Typical examples include the issue of licences to unqualified person(s), failure to issue licences to qualified person(s), and improper imposition of taxes.

COMPLIANCE WITH LEGAL PROCEDURE

Administrative procedure refers to the specific methods and steps for an administrative organ to undertake a concrete administrative act. An administrative decision needs to be made through one or other kind of procedure. Administrative procedure may be classified in different ways. According to the nature and function of administrative acts, it may be classified into administrative legislative procedure, administrative enforcement procedure and administrative judicial pocedure. It may also be classified into legal procedure, *i.e.* the procedure is laid down in legislation, and non-legal procedure, *i.e.* customs or traditions formulated from time to time by the administrative organ for making a particular kind of administrative decisions.

The necessity of judicial review of procedural legality can be illustrated as follows. Firstly, the rule of law principle requires administration according to legal requirements which include both substantive as well as procedural legal requirements. The rule of law principle demands that the administration complies with procedural legal requirements. Though China does not have a uniform administrative procedural law, some general principles on proper administration have been laid down in China's Constitution. Section 5 of the Constitution requires all state organs (including administrative organs) to abide by the law. Section 27 of the Constitution requires all state organs to carry out the principle of simple and efficient administration. However, these are only general principles. Their implementation in practice requires their incorporation into other legislation. The enactment of the *Administrative Penalty Law 1996* has set down the legal procedures for the establishment and imposition of administrative penalties.

Secondly, the breach of procedural requirement is itself an infringement of the rights of the aggrieved party. However, not enough attention has been paid to legislation on administrative procedural requirements. It is true that most substantive administrative legislation such as that on administration of commerce and industry, taxation, customs, public security and so on, has incorporated certain procedural requirements on the exercise of administrative authority. They are however, mainly very general and lack detailed provisions. There are often more procedural requirements for those under administration than those on administrative organs. Consequently, some important administrative procedures have not been incorporated into any legislation. These procedures are the customs formulated over the years in practice and are by no means arbitrary. They are normally followed in practice by the administrative organs in undertaking concrete administrative acts. In principle, the compliance with non-legal procedural requirements is purely voluntary. Whether or not the administrative organ follows the non-legal procedures will not affect the validity and effect of the decisions. Any concrete administrative acts undertaken accordingly will be non-reviewable.

EXCESS OF LEGAL AUTHORITY (*ULTRA VIRES*)

Various attempts have been made by Chinese scholars to define the concept of *ultra vires* in China. Some define the concept according to the contents of *ultra vires* while others define it according to the categories of different kinds of *ultra vires* activities. There are mainly two different views. One approach holds that the concept of *ultra vires* refers to the concrete administrative acts undertaken by the administrative organs, or its personnel, or other organizations either legally authorized, or entrusted by those administrative organs which exceed the scope of authority, either legally prescribed or authorized or entrusted. The other approach maintains that *ultra vires* refers to the circumstances under which the administrative organs either exercise the administrative power which is not legally granted to them or exceed the scope of legally authorized administrative power.

The main difference between the two approaches is whether or not the concept of *ultra vires* should include 'no authority' which refers to if the administrative organs have exercised administrative authority which is neither within their jurisdiction nor entrusted to them by other administrative organs. But both approaches agree that *ultra vires* is only about substantive *ultra vires*, which means that the administrative organs have actually undertaken activities which are in excess of their legal authority.

According to the above discussion of the concept of *ultra vires, ultra vires* administrative activities may be classified firstly into two categories. One is the exercise of authority which is not related to the functions of the administrative organs concerned (no authority). The other is the exercise of authority which is within the types of authority which the administrative organs may exercise but exceeds the scope of the jurisdiction of the specific administrative organ. The second may be further divided into

i	vertical ultra vires, *i.e.* lower administrative organs usurp the authority of the higher administrative organ or vice versa;
ii	horizontal *ultra vires, i.e.* one administrative organ usurps the authority of another administrative organ at the same level either because they are in different geographical locations or they are in charge of different administrative functions;
iii	*ultra vires* in content, *i.e.* the exercise of administrative power exceeds the legal scope.

Judicial control of discretionary power

Discretionary power is authorized by legislation and should be exercised within its defined legal scope and its exercise should be consistent with the objective and fundamental aim of the relevant legislation. Apart from this requirement, the administrative organ may choose to make decision A, which it believes to be accurate, instead of decision B.

As administrative discretionary power is a kind of administrative power, any decision made through the exercise of discretionary power is a unilateral act. The administrative organ has the authority to order the person (natural or legal) concerned to do or not to do something. The person concerned has the obligation to follow such an order. The relationship between the administrative organ and the person under administration is therefore unequal. The improper exercise of discretionary power may infringe upon the legitimate interests of the person concerned.

Administrative discretionary power is very flexible as the administrative organ is granted the authority to choose among different alternatives and the relevant legislation normally does not provide clear guidance with regard to which alternative should be chosen and how to choose. This feature has been claimed to be the essence of discretionary power. Because of this flexibility, an administrative organ may arbitrarily exercise its discretionary power which may lead to obviously unfair results or abuse of its authority. Both of which are the grounds recognized under the ALL upon which a concrete administrative act may be challenged through judicial review.

The traditional approach is that the exercise of discretionary power can only be appropriate or inappropriate. There does not exist the issue of illegality. Therefore discretionary power is not subject to judicial control. The current approach is that there are certain legal requirements upon the exercise of discretionary power, including its legal scope, the legislative objective and fundamental principles. If the exercise of discretionary power exceeds the legal scope or is against the legislative objective or fundamental principles, then that exercise of discretionary power should be regarded as illegal.

Apart from illegal exercise of discretionary power, there also exists inappropriate exercise of discretionary power which is not subject to judicial control. That does not mean no remedies are available to redress inappropriate exercise of discretionary power. If any person has any complaints in this aspect, he may bring the case to the relevant administrative organ at the next higher level for administrative reconsideration. If the inappropriateness attains a certain degree, they may also be subject to judicial review. According to section 54 of the ALL, there are three grounds under which discretionary power can be challenged.

ABUSE OF POWERS

Abuse of powers in administrative law mainly refers to abuse of administrative discretionary powers. Usually, an administrative organ is granted the discretion to undertake a concrete act when certain legal conditions are satisfied. The discretion concerns the activities, not the identification of facts. It may be granted in all kinds of activities. It could be about whether or not to undertake a concrete administrative act, what kind of acts should be chosen, the measures to be chosen, the scope of choice, the time limit or the methods of activities and so on. Two tests need to be satisfied. The first is a subjective one, *i.e.* it must be intentional. In other words, negligent acts can never be classified as abuse of power. The second is an objective test. The concrete administrative act undertaken by an administrative organ is, though within its discretion, against the purpose and principle of the relevant legislation and unreasonable. More specifically, three essential elements must be satisfied for a concrete administrative act to constitute abuse of power. They are: the concrete administrative act exceeds legal authority; the concrete administrative act is against or deviates from the objective and principle of the relevant legislation; the act undertaken is unreasonable. Unreasonableness is caused by improper exercise of discretionary power by an administrative organ.

Abuse of power may be caused by different factors. An unreasonable decision can be classified as abuse of power if it is made due to bad judgment on behalf of the decision-maker. For example, the decision-maker knows that the specific decision is against the objective of the relevant legislation but still makes the decision. It is also abuse of power if the decision-maker, in undertaking a

concrete administrative act, does not take into account the relevant considerations which should usually be considered, and arbitrarily takes an unreasonable
concrete administrative act. Likewise, if the decision-maker takes into account
irrelevant factors which are usually not taken into account, it also constitutes
abuse of power.

OBVIOUS UNFAIRNESS

Obvious unfairness is another ground upon which action can be taken to challenge the exercise of discretionary power. According to section 54(4), this
ground is rather limited. In order to invoke this ground, two conditions need to
be satisfied. One is the concrete administrative act can only refer to administrative penalties as mentioned in section 11(1), not any other kinds of concrete
administrative acts. The other is that the concrete administrative act must be
obviously unfair. There is no legislative interpretation on the meaning of
"obvious unfairness". One academic interpretation is that obviously unfair
administrative penalties refer to those imposed on the wrongdoers which are,
though with the scope of penalties provided by law and regulation, extremely
unfair and incompatible with the wrongs committed.[6] Firstly, the penalty
imposed upon the wrongdoer is incompatible with the wrong committed. It could
either be too heavy or too light. Secondly, quite different penalties are imposed
upon persons with the same responsibility in the same case. Thirdly, in the same
case the person committing serious wrong receives a light penalty while the
person committing a minor offence receives a heavy penalty. Another scholar
has suggested three principles in determining whether or not a concrete administrative act is obviously unfair. They are the principles of proportionality, equal
application and compatibility.[7]

Discretionary power may appear or exist anywhere and at any time. Due to
the impossibility of legislation to provide for details in every aspect and also the
difficulty to foresee what may happen in the future, administrative organs are
often granted discretion. On the one hand, they enjoy discretionary power in
making decisions as to whether or not to undertake concrete administrative acts
either through imposition of penalties or any other punishment. On the other,
they also enjoy discretionary power in undertaking abstract administrative acts.
For example, Chinese national legislation often stipulates that detailed rules for
implementation shall be made by the relevant authority in charge in accordance
with the laws, and be submitted to the State Council for approval. There is no
requirement as to whether or not and when the detailed rules for implementation
should be made. In this sense, the administrative organs enjoy discretionary
power in making subsidiary legislation, *i.e.* regulations or rules. Such discretion
may also be abused.

However, the ALL clearly provides that only concrete administrative acts are
judicially reviewable and abstract administrative acts are not reviewable. That
does not mean discretion in undertaking abstract administrative acts are not

subject to any control. Instead, different procedures of supervision exist. The control is by the administrative authority in charge or at the next higher level, and the legislature, both local and national.

FAILURE OR DELAY IN THE PERFORMANCE OF STATUTORY DUTY

The third ground for legal control of discretionary power is the failure or delay in the performance of statutory power, which is stated in section 54(3) of the ALL. This is concerned with inaction of the relevant administrative organs. There is not much academic writing on this ground. Even in Professor Luo's book on judicial review, judicial review of administrative inaction was only mentioned in passing, while each of the other six grounds of judicial review was discussed in a separate chapter. This ground is rather straightforward and simple in the sense that it is only related to the time when the concrete administrative act should be undertaken and nothing else. But it is at least equally important as any other grounds since failure or delay in the performance of statutory duty may also infringe upon the legitimate rights of those under administration. Much legislation does not stipulate the exact time limit for the performance of statutory duties by administrative organs. They are granted the discretion to determine when they shall undertake the concrete administrative acts. If an administrative organ intentionally delays or fails to commence performance, it will amount to the unlawful exercise of discretionary power. Such an exercise of discretion will not only affect the efficiency of administration but also cause damage to those under the administration.

There are several conditions which need to be satisfied in order to rely on this ground to challenge the administrative organ concerned. The first is that the administrative organ must owe a statutory duty towards the applicant, either to issue a licence or to provide protection. Without the existence of statutory duty, the administrative organ cannot be sued under this ground. Secondly, the statutory time limit must have been passed or a reasonable time period must have passed if there is no statutory time limit. Thirdly, the administrative organ must have refused or failed to respond during the time limit. Fourthly, there are no defences.

Judicial remedies

If an applicant has successfully challenged the concrete administrative acts undertaken by the relevant administrative organ, one of the following remedies may be granted.

ORDER OF RECTIFICATION

The defending party is supposed to undertake the concrete administrative act in accordance with legal procedures. The pre- condition is that there should be a legal procedure available. However, there are no systematic or comprehensive systems on administrative procedures. As a result, there are no existing procedures to be followed for many administrative activities. That is one of the main reasons why administrative organs neglect procedural requirements. But if there are procedural requirements in the relevant legislation, they should be followed. Failure to do so is deemed to be procedural inadequacy. This normally refers to such situations as failure of the defending party to reveal its own identity, or failure to inform the applicant of its rights, or a mistake in the date of the written decision etc. But the ascertaining of facts and application of laws are correct, and the breach of procedural requirements have not directly affected the substantive rights of the applicants. The defending party will only be required by the courts to make up or improve the procedural inadequacy in the concrete administrative act, which remains effective.

This is quite different from the western legal system where procedural justice is so cherished that breach of procedural legal requirements will lead to the act concerned being deemed void. This is because procedural fairness is the only thing which can definitely be achieved and everybody is regarded as equal before the same procedural requirements. Whereas different people will have different perceptions of substantive justice which is influenced by a number of factors such as ideologies, social and economic backgrounds, religious beliefs and so on.

SPECIFIC PERFORMANCE

If the defending party fails to perform the obligations imposed by laws, administrative regulations or regulations, it is a derelict activity. Two situations could arise. One is the defending party's refusal to perform the obligation; the other is the undue delay on the side of the defending party to perform the duties falling within its scope of obligations. The courts may set a fixed time for the defending party to perform the duty.

NULLIFICATION OR CHANGE OF THE CONCRETE ADMINISTRATIVE ACT

If the defending party commits substantive mistakes in the process of undertaking a concrete administrative act, the act shall be annulled, or changed or the defending party may be required by decision to undertake a new concrete administrative act. Substantive mistakes include ambiguity of the main facts, erroneous application of the laws, regulations, rules, or of decisions and orders with a general binding force, violation of legal procedures which affects unfavourably the lawful rights and interests of the applicant, the excess of authority or abuse of powers and obvious inappropriateness of the concrete administrative act.

Relationship between administrative reconsideration and judicial review

Administrative reconsideration and judicial review are different means to redress wrongs committed by administrative organs and to restore justice to the applicant while at the same time protecting the lawful exercise of executive authority by administrative organs. Sometimes the provisions of some laws and administrative regulations stipulate that the person concerned shall first apply for reconsideration and only bring a suit before a people's court if the person concerned does not accept the reconsideration decision. If that is the case, administrative reconsideration is compulsory and a pre-requisite for judicial review. That means all administrative remedies should be exhausted before resorting to judicial remedies. The relatively simple procedure of administrative reconsideration is convenient to both parties and may reduce the burden of the people's courts by solving most administrative disputes at the level of administrative reconsideration. If the applicant does not accept the decision made by the administrative reconsideration organ to reject his application, the applicant may, within fifteen days from the date of receiving the written decision of rejection, bring a lawsuit before the people's court. If the laws or administrative regulations provide otherwise, then those provisions have to be followed. For example, if the laws provide that the administrative reconsideration decision is final, no application for judicial review will be accepted.

Some laws or administrative regulations do not stipulate administrative reconsideration as the prerequisite for judicial review The applicant shall then have the choice, either to lodge an application for administrative reconsideration or to bring a case directly to the people's court for judicial review. If an application for judicial review has already been accepted, then no application for reconsideration will be accepted. On the other hand, if the applicant has lodged an application for administrative reconsideration which has been accepted, then no application for the same case can be filed before the people's court within the statutory time limit for administrative reconsideration.

State Compensation

The *State Compensation Law* (SCL) was adopted by the Standing Committee of the NPC on May 12, 1994 and came into effect on January 1, 1995. The law has for the first time clearly defined the legal basis for claiming compensation from state organs, including the scope and procedure of state compensation. The adoption of the SCL has not only contributed to the establishment of a comprehensive system of state responsibility in China but also filled a gap in the existing legislation of procedural administrative law.

Legislative development

The principle that the state has the responsibility to pay compensation is stated in China's first Constitution (1954) and reappears in the 1982 Constitution with only minor changes. The relevant provision now reads, "Citizens who have suffered losses as a result of infringement of their civic rights by any state organ or functionary have the right to compensation in accordance with the law". This is regarded as the constitutional basis for the establishment of a state compensation system. As specific laws and regulations are needed to implement the constitutional principle. The *Economic Contract Law of the PRC* (1981) and *Regulations of the PRC on Administrative Penalties for Public Security* (1986) are two examples incorporating provisions on the state's responsibility to pay compensation. *The General Principle of Civil Law (GPCL)* (1986) reaffirms the same constitutional principle. Section 121 of the GPCL imposes civil liability on state organs or their functionaries that, while executing their duties, encroach upon the lawful rights and interests of citizens or legal persons and cause damages.

In order to apply section 121 of the GPCL, many issues still have to be sorted out and tested, such as the relation between state organs and their functionaries concerning compensation, the liability of government organs for damages caused by public utilities, the necessity and procedure of compensation for illegal imprisonment and so on. These issues of common concern have perplexed the judiciary. It has become obvious that the broad constitutional principles and section 121 of the GPCL cannot meet the needs of China's changing society. More detailed legal provisions are needed.

The 1989 ALL provided some guidance on the handling of suits brought by citizens, legal persons or other organizations against government organs on "concrete administrative acts". It contains several clauses on the liabilities of state administrative organs to pay compensation. However, the ALL is in nature a procedural law and therefore focuses on procedural issues (such as the criterion for determining, and method of calculating state compensation) rather than substantive provisions. Moreover, the ALL is restricted to concrete administrative acts only, and does not cover either abstract administrative acts or acts carried out by non-administrative organs which nevertheless participate in administration. Therefore, in order to secure the implementation of the ALL, the SCL was finally adopted in May 1994.

Scope of application

The SCL does not include legislative compensation. Several concerns have contributed to the exclusion of legislative compensation from the SCL. Firstly, it is common practice with legislation in China that matters shall not be included if the legislators are uncertain as to whether or not and how they should be covered. Secondly, legislative acts have been claimed by some scholars as State Acts and therefore should be immune from responsibility for compensation. Thirdly, compatibility with the ALL and other legislation demands the exclusion of legislative compensation.

Different opinions have been expressed with regard to whether military compensation should be covered by the SCL. Damages caused by military acts may be classified into three categories. One is those caused by military exercises or training, which are, according to one source, the main ones. They are within the scope of civil disputes and can be recovered through civil claims according of section 121 of the GPCL and the procedure laid down by the *Civil Procedure Law (CPL)*. The second concerns actual military action consisting of lawful acts, and therefore should not be within the scope of the SCL. The compensation for those acts should be provided through administrative indemnity. The third category is concerned with the damages caused by illegal exercise of military power. It has been suggested that these may in the future be governed by a separate military law or other regulations. The main reason for the exclusion of provisions on military compensation, according to a distinguished scholar, Professor Pi Chunxie, is the exclusion of acts of national defence from the ALL. However, as Professor Pi argues, military acts are not equal to acts of national defence, and furthermore military organs were put under state organs under the 1982 Constitution. It is therefore reasonable to subject them to the regulations of the SCL. It has also been claimed that doing so is beneficial to the unification and consistency of the state compensation system nationwide.

As China moves towards a market economy, many public utilities are still owned by the State. How to deal with the damages caused by mismanagement of public utilities, such as roads and bridges, is essential to the protection of the lawful interests of the public. One argument is that there are some provisions in the GPCL on the compensation for damages caused by public utilities. Under those provisions, victims can claim compensation from the enterprises in charge of the administration of the public utilities according to the CPL. They are therefore classified as civil disputes. However, many public utilities are managed by state organs and the damages caused are sometimes enormous. The other argument is that damages caused by public utilities should be covered by the SCL so long as they are still under the management of the state government. But bearing in mind the SCL requirement of the existence of special relationship between the claimant and the state organ concerned, it does not seem easy to prove the existence of a special relationship between a road-user, for example, and the state organ administering the road. It is therefore much easier for the road-user to bring a claim by relying on Article 121 of the GPCL.

The scope of application of the SCL has finally been restricted to administrative and criminal fields. Administrative compensation covers infringement upon both personal and property rights. The infringement upon personal rights includes illegal detention, adoption of compulsory administrative measures, illegal custody of citizens or deprivation of personal freedom by other means, infliction of physical injury or causing death by violent acts or illegal use of weapons and so on. The infringement upon property rights includes illegal use of administrative penalties, illegal institution of compulsory administrative measures, illegal collection of property charges or financial contributions, and "any other illegal acts."

Procedure for state compensation

The SCL combines substantive and procedural provisions. Claimants, including any aggrieved citizens, legal persons and other organizations, must demand compensation according to the procedures provided in the SCL. Before the enactment of the SCL, as far as administrative compensation was concerned, lawsuits could be brought relying on Chapter 9 of the ALL. That chapter, however, contains only three sections setting out general principles. The SCL procedure of compensation (Section 3 of Chapter 2) is therefore a noticeable development on the basis of the ALL general principles. Under the SCL a two-step procedure is provided. Claimants must first file their claims in the form of an application with the state agencies responsible for compensation, which could be any one of the state agencies jointly responsible. The agency which assumes obligation of compensation shall accept the claim and calculate the amount of compensation according to the methods laid down in Chapter 4 of the SCL. If claimants are not satisfied with the amount of compensation, they may then file suit with the people's court within a limited period of time.

Section 14 of the SCL provides that state agencies may seek full or partial indemnity against its functionaries under only two situations, *i.e.* the functionaries either intentionally committed errors or negligently committed grave errors. In other words, if no intention to commit errors can be proved, the functionaries will only be held responsible in negligence if they committed grave or serious errors, not for committing ordinary errors. That is to say that negligence has been divided into two categories, serious negligence and ordinary negligence. The former refers to the condition that the functionaries failed to notice the tortious behaviour which the ordinary persons noticed and were able to prevent happening and their failure leads to the tortious consequence. The main reason to hold the functionaries liable for serious negligence, is to make sure that they do their work properly and exercise their authorities according to law. However, if the functionaries are held liable to pay either full or partial indemnity for all negligent behaviour, then the efficiency of administration will be hampered as they will be over-cautious. It is therefore a balancing exercise between judicial supervision of administration and administrative efficiency. Furthermore, section 14 also provides that the functionaries will face administrative penalties for committing intentional errors or negligently committing grave errors. They may even face criminal penalties if their intentional or negligent conduct constitutes a crime.

The procedure concerning criminal compensation was also very controversial during the legislative process as it involved a series of issues, such as the criminal law system, legal supervision system and reform of judicial and supervision systems. The focus was on whether it was necessary to have pre- trial procedures and if so, which organ should be in charge. The procedure finally adopted by the SCL is a three-step one. The first step is the same as the procedure for claims of administrative compensation. In the second step the claimants may apply to the next higher agency for a review if they object to the amount of compensation. Thirdly, the claimant may apply to the compensation committee of the people's court at the corresponding level for a decision on compensation. This procedure for criminal compensation is a special one which combines administrative reconsideration with administrative litigation. Whether this procedure will work remains to be seen. It is questionable in theory whether this procedure is appropriate, since the fundamental principle of fairness is breached, because the causes of criminal compensation are illegal acts. Both review and litigation will therefore be of little value to the claimant.

Partial or even full indemnity can also be claimed, under section 24 of the SCL, after criminal compensation by the body responsible for paying compensation from the functionaries under certain circumstances. The same is true under section 14 for administrative compensation. As the conduct mentioned under section 24 of the SCL is expressly prohibited by law, it is logical to hold the law enforcers who committed the illegal conduct, responsible for paying indemnity. Moreover, in order to prevent this illegal conduct from happening, those reoponsible will also face administrative penalties, or even criminal penalties if their conduct constitute crimes.

Observation

Though the SCL has a narrow scope of application. The adoption of the SCL is a great achievement towards the improvement of the legal system, especially the public law system in the PRC. The SCL has recognized the uniqueness of the torts committed by state organs for the illegal exercise of power and subjected them to legal regulation. In so doing, not only the lawful interests of the citizens, legal persons and other organizations are better protected, but also the accountability of those state organs regulated by the SCL is enhanced.

The enactment of the SCL has also contributed to the completion of the administrative law structure in China. The ALL was enacted in 1989 with the aim to subject the administrative organs to judicial control in civil affairs. The 1990 RAR promulgated by the State Council is a supplement to the ALL. In the same year, the *Regulation on Administrative Supervision in the PRC* was promulgated by the State Council, under which the Ministry of Supervision shall supervise the work of other administrative organs. However, the Ministry of Supervision is within the executive branch of the Government. Its function is similar to that of Ombudsman in some western countries. The focus of this legislation has been on state organs, *i.e.* to control the exercise of power by state organs. The protection of lawful interests of the claimants and victims and the exact remedies available to them have never been laid down in any detailed legislation. The SCL has filled that gap. In this sense, the adoption of the SCL is a great achievement in the protection of the lawful rights and interests of the citizens, legal persons and other organizations against illegal infringement of their rights or interests by state organs or their personnel.

Conclusion

From 1989 to 1996, China promulgated legislation aimed at the supervision and control of the exercise of administrative authority by administrative organs or their functionaries. There are both internal supervision (administrative reconsideration) and external supervision (judicial review). The aggrieved parties can go through the relevant legal procedures to seek appropriate compensation, including financial compensation. Moreover, the importance of procedural legality has gradually been realized in China. The enactment of the 1996 *Adminstrative Penalty Law* is sufficient evidence of this. The proper operation of the established system shall contribute to the implementation of the rule of law principle in public administration.

Notes

1 See Xu Chongde and Pi Chunrie. *An Overview of Administrative Law in the People's Republic of China*, Legal Science Press, 1991. Beijing, pp. 32–36.
2 The ALL was enacted one year before the RAR.
3 See Legislative Affairs Bureau. *The Interpretation of the Regulation on Administrative Reconsideration*, China Legal System Press, Beijing, 1990, p. 2.
4 See Luo Haocai, *Judicial Review System in the People's Republic of China*, Peking University Press, Beijing, 1993, pp. 324–349.
5 See Luo Haocai, pp. 350–352.
6 See Huang lie, *Interpretation of the Administrative Litigation Law of the PRC*, the People's Court Press, Beijing, 1994, pp. 184–185.
7 See Hua Yang, *Judicial Control of Discretionary Power*, in *Collection of Legal Essays (Administrative Law)*, 1992, Vol. 2, pp. 191–193.

38

CITIZENS v. MANDARINS
Administrative litigation in China*

Minxin Pei

Source: *China Quarterly* 152 (1997): 832–862.

The Chinese government has, in the last 20 years, devoted enormous political resources and effort to revamping its legal system. The resultant legal reforms, part of the government's programme of political institutionalization, have been the subject of intense scholarly interest in the West.[1] One of these legal reforms was the Administration Litigation Law (ALL), passed in April 1989 and implemented in October 1990. The theoretical significance of this law can hardly be exaggerated because, if fully enforced, it would afford Chinese citizens an important legal instrument with which to defend themselves against the abuse of state power by government agencies and officials. Like other legal reforms, the All has attracted the attention of both Chinese and Western legal scholars. However, most early studies do not offer in-depth empirical analysis of the implementation of the law, its effects on China's administrative practices and its political implications. A possible exception was a 1992 study by a group of Chinese scholars who used polling data to assess the public perception of the ALL and relied on two case studies to investigate how the law was implemented at the grassroots level.[2] Nevertheless, the 1992 study has its limitations. Apart from the issue of the reliability of polling in China, it contains no national data on the implementation of the law; nor does it provide an in-depth analysis of sample court cases that went to trial according to the provisions of the ALL. Furthermore, it covers only a very brief period following the implementation of the law and relies on insufficient data, especially at the national level. Other works on the ALL suffer from similar problems, as lack of empirical data apparently restricted their authors mostly to a historical review of the evolution of administrative litigation in China, an analysis of the legal provisions of the ALL and speculation about its effectiveness.[3]

   This study attempts to address several important empirical and theoretical questions left hitherto unanswered. For example, are any patterns demonstrated by the disposition of the lawsuits filed under the ALL since its implementation; and what do such patterns reveal about the political and institutional constraints on the Chinese legal system? Which groups have been the primary beneficiaries of the ALL? Which types of government administrative abuses are more likely to trigger lawsuits under the ALL? What do the results of the implementation of the ALL so far suggest about whether this new institution is undergoing consolidation? How did the institutional innovations in the Deng Xiaoping era reshape state–society relations?

This article uses newly available court cases and official national data on administrative litigation in 1986–96 to explore these issues.[4] The first section analyses the main provisions of the ALL; the second section evaluates its implementation based on the national data for the period between 1987 and 1996; and the third section examines 236 cases that went to trial in China in the early 1990s.[5]

The administrative litigation law

Prior to the passage of the ALL in April 1989, the principal legal basis of administrative litigation was Article 3 of China's Civil Procedure Law (Interim), which was promulgated in 1982. Specifically, Article 3 stated that "this law applies to administrative litigation cases which are legally stipulated to be tried in the People's Court." The legal implications of this were profound. Before the establishment of a legal basis for adjudicating disputes between citizens and the government over various administrative decisions, the only recourse for private citizens who believed they had been unjustly treated or penalized by the government and its officials was to send their written appeals to higher government agencies, the media and China's top leaders; many travelled to provincial capitals and Beijing trying to make direct appeals to high-ranking officials. Such individual efforts rarely succeeded in redressing the grievance, however. One official report revealed that 95 per cent of all the administrative disputes that were appealed to higher government agencies were eventually returned to lower-level (and often the same) government agencies with which the dispute originated in the first place. This practice rarely satisfied the aggrieved individuals. The same report said that more than half the citizens who initiated the complaints were forced to repeat their appeal process.[6]

Although Article 3 of the Civil Procedure Law established a minimum legal basis of administrative litigation after 1982, this provision alone did not constitute a working law, nor did it specify procedural rules. Thus, private citizens seeking judicial relief from injurious and unjust government acts face serious hurdles. The absence of an administrative litigation law and the practical problems it had created attracted the attention of China's law-makers. Under the auspices of the Judiciary Committee of the National People's Congress (NPC), a group of legal scholars began drafting the ALL in 1986 and completed the first draft in 1987.[7] Initial response from government officials was predictably sceptical: a 1987 poll showed that of the 80 municipal, county, and district agencies surveyed, 95 per cent of the officials polled considered the ALL "premature" and urged the passage of the law be delayed.[8]

Despite such reservations on the part of government officials who would probably face legal challenges and restrictions if the law were passed, the leadership of the Chinese Communist Party (CCP) seemed committed to the codification of procedures of administrative litigation.[9] In October 1987 the Political Report of the 13th Congress of the CCP (delivered by Zhao Ziyang, then the CCP General Secretary) cited, as the Party's legislative priorities, the promulgation of administrative laws and the establishment of an appeals system for Chinese citizens. Another legal development made the passage of the ALL both more necessary and desirable. After the PRC Code on Penalties Imposed in the Course of Maintaining Public Order went into effect in January 1987,[10] the judicial branch of the Chinese government was reportedly forced to establish special tribunals to handle legal cases involving the administrative penalties imposed under the Code. These administrative tribunals (*xingzheng shenpan ting*),[11] established an institutional arena in which citizens could seek judicial relief from official abuse of power.[12]

In October 1988 the draft version of the ALL was presented to the Standing Committee of the NPC for debate; the same draft was also circulated to the public for comment.[13] Several revisions later, in March 1989, the ALL was tabled at the second session of the Seventh NPC for passage; and on 4 April 1989, the NPC passed it. Although the ALL did not take effect nationally until October 1990, the government implemented it before then on an experimental basis in several provinces.[14]

The passage of the ALL was hailed in the Chinese legal community. Optimists felt it had the potential to be the key legal instrument for protecting human rights and laying the foundations of the rule of law in China. Preliminary assessment by Western legal scholars was also positive.[15] Judging by the provisions of the law, such optimism was not entirely misplaced.[16] Among other things, the ALL provides ordinary Chinese citizens, "legal persons," and even foreigners the right legally to challenge administrative decisions (various penalties or other measures) that adversely affect their freedom or economic interests.[17] It also sets stringent procedural standards and places the burden of proof on government agencies whose decisions are being challenged. The ALL gives the court the power to uphold, revoke, revise or compel administrative actions. However, it contains several important flaws.[18] Its definition of "concrete administrative actions" subject to judicial review is vague, thus immunizing many government actions from legal challenges. It may not be used to challenge certain government policies that violate citizens' constitutional rights but are "generally binding" (the family planning policy being a clear example). Finally, it makes no provisions regarding administrative actions taken by the CCP, giving the ruling party immunity from judicial review.

The implementation of the ALL

Increase of administrative litigation lawsuits. The data on administrative litigation in China are reported in *Zhongguo falü nianjian* (*Law Yearbook of China*).

In addition, the annual reports by the Chief Justice of the Supreme Court of the People contain some data on administrative litigation. Provincial supreme courts also report the number of administrative litigation cases (ALCs) tried and their disposition (these reports are published in the provincial yearbooks). Although one must treat official data with caution, it appears that the data reported in these yearbooks are relatively reliable because they reflect the patterns of change consistent with the findings by more independent analysts.[19]

The statistical data on ALCs gathered for this study indicate that the ALL has had a considerable impact since its implementation in 1990. It is true that similar lawsuits against government agencies and officials had been filed and tried prior to the passage of the ALL, but the number of such cases was relatively small in the late 1980s (fewer than 10,000). In the 1990s the number of such cases processed by the legal system each year continued to rise, reaching 79,527 in 1996 (Table 1).

The pattern of the increase in the number of ALCs seemed to have been influenced in part by the stop-and-go nature of political liberalization in the Deng era and by the changes in the Chinese legal system. The rapid increase in 1988 was apparently the result of the relatively relaxed political environment created by the policies of then CCP General Secretary Zhao Ziyang. Conversely, in the aftermath of the crackdown on the pro-democracy movement in 1989, the increase of ALCs slowed down.

On the whole, however, other changes in China's legal system had a greater impact on the number of ALCs accepted and tried in the court. The spectacular rise in 1987 was a result of the implementation that year of the PRC Code on Penalties Imposed in the Course of Maintaining Public Order. The enforcement of this code occasioned more opportunities for disputes between citizens and

Table 1 Number of cases accepted (*shouli*) and tried (*shenli*) by the Court, 1986–96

	Accepted	Change (%)	Tried	Change (%)
1986	632	–	–	–
1987	5,240	729	4,677	–
1988	9,273	77	8,751	88
1989	9,934	7	9,742	11
1990	13,006	31	12,040	24
1991	25,667	97	25,202	109
1992	27,125	6	27,116	8
1993	27,911	3	27,958	3
1994	35,083	26	34,567	24
1995	52,596	50	51,370	49
1996	–	–	79,527	55

Sources: Zhongguo fazhi nianjian (Law Yearbook of China), various years; *Falü yu shenghuo (Law and Life)*, No. 82 (October 1990), p. 19; *Renmin ribao*, 21 March 1997, p. 2.

state agents over the latter's discretionary power in imposing penalties; it also entailed, as mentioned earlier, the establishment of the administrative tribunals to process cases involving administrative penalties. The doubling of ALCs in 1991 was clearly the consequence of the implementation of the ALL after October 1990. The rapid rise registered in 1994 (up 24 per cent), 1995 and 1996 (up almost 50 per cent) was not the direct result of any specific legal changes affecting the ALL. As will be demonstrated, this upward trend reflected a higher level of public awareness of the ALL and its legal implications. Although the results of the implementation of the ALL since 1990 showed that the law remained an imperfect legal instrument for Chinese citizens, the very fact that filing a lawsuit based on the ALL can lead to some form of judicial relief has probably encouraged an increasing number of citizens to take this option.

Regional variation. The regional distribution of ALCs filed in 25 of China's 27 provinces and three municipalities is presented in Table 2.[20] Using the differential between a province's share of the national population and its share of ALCs filed in 1994 as a measure of the level of administrative litigation (a proxy for citizens' assertiveness of their legal rights), it is shown that more economically developed areas do not necessarily lead the nation in litigation against the government. The provinces with the highest positive differentials were either among the poorest (Hunan and Henan) or the mid-income (Shandong and Heilongjiang). Indeed, some of the most prosperous regions (such as Guangdong, Beijing and Fujian) lagged behind the poorest regions (such as Henan, Hunan and Guizhou) in this respect. This evidence casts doubts on a positive relationship between the level of economic development and frequency of administrative litigation. However, there does seem to be a negative relationship between economic development and administrative litigation because the less developed provinces in China made up the majority of the laggards shown in Table 2. Of the 14 provinces with negative differentials, seven were among the poorest provinces (Sichuan, Anhui, Jiangxi, Yunnan, Gansu, Ningxia and Shaanxi); two were relatively poor provinces (Qinghai and Inner Mongolia).

One possible explanation of the regional variation in administrative litigation is that it may be related to differing degrees of judicial fairness in different regions. In regions where the system of judicial review has been better established and fairer, citizens are less fearful of filing ALCs. Evidence from Henan, which led the country in the number of ALCs filed in both absolute and relative terms in 1994, provides some support for this view. The disposition of ALCs in Henan in 1993 and 1994 shows that the proportion of rulings favourable to plaintiffs is much higher than the national average. Of the 4,910 ALCs tried in the courts in 1994, administrative actions were upheld in 13.9 per cent of the cases and revoked in 27.2 per cent; of the 3,764 ALCs tried in the courts in 1993, administrative actions were upheld in 16 per cent of the cases and revoked in 16 per cent, but in addition, the courts changed administrative actions in 2.4 per cent of the cases and compelled government agencies to

Table 2 Regional distribution of ALCs accepted by the Court in 1994

Provinces	Number	Percentage	Share of population	Differential[a]	Wealth rank[b]
Hunan	4,857	13.84	5.3	8.54	20
Henan	5,187	14.78	7.53	7.25	26
Shandong	3,961	10.5	7.23	3.27	10
Guizhou	1,609	4.58	2.88	1.70	30
Heilongjiang	1,602	4.56	3.0	1.56	11
Jilin	917	2.6	2.1	0.5	13
Shanghai	478	1.36	1.1	0.25	1
Hubei	1,761	5.0	4.77	0.23	15
Xinjiang	552	1.57	1.36	0.21	12
Liaoning	1,247	3.5	3.3	0.2	4
Zhejiang	1,282	3.65	3.58	0.07	6
Shaanxi	1,047	2.98	2.9	−0.08	27
Ningxia	115	0.3	0.4	−0.1	21
Beijing	246	0.7	0.9	−0.2	2
Qinghai	70	0.19	0.39	−0.2	17
Hainan	22	0.06	0.59	−0.53	9
Inner Mongolia	462	1.31	1.88	−0.57	16
Fujian	725	2.06	2.65	−0.59	8
Gansu	465	1.32	1.98	−0.66	29
Guangdong	1,675	4.77	5.58	−0.81	5
Yunnan	829	2.36	3.28	−0.92	25
Jiangxi	766	2.18	3.35	−1.17	22
Hebei	1,327	3.78	5.3	−1.52	14
Anhui	702	2.0	4.96	−2.96	23
Sichuan	2,118	6.0	9.3	−3.3	24
Subtotal	34,022	96.97	–	–	–
Other	1,061	3.03	–	–	–
Total	35,083	100	–	–	–

Sources: Provincial Yearbooks and *Zhongguo falü nianjian* (1995), pp. 823–885; per capita income data were from Zhou Zhenghua (ed.), *Zhongguo jingji fengxi 1995* (*Analysis of the Chinese Economy in 1995*) (Shanghai: Shanghai renmin chubanshe, 1996), p. 94.

Notes
a The difference between the province's share of ALCs and national population. A positive number indicates above-average use of the law in the province.
b Per capita income in 1994.

perform their legal responsibility in 15 per cent. Altogether, plaintiffs obtained favourable or partially favourable rulings in nearly 33 per cent of the cases (compared with 16 per cent for the government). The data for 1993 and 1994 show that plaintiffs enjoyed a two-to-one advantage over the government in all the cases that went to trial in Henan. Moreover, the rate of withdrawal in Henan was also lower than the national average. In 1993, 39.3 per cent of ALCs were withdrawn (the national average was 41 per cent); in 1994, 34.8 per cent (14.8 per cent of ALCs were withdrawn after the defendants changed the disputed administrative actions). Henan's withdrawal rate in 1994 was 9 per cent lower than the national average.[21] The data for Hunan and, to a lesser degree, Shandong were similar. The data for 1994 showed that the courts in Hunan revoked administrative actions in 15.2 per cent of the cases and upheld them in 13.8 per cent (with a withdrawal rate of 50 per cent). Shandong's courts revoked administrative actions in 9.6 per cent of the cases and upheld them in 9.5 per cent (with a high withdrawal rate of 65 per cent).[22] The above data indicate that the greater likelihood of obtaining favourable rulings from the court may be an important reason for the large number of ALCs filed against the government in Henan and Hunan. The data from Shandong suggest that out-of-court settlement may have become a principal form of dispute resolution between the state and private citizens.

Scope of administrative litigation. As the number of ALCs rose, the scope of the ALL also expanded. Given the intrusiveness of the Chinese state, the broad discretion enjoyed by government agents and the lack of clearly defined property rights, the ALL provided one of the few state-sanctioned means for private citizens to challenge the actions of government officials on many regulatory and administrative issues. According to an official report, more than 40 types of administrative branches of the state (such as law enforcement, urban development, commercial administration, tax collection, environmental protection and so on) were targets of lawsuits in 1995.[23] The breakdown of the type of ALCs in the court from 1988 to 1994 reveals two trends. First, the composition of such cases is basically consistent over time, with most ALCs involving disputes over law-enforcement agencies (the public security bureau and committee of reform through labour), land use, forestry, urban zoning, and real estate (see Table 3). Disputes in these four areas constituted about 80 per cent of all ALCs in 1988 and 52 per cent in 1995. Secondly, the scope of the ALL has been expanded over the years, as the law has been increasingly invoked to challenge government actions in many other areas; this has led to a relative decline of the proportion of ALCs involving law-enforcement agencies and land use, and a gradual rise in the proportion of cases labelled as "other" (about 41 per cent in 1995).[24]

The data in Table 3 also reflect a stark political reality in China. Citizens sue the government to protect their liberty and property only as a last resort. Thus, they often refrain from suing not because their rights have not been violated, but because the stakes are not high enough. A survey of plaintiffs showed that 57 per cent stated that they filed suits under the ALL because they felt they had no other choice.[25] According to one study, disputes over land use made up most of the ALCs in an agrarian region in Henan because the very livelihoods of the aggrieved peasants were at stake. Similarly, a large number of lawsuits were filed against law-enforcement agencies because the aggrieved citizens felt their liberty was threatened. From this perspective, one should not view the relatively small share of suits filed against the state's regulatory and extractive agencies (industrial and commercial administration and tax collection agencies) as evidence that they are less likely to be embroiled in disputes

Table 3 Composition of Cases, 1988–95

Type	1988ᵃ number (%)	1990ᵇ	1992ᵇ	1993ᵇ	1995ᵇ
Public security	3,385 (38.6)	4,519 (34.7)	7,863 (29.0)	7,018 (25.1)	11,427 (22.2)
Land use	2,719 (31.1)	4,038 (31.0)	8,330 (30.7)	8,063 (28.9)	10,009 (19.5)
Urban zoning and real estate	433 (4.9)	–	–	2,038 (7.3)	2,949 (5.7)
Forestry	422 (4.8)	–	–	1,971 (7.1)	2,568 (5.0)
Industrial and commercial adm.	204 (2.3)	–	710 (2.6)	571 (2.0)	1,388 (2.7)
Public health	250 (2.9)	–	548 (2.0)	456 (1.6)	892 (1.7)
Traffic	–	–	–	–	1,275 (2.5)
Other	1,253 (14.3)	4,449 (34.3)	9,674 (35.7)	7,794 (28.0)	20,862 (40.7)
Total	8,753	13,006	27,125	27,911	51,370

Sources: Zhongguo falü nianjian, various years; *Renmin fayuan nianjian* (1992) (Beijing: Renmin fayuan chubanshe, 1995), p. 839; figures for 1988 were obtained from Susan Finder, "Like throwing an egg against a stone? Administrative litigation in the People's Republic of China," *Journal of Chinese Law*, Vol. 3, No. 1 (Summer 1989), p. 11.

Notes:
a The number of cases tried by the court.
b The number of cases accepted by the court.

with citizens. According to the same study, fewer suits were filed against those two agencies because they were in a better position to retaliate against plaintiffs even if they lost. A private citizen could thus "win once but lose the rest of his life."[26]

Analysis of outcome: who wins. A key test of the effectiveness of the ALL is whether the Chinese legal system has displayed judicial impartiality in adjudicating ALCs. This test is conducted in the following section, based on the data from 1987 to 1995 (Table 4). Despite the incompleteness of the official data on the implementation of the law, this analysis indicates that its success at providing impartial judicial review has been mixed, for a number of reasons.

A relatively high percentage of suits were dismissed. An examination of official data on the disposition of ALCs shows that the proportion of dismissed suits was unusually high and has been climbing steadily since 1991. Although this category (ALCs dismissed by the court of first instance) was not explicitly identified in most official annual reports on administrative litigation, the data for 1992 revealed that 8 per cent of ALCs were dismissed by the court of first instance. The Supreme People's Court's annual report for 1995 showed that about 16 per cent of all the ALCs (8,349) were dismissed by the courts after the first ruling (*caiding*).[27] This shows that dismissed cases constituted most of the court decisions under the "other" category (comprising 10–15 per cent of the ALCs processed in 1987–95). The rest of the "other" category includes the transfer of the cases to a different judicial branch (such as the civil litigation court) and "termination" of the proceedings (presumably without rendering any judgment).

Low probability of winning ALCs against government agencies. Data for this period show that plaintiffs had only a 15–21 per cent chance of obtaining a favourable ruling from the courts of first instance that tried the cases (a favourable ruling results in revoking or, on rare occasions, changing the disputed administrative actions).[28] In comparison, the government had a higher chance (17–50 per cent) of having its actions upheld by the court. One should observe, however, that there has been a remarkable convergence between the ratio of rulings favourable to the plaintiff and those favourable to the defendant since the early 1990s. Such a convergence resulted not from a rising ratio of rulings favouring plaintiffs (which remained constant), but from a falling ratio of rulings favouring defendants (from 50 per cent in 1987–88 to 17 per cent in 1995). The data for the disposition of the ALCs in 1995 show that, for all the ALCs that went to trial that year, the odds of winning their cases were about the same for plaintiffs and defendants. If we include the percentage of the ALCs dismissed by the courts without trial (8 per cent in 1992 and possibly 16 per cent in 1995), the government maintained a nearly two-to-one advantage in having its actions effectively upheld by the court.

The puzzle of withdrawn cases. The most intriguing puzzle in analysing the effect of the ALL is presented by the large proportion of ALCs filed but later withdrawn by plaintiffs. Data in Table 4 indicate that the rate of withdrawal was increasing rapidly in the early 1990s – from 37 per cent in 1991 to 51 per cent in 1995. The share of withdrawn ALCs in 1995 nearly doubled that in 1988.

A closer examination of the data on the withdrawn ALCs shows, however, that a large number of such withdrawals represent out-of-court settlements (with the government agencies being sued unilaterally rescinding or changing their administrative actions). Official data reported (Table 4) that of the suits withdrawn by plaintiffs in 1994, 38 per cent of them (or 16.7 per cent of the total cases processed by the courts that year) were withdrawn after the defendants (government agencies) rectified the disputed administrative actions. Of the suits withdrawn in 1995, 45 per cent (or 22.5 per cent of the total cases processed that year) were withdrawn after the defendants rectified the disputed actions. In the sample cases, there were altogether 14 cases of withdrawal of suits by plaintiffs. In 12 of the 14 cases, plaintiffs withdrew their suits after the defendants rescinded the disputed administrative actions to the satisfaction of the plaintiffs. There were only two cases in which plaintiffs withdrew their suits after realizing that their suits lacked merit or were not covered under the ALL.[29]

Table 4 Disposition of tried cases (%)

	RAA	UAA	SWP	CAA	Other[a]
1988	11	49	27	5	8
1989	14	42	31	6	7
1990	17	36	36	3	8
1991	19	32	37	2	10
1992	21	28	38	2	11
1993	19	23	41	2	15
1994	19	21	44[b]	1	15
1995	15	17	51[b]	1	16

Source: Zhongguo falü nianjian, various years.

Notes
RAA: Revoking administrative actions.
UAA: Upholding administrative actions.
SWP: Suits withdrawn by plaintiffs.
CAA: Administrative actions revised by the court.

a. The "other" category remains a mystery. In the data for 1988 "other" explicitly consisted of two types of disposition: cases that were "terminated" (*zhongjie*) and presumably dismissed, and cases that were transferred (*yisong*) to other authorities. The data for 1992 explicitly identified the number of cases dismissed (*bohui qisu*) (2,116) for that year. This accounted for about 8% of all the cases processed by the courts. The data for 1995 explicitly identified the number of dismissed and terminated cases (8,349) for that year.
b. In 1994, 38% of all the cases in this category were withdrawn after the defendants changed "concrete administrative acts"; in 1995, about 45% of all the cases in this category were withdrawals after original administrative actions were revised or changed.

These results show that the very act of filing a lawsuit can generate substantial benefits for the plaintiffs even without going to trial. Compared with either not filing the suit (and enduring the adverse consequences of unjust government actions) or going to trial (facing poorer odds of winning), filing a suit and then hoping that the government agency being sued will rectify its original actions before trial amounts to taking a calculated risk that redress can be achieved indirectly. In fact, according to the preceding analysis, filing a suit to induce the government agency to change its actions before trial has about the same probability of obtaining effective relief as filing the suit and receiving a favourable ruling after trial (about 16 and 20 per cent in 1995 and 1994, as shown in Table 4). The costs are, of course, much lower.

Thus, if the ratio of court-revoked administrative actions and administrative actions rectified by the government agencies without going to trial are combined, it seems that the very act of filing an ALC gives the plaintiff a considerable chance (36.7 per cent in 1994 and 38.3 per cent in 1995) of obtaining the desired judicial relief one way or another. The risk of filing an ALC is therefore justified. This may be the reason why the rate of filing ALCs rose rapidly in the mid-1990s (especially 1994 and 1995), even without major legal or political reforms that would increase the effectiveness, impartiality and enforceability of the ALL.

This analysis is counter to the assertion made by some Chinese legal scholars that the large number of withdrawn ALCs was indicative of the failure of the ALL as a legal instrument to provide judicial relief to ordinary citizens.[30] Such criticism is based on the fact that of all the withdrawn ALCs in 1994 and 1995, 62 per cent and 55 per cent, respectively, were withdrawn by plaintiffs "abnormally"; that is, they withdrew their complaints without having the disputed actions rescinded by the government authorities being sued. However, our analysis of the data suggests a different explanation. The decision to withdraw ALCs seemed to be based on rational reasoning, not merely fear of reprisal or distrust of the legal system. Plaintiffs decided not to pursue their cases against government agencies and officials in the court because of the high odds against winning. As analysed above, when the ratio of dismissal by the court of first instance (roughly 10 per cent) and winning ratio for the government (averaging about 28 per cent over the same period) are combined, the government had a probability of effectively winning 38 per cent of all ALCs tried in the court, double the probability of winning for plaintiffs (19 per cent).

Such odds may force a rational plaintiff to adopt a different strategy, one aimed at obtaining judicial relief without the negative ramifications of winning a suit against the government. This strategy consists of filing an ALC in the hope of obtaining a pre-trial settlement (not very different from the practice in civil litigation in the United States). Clearly, administrative litigation is a costly process both to the aggrieved citizens and to the government agencies being sued. For the plaintiffs, there is a higher probability of losing the case than winning it in the courts; the benefits of actually winning were dubious because of the difficulty in enforcing rulings against the government; and the government agency and officials that lose in court may then retaliate against the plaintiffs in the future.

Government agencies and officials face real risks in fighting ALCs in the courts. Although their overall probability of effectively winning is about 40 per cent, the 20 per cent probability that they will lose poses a non-trivial threat. Losing an ALC may undermine the authority of the government agency and blemish the record of the responsible officials. In the court proceedings government agencies and officials risk unfavourable public scrutiny. If their abuse of official power is rampant, such misdeeds may be publicized or reported to higher authorities. Although the Chinese political system is undemocratic and unresponsive, certain egregious cases of abuse of citizens' rights, if subjected to sufficient exposure, can force national authorities to take drastic action against the culpable officials in order to appease public opinion and popular demands for justice.

This means that both sides have a considerable incentive for an out-of-court settlement. Moreover, the administrative tribunals, caught in the middle of the legal proceedings, apparently see out-of-court settlement as the most convenient way out of a no-win situation. On the one hand, given the lack of judicial independence, the court can ill afford to rule consistently against the government's administrative authorities even if their actions must be revoked under the ALL. On the other hand, the court's persistent bias in favour of the government may not only jeopardize its credibility, public image, institutional identity and sense of professionalism, but also force determined plaintiffs to pursue their grievances with higher-level government authorities or make appeals to higher courts. Thus, the administrative tribunals, too, have a strong incentive to encourage a settlement. According to one source, many ostensibly out-of-court settlements were actually mediated by the administrative court. Especially in cases in which the administrative court found it hard to uphold the government's action, the court would informally ask the defendants to rescind the disputed actions while trying to persuade the plaintiffs to withdraw the suits.[31]

Variation in disposition of ALCs against different agencies. Not all government agencies are equal in terms of their influence on judicial proceedings. Everything else being equal, the more powerful government agencies should enjoy greater advantages in the judicial proceedings in administrative litigation. Such advantages should be reflected in the disposition of ALCs filed against these agencies. Based on available data on the disposition of ALCs filed against different government agencies (Table 5), there is evidence that more powerful agencies (local governments and important functional departments) are likely to receive more favourable treatment in the court. The data for 1992–94 show that local government (which is often sued in cases of disputes over land ownership, land use, forestry, urban real estate and zoning) consistently enjoyed a significant advantage in the court. This advantage can be measured in terms of two comparisons. First, the percentage of court rulings favourable to the local government in these cases is compared with the overall percentage of rulings favourable to the government in all cases. This reveals that, with the exception of urban zoning, the percentage of rulings favourable to local governments was consistently above the national average. Law-enforcement agencies enjoyed a similar advantage in administrative litigation proceedings although their advantage has been shrinking over the years and, in 1995, disappeared altogether. Secondly, the percentage of rulings favourable to defendants is compared with that favourable to plaintiffs. Here local government also enjoyed a visible, though gradually shrinking, edge over plaintiffs (2–8 per cent).

Conversely, second-tier, less powerful administrative agencies may have no inherent advantage in administrative litigation proceedings. It is clear from Table 5 that, with the exception of 1995, industrial and commercial administrations enjoyed no advantage when compared with other government agencies, as reflected in a lower-than-average percentage of favourable rulings for these administrations (3–5 per cent). Moreover, the advantage for industrial and commercial administrations as defendants disappeared completely in 1993 and 1994 (but not in 1995). The story was the same for other local government agencies. The data for 1992–94 show that cultural and public hygiene agencies were less likely to have their administrative actions upheld and more likely to have them revoked.[32]

Table 5 Disposition of Major Categories of ALCs (%)

	UAA	RAA	CAA	SWP	Other
1992					
Law-enforcement	31	19	3	37	10
Land use	32	26	1	35	6
Industrial and commercial adm.	25	16	1	44	14
All cases	28	21	2	38	11
1993					
Law-enforcement	26	17	2	43	12
Land use	31	23	1	37	8
Urban zoning	20	12	1	33	34
Industrial and commercial adm.	19	18	1	45	17
All cases	23	19	2	41	15
1994					
Law-enforcement	20	16	2	47	15
Land use	30	25	1	34	10
Urban zoning	19	13	0.5	54	13.5
Industrial and commercial adm.	16	17	0	46	21
All cases	21	19	1	44	15
1995					
Law-enforcement	17	16	2	50	15
Land use	29	22	1	34	14
Urban zoning	22	15	0	50	13
Industrial and commercial adm.	30	17	0	40	13
All cases	17	15	1	51	16

Source: Zhongguo falü nianjian, various years.

Notes
UAA: Upholding administrative action;
RAA: Revoking administrative action;
CAA: Changing administrative action;
SWP: Suits withdrawn by plaintiffs;
SD: Suits dismissed.

The appeals. The ALL gives the losing party the right to appeal. Based on the data for 1988, 1990, 1992 and 1995 (Table 6), the rate of appeal of the rulings of the first trials was within the range of 19 to 31 per cent. The appellate court makes four types of rulings: upholding first-trial decisions; changing first-trial decisions; returning the case to the lower court for retrial; or an unspecified other decision. Appellants can also withdraw their appeals. Available data on the disposition of the appealed cases for 1992 and 1994 indicate a stable pattern. First, the appellate courts tended to uphold the first-trial decisions in most cases (64 per cent in 1992 and 1995). Secondly, a modest percentage of the rulings by the appellate court (16 per cent in 1992 and 15 per cent in 1995) favoured the appellants. Thirdly, an even smaller percentage of the appealed cases were sent back to the lower courts for retrial (8 per cent in 1992 and 7 per cent in 1995).

Table 6 Disposition of appealed cases, 1988–95

	1988	*1990*	*1992*	*1995*
First trial cases completed	8,029	12,040	27,116	51,370
Appeals accepted	2,359	3,431	8,334	9,694
Appeals completed	2,218	3,325	8,273	9,536
FTDU	1,573	2,192	5,333	6,086
FTDR	246	662	1,332	1,408
RFRT	—	258	687	676
AW	—	102	397	658
Other	399	111	524	708

Source: Zhongguo falü nianjian, various years.

Notes: FTDU: First-trial decisions upheld;
FTDR: First-trial decisions revised;
RFRT: Returned for re-trial;
AW: Appeals withdrawn.

Finally, unlike the high rate of withdrawals in the first trial, few appellants withdrew their appeals (5 per cent in 1992 and 7 per cent in 1995).

Given the fact that for 1992, the government had a higher chance of obtaining a favourable first-trial ruling than the plaintiff (28 per cent versus 21 per cent), it seems that the appellate court decisions also favoured the government (since 64 per cent of all first-trial decisions were upheld, assuming that losing plaintiffs and defendants were equally likely to appeal). This bias, if the assumption about the defendants' and plaintiffs' equal propensity to make appeals holds, seemed almost to have disappeared by 1995. Since the probability of obtaining a favourable first trial ruling was nearly identical for plaintiffs and defendants that year (15 versus 17 per cent), the appellate courts appear to have reduced their pro-government bias. Given the higher professional qualifications of judges and legal staff in the appellate courts and their relative insulation from local government agencies involved in the lawsuits, it is reasonable to assume that Chinese appellate courts exercise a higher level of impartiality and autonomy in judicial review.

How the ALL works: evidence from case studies

This section analyses the information provided by 236 cases that were tried in China's administrative tribunals in the early 1990s. Because these cases were not randomly selected by the Chinese sources that published them, they should not be considered fully representative. Indeed, they may contain one major bias. Intended mainly as legal precedents and textbook cases for future Chinese judges and lawyers, they may include cases considered exemplary in terms of compliance with the procedures of the ALL. In other words, the application of the ALL documented in these cases may reflect the ideal image of the ALL held by those who selected the cases, rather than the reality. Another problem caused by the non-random selection is that these cases cannot be used to generate information on how different factors (such as socio-economic backgrounds of litigants, the branches of government agencies being sued and access to legal representation) may affect trial outcomes.

However, the pitfalls caused by these two short-comings can be avoided if they are not relied upon to analyse either procedural fairness or factors that affect trial outcomes. On the other hand, several factors enhance the value of the these cases. First, most of them were contained in specialized volumes edited by leading legal Chinese scholars. The small number of copies printed (8,000 for each volume) and high prices (110–198 *yuan*) were evidence that these case books were not intended by the authorities as mass propaganda tools. The government was thus less likely to put pressures on the editors concerning the selection and presentation of the cases. Secondly, the non-random selection of the original data may have less effect in terms of understanding several important issues about the ALL, such as who sues, who sues whom, who has legal representation and what types of violation are most frequently committed by government agencies. Thirdly, if the composition of the 236 sample cases included in this study resembles that of the general population of ALCs (Table 3), it means that, at least in one important aspect, the sample cases represent the general population.

A breakdown of the 236 cases is presented in Table 7. On the whole, the composition of the sample cases collected here is similar to that of the general population (Table 3) although the cases here over-represent the ALCs involving taxation and industrial and commercial administration. A close analysis yields answers to a number of question.

Who sues? Although no study has been conducted to examine the composition of plaintiffs in ALCs, the 236 cases studied here shed some light on this problem (Table 8). A surprising finding is that state-owned enterprises (SOEs) and private firms/entrepreneurs made up the largest proportion of plaintiffs (20 per cent each). However, the over-representation of cases against industrial

Table 7 Types of cases in the sample

Type	Number	Percentage
Law-enforcement	59	25
Land use, urban zoning and real estate	50	21
Industrial and commercial adm.	36	16
Taxation	13	6
Public health	8	3
Environment	5	2
Traffic	5	2
Other	60	25
Total	236	100

Table 8 Who sues: types of plaintiffs from the sample

Plaintiffs	Number of cases	Percentage
State-owned enterprises	48	20
Private entrepreneurs/firms	47	20
Peasants	39	17
Workers	27	11
Collective firms/organizations[a]	22	9
Unemployed	9	4
Foreign joint ventures	9	4
Professionals	9	4
Cadres	9	4
Collective suits[b]	7	3
Other	10	4
Total	236	100

Notes
a. Collective firms and organizations include urban collective firms, township and village enterprises, villagers' committees and villagers' teams.
b. Collective suits are filed by a group of individuals, ranging from 25 households to 505 individuals in the sample.

Table 9 Who sues whom: plaintiffs and defendants in most frequently filed cases

Defendants	Law enforcement	Land use, zoning and real estate	Industrial and commercial adm.	Taxation	Other
Plaintiffs					
State-owned enterprises	3	6	15	2	22
Private firms/ entrepreneurs	13	3	11	4	16
Peasants	12	11	0	3	13
Workers	18	5	0	0	4
Collective firms/ organizations	1	8	4	2	7
Unemployed	4	1	0	0	4
Professionals	4	4	0	0	1
Collective suits	0	3	1	2	1
Foreign joint ventures	1	1	2	0	5
Cadres	3	5	0	0	1
Other	0	3	3	0	4
Total	59	50	36	13	78

and commercial administrations may be responsible for the large number of SOEs in the sample (see Table 9). In any case, the ALL has provided SOEs a useful legal instrument for resolving their disputes with state agencies that regulate them. Compared with aggrieved private individuals, SOEs are less afraid of taking government agencies to court. Another explanation for their legal activism is related to disputes over property rights. Since the property rights of SOEs are poorly defined in China, they are subject to local interference in their managerial affairs and often become attractive targets for other government agencies hungry for various fees. The ALL enables them to use the legal system to challenge such illegal levies and interference.

China's emerging private entrepreneurs and firms also have taken advantage of the legal protection provided by the ALL. They account for 20 per cent of the plaintiffs in the sample cases.[33] Given the unpredictable regulatory environment in which China's new private entrepreneurs and firms operate, they are more likely to encounter bureaucratic intrusion and harassment than are other individuals. Moreover, their relative economic autonomy from the state and their enormous personal stake in the success (and often the very existence) of their businesses give them both more economic resources and greater incentives to seek judicial relief by filing ALCs against government agencies that interfere with their private enterprise. Therefore, despite the small share of private entrepreneurs in the Chinese population, they seem to be the most active litigants against the state.

Data in Table 8 show that peasants and workers accounted for, respectively, 17 and 11 per cent of the plaintiffs in the sample. It may be that more peasants than workers file ALCs against the government because they account for the majority of the population and their relatively low social status makes them more likely to be victims of the abuse of power by low-level state agents. In comparison, ALCs filed by individuals of higher socio-economic status (such as professionals and cadres) accounted for a small percentage of the sample cases (4 per cent for both groups), reflecting their relatively privileged positions, as well as their small presence in the Chinese population.

The analysis of the data in Table 8 suggests that the ALL has benefited the three social groups with relatively low political or social status: private entrepreneurs, peasants and workers.[34] Therefore, if the implementation of the ALL becomes more effective and impartial, it can become a valuable institutional device to reduce the tensions between the state and the three largest social groups in China.

Table 8 shows that there are two types of collective suits, one filed by urban and rural collectives such as township and village enterprises and villagers' committees, and the other filed by *ad hoc* groups of private citizens whose rights were violated by government actions. Most of the actual cases filed by urban and rural collectives resemble those filed by SOEs and involve disputes over government regulations and rights to land and mineral resources. The second type of collective suits is politically more interesting. Although such spontaneously organized collective lawsuits were only 3 per cent of the sample, they serve as a telling indicator of *organized* political and civic activism in present-day China. Of the seven cases included in the sample, five were filed by urban residents and two by rural residents. Plaintiffs in three of the five cases filed by urban residents tried to stop construction of commercial projects that would threaten their property and impair their quality of life, suggesting that the ALL might become a potentially useful legal weapon for community activists in the future.

The two sample cases from rural China, both in 1992, show that the ALL could provide limited legal protection against unlawful taxes imposed by local government. In the first case, 32 peasants in a village in Sichuan sued the local township government for imposing taxes that exceeded the legal limit set by the provincial government. They won the case. In the second case, 25 peasants in Sichuan sued the local township government for imposing various illegal levies in violation of the provincial government's limits on taxes and fees. They also won the suit.

Who sues whom? The preceding section analyses the socio-economic and organizational backgrounds of plaintiffs; this section examines whether certain types of plaintiffs are more likely to sue certain types of government agencies. Such analysis may yield important clues as to the relative role of different government agencies in regulating the lives and activities of different social groups and economic organizations in China. The data from the sample (Table 9) reveal several patterns.

First, state-owned enterprises are more likely to sue government regulatory agencies, such as industrial and commercial administrative agencies. One-third of the ALCs in the sample filed by SOEs was against such agencies. Of the remaining 22 cases under the category of "other" in Table 9, all were against various government regulatory agencies (the environmental protection department, public health bureau, the department of standards and others).

Secondly, most lawsuits against Chinese law-enforcement agencies were filed by individuals of low socio-economic status. Workers, private entrepreneurs, peasants and the unemployed accounted for 47 of the 59 ALCs against law-enforcement agencies. The implications are twofold. First, those agencies may be more abusive of their power in their dealings with lower-status individuals than in their dealings with higher-status citizens. In addition, China's lower-status groups seem to have a rising level of awareness of their legal rights and to be growing more assertive in seeking judicial relief from abuse of power by law-enforcement authorities.

Thirdly, judging by the relatively large number of ALCs involving disputes over land ownership and use filed by peasants and rural collectives (19 of 50), the determination of property rights appears to have become a major source of conflict in rural China.

Finally, as shown by the fact that a large portion (23 per cent) of the ALCs filed by private entrepreneurs was against industrial and commercial regulatory agencies, it may be inferred that despite two decades of economic reform, Chinese private entrepreneurs still operate in a difficult regulatory environment.

Access to legal counsel. The ALL allows plaintiffs to represent themselves in the proceedings, or they may appoint others to do so: professional lawyers, social groups, their close relatives, individuals recommended by their work units or other citizens permitted by the court to represent their cases. For plaintiffs, access to professional legal counsel is a reasonable indicator of the extent of their economic resources and, perhaps more importantly, of their determination to pursue judicial remedy of unjust government actions (assuming that the more determined plaintiffs tend to devote more resources to such lawsuits). For defendants, the decision to seek representation by professional counsel may be an indication of how seriously they treat ALCs filed by ordinary citizens.

The national data (Table 10) on legal representation in administrative litigation show that, with the exception of 1991, more plaintiffs retained legal counsel than defendants. This suggests that plaintiffs tended to invest more resources in ALCs than defendants. However, the rate of legal representation for plaintiffs, after first rising dramatically from 21 per cent in 1991 to 38 per cent in 1992, fell gradually in the following years. There are three likely explanations.

First, the rate of professional legal representation for plaintiffs nearly doubled from 1991 to 1992, perhaps as a response to the government's high rate of legal representation at that time. The decline of legal representation thereafter might be related to the perceived impact of such representation on trial outcomes. More specifically, the lawyers' role turned out to be less critical in litigation proceedings than expected because, according to the findings of a 1992 study, plaintiffs thought that their own legal knowledge was the most important factor in winning a case (a good lawyer ranked as the fourth most important factor, behind a "sense of justice" and "good social *guanxi* (connections))."[35] China's legal system also prescribes a limited role for lawyers, a factor that hampers their ability to defend the rights of their clients. The same study found that 90 per cent of the lawyers surveyed agreed that the "limited role of lawyers" was one of the factors that made administrative litigation difficult in China.[36]

Secondly, plaintiffs who filed suits in 1992–93 might have been more determined to pursue their cases to the end and thus hired professional lawyers to increase their chances of winning. But as out-of-court settlement between plaintiffs and defendants began to predominate, plaintiffs might not need to retain professional legal service in order to reduce the financial costs of litigation.[37]

Table 10 Access to legal counsel, 1991–95

Year	Percentage of plaintiffs with professional counsel	Percentage of defendants with professional counsel
1991	21	36
1992	38	28
1993	35	19
1994	30	17
1995	21	14

Source: Zhongguo falü nianjian, various years.

Finally, decreasing rate of professional legal representation might be the result of the rapid increase of administrative litigation cases. The rate of legal representation fell in relative terms when the rate of growth of ALCs was faster than the rate of growth of professional lawyers. This may be the case in 1994 and 1995, when the number of ALCs rose 26 per cent and 50 per cent, respectively. In the same period, the growth of the legal profession was slower. In 1994, the total number of lawyers rose by 22 per cent; in 1995, the growth of the number of lawyers was only 8 per cent.[38]

The data on the legal representation for defendants show a steady decline, from 36 per cent in 1991 to only 14 per cent in 1995. This trend has several implications. The high rate of legal representation for the government in 1991 is an indication that the formal implementation of the ALL that year might have caused much anxiety among government officials about their chances of winning ALCs under more formalized and stringent rules stipulated by the law. The high rate of legal representation in 1991 was a defensive measure. But as the court continued to maintain its pro-government bias (albeit the bias declined in the early 1990s), the government might have decided to forego the precautionary measure of retaining professional counsel. Another significant factor for the low rate of legal representation for the government was that most law-enforcement agencies – in this sample 90 per cent – did not retain professional counsel (probably because these powerful agencies did not view legal representation very seriously). The most important reason for this general trend is, however, the emergence of out-of-court settlement as the dominant form of resolution, which greatly reduced the need of professional counsel.

Comparatively speaking, the rate of legal representation in administrative cases was lower than that in criminal cases (ranging between 47 to 41 per cent from 1993 to 1995) but higher than those in civil and economic cases. However, because official Chinese data on civil and economic cases are not detailed enough to show the rate of legal representation for plaintiffs and defendants, it is only possible to draw estimates from such data. To be precise, official data on legal representation in civil and economic cases should be termed "rate of lawyer participation." This rate specifically means the number of lawyers who participated in a given year's civil and economic cases, without revealing which side they represented. If it is assumed that plaintiffs and defendants in civil and economic cases are equally likely to hire professional legal counsel, the rate of legal representation for each side may be derived by halving the rate of lawyer participation. The rate of lawyer participation in civil cases was stable in the early 1990s: 10.2 per cent in 1993, 11.1 per cent in 1994 and 11.6 per cent in 1995. The rate in economic cases fluctuated in the same period: 20.6 per cent in 1993, 26.5 per cent in 1994 and 25.6 per cent in 1995.[39] Thus the rate of legal representation for each side may be in the range of 5–6 per cent for civil cases and 10–14 per cent in economic cases – considerably lower than that in administrative cases.

Table 11 shows the access to professional legal counsel by plaintiffs in the 203 of the sample cases for which such information was given. Although the rate of

Table 11 Plaintiffs' access to legal counsel in 203 sample cases

Plaintiffs	Represented by professional counsel	No legal counsel	Represented by non-professional counsel
State-owned enterprises	37	7	1
Private entrepreneurs/ firms	33	6	3
Peasants	17	11	4
Workers	16	8	1
Collective firms/ organizations	15	1	2
Unemployed	6	1	–
Collective suits	4	3	–
Other	17	8	2
Total (%)	145 (71%)	45 (22%)	13 (7%)

legal representation in the sample (71 per cent) is much higher than the overall national rate described above, it is the case that access to professional legal counsel depended on the plaintiffs' economic resources. Plaintiffs who were commercial or collective organizations (SOEs or township and village enterprises) had above-average rates of professional legal representation (about 83 per cent for SOEs and rural collectives). Private entrepreneurs also had high rates of professional legal representation (79 per cent). Plaintiffs with fewer economic resources had below-average rates of professional legal representation. For workers, the rate in the sample was 64 per cent; for peasants, the rate was 53 per cent.[40] Unemployed plaintiffs had a high rate of professional legal presentation in the sample (six out of seven) because the unemployed plaintiffs who had income-earning family members all had hired professional legal counsel. The only unemployed plaintiff who did not have professional legal counsel was a homeless migrant labourer.

Bones of contention: administrative violations. The ALL permits private citizens, commercial entities and other organizations to challenge specific administrative actions in court. The analysis in the preceding sections gives some clues as to the types of plaintiffs and the suits they are likely to file. This section studies the types of violations committed by government agencies or agents that may prompt aggrieved citizens or commercial entities to file ALCs.

According to Article 54 of the ALL, seven types of violations by government agencies may cause the court to rule in favour of the plaintiffs by revoking or partially revoking the disputed administrative acts, ordering the defendant to perform a new specific administrative act, modifying administrative penalties, and ordering the defendant to perform its legal duties. The seven are as follows:[41]

1   The disputed specific administrative actions are based on insufficient principal evidence.

2   The disputed specific administrative actions are reached through an incorrect application of law or rules and regulations.
3   The defendant violated legally prescribed procedures.
4   The defendant exceeded its legal authority.
5   The defendant abused its power.
6   The disputed administrative penalties are clearly unjust.
7   The defendant failed to perform or delayed the performance of its legal responsibility.

The final rulings favourable to plaintiffs issued by the courts of first instance and by the appellate courts are examined in the sample to ascertain the frequency with which such violations occur. The court may rule in favour of the plaintiffs on the basis of one or more violations in the same case. These legal rulings provide a rare look at how power is exercised by the Chinese government. The findings are reported in Table 12.

The court-established violations by government agencies tabulated in Table 12 suggest the following features of China's administrative system and offer some clues as to why actions taken by state agencies are often subject to legal challenges under the ALL.

Agency-specific characteristics

Law-enforcement. It is evident that China's law-enforcement agencies, as shown by Table 12, seem most prone of all state agencies to all types of violations.

Table 12 Types and frequency of violations by government agencies in sample cases

Type of violations	Law enforcement	Land use zoning and real estate	Industrial, commercial administration	Taxation	Other	Total
ELA	14	12	11	4	19	60
IPE	9	11	3	3	22	48
IAL	12	10	7	3	8	40
VLP	12	8	3	1	8	32
AOA	6	1	3	2	4	16
FPL	6	7	0	0	1	14
UAP	7	1	1	0	0	9
Total	66	50	28	13	62	219

Notes
ELA: exceeding legal authority, including acts with no legal basis;
IPE: insufficient principal evidence;
IAL: incorrect application of law and rules;
VLP: violation of legal procedures;
FPL: failure to perform legal responsibility;
AOA: abuse of authority;
UAP: unjust administrative penalties.

The three most frequent violations committed by law-enforcement agencies are exceeding their legal authority; violating legal procedures; and incorrectly applying laws and rules or taking actions with no legal basis. That law-enforcement agencies have engaged in widespread violation of Chinese laws – such as abuse of authority, gathering insufficient evidence, imposing unjust penalties and failing to perform their legal duties – is a troubling indicator of their organizational problems and corroborates the widespread popular impression that China's law-enforcement agencies are plagued by serious abuse of power.

Land use and zoning agencies. The most frequent violations committed by such agencies are exceeding legal authority; taking actions on the basis of insufficient principal evidence; incorrectly applying laws and rules; and violating legal procedures. These agencies (mostly local governments) exceed their legal authority chiefly because China's national and local laws on property rights are relatively new, unclear and often non-existent.

Industrial and commercial administration. Like law-enforcement agencies, China's regulatory agencies in the industrial and commercial sectors are particularly prone to exceed their legal authority because they are not accountable to other supervisory bodies. More importantly, they also frequently misapply laws and rules because China does not have a uniform commercial code. Furthermore, its laws and regulations governing commerce are simultaneously excessive and insufficient: excessive because there are too many restrictive regulations (especially on the private sector), insufficient because existing laws and regulations lack precision and transparency.

The institutional origins of violations. Table 12 shows that government agencies tend to commit some types of violation more frequently than others. The four most often-committed violations are:

1　Exceeding legal authority, including making administrative decisions without any legal basis (60 out of 219 violations).
2　Actions based on insufficient principal evidence (48).
3　Incorrect application of laws and rules, or no legal basis for administrative actions (40).
4　Violation of legal procedures (32).

It is suspected that the high frequency of such administrative violations is symptomatic of three major problems in China's legal, economic and political systems. First, the Chinese state still maintains excessive control over socio-economic activities through its system of laws and regulations. Secondly, the laws, rules and regulations that govern socio-economic activities are in great need of clarification. Close analysis of the sample cases shows that national, provincial and local laws often conflict with and even contradict each other. Many also lack transparency, thus allowing administrative authorities unwarranted additional power to interpret them to their advantage. Such systemic legal confusion and opaqueness is also exacerbated by unclear specification of the limits of jurisdictional authority and power of the various government agencies. The combined effects of imprecise, opaque and conflicting laws, rules and regulations inevitably lead to a high rate of the misapplication of laws and the exceeding of legal authority by government agencies.

Thirdly, decision-making in Chinese administrative agencies remains highly arbitrary, such that there is no accountability. Rather, there is a tendency to reach important administrative decisions that affect the lives and livelihoods of ordinary citizens on the basis of insufficient evidence. Legal procedures are frequently violated, and the limits of agencies' legal authority are often exceeded. The analysis in this study shows a consistent pattern of "administrative opportunism" whereby government agencies tend to base their decisions on laws and regulations that would favour them, even though such laws and regulations did not apply. In other words, misapplication of laws was often not accidental but intentional. In many sample cases reviewed in this study, government agencies misapplied laws and exceeded their authority primarily to impose heavy fines or seize the property of ordinary citizens and commercial entities.

Fruits of victory: what did plaintiffs get? In the 236 sample cases, plaintiffs obtained 148 favourable or partially favourable rulings from the court, excluding cases where plaintiffs withdrew their lawsuits after the defendants voluntarily revoked or changed the disputed administrative actions. Most favourable rulings led to a complete revocation of an administrative action, a partial revocation of an administrative action, an order to compel the performance of a delayed legal responsibility by the defendant, or an order to take a new administrative action. When plaintiffs won ALCs, defendants usually paid more than half, and sometimes nearly all, of the litigation costs. A litigant who lost an appeal was responsible for the costs of the appeal.

Of the favourable rulings obtained for plaintiffs in the sample, most did not award compensation to plaintiffs because such compensation was not demanded. Out of the 148 rulings for plaintiffs, this was the case for 96 (65 per cent). Of the remaining rulings favourable to plaintiffs, 17 plaintiffs demanded compensation but the court denied it; 18 demanded compensation but were awarded lower amounts (some then appealed to the higher court for more compensation); and 17 demanded compensation and received amounts apparently satisfactory to them. All compensation awards were for direct economic losses resulting from disputed administrative actions; there were no consequential compensation or damage awards. This suggests that the primary motive for plaintiffs was to revoke an injurious and unjust administrative action. Although many plaintiffs demanded compensation, the sample cases show that it was difficult to get the court to award such compensation or award it in a satisfactory amount.[42]

Conclusions

The evidence presented and analysed in this study shows that, although the constraints of China's closed political system seriously limit the effectiveness of the

ALL, the institution of judicial review of administrative actions is gradually being consolidated. The findings tend to support some of the earlier predications made of the ALL by one scholar who noted that it could be used by more powerful organizations (such as SOEs) in challenging government administrative agencies; he also saw the ALL as a useful legal instrument for China's emerging private sector.[43] Indeed, SOEs and private entrepreneurs and firms were among the most active litigants in the sample. Analysis of the national data on the increasing scope of administrative actions subject to challenge under the ALL similarly bears out the predication by another scholar who foresaw the expansion of the application of the ALL to "include within the ambit of judicial scrutiny an increasingly broad range of administrative activity."[44] Moreover, the embedded flaws of the ALL identified earlier by other scholars were also reflected in the results of the implementation. For example, the law's "focus on judicial review of the legality rather than the propriety of administrative decisions" has prevented Chinese citizens from invoking the ALL to challenge substantive government policies, as shown by the fact that none of the sample cases contained such suits.[45] The lack of judicial autonomy was also an important factor in the court's persistent bias in favour of the government (as indicated by their greater odds of winning these suits).

Therefore, in several important aspects, one may argue that the ALL has failed to live up to the expectations of its liberal proponents: it has not become a fully reliable or effective legal instrument that enables ordinary citizens to defend themselves against government infringements of their rights. But it has not been a total failure. The evidence indicates that it has gained a limited role in curbing and rectifying unjust treatment of citizens by government officials. One of the important findings of this study, which was not foreseen by other scholars in their earlier studies of the ALL, is the rising rate of settlements that provide effective judicial relief to the plaintiffs. The evidence gathered in this study offers some preliminary signs of the gradual consolidation of the ALL as a legal institution, including the consistent and dramatic rise of administrative litigation suits since its implementation; the decline in the percentage of rulings in favour of government agencies; the rise in the percentage of effective victories for plaintiffs; and the public perception of the ALL as a useful, albeit limited, legal instrument for protecting their rights.

A 1992 poll showed that 92 per cent of the respondents agreed that "it is better to have the ALL than not have it because, although the ALL is not perfect, citizens' rights have gained some protection."[46] In the same poll, 68 per cent of the ordinary citizens surveyed agreed that the ALL made a difference in limiting unlawful practices in society.[47] Under it, administrative litigation has also become an important option for ordinary citizens. When asked what recourse they would have when their rights are violated by the government, 35 per cent of the respondents said that they would bring their complaints directly to "relevant government agencies," while 30 per cent said that they would sue the government in the court (under the ALL).[48] The ALL also had an impact on government officials. The 1992 poll found that 74 per cent of the government officials surveyed said that they had begun to exercise greater caution in their work because of the ALL.[49]

This initial evidence of the institutional consolidation of China's administrative litigation system also sheds some light on the process of institutional evolution. The case of the ALL offers some evidence that institutions evolve through a process of *mutual adaptation* – new institutions adapt to the existing political system and its constraints and the existing political system adapts to the new norms and rules stipulated and embodied in the new institutions. As a result, the proposed institutional experiment tends to realize less than its full potential in terms of structuring political behaviour and enforcing new norms. At the same time, even such partially effective institutional experiments have a real impact on the existing political system, with its components (that is, various bureaucracies and organizations) struggling to adjust their behaviour to meet at least some of the requirements set by the new institutional experiments. There is evidence of such adjustments made by various agencies of the Chinese state. For example, a one-in-five chance that they may lose a case forces them to be increasingly open to settling with plaintiffs. Government officials also admitted that the ALL made them more careful in exercising administrative power. The immediate result of this mutual adaptation is a novel and complex arrangement of conflict resolution between the Chinese state and its citizens unanticipated by the designers of the ALL.

On the one hand, the ALL has set a series of legal precedents and procedures for citizens to seek judicial relief through a complete litigation process. On the other hand, the high costs of this process and the severe constraints placed by the Chinese political system on the judiciary induced plaintiffs and defendants to seek compromises through court-mediated settlements in many cases. This has certainly fallen short of the ideal of the rule of law, but even this imperfect outcome has generated real benefits both for the Chinese state (in terms of opening an institutional channel for addressing public discontent) and for individual citizens (in terms of redressing government-inflicted wrongs).

An intriguing question is why the old political system should accommodate the requirements of new institutions and refrain from reversing such accommodations. Scholars who have followed recent Chinese legal reforms argue that such accommodation was necessitated by the post-Mao regime's search for a new basis of legitimacy.[50] Other than legitimation concerns, it is contended that such accommodations, once made, may be difficult to withdraw unilaterally because of the high political costs that would entail. First, in many cases, the accommodations were initiated by reformers within the old regime who saw political benefits of a more institutionalized legal system. An attempted reversal of reform would lead to a bitter intra-elite struggle with high risks for both sides. Secondly, institutional development tends to be path-dependent. Legal reforms are no exception. The path-dependency of legal reform in China has been recognized also by other scholars, as one wrote, "... the operation of law is subject to evaluation and challenge by reference to external standards: once a principle of law is enunciated it becomes part of the public domain and open to uses that the regime may not be able to control."[51] In addition to setting new norms that eventually become benchmarks for evaluating individual or organizational behaviour, a new institution also acquires its defenders who are beneficiaries of the new system. Therefore, although institutional innovations may start as experiments, the longer such experiments continue, the higher the costs entailed in their reversal. Initially, the costs of reversing an institutional experiment are mainly reputational; the ruling elite risks losing political legitimacy or credibility if part of its new policy package is abandoned without justifiable reasons. In the Chinese context, since the ALL was promoted and implemented as an important element of China's overall legal reforms, any official action that overtly suspended or weakened its enforcement would have discredited the entire programme of legal reform.

Gradually, as an institutional experiment continues, political and economic entrepreneurs begin to perceive its potential benefits and capture them. Consequently, despite the limited nature of most institutional experiments, they attract entrepreneurs who then become the beneficiaries of these experiments (it is no mere accident that, in this sample, Chinese private entrepreneurs were the most active private litigants). The benefits won by these entrepreneurs are widely publicized by the reformers, who try to disseminate the information to more groups and attract a larger political following to defend the new institutional arrangement. Hence in the early days, lawsuits filed under the ALL received enormous publicity in the media. Once the benefits of the experiments have been conferred on many important groups (as the ALL has done for SOEs, township and village enterprises, the legal community, village groups, peasants, workers and entrepreneurs), it becomes more politically costly to reverse the reform.

This study also suggests that China's legal reforms, though far from establishing the rule of law in the short term, have made measurable progress in promoting legal norms and awareness of such norms at the grassroots level. For example, a majority of Chinese citizens know of the existence of the ALL.[52] The 185 cases examined here reveal that private citizens are more assertive of their rights. In the sample cases there are citizens who sued authorities for illegal search, seizure, fines and detention, who challenged regulatory agencies for failure to issue permits or licences, and who demanded rectification of unjust administrative penalties levied against them. The fact that a considerable proportion of suits filed under the ALL (about 39 per cent in 1995, according to this analysis) led to full or partial correction of wrong or unjust administrative actions shows that such legal risk-taking by ordinary Chinese is not completely futile. If this trend continues, a virtuous cycle may emerge: rising public awareness of legal norms and resources leading to increasing assertiveness by citizens and more frequent use of laws like the ALL, which creates more a credible threat to arbitrary government agents and places greater pressure on them to be accountable for their exercise of power.

Finally, this study indicates that state–society relations are changing in post-Mao China and that the boundaries between the state and society are being redrawn. A principal force of such changes is undoubtedly China's economic reforms that have restructured authority relations in virtually all sectors of the economy and society as a result of redistribution of economic resources from the state to society. However, the study shows that institutional changes such as legal reforms are a critical factor in the redefinition of state–society relations in China. These changes have more explicitly set limits on state power and established procedures for citizens to defend themselves against intrusion or infringement by the state and its agents. If such institutional changes continue, the new state–society relations in China will be not only based on structural factors (the distribution of economic resources and organizational capital between the state and society) but also underpinned by an increasingly sophisticated set of institutions that embodies norms and enforcement mechanisms which make such relations more sustainable and less prone to open conflict.

Notes

* The financial support for the research was provided by the United States Institute of Peace (SG-71–94). The opinions, findings, and conclusions or recommendations expressed in this article are those of the author and do not necessarily reflect the views of the United States Institute of Peace. The author wishes to thank the helpful comments from Larry Diamond, Elizabeth Perry, Stanley Lubman and Jonathan Hecht.

1 See Anthony Dicks, "The Chinese legal system: reforms in the balance," *The China Quarterly*, No. 119 (September 1989), pp. 540–576; Pitman Potter (ed.), *Domestic Law Reforms in Post-Mao China* (Armonk, NY: M. E. Sharpe, 1994); and Stanley Lubman, *China's Legal Reforms* (New York: Oxford University Press, 1996).

2 See Gong Ruixiang (ed.), *Fazhi de lixiang yu xianshi* (*The Ideal and Reality of the Rule of Law*) (Beijing: Zhongguo zhengfa daxue chubanshe, 1993).

3 Susan Finder, "Like throwing an egg against a stone? Administrative litigation in the People's Republic of China," *Journal of Chinese Law*, Vol. 3, No. 1 (Summer 1989), pp. 1–28; Pitman Potter, "The Administrative Litigation Law of the PRC: judicial review and bureaucratic reform," in Potter, *Domestic Law Reforms in Post-Mao China*, pp. 270–304; Song Bing, "Assessing China's system of judicial review of administrative actions," *China Law Reporter*, Vol. 8, Nos.1–2 (1994), pp. 1–20.

4 Lawsuits against government officials and agencies had been filed and tried even before the passage of the ALL, but the number of such cases grew dramatically after the passage of the law.

5 These 236 cases include 189 from a series of textbooks for Chinese judges. They are collected in *Zhongguo shenpan anli yaolan* (*Selected Major Trial Cases in China*); this series is edited by Zhongguo gaoji faguan peixun zhongxin (The National Training Centre for Senior Judges) and the Law School of the People's University; it is published by Zhongguo renmin gongan daxue (The Chinese People's Public Security University) Publishing Company. The 189 cases were from *Zhongguo shenpan anli yaolan* (hereafter *ZSAY*) (1992, 1993, 1994, 1995). Forty cases were published in *Renmin fayuan anli xuan* (*Selected Cases from the People's Court*), Nos. 11–15 (Beijing: Renmin fayuan chubanshe, 1995). Seven cases were published in *Zhongguo falu nianjian* (*Law Yearbook of China*), various years.

6 Liu Jinghuai, "Min gao guan you fa keyi" ("The legal basis for private citizens to sue government officials"), *Liaowang* 29 October 1990, p. 14.

7 Also see Potter, "The Administrative Litigation Law of the PRC," pp. 274–76; Finder, "Like throwing an egg against a stone?" pp. 8–10.

8 Liu Jinghuai, "Min gao guan you fa keyi," p. 14.

9 The CCP Politburo reportedly held two special meetings on the ALL. Peng Zheng, the chairman of the National People's Congress, strongly supported the ALL. Interview with the head of the Institute of Law at the Shanghai Academy of Social Sciences, May 1997.

10 The Chinese title of this law is "Zhonghua renmin gongheguo zhi an guanli chufa tiaoli." It gave the Chinese law-enforcement authorities broad powers to impose penalties (including administrative detention) on Chinese citizens.

11 For a brief discussion on this development, see Tong Shuisheng, "Min gao guan bei-wanglu" ("A memo on citizens suing officials"), *Falü yu shenghuo* (*Law and Life*), No. 82 (October 1990), p. 20.

12 At the end of 1988 there were 1,400 administrative tribunals; in 1990 the number rose to 2,638. *Xinhua yuebao*, No. 534 (April 1989), p. 36; Liu Jinghuai, "Min gao guan you fa keyi," p. 15.

13 According to Wang Hanbin, the chairman of the Judiciary Committee, the NPC received commentaries on the law from 130 government agencies and courts and only 300 commentaries directly from private citizens. *Xinhua yuebao*, No. 534 (April 1989), p. 36.

14 Henan, Guangdong, Sichuan and Tianjin were mentioned in Liu Jinghuai's report. Liu Jinghuai, "Min gao guan you fa keyi," p. 15.

15 Yang Haikun, "Baituo xingzheng susong zhidu kunjing de chulu" ("A solution to the besieged administrative litigation system"), *Zhongguo faxue* (*Chinese Legal Science*), No. 3 (1994), p. 51; Potter, "The Administrative Litigation Law of the PRC," pp. 287–290; Finder, "Like throwing an egg against a stone?" pp. 27–28.

16 The official text of the All can be found in *Xinhua yuebao*, No. 534 (April 1989), pp. 32–36; an English translation is available in *China Current Laws*, Vol. 1, No. 9 (October 1989), pp. 6–16. The references to the text of the ALL in this article are mostly based on this translation.

17 For detailed analysis of the provisions of the ALL, see Potter, "The Administrative Litigation Law of the PRC," pp. 276–281; Finder, "Like throwing an egg against a stone?" pp. 11–27.

18 See Potter's excellent analysis of the limits of the ALL, in "The Administrative Litigation Law of the PRC," pp. 282–87.

19 See, for example, Gong Ruixiang, *Fazhi de lixiang yu xianshi*.

20 The 1994 data for several provinces are unavailable. We use the data for 1993 and 1992 for these provinces to estimate their share of ALCs. Our estimates show that Tianjin's share (based on 161 ALCs in 1993) was 0.78% with a differential of –0.72; Shanxi's share (631 in 1993) was 2.2% with a differential of –.03; Jiangsu's share (906 in 1992) was 3.3% with a differential of –2.55. The number of cases accepted for trial by individual provinces seemed slightly to exceed the number given by the Supreme People's Court.

21 *Zhongguo falü nianjian* (1994), p. 236; *Zhongguo falü nianjian* (1995), p. 847.

22 *Hunan nianjian* (*Hunan Yearbook*) (1995), p. 88; *Shandong nianjian* (*Shandong Yearbook*) (1995), p. 844.

23 *Renmin ribao*, 22 March 1996, p. 3.

24 Court cases provide some clues as to what are labelled under the "other" category. They include the following: cases against the bureau of standards, against the patent bureau, against local governments on matters other than land use or zoning, against

tax collection agencies, against the supervisory agencies of state-owned enterprises, and against the bureau of civil affairs.

25 Tang Yongjin, "Yichang jingqiaoqiao de geming" ("A quiet revolution"), in Gong Ruixiang, *Fazhi de lixiang yu xianshi*, p. 60.

26 Zhang Shuyi and Zhan Zhongle, "Qiantu guangming, daolu quzhe" ("Bright future and tortuous road"), in Gong Ruixiang, *Fazhi de lixiang yu xianshi*, pp. 113, 121.

27 Compared with the data for previous years, the number of dismissed cases in 1995 might be too high.

28 Few court decisions change original administrative actions because the ALL restricts the court's authority to modify administrative actions. Such actions may be revised only when administrative penalties are deemed "clearly unjust."

29 See cases nos. 11, 12, 13, 22, 35 in *Yaolan 1992*; nos. 15, 23, 38, 43, 44 in *Yaolan 1993*; nos. 47, 59 in *Yaolan 1994*; nos. 10 and 30 in *Yaolan 1996*.

30 Yang Haikun, "Baituo xingzheng susong zhidu kunjing de chulu," p. 51; Zheng Hangsheng (ed.), *Report on Social Development by Renmin University of China, 1994–1995* (Beijing: Renmin daxue chubanshe, 1995), p. 68.

31 This claim was based on a report on the implementation of the ALL conducted by the Sichuan Supreme People's Court. It was cited in Tang Yongjin, "Yichang jingqiao-qiao de geming," pp. 43–44.

32 For cultural agencies, the court upheld their administrative actions in 20% of the law-suits in 1992, 12.5% in 1993, 9.2% in 1994 and 11.4% in 1995 while revoking their administrative actions in 22% of the cases in 1992, 26.7% in 1993, 17% in 1994 and 16.2% in 1995. The court upheld the actions of public hygiene agencies in 16.3% of the cases in 1993 and 17.2% in 1994, while revoking their actions in 18% of the cases in 1993 and 13% in 1994. *Zhongguo falü nianjian* (1994), p. 1029; (1995), p. 1065; (1996), p. 959; *Renmin fayuan nianjian* (*Yearbook of the People's Court*) (1992), p. 839.

33 Because the sample includes many lawsuits against industrial and commercial admin-istrations, the share of the suits filed by private entrepreneurs and firms might be larger than in a random sample. However, the information in Table 9 shows that only 11 private entrepreneurs and firms were plaintiffs in cases against industrial and com-mercial administration, indicating that the selection bias is not too severe in this sample. In terms of the outcome of the suits, private firms and entrepreneurs won 25 cases (53%), obtained partial favourable rulings in six cases (13%), lost 12 cases (26%), and withdrew in four cases (three cases were withdrawn after the defendants revoked the disputed actions).

34 The previously cited 1992 study based on primary research reported similar findings. Of the 96 plaintiffs surveyed, about 19% reported that their economic status was "rel-atively poor or poor"; 68% reported that their economic status as "average." Tang Yongjin, "Yichang jingqiaoqiao de geming," p. 7.

35 Tang Yongjin, "Yichang jingqiaoqiao de geming," p. 35.

36 *Ibid.* p. 29.

37 According to two Chinese researchers, most peasants were unwilling to spend money on legal representation. Zhang Shuyi and Zhan Zhongle, "Qiantu guangming, daolu quzhe," p. 117.

38 The data on the number of lawyers in China were obtained in *Zhongguo falü nianjian* (1994), p. 1045; (1995), p. 1079; (1996), p. 975.

39 *Zhongguo falü nianjian*, 1993, 1994, 1995.

40 In addition to lack of economic resources, Chinese peasants have less access to legal counsel because there are very few lawyers in the countryside.

41 The following text is based on "Administrative Procedure Law," *China Current Laws*, Vol. 1, No. 9 (October 1987), p. 10.

42 Before the implementation of the Law on State Compensation on 1 January 1995, citizens could not sue the state for damages.

43 Potter, "The Administrative Litigation Law of the PRC," p. 288.

44 Finder, "Like throwing an egg against a stone?" p. 28.

45 Potter's insight on the "legality" focus of the ALL is invaluable in understanding why it was enacted and how it was implemented. Potter, "The Administrative Litigation Law of the PRC," p. 288.

46 Zhan Zhongle, "Xingzheng susongfa shishi xianzuang yu fazhan fangxiang diaocha wenjuan baogao" ("Report on the survey on the implementation and trends of the ALL"), in Gong Ruixiang, *Fazhi de lixiang yu xianshi*, p. 280.

47 Tang Yongjin, "Yichang jingqiaoqiao de geming," p. 11.

48 *Ibid.* p. 59.

49 *Ibid.* p. 14.

50 See Pitman Potter, "Riding the tiger: legitimacy and legal culture in post-Mao China," *The China Quarterly*, No. 138 (June 1994), pp. 325–358; Edward J. Epstein, "Law and legitimation in post-Mao China," in Potter, *Domestic Law Reforms in Post-Mao China*, pp. 19–55.

51 Potter, "Riding the tiger," pp. 325–26.

52 According to a 1992 poll, 88% of the ordinary people surveyed said that they had heard about the ALL. Tang Yongjin, "Yichang jingqiaoqiao de geming," p. 10.

39

BETWEEN DREAMS AND THE REALITY

Making of the administrative procedure act in China*

Xixin Wang

Source: *Journal of Korean Law* 7:1 (2007): 157–182.

I Developments of administrative procedures since 1989: a brief survey

The past two decades of law reforms since late 1970s have seen remarkable developments with respect to administrative procedural system. The ideas of procedural legality, fairness, legitimacy, and procedural rationality have been greatly improved and come into play in China's administrative process. In the meanwhile, however, the process of the administrative procedural reforms has also revealed a series of problems and challenges ahead. For instance, there exist crying problems in terms of procedural openness, systematization, institutionalization, and procedural reasonableness, to name just a few. The law reformers come to recognize that the making of a unified Administrative Procedure Act, which is now under the way, is of critical importance to the ideas of "administration in accordance with law" and rule of law. Yet it is in no sense an easy job. In fact, the making of APA in China, deemed as an opportunity for "*reinventing government*", requires subtle integration of ideas and realities and of fundamental principles and practices of the administrative process.

In this regard, it is helpful to begin with a brief survey of developments of administrative procedures, in terms of both ideas and realities, for a better understanding of the context in which the making of administrative procedure act is under its way.

1 Procedural legality: legislative requirement and its practice

It is widely believed, in today's China, that procedural legality is one of the fundamental elements of the Rule of Law. Reforms in contexts of civil, criminal, and administrative procedures have reflected the practical attentions given to legal procedures. The Administrative Litigation Law as adopted by the National People's Congress in April 1989, which for the first time raised the issue of procedural legality to regulate exercise of administrative power by providing that courts may repeal an administrative action that "violates statutory procedures". "Procedural rule of law" has since then become an aspect of the practice of the "administrative rule of law". In the legal reforms of promoting the modernization of the legal system of China, as many believe, the Administrative Litigation Law has been a milestone, for its contribution to the establishment of the system of judicial review over administrative actions. However, there still exist good reasons for us to believe, from the perspective of institutionalization of administrative procedures, that the Administrative Litigation Law has also made another important achievement by highlighting the significance of legal procedures for curbing abuse of administrative power and safeguarding individual rights, as is mentioned here. This law provides for the first time that the court "may repeal through judgment" a specific administrative action that "violates statutory procedures";[1] therefore, the legal requirement of procedural legality in the process of exercising administrative power has been established in the form of legislation for the first time.[2]

However, while the requirement of procedural legality in administrative process by the Administrative Litigation Law should be deemed as a gigantic progress for China's construction of the rule of administrative law and the modernization of China's legal system, the practice of procedural legality may be a different story. It can be observed from the current administrative law system that two facts with respect to administrative procedures may practically hamper the functioning of principle of procedural legality.

Firstly, the requirement as articulated by the Administrative Litigation Law is limited to the context of "statutory procedures" only. In other words, courts can repeal administrative actions, when, and only when, they believe that agency violates "statutory procedures". If there were no such "statutory procedures" governing agency actions, it would be very difficult for courts to apply the principle of procedural legality to review agency action. Unfortunately, the reality is that there exist wide varieties of administrative actions that are not governed by "statutory procedures."

Secondly, in the practice of administration, the legal effect of the principles, such as procedural justice and reasonableness, have largely failed to be practically acknowledged and judicially enforceable, and the principle of the rule of procedural law could hardly serve directly as the "statutory procedures" for governing the exercise of administrative power. Therefore, when there is no clear provision in laws and regulations concerning legal procedures for administrative actions, there shall be no "playground" for the principle of procedural legality as established by the ALL. To put it more simply, the ALL, by requiring procedural legality, has left a huge task of developing legalized procedures governing agency actions.

As for us, a review of the requirement of procedural legality as described above has also pointed out a direction for administrative procedural reform in this country. With regard to administrative procedures, to take the requirement of procedural legality more seriously, we believe huge efforts must be made primarily in the following two aspects: First, fair and rational procedural rules must be made through legislation to govern any and all administrative actions that may affect rights and interests of private parties or public interest in administrative process, and such legislation should be available at a practically earliest possible time. Secondly, in the practice of administration and judicial review, legal effect must be attached to fundamental procedural principles that aim to guarantee procedural fairness, rationality, and reasonableness, because there exist huge discretion in agency's procedural activities. In order to curb abuse of discretion, and to ensure procedural fairness and reasonableness, those basic principles of administrative procedure highlighting fundamental values such as impartiality, fairness, consistency, credibility, and reasonableness must be declared and, more importantly, to be judicially enforceable through judicial review.[3] In other words, the basic principles of due administrative procedures shall have the same legal effect as statutory procedural rules. In this regard, the making of an Administrative Procedure Act is to govern exercise of administrative powers by providing both governing procedural rules and guiding procedural principles as well.

2 Wakening up of the consciousness of procedural reasonableness

In the early stage of China's administrative procedure reforms, although the legal system has failed to show concerns for the idea of procedural reasonableness, it should not be taken for granted that awareness of general public and law reformers on procedural reasonableness have been remaining in silence. As a matter of procedural practice, the consciousness of procedural reasonableness in the process of administration has been awakened and constantly increased. The Regulation on Administrative Reconsideration as promulgated by the State Council in 1990 and amended in 1994, and thereafter the Administrative Reconsideration Law, enacted in 1999 by the Standing Committee of China's National People's Congress, may be regarded as further efforts made for awakening China's dormant consciousness of procedural reasonableness and for institutionalization of mechanisms to attain reasonableness. As we have pointed out, although the Administrative Litigation Law has provided for the scope and principles as well as an institutional framework for the courts to conduct judicial review over administrative acts, this law also embodies a conspicuous defect – according to this law, it is the general principle that the courts can only review the lawfulness of concrete administrative acts. In other words, to a large degree, the court is not empowered to do anything to review the reasonableness of challenged administrative actions. By comparison, the Regulation on Administrative Reconsideration and the Administrative Reconsideration Law enacted thereafter have empowered the administrative reconsideration organs to review both the lawfulness and reasonableness of a concrete administrative acts.[4]

Logically speaking, the reasonableness of concrete administrative acts includes both substantive reasonableness and procedural reasonableness. The reconsideration organs may annual any administrative decision if they believe that it has contravened the requirement of procedural reasonableness. As the key issue of procedural reasonableness is, in its essence, procedural fairness, the Administrative Reconsideration Regulation's concern for the issue of procedural reasonableness implies that procedural fairness has caught attention of the law reformers and the general public as a basic requirement for administrative decision-making. We have great reason to believe that, with the wakening up of public consciousness of procedural fairness, procedural reasonableness will become a focus in the context of administrative procedure reforms.

3 Efforts for institutionalization of procedural fairness

In pace with the wakening of the consciousness of procedural fairness reflected in laws and regulations, institutionalized efforts have been made in administrative procedure reforms to attain procedural fairness. As viewed from the process of administrative decision-making, the basic elements of administrative due process, such as the neutrality of the administrative decision maker, the participation of the affected party, procedural openness, and rationality of decision-making, and so forth, have transformed from concepts of procedural fairness into procedural rules and workable mechanisms to regulate administrative decision-making process. All these may be regarded as institutionalized efforts to attain procedural fairness in the process administrative decision-making.

For example, the Law of the People's Republic of China on Assembly, Procession and Demonstration as adopted by the Standing Committee of the National People's Congress in 1989 provides that, for an application for assembly, procession or demonstration, the public security organ shall inform the citizens concerned, at least two days before the date as applied for, of its final decision of approval or disapproval. If the public security organ fails to make a decision within the legally prescribed time limit, it shall be deemed that the application has been approved.[5] From the perspective of procedural impartiality, the aforementioned provision has begun to treat seriously some of the basic elements of procedural fairness, say, explaining the reason for the decision, informing the affected party, and providing the legal remedies for the adversely affected parties, among other things.

As for the institutionalized efforts to guarantee procedural fairness, the Law of the People's Republic of China on Administrative Punishment (hereafter the "Administrative Punishment Law") as promulgated in 1995 is a remarkable starting point in this regard. As we can observe and analyze from procedural requirements concerning imposing administrative penalties by agency, this law has made giant steps for the institutionalization and realization of procedural fairness in the following major aspects:

A Ensuring the neutrality of the decision maker

The Administrative Punishment Law has for the first time clearly showed its concern to the neutrality of the decision makers in the process of making administrative punishment decisions. According to this law, if the affected party believes that an administrative decision maker has an interest, bias, or prejudice in the administrative punishment decision, he or she is entitled to apply for the withdrawal of that decision maker. A prejudice may be that the maker of administrative punishment decision has a direct interest in the case in question or that the maker has personal relations with the party concerned in the case in question. In the hearing procedure for administrative punishment, the affected party may also apply for the withdrawal of the presiding hearing officer whom is believed to be biased, interested or prejudiced.[6] On the other hand, this law has also tried to prevent and eliminate the preference of the administrative decision maker by separation of functions. For example, this law provides that, in the process of imposing administrative punishment, the officer taking charge of the investigation may not participate in the making of final administrative punishment decision.[7]

B Introducing formal hearing procedures into administrative decision-making

The Administrative Punishment Law has, for the first time, introduced formal hearing as a procedural requirement into administrative decision-making process in the form of legislation. This is, undoubtedly, remarkable progress forward in realizing procedural fairness in the process of making administrative decisions. The establishment of the hearing system makes it possible for the realization of an important procedural right of affected parties, namely, the right to be heard. For administrative organs, when imposing administrative penalty upon individuals, such administrative punishment as revoking a license or imposing a considerably large amount of fine, the affected party shall be entitled to apply for a formal hearing.[8] According to this law, in the process of hearing, the private party concerned is entitled to obtain relevant information about the hearing activities within a reasonable period of time, to retain professional legal assistance, to defend herself, to demand the holding of the hearing to be made public, and so forth. The introduction of formal hearing system and the procedural rules aiming at ensuring procedural fairness of the hearing process have provided an institutionalized channel to realize procedural legality and fairness in administrative decision-making process.

C Separation of functions

Though the Administrative Punishment Law fails to clearly articulate separation of functions as a general principle for decision-making in the context of imposing administrative penalty, it has nonetheless embodied the spirit of separation of the functions of investigation, decision-making, and enforcement in the process.[9] To put it simply, separation of functions is reflected in two aspects. Firstly, according to this law, the officer taking charge of the investigations may not participate in the making of punishment decisions. The essence of this provision is to separate the function of investigation or the function of prosecution from that of making decision, the purpose of which is to prevent the decision maker from being prejudiced that otherwise might occur as result of mixture of functions. Secondly, this law has separated the function of imposing administrative fine from the function of collecting that fine. From the theory of procedures, the former is an "internal separation of functions", while the latter is an "external separation of functions". Whatever the form, the purpose of separating the functions is to ensure procedural impartiality. If, under any procedure, the function of investigation and that of decision-making is integrated and vested in the same body, the decision maker would be the "judge of his own case". If, in the process of making administrative punishment decisions, the person who makes the decision of fine is able to collect the money, it may imply or indicate a fact that the decision maker has a "direct interest" in the final decision that he makes.

D Reason-giving and pre-notice

These two procedural requirements are not only the requirements of administrative transparency, but also the requirements of administrative rationality. The Administrative Punishment Law provides that before a final decision-making, agency must notice facts, charges, reasons and legal bases for its proposed final decision to the affected party, and inform that affected party of her right to defend for herself, and that when final decision is made, it again must be noticed to the affected party with clearly stated reasons and legal bases. Such procedural requirements are believed to be critical to curb arbitrary use of agency power and to safeguard individual rights, and to facilitate consequent judicial review if the affected party is not satisfied with the final decision.

Further, the Administrative Licensing Law, as enacted by the NPC in 2003, has reaffirming the basic principles of procedural openness, fairness, impartiality, and reasonableness in contexts of establishing and deciding on administrative licenses. It has also developed mechanisms of procedures to institutionalize such principles. What is more, the Licensing Law introduced formal hearing procedure and other forms of public participation into policy-making process. For instance, when agency intends to create a licensing regime, the Law requires that some "appropriate sorts forms for soliciting public opinion" must be taken, including formal hearing and some sorts of public notice and comments procedures. In this regard, it is believed that the implementation of the Administrative Licensing Law may contribute to improvements of administrative procedures, in terms of both procedural ideas and practice.

4 The rise of public participation: procedural reforms of the administrative regulatory process and the rule making process

Spurred by the procedural reform in the area of administrative decision-making process, the procedural reform in the administrative regulatory process and the rule-making process of China has also been carried out and some achievements have been scored. Being different from administrative decision-making, the administrative power as exercised in administrative regulatory process may produce an impact on the rights and interests of the general public rather than on particular parties. The typical administrative regulatory acts include the price fixing as dominated by the government in some regulatory contexts, the setting of industrial standards, city planning, management of public facilities, and so forth. The administrative regulatory process is closely connected with the rule-making process, yet there exist some procedural differences between the two processes. The rule making process is, in practice, a process of making administrative regulation and rules, as well as formulating and issuing of administrative normative documents that also bear practical legal effect. There are different procedures governing administrative regulatory policy-making and rulemaking, but generally speaking, rulemaking is required to follow more complicated procedures, while procedures for policy-making are relatively flexible. In both processes, the recent five years have seen the rise of idea and practice of public participation; consequently, it should be no surprise to find that public participation has been increasingly a keyword in the procedural reforms. Since the time when the price hearing system was introduced by the Price Law, the means for participation by the general public in the administrative regulatory process has developed from the various forms of hearings into diversified means for public participation. In the process of rule making, the concept of legislative hearing and encouragement of various forms of public participation are provided by the Law on Legislation, and further required by two State Council regulations concerning Procedure of Making Administrative Regulations and Procedure for Making of Administrative Rules, which have introduced legislative hearings into a wider scope of practice, particularly in the practices of rulemaking by local governments. What's more, a procedural practice similar to notice-comments has also been introduced into the process of rule making by both central and local governments in recent years. The practice of public participation in administrative regulatory process and rule making process, while has shown an exciting new trend of procedural development in terms of rationality and democracy, has also revealed practical problems that are crying for solutions.

II Major problems of the administrative procedure system: a summary

While it is acknowledged that, since the reform and opening up policies were carried out and with the efforts of the construction of democracy and rule of law, the administrative procedure system has witnessed much progress, examination from a macroscopic point of view on the legal procedure construction nonetheless indicates the reality that procedural system is yet far from being able to satisfy the demand of the principle "administration according to law and building the rule of law state", as adopted by the Constitutional amendment in 1999. Therefore, a summary of those procedural problems may be helpful for the ongoing administrative procedural reform. To be specific, major problems plaguing the administrative process may include:

1 The existing administrative procedural rules are sporadic and lack necessary cohesion and uniformity which have resulted in conflicts among the principles or rules within the procedural system;

2 The process of making some important administrative decisions still lack statutory provisions of legal procedure, and in the exercise of administrative power too much discretion is left to agency, therefore, it is hard to ensure the fairness of procedure;

3 Procedural rights are not taken seriously by administrative agency, or even courts. In administrative process, agency may give its major attention to substantive matters, such as facts and criteria, but very little attention to respecting individual procedural rights; so is the court in judicial review over agency actions. In addition, procedural mechanisms safeguarding procedural rights are not well developed, leaving those rights largely unrealistic.

4 As compared to the enhancement of the consciousness of the "procedural legality" in the legislation and practice, the value and significance of "procedural reasonableness" has not received enough attention, resulting in arbitrary and capricious use of administrative powers;

5 There are serious conflicts among existing procedural rules, which demonstrates that such procedural rules have been arbitrarily designed and therefore lack minimum consistency;

6 Some of the basic procedural principles containing crucial values of procedural fairness have not been recognized by legislations and their legal effect usually denied by agency and the court;

7 There are no clearly defined and specific conditions for the use of summary procedures, which has left too large rooms for arbitrary exercise of administrative power in procedural operations;

8 The participation of the general public in the administrative regulatory process and rule making process is not sufficiently ensured by law in terms of scope and degree, and the institutionalization of public participation remains to be improved, and the constitutive elements for effective participation (e.g., information disclosure, organization of interest groups, etc.) remain poorly defined;

9 The liabilities for the agency violation of statutory procedures or infringing upon individual's procedural rights are not defined clearly, and some violations of administrative procedures by agency still remain unaccountable at all;

10 The administrative organs and officials are not equipped with a good sense of procedural legality and reasonableness, instead, the instrumentalism has been for a long time a dominant ideology with respect to legal procedures;

11 Consciousness of citizens, legal persons and other organizations concerning procedural rights has been remaining very weak.

As summarized above, the problems faced by the procedural reform may fall into two categories. The first category is problems resulting from subjective factors. Subjectively speaking, the Chinese traditional legal culture has for a long time shown misunderstanding, bias and even indifference to values and functions of legal procedure. For example, agency officials believe that legal procedures are only a means for managing the society and controlling people, and can only govern the "governed" rather than to "govern the governor", otherwise legal procedures may "bind up agency's own hands and feet". They believe that procedures are merely means for attaining administrative ends; therefore, if procedure cannot serve particular administrative ends, they may go beyond the procedures.[10] Similarly, the fact that the social members have a faint consciousness of significance of legal procedures, values of procedural rights and procedural fairness is also a problem of procedural ideology. The second category is resulted from objective factors. The objective factors mainly include technical factors, such as empirical research and procedural designing, particularly the insufficient knowledge and mastery of the structure of legal procedures, the conditions for procedural reasonableness and procedural fairness, and the institutional arrangements for attaining due process. All such factors may lead to the corresponding problems in procedural arrangements. Accordingly, we strongly recommend that reform of administrative procedures must also be tackled from the aforementioned aspects.

III Theoretical research as a preparation for making of administrative procedures Act: a review

Chinese scholars have begun to pay remarkable attention to the study of administrative procedures and the practical problems relating to them since early 1990s, resulting in great scholarship on administrative procedures and theoretical proposals of reforming the administrative procedural system. Such theoretical studies are undoubtedly of pivotal guiding significance to the making of Administrative Procedures Act that has been initiated in late 1990s.

To sum up, theoretical studies that have been done are basically focused on the following areas. First, emphasizing of importance and values of administrative procedures and conceptual enlightenment. Studies with regard to this aspect involve the basics of legal culture regarding administrative procedures, the significance of administrative procedures in the rule of law context, concepts of the rule of procedural law and the meanings thereof, procedural fairness and the interpretation of due process, procedural rights, and relations between procedural law and substantive law. Such studies done by the Chinese legal community on the above important theoretical issues may lay a conceptual foundation for the making of Administrative Procedure Act.

Secondly, research on the basic principles and rules regarding administrative procedures. Such studies concern with basic principles and rules for setting the framework of the Chinese APA, including debate over fundamental goals or values of administrative procedural legislation, particularly the potential intension between procedural fairness and procedural efficiency.

Thirdly, comparative studies of administrative procedures. The theoretical study done by the administrative law community on the administrative procedure legislation had highlighted a global vision; they have made an all-round investigation and study of administrative procedure legislations and practices of major western countries. The Administrative Legislative Research Group, a group responsible for drafting the Chinese APA under the sponsorship of China's NPC Standing Committee, has organized many seminars and conference on comparative studies of administrative procedures, plus study tours to many countries, including the United States, the UK, Germany, France, Spain, Japan, and South Korea. Through comparative studies, the Chinese administrative law community has not only translated legislative documents of administrative procedure law in major countries, but also studied experiences or lessons from practices of administrative procedure abroad. Such comparative studies have provided necessary reference for China's legislation on administrative procedures.

Finally, studies on format and legislative techniques for the making of APA. Apart from the general theoretical and comparative studies, Chinese administrative law scholars have also conducted some research works directly relating to the making of APA itself. Such studies focused on the formats of the APA, the framework and the structure of the Law, techniques of coordinating uniformity and specialty of administrative procedures. Some scholars have even completed "Model Drafts" of the Administrative Procedure Act.

IV Empirical research for the making of Administrative Procedure Act

It is unimaginable to reform the administrative procedure system and to make a law governing administrative procedures without full understanding of the real situation of administrative procedures. It is widely agreed that empirical studies of administrative procedure is critical to the making of the Chinese APA.[11] However, such studies have not been given sufficient attention until now. When the Chinese Administrative Legislation Research Group started its drafting work on the Administrative Procedure Act in late 1990s, it was fully aware of the significance of systematic empirical studies on situations of administrative procedures.

At the "Sino-US International Conference on Administrative Procedure Law" held in Dalian, northeastern city of Liaoning Province in July 2000, the Group proposed that, during the stage of preparing for the drafting of the Administrative Procedure Law, it would be necessary to make a systematic investigation and study on China's status quo of the rules on administrative procedures so as to enable the draft law to respond exactly to practical problems existing in the area of administrative procedures. This proposal met with the support of the attendees coming from both China and the United States. The objectives of the empirical study are to conduct investigations and studies on the major administrative procedures of the Central Government and those of the selected local governments from the beginning of 2001 to the end of 2002, and to submit a general report and corresponding legislative suggestions to the legislature for reference of legislation.[12]

Between September 2001 and May 2002, the Group started its investigation of the major administrative procedures of the organs of the Central Government. The main purpose is to make an observation and understanding of the status quo of the administrative procedures in China in an effort to offer an outline of the operation of administrative procedures. Therefore, the purpose of this investigation was not to offer an all-round "knowledge" about the relevant procedural operations. The purpose was to attract the examination and concern of the reformers and the objects of reform, and to call on the legislators to carefully observe and construe the local context of administrative procedures legislation. From the investigations we have identified some key issues to which the coming administrative procedure reforms must respond.

1 The necessity for uniform legislation on administrative procedures

Is it necessary to make a uniform law so far as the present situation is concerned? From the data that we have acquired from the investigation in the organs of the Central Government, we believe that the following three aspects may be helpful to our deliberation over this issue. Firstly, at the present time, the ministries and commissions of the Central Government are not short of regulatory provisions regarding administrative procedures; on the contrary, the provisions on administrative procedures are large in amount and plenty in variety and the procedural operations are diversified. The problem is that many of the procedural provisions are overlapping in content; they "check" or even conflict with each other. For example, in the area of foreign trade regulation, the existing administrative procedures include at least the procedures for management of quotas, procedures for management of import and export licenses, antidumping procedures, countervailing procedures, and so on. Let's take the antidumping and countervailing procedures as an example. The procedure for accepting cases alone concerns the MOFTEC (now the Ministry of Commerce), the State Economic and Trade Commission, the General Administration of Customs, the Tariff Policy Commission of the State Council, and all these government organs have their own procedural provisions. Their different provisions have displayed a procedural network with "mutual check" and conflicts, which has affected the efficiency of administration and the reasonability of control.

Secondly, the procedural rules of different departments mostly concern very specific matters, and with the progress of situation, corresponding rules will show much variance. The procedural rules lack governing principles and necessary concerns for continuity and consistency of administrative activities.[13]

Thirdly, the procedural rules of the departments concerned are not dovetailed well and concerted with each other, and application of procedures by different departments is characterized by inconsistency and arbitrariness.

Undoubtedly, all these existing problems indicate practical necessity of making a uniform law on administrative procedures; however, it is no easy task. If uniform legislation is necessary, then how shall we deal with the relationship between uniform legislation on administrative procedures and the procedural particularities in different administrative areas? How should this relationship be positioned? How can it be concerted through the uniform procedural legislation?

2 Feasibility of uniform legislation on administrative procedures

Is it feasible to make a uniform law on administrative procedures? So far as the present situation is concerned, we believe that it is feasible to make a uniform law on administrative procedures. Firstly, after more than a decade of building the administrative rule of law, the consciousness of "procedural lawfulness" of public power and the exercise of such power is growing,[14] which has provided a "manpower" basis for the carryout of lawfulness in procedural operations because the legislative feasibility does not only include the feasibility of making laws but also the feasibility of implementing the laws. Secondly, we have accumulated rather rich experiences during the past years in the relevant legislation on administrative procedures and law enforcement thereof, and some major administrative departments have begun to make a lot of attempts in regularizing their procedures. For example, the customs and the foreign trade departments have made some future-oriented legislative efforts to reform their procedures in accordance with requirements of WTO. Thirdly, some important administrative procedural systems have been established and have produced good results, e.g., the procedures for hearing and the procedures for information disclosure in the antidumping investigations, etc. The establishment and application of such procedural systems has formed the basis and offered important practical experiences for the uniform legislation on administrative procedures.

3 The format of the uniform legislation on administrative procedures

What format should be employed for the legislation on administrative procedures? Should it be a uniform and detailed code or a legislation of general provisions? With regard to this question a lot of discussions have taken place.[15] From the practical situation, the format of legislation on administrative procedures should be able to meet the need of the procedural operations. On the one hand, we should be aware that different administrative departments have their substantive and procedural particularities in the administrative regulatory process, therefore a uniformed and detailed procedural code might result in "cutting the feet to suit the shoes" or "attending to one thing but losing sight of another". On the other hand, though different administrative processes are somewhat different in procedural operations, they are in essence exercise of government power, and such exercise of power should satisfy some common and general procedural requirements, e.g., transparency, consistency, procedural efficiency, and fairness, etc. If these general principles and values are not provided for in the procedural legislation, the legislation itself would be meaningless. Taking these two aspects into consideration, we believe that, in terms of the legislative format, we may adopt the format of "a law on general principles and mechanisms of procedure", namely, the legislative structure may adopt a model of "principles guided general provisions and special provisions". The principles shall apply to all the administrative processes, and the general provisions shall apply to all circumstances for which there are no special provisions of law, while the special provisions shall apply to the special administrative processes only. The legislation should be a combination of principles and general provisions and the concretization of particular administrative processes.

4 Institutional innovation of the legislation on administrative procedures

From the present situation of administrative procedures, the Administrative Procedure Act should pay much attention to the following institutional arrangements: Firstly, provisions about the general principles of administrative procedures. For the time being, the diversity of the practice of administrative procedures has reflected the various procedural requirements, but it also has revealed the disarray of administrative procedures. An important objective of legislation on administrative procedures should be offering a basic "model procedure" so as to ensure that the diversified administrative procedures are operated under the guidance of the basic procedural principles, and to promote uniformity with necessary diversity. The objective of general procedures is also to provide, by setting models, standards for judging the reasonableness of the non-statutory procedures or discretionary procedures and to work out a basic procedural framework for the special procedures of different departments.[16] Secondly, the hearing procedures need to be further improved and rationalized. At the present time, the provisions regarding the hearing procedures in administrative processes are diversified in kind but lack basic consistency.[17] To this end, the Administrative Procedure Law should include general provisions for the "minimum requirement" for the hearing procedures – the opportunity to be heard. In the meanwhile, the requirements for the hearing procedures under different circumstances should be provided for in other separate laws. By doing so, the principle and flexibility can be balanced. Thirdly, it should articulate the principle of disclosure of government information. Though it is believed that openness and participation are the basic procedural requirements in administrative processes, due to the "concealing" of information by the government, the general public is largely restrained in their participation in administrative activities. Fourthly, the legal liabilities for agency's violation of procedures should be clarified and made practically accountable. In the relevant legislations on administrative procedures today, the crying problem is that the provisions regarding legal liabilities of the illegal procedural activities of administrative agencies are too vague, and there may even be no corresponding provisions at all. This situation has resulted in the rampancy of various illegal activities in administrative procedural operations, or even procedural nihilism.

V The basic framework and suggestions for China's legislation on administrative procedures

With the tremendous support of the Legislative Affairs Working Commission of the National People's Congress, the Chinese Administrative Legislation Research Group (the Group) started to work on the framework of the Administrative Procedure Act at the beginning of 2001. At the beginning of 2002, the Group produced the Framework of the Administrative Procedure Act (initial draft). After the Framework was completed, the Legislative Affairs Working Commission of the National People's Congress held a symposium in Beijing and Tianjin in April and June 2002, respectively, to discuss and solicit advice for revising and supplementing the initial draft. On the basis of this and after making study visits to other countries, the Group absorbed the advices from all sides and completed the expert initial draft of the Administrative Procedure Act, which has been discussed, and advice for it solicited as many as 15 times so far. In December 2004, the Draft Administrative Procedure Act was submitted to the Legal Affairs Working Commission of NPC for intensive review and discussion.

1 Basic features of the content of the Draft Administrative Procedure Act

1 Apart from general provisions that may applicable to all administrative actions, for instance, procedural principles and hearing procedures and general provisions of procedures, the Draft also provides for the specific procedures for particular administrative acts, such as decision-making, rulemaking, and administrative planning, and government contract, thus featuring a combination of generality and particularities.

The Administrative Procedure Act is expected to be a general law on the procedures for administrative acts, but it is not a simplistic enumeration of the various administrative procedures. Rather, provisions regarding the common procedural rules for the various administrative acts show that there exists a relationship of overlapping between procedural rules and administrative acts: a procedural rule may be applied to more than one administrative act, and an administrative act needs the application of more than one procedural rule. If the chapters of the Administrative Procedure Law are arranged in such a structure as they are arranged according to specific categories of administrative acts, the result would be that procedural rules must be provided in great detail for each administrative act, and the Administrative Procedure Law so arranged would be a "compilation" of procedural laws for various types of administrative acts and would be verbose, lengthy and overlapping in content, and would not be able to form an organic system. Therefore, some countries, such as the United States, have followed the format of providing for the common procedural rules for the various administrative acts in making their administrative procedure laws.

The Draft of the Administrative Procedure Act has to large extent taken the practice and legislative model of German administrative procedure law as a reference. It provides general provisions for procedures of making administrative decisions, and procedures for particular types of administrative acts. After careful deliberation, the particular types of administrative acts as provided in the final Draft include administrative rulemaking, decision-making, administrative programs and planning, government contract, and administrative guidance. Considerations on selection of these particular types of administrative actions relate to the fact that previous to the making of Administrative Procedure Act, there are already the Administrative Punishment Law (1995), the Administrative Licensing Law (2003), and the Administrative Compulsory Enforcement Law (expected to come very soon), all of which lay down specific procedures governing corresponding administrative actions and measures; therefore, general guiding provisions on procedures for those specific administrative actions would be enough, leaving detailed and specific procedure provisions to those separate laws. On the contrary, there exist no separate laws providing even guiding principles and general provisions of procedures for administrative actions and measures such as making of administrative normative documents, administrative planning, government contract, and administrative guidance. Meanwhile, procedural problems with these types of administrative actions are among the most serious ones that need to be dealt with in practice.

2 Apart from procedural provisions, the Draft also includes provisions on substantive matters, thus featuring the combination of procedural and substantive provisions.

The reasons for this arrangement are that there lack unambiguous legal provisions regarding such important issues as the basic principles, the validity, and the legal effect of administrative acts; there also lack necessary arrangements for principles guiding allocation and exercising of administrative powers

297

within the administrative system; and still, there lack clear and accountable legal liabilities for violations of administrative procedures. With those facts, it would be hard to imagine the practical effect of legal procedures if there are not such substantive provisions concerning the above-mentioned key issues in administrative process.

3 Apart from external administrative procedures, the Draft also provides for internal administrative procedures, thus featuring the combination of internal and external procedures.

From the administrative law perspective, administrative procedures mainly refer to external administrative procedures governing agency actions that may directly affect private parties concerned. However, although agency internal administrative action may not directly affect rights or interests of parties concerned, it may nonetheless influence rights or interests of private parties in terms of procedural fairness and efficiency. Given the fact that in China today there exist huge amount of chaotic and bureaucratic agency internal procedures that usually impose great impacts on private parties in particular administrative context, including, but not limited to conflict of administrative jurisdiction between administrative organs (positives and negative conflicts), and assistance among administrative organs, we perceive a compelling demand for regulating agency internal procedures through the Administrative Procedure Act.

4 The Draft concentrates on laying down prior procedures for administrative actions, but leave posterior procedures such as administrative appeal and judicial review procedures for regulation by other laws.

It might be surprising to some US legal scholars that the Draft says nothing about judicial review relating administrative procedures. Yet the fact is that the already existing laws, including the Administrative Reconsideration Law (1999), the Administrative Litigation Law (1989) and the State Compensation Law (1994) have already provided for procedures for administrative appeal, judicial review, and state compensation. There is the call for integration of all these laws into a unified administrative procedure code in the future, but at present stage, the Draft of Administrative Procedure Act remains to be a law concerning procedures of exercise of administrative power within administrative process.

2 Main contents and structure of the framework of the Administrative Procedure Law

From the above description about the Draft, we could see that the draft of the Administrative Procedure Act has a large volume of contents; therefore the lawmaking in this case requires huge legislative techniques in terms of arranging the contents scientifically, reasonably and logically. With reference to the experience of other country, we have proposed that the contents of the Law be arranged in the following way:

1   General provisions precede special provisions. Chapter I of the Draft law lay down the general provisions and Chapter II provides for principles governing organization of administrative organs and relations among them; Chapter III contains general provisions for procedures of administrative decision-making. Chapters IV through VIII are provisions for specific types of administrative actions, including administrative rulemaking and making of normative documents, administrative planning, government contract, and administrative guidance.

2   Procedural provisions precede substantive provisions. As for the arrangement of the general provisions, we believe that the administrative acts by which the subjects exercising administrative power makes decisions through certain procedural operations, so the initial draft should take administrative power as the axis, and arrange the relevant contents according to the sequential order of "administrative bodies → procedures governing operation of administrative power → legal effect and consequence of administrative actions". That is to say, the Draft first lays down basic principles for structure of administrative organs and relations thereof, and then provides for procedures for different administrative actions, and then clarifies conditions for validity and legal effect of administrative actions.

3   Some of the provisions regarding internal administrative procedures are provided in Section 1, Chapter II: "Administrative Organs".

3 Choice of the legislative format for the Draft Administrative Procedure Act

So far as the structure of the aforesaid contents is concerned, there exists the question of how to choose a legislative format in the entire process of making the Administrative Procedure Act. According to the experience of foreign countries, the legislative forms are mainly as follows:

1   Highly codified format, as adopted by, for example, Germany and China's Taiwan. The feature of this form is that all the contents relating to administrative procedures are incorporated into the administrative procedure code, and the advantage thereof is that the provisions regarding administrative procedures are unified to the largest possible extent.

2   The format of separate general provisions. This form can make the separate general provisions and other relevant laws form into an integrated system so as to co-regulate the procedures for administrative activities. This form has been adopted by some countries, including Japan and Italy.

3   The format of a separate procedure law with eventual codification, as adopted by, the United States. A feature of this legislative format is that a procedural code of general provisions is formulated first, and then the relevant separate laws are incorporated into the administrative procedure law by

means of codification, which may make the administrative procedure law an open-ended legislative process.

The legislative formats as described above have their own advantages and disadvantages. We are holding the view that, to select the legislative format for the Administrative Procedure Act, we should take the following factors into consideration: the costs of legislation, the demands of legislation, the coordination between the administrative procedure act and other already existing separate laws, and practical possibility. Based on these considerations, we have recommended that the Draft Administrative Procedure Act take the format of a separate law of general provisions. That is to say, the Administrative Procedure Act mainly provides for general principles and provisions of procedures governing administrative activities, general procedural rules, and some specific procedural rules. At present stage, it may be unrealistic to make a unified and detailed administrative procedure code. However, we also recommended that along with the administrative procedure reforms, efforts to codifying administrative procedures be made for the concern of attaining uniformity, and consistency of administrative procedure system.

VI Challenges ahead: difficult issues in the making of China's Administrative Procedures Act

While it has received great enthusiasm and intellectual support form legal communities both home and abroad, the ongoing process of making China's APA is still facing great difficulties and challenges ahead. Those difficulties include practical resistance from some government agencies at both central and local level. Since the making of APA intends to regulate administrative process and to control administrative power, it should be no surprise to perceive reluctance or even resistance from the bureaucratic system. In the meanwhile, the process of making APA can also be understood as a process for reallocation of regulatory powers between the central and local governments; therefore, power struggles in the lawmaking process should not surprise either. For the lawmakers, in addition to balance practically involved interests in the lawmaking process, technical and legal issues concerning the law itself also present a huge challenge. With this respect, there still exist a number of key and difficult issues, demanding further comparative and empirical studies and great wisdom for resolutions. Such key issues include at least the following:

First, there comes the question concerning the legal effect of the principles of the administrative procedure law. The basic principles of the administrative procedure law are essentially important in legislation. Should these principles bear direct legal effect and binding force? Can courts apply and enforce legal principles of procedures in judicial review cases? How should we deal with them in legislation? How should we coordinate the relationship between the principles? How should we deal with the relationship between the basic principles and the specific procedural rules?

Secondly, questions concerning the relationship between the general provisions for administrative procedures and the specific procedures for particular administrative acts. Are the general provisions a "benchmark" requirement for administrative procedures? Or shall the special procedural provisions prevail over the general provisions?

Thirdly, questions concerning the relationship between the general administrative procedure act and other relevant laws. Should the relationship be that of one between a new law and old laws, or between a general law and special laws? For example, for administrative licensing and punishment procedures, shall the Administrative Licensing Law and the Law on Administrative Punishment apply, or shall the Administrative Procedure Law apply? Should this relationship be handled and coordinated by the general provisions or by particularized legislations?

Fourthly, questions concerning legal liabilities and means of accountability for violations of administrative procedures. What shall be the legal consequences or liability for a violation of administrative procedure? What are the means and mechanisms for account agency liabilities for violation of administrative procedures, and what kind of remedies shall be available for individuals to challenge agency's violations of procedural requirements?

Fifthly, questions concerning the choice of legislative format of the APA.

Finally, questions concerning the national uniformity and local diversities of administrative procedures. The Draft APA has paid much attention to attaining procedural uniformity for the administrative system. However, given the fact that local governments may also demand procedural flexibility and diversities in local administration, how to coordinate the uniformity dream and diversified realities? Should local government be given authorities to modify general procedural requirements based upon local and practical realities? If that is case, how to maintain a balance between the uniformity and diversity?

To sum up, the making of administrative procedure Act in China, while widely believed to be a work of great urgency and importance, is also facing considerable difficulties and challenges. Fortunately, there is the increasing consensus among government leaders and the general public on the demanding need for making of the APA. The process of the lawmaking has been ongoing, and steps seem to be accelerating. All these might again give us reasons and sources for a modest optimism toward the future.

Notes

* This article was originally a working report to the Standing Committee Legal Affairs Working Commission of China's NPC on drafting the China's Administrative Procedure Act. A more detailed and comprehensive Chinese version of this report can be found in *Chinese Legal Science*, volume 5, 2003. As one of the major draftsmen of the Chinese APA, the author has been in charge of most of the research and drafting works for this law. The Author wants to express his deep appreciations and high respect to Members of the Drafting Group led by Professor Ying Songnian and to the

foreign experts involved, especially, Professor Paul Gewirtz, Professor Stanley Lubman and Professor Peter Strauss, among others. Leading figures of the foreign expert group, they have been for many years deeply involved in the making of China's APA and have made tremendous contributions to the drafting process of this law.

1 The Administrative Litigation Law of the People's Republic of China (hereafter "the Administrative Litigation Law"), Article 54.

2 Of course, before the enactment of ALL, there were some sorts of "policy requirements" of procedures and procedural legality, but such requirements were largely in the bureaucratic system, referring to internal administrative procedures. Procedures governing agency actions affecting individuals were very vague and subject to administrative discretion.

3 For a detailed discussion of the basic principles and requirements of due administrative process, see Wang Xixin, *The Basic Requirements of Procedural Fairness Explained*, 3 ADMINISTRATIVE LAW REVIEW (2000); Wang Xixin, *Due Process and 'Minimum Impartiality'*, 2 LAW REVIEW (2002).

4 The Regulation on Administrative Regulation, Article 5.

5 The Law of the People's Republic of China on Assembly, Procession, and Demonstration, Article 9.

6 The Law on Administrative Punishment, Article 42 (4).

7 The Law on Administrative Punishment, Article 38, Article 42 (4).

8 The Law on Administrative Punishment, Article 37.

9 For a discussion of the legislative spirit of the Law on Administrative Punishment, see Wang Xixin, *On the Legislative Spirit of the Law on Administrative Punishment*, 6 STUDIES IN LAW AND BUSINESS (1996).

10 Objectively speaking, all legal procedures serve certain "purposes". In this sense, the 'instrumentalist view of procedure" is not unacceptable, and in fact, in any legal system, legal procedures possess certain instrumentalist functions to a certain degree. But if this is why we believe that legal procedures can only serve substantive results, and when the procedures cannot serve the results and they are not to be observed, then it is not "instrumentalism of procedures", but "nihilism of procedures".

11 In the history of legislation on administrative procedures in other countries, the relevant positivist research has formed a basis of legislation. To take the making of the United States' Federal Administrative Procedure Act as an example. In the process of enacting this law, the American Bar Association ("ABA") organized long-term positivist study, and the relevant authorities also conducted large-scale positivist studies. In 1939, President Roosevelt established an Attorney General's Committee on Administrative Procedure consisting of outstanding scholars, private lawyers, and judges, aiming at conducting an extensive investigation and study on the status quo of administrative procedures. During the subsequent two years, a positivist study was conducted on the administrative procedures of 27 federal government departments by various ways, including interviewing administrative officials, lawyers, the general public, attending the meetings of administrative organs, consulting relevant archival files, etc., and formed a 474-page-long report in 1941. This report was believed to be "a landmark in the administrative law of the United States", which has formed an important basis for the making of the Administrative Procedure Act. See: 1941 Final Report of Attorney General's Committee on Administrative Procedure.

12 The task force "Positivist Study on Chinese Administrative Procedures" was chaired by Professor Ying Songnian with the National Institute of Administrative and Dr. Wang Xixin, Associate Professor with Peking University Law School. Over a dozen postgraduates and doctoral postgraduates of Peking University Law School participated in the practical investigation work. For the time being, we have finished the investigation of the administrative procedure rules and practice of some of organs

of the Central Government and local governments, and are now in the final stage of writing the investigation report. The Legislative Affairs Committee of the National People's Congress has provided tremendous support to this study, and the Asia Foundation has als provided funds to the said study.

13 See *Investigation Report* (Concerning the organs of the Central Government, quoted from the materials obtained from the 2002 annual conference of China Administrative Law Society).

14 This is an initial impression that we get in the investigations and interviews.

15 For representative discussions, see Ying Songnian, *Law on Administrative Acts*, PEOPLE'S PRESS (1993); Jiang Ming'an, *How Should China Select Its Legislative Mode on Administrative Procedures?*, 6 CHINA LEGAL SCIENCE (1995).

16 The Framework of the Administrative Procedure Law, which has been finished so far, has included good provisions in this aspect, which can basically satisfy the aforesaid requirements.

17 According to the statistics done by the authors, there are at least several dozens of hearing procedures. There is sharp difference between the different procedures as well as the provisions of the different regions and different departments.

Part 15

ECONOMIC AND COMMERCIAL LAW

40

FUNDAMENTAL PRINCIPLES OF CHINA'S CONTRACT LAW

Wang Liming and Xu Chuanxi

Source: *Columbia Journal of Asian Law* 13:1 (1999): 1–34.

I Introduction

On March 15, 1999, the Contract Law of the People's Republic of China[1] was adopted by the Second Session of the Ninth National People's Congress (NPC) and scheduled to take effect on October 1, 1999. The Contract Law's promulgation constitutes not only a major development of China's contract law, but also an important step in China's enactment of its much-awaited Civil Code (*minfa dian*).[2] The Contract Law provides general provisions (entitled *zongze* in Chapters 1–8 in the Contract Law) for governing all types of contractual relationships,[3] as well as particular provisions (entitled *fenze* in Chapter 9–23) for further regulation of 15 particular categories of contracts, respectively.[4] As the statute that deals specifically with contracts, the Contract Law can be expected to play a crucial role in regulating China's burgeoning market economy and in contributing to China's further legal development.

This Article attempts to discuss some of the fundamental guiding principles of the Contract Law. There are three major principles/policies, namely, those of freedom of contract (*hetong ziyou*), good faith (*chengxin*), and the fostering of transactions (*guli jiaoyi*), that have been conscientiously followed by the law's drafters[5] and that have been essentially embodied in the law's final formulation. By examining major provisions of the Contract Law that embody these three fundamental principles, respectively, we hope to elucidate the main spirit of the Contract Law as well as its general doctrinal structure. For ease of presentation and for want of space, we devote our primary attention to the general provisions (*zongze*), although particular provisions (*fenze*) are occasionally touched upon where relevant.

To provide some necessary background to our discussion, Part II of this Article briefly examines major reasons for the promulgation of the Contract Law and the previous contract laws it is intended to supercede. Parts III, IV and V are then devoted to elucidating the Contract Law's three fundamental principles, viz., freedom of contract, good faith and the fostering of transactions, respectively. In these sections, we attempt to identify major provisions of the Contract Law that reflect these principles and explain how these principles apply at various stages of a contractual relationship. Part VI offers our brief concluding remarks.

II The necessity of the Contract Law

The Contract Law unifies and improves upon China's three previous contract laws, namely, the Economic Contract Law,[6] the Foreign Economic Contract Law,[7] and the Technology Contract Law.[8] By superceding the previous contract laws,[9] the Contract Law seeks to establish a more advanced, systematic, and comprehensive contract law to better suit the particular needs of China's transitional economy. Specifically, the Contract Law has been necessitated by the following major problems with the previous contract laws:

A The problematic notion of "Economic Contract"

China's previous contract laws, especially the Economic Contract Law and the Foreign Economic Contract Law, espoused a problematic notion of contract, that of "economic contract" (*jingji hetong*). Originated in the former Soviet Union (USSR), this concept has figured prominently in USSR's economic law regime. In China, the concept of economic contract was adopted for the first time in 1956.[10] With the promulgation of the Economic Contract Law in 1981, the concept was officially adopted by the Chinese legislature. Many scholars have held that economic contracts belong to the field of economic law, while non-economic contracts (i.e., civil contracts; *minshi hetong*) belong to civil law. In connection with the distinction between economic and non-economic contracts, there has been a division of economic courts (*jingji ting*) and civil courts (*minshi ting*) within each of China's people's court (*remin fayuan*). The economic courts have been in charge of handling economic disputes, while the civil courts have been responsible for hearing non-economic, civil cases.

The concept of economic contract is seriously imprecise and of little use in practice. According to the Economic Contract Law, an economic contract is made between legal persons for the pursuit of a certain economic purpose.[11] This definition, however, does not distinguish the so-called economic contracts from other types of contracts, because in entering a contract the parties almost always have some economic purpose in mind and thus most, if not all, contracts have an economic dimension. As necessitated by the notion of economic contract, all particular categories of contract were divided into economic vis-a-vis civil contracts, to which different rules were to apply. Thus, for example, sales contracts (*maimai hetong*) were divided into "purchase and marketing" (*gouxiao*) and "general sales" (*yiban maimai*) contracts, storage contracts (*baoguan hetong*) into "warehouse storage" (*cangcu baoguan*) and "non-warehouse storage" (*fei cangcu baoguan*) contracts, and so on. In practice, judges often found it difficult to make such distinctions and to apply different rules to contracts based on these distinctions.

To be sure, some unique transactions in the marketplace may indeed give rise to contracts that are markedly different from other contracts. Nonetheless, there are important common grounds among all contracts, economic and non-economic alike. For instance, in forming any contract, the parties must follow general principles such as voluntariness, fairness and good faith; contract performance must be in accordance with terms of the contract and such principles as good faith; breach of contract must entail liability for damages, and so on. These common grounds call for the unification of China's previous contract laws and have formed the basis of the general provisions in the Contract Law. To the extent that particular types of contracts may have their unique features, they can be adequately addressed with the secondary, specific provisions relating to particular types of contracts in the Contract Law.[12]

The division of economic and civil contracts and of their respective sets of rules, in addition to being inherently dubious, also failed to meet the needs of China's developing market economy. A market economy calls for a uniform market, one that is open on equal terms to all types of enterprises, organizations, and individuals. However, the three previous contract laws applied only to economic contracts, which by definition existed only between legal persons (*faren*), not natural individuals (*ziranren*).[13] On the other hand, civil contracts were between natural individuals only.[14] The dichotomy between economic and civil contracts was thus unfavorable to developing a uniform market in China and to providing a uniform contract law to all types of parties and transactions.

Although the Economic Contract Law underwent a significant revision in 1993,[15] that revision did not eliminate the need for a uniform contract law. A chief reason is that the Revised Economic Contract Law still retained the concept of economic contract. In addition, the revision of the Economic Contract Law failed to successfully coordinate the interrelationship among the three previous contract laws and between these laws and the General Principles of Civil Law,[16] as will be discussed in greater detail below.

B Contradictions and redundancies among the previous Contract Laws

There were many contradictions and redundancies among the previous contract laws. For instance, modeled more closely on Western contract laws, the Foreign Economic Contract Law accorded the contracting parties greater freedom of contract than did the Economic Contract Law.[17] Article 17 of the Foreign Economic Contract Law stipulated, for example, that "[a] party may temporarily suspend its performance of the contract if it has conclusive evidence that the other party is unable to perform." This stipulation, however, was absent from the Economic Contract Law, which provided a mandatory rule for specific performance.[18]

The Revised Economic Contract Law created some additional discrepancies among the previous contract laws. For example, Article 27 of the Economic Contract Law provided that only where performance of an economic contract was rendered unnecessary by one party's breach, might the other party terminate the contract. To accord greater respect for a party's right of termination upon the other party's breach, the Revised Economic Contract Law abandoned this provision. However, the Technology Contract Law still followed Article 27 of the Economic Contract Law in stipulating that a party could only terminate a technology contract where its performance was rendered unnecessary or impossible by the other party's breach.[19] Thus there existed an obvious contradiction between the Revised Economic Contract Law, on the one hand, and the Technology Contract Law, on the other.

As they contradicted and duplicated one another, the previous contract laws also failed to cover certain common situations. For instance, the Economic Contract Law governed economic contracts only, leaving non-economic contracts to be governed by no particular statute. (This was so although the economic-noneconomic distinction was unclear and imprecise). In addition, with the Foreign Economic Contract Law governing economic contracts involving foreign parties[20] and the Economic Contract Law governing domestic contracts only, there was no legal basis for deciding disputes concerning non-economic contracts involving foreign parties. For example, when a foreign citizen rented a house from a Chinese citizen, thus giving rise to a so-called non-economic contract, the previous contract law provided no clear guidance on which statute should govern the contract in question.

Similarly, because the Technology Contract Law applied to domestic technology contracts only[21] and the Foreign Economic Contract Law did not apply to technology contracts involving foreign parties,[22] foreign-related technology contracts were left outside the realm of the former contract laws.[23]

There also existed inconsistencies between the three contract laws, on the one hand, and the General Principles of Civil Law ("GPCL"), on the other. For instance, the GPCL stipulates that, "civil acts should follow the principles of voluntariness, fairness, equal compensation, and good faith."[24] By contrast, Article 5 of the Economic Contract Law provided that, "[i]n forming economic contracts, [parties] must follow the principles of equality and mutual benefit, consultation and agreement, and equal compensation," whereas Article 3 of the Foreign Economic Contract Law provided that, "contract formation should follow the principles of equality and mutual benefit, and consultation and agreement." Neither of the two contract laws mentioned the principle of good faith, as does the GPCL.

According to Professor Liang Huixing, such problems with China's previous contract law were primarily attributable to the executive branch's undue influence on legislation.[25] Many laws as well as administrative regulations (*fagui*) and rules (*guizhang*) have been drafted by various ministries and commissions under the State Council, who often have been too confined by their own perspectives to take account of the general legal structure.[26] It is clear, therefore, that only by the legislature's drafting an overarching Contract Law to replace the three previous contract laws can the previous contract laws be unified and improved.

C The lack of basic contract rules in the previous Contract Laws

Since the promulgation of the Economic Contract Law in 1981, China saw the production of several major laws and regulations in the field of contract. Despite all of this, however, China always lacked some basic contract rules, such as those on offer and acceptance. As a consequence, such crucial issues as what constitutes an offer or acceptance, what distinguishes an offer from an invitation to deal, and so on, were left to the discretion by individual judges. This created much discrepancy and many similar problems in practice.

Similarly, the previous contract laws lacked any legal rules on precontractual liabilities. For instance, as has been quite common in China, prior to the formation of a contract, one party may accidentally or maliciously cause significant damage to the other party. Can the injured party demand compensation in such cases? There was no rule in the previous contract laws that addressed this question and the new Contract Law should provide such a rule.

The lack of such basic rules in China's previous contract law is seriously troublesome if one takes into account the many recent developments in contract law in other legal systems. Since World War II, contract laws in many advanced countries have had tremendous developments as their market economy has experienced further growth. By means of case law or codification, these countries have established many new contract rules to reflect their current market practice.[27] Similarly, there have been substantial changes in international regulations on contracts.[28] In order to further develop its economy and integrate itself into international market, China must learn from the contract legislation in other legal systems and bring its contract law to maturity and modernization.[29]

D The Contract Law and the civil code

In addition to rectifying the problems identified above, the Contract Law is also a part of China's efforts to develop a civil code. China started to design a civil code in the early 1950s. More than 40 years later, however, a civil code still remains a mere wish for Chinese legal scholars. Nonetheless, with the drastic changes in China's social and political life as well as the development of China's market economy, to enact a civil code has now become the consensus of all that are concerned. In order to reach the goal of developing its market economy and that of administering the country according to law (*yifa zhiguo*), the Chinese government has resolved to complete, by the year 2010, a comprehensive, modern legal system. The promulgation of the civil code will mark the eventual establishment of this legal system.

However, the drafting of a civil code is a tremendous, complicated project that can only be undertaken step by step. The promulgation of the Contract Law is a necessary, major step in producing the civil code. Upon the promulgation of the Contract Law, legislation of the law on obligation and on contracts has been essentially completed; in the future it can be directly incorporated into the civil code.

When drafting the Contract Law, there were two differing opinions among the drafters and legal scholars as to its contents. Some scholars were of the opinion that the law should include general provisions and, whenever possible, particular provisions that will govern various specific types of contracts. Other scholars held that, in order to expedite the law's promulgation, we should first promulgate the general provisions and, as does the UCC, provide particular rules only on sales contracts but not any other types of contracts. The legislature has adopted – correctly in our opinion – the first position. This is because the previous contract laws provided rules on many particular types of contracts. To unify and supercede the previous laws, the Contract Law must necessarily provide for those particular types of contracts as well.

III The principle of freedom of contract

The fundamental principles of a contract law represent the law's essence and spirit. As the law's guiding principles, they are the starting point for drafting, interpreting, implementing, as well as for studying the law. In practice, such principles may oftentimes be employed to guide or inform, or even serve as the legal basis for, the resolution of various contractual disputes.[30] We believe that the Contract Law has been primarily influenced by three fundamental principles: freedom of contract, good faith, and the fostering of transactions. This section focuses on explicating the principle of freedom of contract, whereas the following two sections are devoted to the principles of good faith and the fostering of transactions, respectively.

As a fundamental legal principle, freedom of contract recognizes a contracting party's freedom in choosing the other contracting party, forming a contract, determining the terms and contents of the contract, modifying or terminating the contract, stipulating the remedies for a breach, and so forth. The principle of freedom of contract governs every stage of the contracting process and is in many ways the most crucial of all contract law principles.

In drafting the Contract Law, there existed differing opinions on whether we should adopt the principle of freedom of contract. Some scholars held that the notion of freedom of contract originated from classical Western contract law models; by the 20th century, however, as nation-states have strengthened their intervention in contracts, this principle has gradually become defunct. China's contract law, so the argument goes, "must follow the new trends in the world's contract law, i.e., to place necessary limitations on freedom of contract in order to realize social public interest and the protection of the weak in society."[31] Another opinion held that the principles of equal consultation (*pingdeng xie-shang*), equal compensation (*dengjia youchang*), and so on, have essentially embodied the contents of freedom of contract. Therefore, there is no need in the new Contract Law to stipulate the principle of freedom of contract.

We believe that both of these opinions are incorrect. To be sure, since the beginning of this century, many developed nations have indeed strengthened state intervention in contracts. Nonetheless, freedom of contract remains a fundamental legal principle.[32] In China, the long history of intense centralized planning and the elimination of freedom of contract now calls for an expansion of contractual freedom, rather than its restriction. This is necessary because, although the economic reforms have greatly strengthened various parties' autonomy to engage in economic activities, in reality there still exist many limitations on and deprivations of the parties' freedom of contract.[33]

The principle of freedom of contract must be adopted also because it is needed for the fostering of transactions and for the further development of China's market economy. As Professor Jiang Ping has pointed out, "To accord parties freedom of action to the greatest extent possible is the common demand by the market economy and the autonomy of the parties' free will."[34] The more developed and widespread the various contractual relationships, the livelier the transactions, and the more dynamic the market economy. Only with a developed market economy and its active transactions can the society's wealth substantially increase. All this will depend on how much freedom of contract the parties will enjoy according to law. Under the current circumstances, China's contract law must thus embrace freedom of contract as its most fundamental principle. This principle will not only substantially improve China's contract law but also, for China's legal system in general, lay down a novel rule-of-the-law precept that fully respects the freedom and rights of enterprises, organizations, and citizens.[35]

To be sure, China's civil law has established the principles of equal consultation and equal compensation.[36] These principles, however, do not amount to and cannot replace freedom of contract. On the one hand, these principles do not express a notion of freedom, but of equality. They are concerned primarily with the relationship between two equal parties and emphasize equality as the relationship's guiding principle. However, the principle of freedom of contract is not limited to the relationship between two parties, but recognizes instead genuine freedom that any contracting party may lawfully enjoy. On the other hand, although these principles are directly applicable to contractual relationships, their scope is not limited to contracts but covers other civil legal acts as well. By contrast, freedom of contract is a particular principle for contracts; it governs contractual relationships but not any other civil legal relationships.

Furthermore, the principles of equal consultation and equal compensation apply primarily to contract formation, whereas freedom of contract not only covers contract formation, but also the contents and form of the contract, the modification and termination of the contract, the transfer of contract, and any other segments of the entire contract process. For the reasons stated above, the principles of equal consultation and equal compensation can not, contrary to the opinion of some researchers, replace freedom of contract.

A major reflection of the Contract Law's adoption of freedom of contract – in spirit if not in the exact words – is that it has, to the greatest extent possible, limited the mandatory provisions in the previous contract laws and, at the same time, broadened the scope of elective provisions.[37] Generally, under the Contract

Law, if the contracting parties have reached an agreement as to matters of their transaction, their agreement shall govern; only where no agreement exists will the law be triggered. For instance, many articles of the Contract Law include the important qualifier "except where the parties have otherwise agreed,"[38] indicating the law's respect for the parties' free will. The Contract Law's affirmation of the principle of freedom of contract is, additionally, reflected in the following respects:

A Contract formation

With respect to contract formation, the Contract Law has substantially reduced or eliminated the restrictions by the previous contract laws, regulations and rules on the parties' freedom to form contracts and to select their contractual partners. According to Article 4 of the Contract Law, "[p]arties have the right to voluntarily enter into a contract, no entity or individual may unlawfully interfere [with this right]." It is true that Article 38 of the Contract Law provides that "[w]here the State according to its need issues mandatory plans or state purchasing tasks, the concerned legal persons and other organizations shall form contracts in accordance with their rights and duties as provided in relevant laws and administrative regulations," thus placing some limitation on the parties freedom to form a contract. Nonetheless, because the State currently only imposes mandatory plans in truly exceptional situations, this provision does not seem to significantly restrict the parties' freedom with respect to contract formation.

B Contract validity

The Contract Law respects the parties' freedom in validating their contract and has significantly reduced the government's unnecessary intervention in that area. The Contract Law no longer grants state executive agencies the power to determine the effectiveness of a contract and places serious restraints on their power to supervise and examine (jiandu jiancha) contracts.

For example, Article 127 of the Contract Law stipulates that "[w]ithin the scope of their respective authority and responsibilities, departments of the industry and commerce administration and other relevant administrative agencies in charge shall, according to provisions by law and administrative regulations, take charge in supervising and handling any illegal act that, by the means of a contract, harms the state interests and public interests." This article does not provide a cover-all contract management power to executive agencies, as did the previous contract laws,[39] but requires the administrative organs to obey the law and regulations when supervising contracts. More important, this article explicitly limits the scope of contracts to be monitored by administrative organs to those that "harm State interests and public interests."[40] This will help prevent the executive branch from willfully expanding its power to managing contracts to the detriment of the parties' necessary freedom of contract.

C Terms of a contract

The Contract Law provides that the terms of a contract are to be decided by the parties through agreement.[41] Although the law lists some terms that are generally included in a contract, such as the parties' names and domiciles, the subject matter of the contract, and the quantity and quality of the goods involved, it does not require that all contracts contain all these terms. The law does not impose uniform provisions on the terms in all types of contracts. The contracting parties enjoy freedom and flexibility in determining what to include in their contract.

By contrast, Article 12 of the Economic Contract Law stipulated that economic contracts were to have five major terms: namely, subject matter; quantity and quality; price or compensation; the time period, location, and form of performance; and liability for breach of contract. The law's listing of major terms that were to be included in a contract had in practice been easily misunderstood as meaning that absence of any of such terms would entail an invalidation of the contract. The Contract Law has discontinued such provisions from the Economic Contract Law in order to avoid such misunderstandings.

D Contract termination

China's previous contract laws recognized that parties might terminate a contract through consultation with each other.[42] They did not recognize, however, that parties might terminate their contract through the exercise of an agreed-upon right of termination. An agreed-upon right of termination is the right to terminate a contract under certain stipulated circumstances; the right is normally assigned to a party as a result of the parties' negotiation. The parties' agreement as to this right may be reached when the contract is formed or it may be reached independently thereafter.

The Contract Law now explicitly recognizes the parties' right to agree upon contract termination and allows the parties to stipulate — e.g., at the time when the contract is formed — a right to terminate the contract. After the contract takes effect, if the conditions for terminating the contract are materialized, a party that holds the right of termination shall be allowed to terminate the contract by exercising its agreed-upon termination right.[43]

E Liability for breach of contract

The Contract Law accords substantial respect for a non-breaching party's freedom to choose the form of remedy where the other party breaches. For example, Article 107 of the Contract Law stipulates that "[w]here one party fails to perform its contractual obligations or fails to perform its contractual obligations in accordance with the contract, it shall bear the liability for breach by continuing its performance, taking remedial measures, or paying damages." This provision has essentially abandoned the traditional mandatory rule of specific performance.[44] It allows the non-breaching party to choose the form of remedy, including liquidated damages, damages, as well as specific performance (excepting special situations where the law recognizes that specific performance is impossible). With regard to the terms of liquidated damages, the Contract Law will generally follow the agreement between the parties. Even where the liquidated damages do not correspond to the damages as determined by law, the liquidated damages are to be deemed valid unless they are determined to be unduly high or low.[45]

It should be pointed out, however, that the freedom of contract as embodied by the Contract Law is relative, not absolute. In order to ensure that China's market economy develops in an orderly fashion, it is necessary for the State to exercise some measure of intervention and control. State invention is appropriate especially where it is needed to ensure that contracts are adequately fair and equal, that they balance the parties' conflicts of interest sufficiently well, that they do not serve the parties' interest to the detriment of the welfare of the state and the society, and so on.

The justification for state intervention in contracts is often summarized in China as the principle of contract justice (*hetong zhengyi*), for it is justice that state intervention is called upon to achieve. There are a number of scholars who believe that contract justice and freedom of contract are the two major principles of contract law, with one principle supplementing and assisting the other. Contract justice can function to counteract the shortcomings of freedom of contract and to supplement its insufficiencies.[46] That the Contract Law has embodied the spirit of contract justice can be seen in Articles 39–41 and Article 53, which impose restrictions on the use of form contracts and on clauses of indemnification.[47]

IV The principle of good faith

The principle of good faith (*chengxin*; literally, honesty and trustworthiness) requires parties to a civil act to conduct themselves honorably, to perform their duties in a responsible matter, to avoid abusing their rights, to follow the law and common business practice, and so on. In civil law countries, the principle of good faith is often called the highest guiding principle or the "royal principle"[48] for the law of obligations. Why should the Contract Law recognize and embody the principle of good faith? We believe the major reasons are the following:

A Norms of commercial conduct

The principle of good faith will help to maintain China's traditional mores and commercial ethics. Chinese society has been under the crucial influence of Confucianism and has constantly been holding up the value of good faith. Good faith has not only been one of the general principles for people's everyday conduct but has also been a crucial moral precept in China's commercial practice. By embracing the principle of good faith, the Contract Law is recognizing China's traditional morality and business ethics, which is also consistent with the norms of international commercial practice. With its strong moral force, the principle of good faith can be expected to contribute much to the establishment of a normal transactional order in China.

B Respect for and performance of contract

On a more specific level, the principle of good faith will help to ensure that contracts are respected and performed. Good faith requires that one keep one's word and be trustworthy. Only when parties to a transaction abide by the principle of good faith can their contract be adequately respected and executed. If people take the notion of good faith seriously, even if their contract is deficient in some way, they will endeavor to cure the contract's defects and fulfill their obligations. Conversely, in a situation where the contract is perfectly complete, if the parties do not act in good faith, the contract is unlikely to be faithfully carried out. Therefore, the strengthening of the principle of good faith is a necessary foundation for the establishment of an optimal transactional order for China.

C Other functions of the principle of good faith

As a fundamental principle underlying the transactional order, the principle of good faith should not only help balance the parties' conflicts of interest during their transaction but also help guide the interpretation of the law and the contract in question. In view of the many social and economic changes occurring in China, many laws and regulations are no longer suitable to the current economic situation. Thus, if we adopt the principle of good faith and enable judges to fill the legal loopholes/vacuums accordingly, this will help to develop and improve China's legal system.[49]

The Contract Law requires the contracting parties to exercise their rights and fulfill their duties in strict accordance with the principle of good faith, not only at the stages of contract formation, performance, modification and termination, but also after the contractual relationship is terminated. The law recognizes that parties to a transaction should act in good faith at every stage of their transaction. Only with good faith can they be made to follow not only commercial ethics, but also their contract, thus helping to develop a normal order for transactions.

1 Good faith at the stage of contract formation

At the stage of contract formation, although the contract has not yet been formed, the parties have already been in contact and may have even reached some preliminary agreement. They therefore should, according to the principle of good faith, observe some necessary ancillary (*fusui*) duties. In accordance with the principle of good faith, contracting parties owe to each other the following duties when forming their contract:

317

A THE DUTY OF LOYALTY IN FORMING THE CONTRACT

The parties should engage in the making of their contract out of good will. They shall not, under the disguise of forming a contract, viciously conduct negotiations with the other party in order to cause losses to the other party. For example, they are not to negotiate with the other party in order to prevent that party from forming a contract with a third party;[50]

B THE DUTY OF HONESTY AND NON-DECEPTION

The parties should truthfully state to each other the defects and qualities of their products and may not otherwise seek to deceive the other party. The parties should also, at the same time, state to each other certain important facts, such as their financial situation, their abilities (or the lack thereof) to perform, and so on. On the whole, they should be faithful to the facts and should not make any false statements. If they intentionally conceal important facts or provide false information in connection with contract formation, thus causing losses to the other party, they must be liable for damages;[51]

C THE DUTY TO KEEP PROMISES

During their negotiations, parties should strictly keep their promises. When a party sends out an offer, it should be prepared to be bound by the offer. After the offer reaches the offeree and the offeree reasonably relies on the offer, if the offeror by canceling its offer causes damage to the offeree, the offeror should bear liability for such damage. If the contract is to be formed by telegram, facsimile or other similar means, and one party demands the signing of a confirmation letter before the contract is formed, the other party should agree.[52] But where the parties have formed a preliminary agreement or where one party has made a promise that has caused reasonable reliance by the other party, if the party who requests the signing of a confirmation letter eventually fails to accept the offer, it should, by implication, pay for the other party's reliance damages;

D THE DUTY OF CONFIDENTIALITY

The contracting parties must not reveal or improperly use commercial secrets they have learned during the process of contract formation, whether or not the contract is actually formed or becomes effective. Otherwise, they shall pay damages to the injured party for its losses resulting therefrom.[53]

2 Good faith after contract formation and before contract performance

After the contract is formed but performance has not yet begun, parties should, according to the principle of good faith, strictly keep their promises and diligently prepare for their performance of the contract. If, prior to its performance, one party suffers serious losses from its ill-management/operation or encounters other adverse situations as specified by law, the other party may temporarily cease its own performance and demand insurance for performance by the first party. However, in thus exercising its right of termination, the other party should strictly follow the spirit of good faith as well as conditions stipulated by law. It should not, because of temporary or non-serious difficulties restricting the other party's ability to pay, use that as a pretext for terminating its own performance. If its failure to thus follow the principle of good faith causes losses to the other party, it shall pay damages for such losses.[54]

If, without the reasons as outlined above, one party during this period explicitly informs the other party or manifests by its conduct that it will not perform the contract, the other party may demand that it bear liability for breach of contract before the term of the contract expires.[55] But where one party does not signal that it will not perform the contract, or its signaled non-performance has a proper legal excuse, the other party should, in accordance with the principle of good faith, refrain from terminating the contract.[56]

3 Good faith in contract performance

Contract performance should strictly follow the principle of good faith. When performing their contract, parties should observe various ancillary duties created by the principle of good faith, in addition to their duties as stipulated by law and the contract. As has been discussed above,[57] such ancillary duties include the duty of loyalty, the duty to disclose defects and to notify the other party of important situations, duty to cooperate with and assist each other, the duty to convey instructions for use, and so on.

As to duties that are stipulated by the law or the contract, if they are unclear, insufficient or lacking, the principle of good faith requires that parties perform their duties in good faith. For instance, if a contract does not specify any quality requirements for its subject matter, the obligor should not, contrary to the principle of good faith, intentionally select and deliver goods and services that are of inferior quality.[58] If the contract does not specify the time of performance, when the obligor offers to perform, it should according to the precept of good faith allow the obligee some necessary, reasonable period of time for preparation. If the contract stipulates the time limits for its performance, the obligor in selecting the actual time of performance must follow the principle of good faith as well. In this situation, if the obligor has a proper reason to perform before the deadline and this advance performance will not cause any damage to the obligee, the obligee should accept the obligor's performance unless he has a proper reason not to. One such reason would be that this advance performance would somehow harm or seriously inconvenience the obligee.

4 Good faith in terminating a contract

In comparison with China's previous contract laws, the Contract Law provides unequivocal limitations on how a contract is to be terminated. For example, it provides that only where one party's delay of its performance or some other breaching act frustrates the purpose of the contract, may the contract be terminated.[59] In general, termination of a contract must follow the principle of good faith. For instance, where the goods delivered by one party are deficient but these goods comprise but an insignificant part of the entire order, the other party generally should not terminate the contract on that basis alone. Similarly, in the case of a long-term contract, should either party decide to terminate the contract according to conditions specified therein, it should notify the other party as far in advance as practicable, so that the other party may have enough time to cope with the termination.

5 Duties of confidentiality and loyalty after the contract is terminated

Following contract termination, the contracting parties no longer owe each other any contractual obligations. They should, however, in accordance with the principle of good faith, bear certain necessary ancillary duties, the most important of which are the duties of confidentiality and loyalty. Such duties are thus called post-contractual duties (*hou qiyue yiwu*) as are imposed by the principle of good faith. A number of scholars have argued that imposition of these duties is unjustified. According to them, once the contractual relationship is terminated, there will no longer exist any relationship between the contracting parties as regards that contract. Neither party should bear any contractual duty to the other, otherwise we would be imposing on parties duties they have not contracted for.[60]

This opinion apparently has a kernel of truth. In general, contractual duties are to be terminated when the contract is ended and neither party should bear any further contractual duty to the other party unless the contract stipulates otherwise. Under certain circumstances, however, although the contractual relationship is terminated, it is necessary to impose some post-contractual duties under the principle of good faith. For example, suppose A hires B for a number of years. At the end of B's term, A does not renew B's employment contract because he has not been satisfied by B's performance. B goes to work for A's competitor C and divulges A's operational secrets to C, thus causing serious damage to A. Because the secrets do not come under the protection of patent law nor do they qualify as privacy, A will not be able to sue B except on the basis of B's post-contractual duties to A. To deal with cases such as in the hypothetical above, Article 92 of the Contract Law thus recognizes a series of post-contractual duties under the principle of good faith.[61]

6 Good faith in contract interpretation

In practice, the language used by parties in their contract may be imprecise or ambiguous, and the contract may fail explicitly to stipulate the parties' rights and duties. Such problems may prevent the contract from being correctly performed and thus engender disputes. In these situations, the court or arbitration tribunal should according to the law invoke the principle of good faith, taking into account relevant factors (such as the nature and purpose of the contract, the business customs at the location of the contract's formation, and so on), so as to arrive at the parties' true intention and meaning, and thus correctly interpret the contract and the parties' respective rights and duties.

In interpreting a contract, the court or arbitration tribunal should, in accordance with the principle of good faith, balance the parties' interests and determine the terms of the contract fairly and reasonably. For example, in case of a gratuitous contract (*zengyu hetong*), the interpretation should favor a less burdensome obligation by the obligor, whereas in a contract for consideration, the interpretation should generally be equitable to both parties. That contract interpretation should follow the principle of good faith is explicitly provided for in Article 125 of the Contract Law.

V The principle of fostering transactions

A transaction is an exchange of property and/or other forms of interest between independent entities or individuals in the marketplace. Transactions are expressed as contractual relations and thus are governed by contract law. That the Contract Law has adopted the principle of fostering transactions is reflected not only by the fact that the law regulates transactions, but also by the following:

A Fostering transactions in order to promote China's market economy

Under a market economy, all transactions are essentially conducted by forming and performing contracts. The market itself consists of transactions, the totality of which in turn constitutes the aggregate market. From this perspective, contractual relationships constitute the most basic legal relationships in a market economy.[62] In order to promote the continuing development of China's market economy, a fundamental objective of the contract law must be to foster and encourage transactions. This is because encouraging parties to engage in transactions is tantamount to encouraging their participation in the market. Only when transactions on the market, under the protection of contract and other related laws, become increasingly numerous and frequent can China's market economy achieve genuine development.

B Fostering transactions in order to increase efficiency and social wealth

Similarly, transactions must be encouraged so that economic efficiency and the overall wealth of society can be increased. This is not only because different entities and individuals can satisfy their needs for different goods or services and their desire to increase their wealth only through transactions, but also because only through freely-negotiated transactions can resources be distributed optimally and utilized most efficiently. According to Professor Wang Weiguo, the value orientations of contract law consist in efficiency, security for transactions, and fairness.[63] The goal of efficiency depends very much on a secure legal environment for voluntary transactions.[64] Voluntary transactions can, through a process similar to bidding, allow resources to go to the party who values them the most. This party can in turn use the resources to produce the greatest value. Thus, although contract law itself can not create social wealth, it can foster efficient transactions and therefore induce the creation of and increase in social wealth.

C Fostering transactions and the protection of freedom of contract

The contracting parties' autonomy and free will are the basis of and premise for genuine transactions. Without autonomy and free will, transactions cannot be fair and equitable. Where the parties voluntarily agree to be bound by a contract, and where the contract does not violate the law or public morality, it will violate the parties' autonomy and free will if any third party – including the State – forces the parties to terminate their contract. It is clear, therefore, that encouraging transactions and assisting the parties to realize their purpose in forming the contract is in compliance with their free will and the notion of freedom of contract.

It is worth noting that by fostering transactions, we mean primarily the encouraging of lawful transactions. The legality of a contract is a chief premise for the validity of a contract. That is to say, only where the parties' agreement does not violate the state's law and public interest will it be legally enforceable. In situations where the contract violates the law or public interest, the law should not only refrain from fostering that transaction but should find the parties liable for their violation. Moreover, the transactions to be encouraged should be voluntary and reflect the parties' true intentions. Transactions that are based on fraud, duress or other faulty expressions of intentions typically do not accord with one or both parties' will and interest. As a result, they are often unfair and unjust. With respect to such transactions, we should protect the disadvantaged party with rules such as those on contract modification and voidability, discussed below, and enforce such contracts only after their defects have been cured by the parties.

To regulate contracts based on the principle of fostering transactions is especially important in China. Because of the underdevelopment of the market economy in China, legislators have long ignored the importance of using contract rules to encourage transactions. For instance, Article 58 of the GPCL provides an over-broad list of invalid civil acts. In particular, it regards as invalid all civil acts that are conducted through fraud, duress, exploiting a party's emergent situation and other means that violate a party's true intention.[65] To be sure, such provisions may be, to some extent, helpful in maintaining social order. However, by treating such contracts not as voidable, but as void or invalid per se, these provisions have improperly expanded the scope of invalid contracts. This is because whether an expression of one's intent is truthful is typically known only to the party itself; outsiders – including the court or arbitration tribunal – often have difficulty in making a judgement thereof. After all, if the victim of fraud or duress does not voluntarily divulge the fraud or duress (such as by filing a lawsuit with the court), the outsiders will typically have no way of knowing its existence.

Granted that such contracts are defective, there are situations where the victim may want the contract to remain binding on herself as well as the other party, rather than voiding the contract entirely. Even under such circumstances, however, the GPCL will, per Article 58, require the contract to be declared invalid and the victim's wish to go unfulfilled. Under the previous contract laws, because the state was given substantial authority to voluntarily declare such contracts as invalid, there occurred many instances where transactions were unnecessarily eliminated and the victims and well-intentioned third parties failed to be sufficiently protected.

As the previous contract laws were problematic in voiding too many contracts, they also lacked necessary limitations on contract termination where there was a breach. For instance, Article 26 of the Revised Economic Contract Law provided that where "one party [did] not perform ... within the time limit specified in the contract," the non-breaching party had the right to notify the other party and terminate the contract. According to this provision, as long as the obligor failed to perform within the specified time period, no matter whether the breach had produced any significant consequence, the obligee had the right to terminate the contract. In fact, it thus allowed one party to freely exercise its termination right even when the other party was merely delaying its performance.

This provision was apparently improper. In practice, many courts had decided, based on Article 26, that once a party breached, no matter how trivial the breach might have been, the contract could be declared to be terminated; and where a contract was declared invalid or terminated, the transaction dissolved, even though the parties may have wished to have it continue. Upon a contract's invalidation or termination, the parties were to return to each other, according to the principle of restitution, the property that had been delivered or to pay damages where the situation demanded. This not only means that the expenses of the parties' performance were uncompensated and the purpose of their contract frustrated, but also that additional costs had to be incurred for the return of property, thus resulting in even greater loss and waste. The loss and waste would be especially serious where a product had been custom-made for a party and no other user could be located for that product. To promote economic efficiency as well as freedom of contract, transactions must be fostered and the law must refrain from invalidating or terminating contracts in disregard of the parties' wishes.

To rectify such weaknesses and deficiencies in the previous contract laws, especially those concerning contract validity and termination, the Contract Law follows the principle of fostering transactions and effects many substantial revisions. Specifically, the Contract Law has embodied the principle of fostering transactions in the following major respects:

1 The concept of an invalid contract

In addition to listing four special types of invalid or void contracts,[66] the Contract Law explicitly provides that invalid contracts are those that "violate mandatory provisions of a law or administrative regulation."[67] This provision is crucially important in that it signifies that not any just regulatory document (*guifanxing wenjian*) will invalidate a contract; only where a national law (*falü*) or administrative regulation (*xingzheng fagui*) is violated may a contract be declared invalid. Furthermore, it is not that any violation of any provision of a law or regulation will entail contract invalidation. Only where a mandatory, not merely an elective, provision is violated may the contract be invalidated. In comparison with the previous contract laws, this has greatly limited the scope of invalid contracts.

2 The distinction between void and voidable contracts

The Contract Law strictly distinguishes void contracts from voidable contracts. Voidable contracts are generally contracts that lack a genuine expression of the parties' intention.[68] In the case of a voidable contract, if the party holding the right of termination does not voluntarily request the contract to be terminated, then it shall be valid.[69] Where the party requests to modify the contract and is silent about termination, the court shall not terminate the contract and thus eliminate the contracted-for transaction.[70]

But even if the disadvantaged party wishes to terminate the contract, if by modifying terms of the contract the court can sufficiently protect the party's interest without violating the law or public interest, the court should generally refrain from terminating the contract. This will help foster transactions and avoid or reduce loss and waste that will result from terminating a contract and having the parties return each other's property.

Therefore, under the Contract Law, the disadvantaged party to a contract that is formed through fraud, duress or the exploitation of the party's emergent situation shall have the right to ratify the contract as long as such contracts do not harm the State interest. Being voidable and not void per se, the contract can be validated in accordance with the victim's free will. This treatment is clearly in line with the principle of fostering transactions.

3 The distinction between void contracts and contracts of pending validity

The Contract Law also distinguishes contracts that are void from contracts whose validity is pending (*xiaoli daiding*). A contract with pending validity means that although the contract has been formed, because it does not fully comply with the relevant provisions on validity, whether it is valid will hinge on the right-holder's manifest ratification.[71] Such contracts mainly include those 1) that are concluded by persons with no capacity or with limited capacity for civil acts; 2) that are concluded in the name of a principal by a person who has no authority as agent or who in concluding the contract exceeds her authority as agent; and 3) that are formed by persons with no authority to dispose of the property specified in the contract.[72]

Such contracts were all treated as invalid per se by the previous contract laws. This is apparently improper. On the one hand, the defects of these contracts can be easily cured by the right-holder if she determines that the contract is in her interest. For instance, where a person with no agency authority concludes a contract for an intended principal, the contract may very well be what the principal would have wanted. It is entirely proper, therefore, to validate the contract upon the principal's voluntary ratification. This is because the ratification indicates that the contract is in accord with the right-holder's will and interest and thus constitutes a valuable transaction for both parties. If we treat these contracts as invalid, we will be depriving the right-holder of his right to ratify the contract.

Moreover, to validate a contract with the right-holder's ratification does not violate the law and public interest. On the contrary, it promotes more transactions that are in the contracting parties' interest and better protects the parties' interest and free will.

For the reasons stated above, the Contract Law distinguishes invalid contracts from contracts of pending validity, treating the latter as a particular type of contract and providing reasonable special provisions thereon.[73]

4 The distinction between contract formation and contract validity

In comparison with the previous laws, the Contract Law draws a much clearer distinction between contract formation and contract validity. For a long time, because China's previous contract laws made no such distinction, many courts treated contracts that were formed but lacked certain conditions for taking effect as invalid contracts, thus invalidating a great number of contracts that should have been deemed valid.

In fact, contract formation and validity are categorically different. Contract formation refers to the completion of the process whereby the parties through equal consultation come to agree on the terms of their contemplated transaction. However, a contract does not automatically become valid as it is formed. Contract validity largely depends on the state's attitude to and evaluation of the contract in question. In other words, contract formation is mainly governed by the parties' free will and the principle of freedom of contract. In contrast, contract validity chiefly reflects the state's evaluation of and intervention in contractual relationships.

The Contract Law follows the principle of fostering transactions in designing its rules on contract validity. For instance, the law allows various ways to validate a contract despite its deficiencies. If a contract lacks major terms or if these terms are ambiguous, the court should reasonably interpret the contract to allow the parties, if they so wish, to be bound by it, rather than simplistically declare the contract as invalid and thus eliminate the transaction. The Contract Law provides for contract formation and validity in Chapters 2 and 3, respectively. In section 5, below, we discuss contract formation in greater detail, whereas section 7 will again touch on the subject of contract validity and interpretation.

5 Rules on contract formation

China's previous contract laws lacked provisions on contract formation, or offer and acceptance. This not only made it difficult for parties to form a contract but also created a situation where there was no standard for determining if a contract had been formed when this became an issue of dispute between the parties. The lack of provisions on contract formation was closely connected to the invalidation of many contracts that were already formed. Because the previous contract laws and regulations did not provide any clear rules on contract formation but instead enumerated major terms for various contracts,[74] and because the legislators had not offered any clarification as to the nature of these terms, there had been a widespread misunderstanding, viz., that the contracts specified must contain these enumerated terms. As a result, many courts had held that contracts lacking any of these major terms were invalid, thus creating a great number of invalid contracts.

In response, the Contract Law establishes a complete set of rules on contract formation, which substantially reflects the principle of encouraging transactions. Article 12 of the Contract Law explicitly provides that the contents of a contract are to be decided by the parties through mutual agreement,[75] thus allowing parties freely to determine the terms of their contract. In addition to upholding freedom of contract, this provision is exceedingly favorable to parties' structuring their own transactions.

Similarly, the Contract Law's rules on offer and acceptance[76] are designed to facilitate formation of contracts and transactions. For instance, according to the traditional continental theory, offer and acceptance must be identical in their contents. A reply that adds to, limits or modifies the original offer is equal to a refusal of the offer. This traditional view, however, has come to be regarded as unfavorable to the formation of contracts and the fostering of transactions. The United Nations Convention on the International Sale of Goods, for example, now adopts the rule that where the acceptance modifies immaterial contents of the offer and the offeror does not promptly manifest her objections thereto, the contract shall be deemed as formed.[77] The same rule has been adopted by Article 31 of the Contract Law.

6 Form of a contract

There have always been two differing views in China as to the proper form of a contract. One view held that the provision in the previous contract laws, that contracts should be in written form,[78] was mandatory. If the parties did not put their contract in writing, then the contract was not yet formed, and thus could not be valid. The other view pointed out that the rationale for this written requirement was that the written form would best prove the existence and terms of the contract. If the parties failed to put their contract in writing, then there was difficulty in proving the contract and its terms.[79]

The courts had generally adopted the first view. But although this interpretation would compel the parties to use the written form and thus reduce contractual disputes, it constituted an overly rigid requirement that may have prevented many transactions from taking place. On the one hand, there are situations where, although the parties have for various reasons failed to adopt the written form, they have already partially or fully performed or, although the contract has not yet been performed, the parties have no disputes as to the contract's existence and major terms. Under these circumstances, denying the contract's formation will be eliminating a transaction that is desired by both parties. For speediness and convenience, many parties in today's marketplace have taken to telephone, audio-recording, video-recording and other means in forming their contract. To refuse to recognize all such contracts as properly formed will undoubtedly frustrate or at least inconvenience many significant market activities.

In the spirit of fostering transactions, the Contract Law has now adopted the view that the form of a contract is evidence for the contract's existence, rather than a criterion in deciding whether the contract has been formed. Article 10 of the Contract Law provides that "[f]or parties to form their contract, there are written, oral, and other forms." It is clear that, except for contracts that according to a law or administrative regulation must be in writing[80] or that need to be registered and approved,[81] parties in forming their contract may now adopt the oral form. Where the parties have not put their contract in writing, the parties should be allowed to adduce evidence to prove the existence of their contract and its major terms. If the parties fail to produce adequate evidence, then the contract is to be declared non-existent. But when adequate evidence is presented, the contract shall be deemed as properly formed and valid.

7 A system for contract interpretation

Because the previous contract laws did not provide for a system of contract interpretation, in practice the courts often treated contracts whose contents were unclear or ambiguous as invalid, thus causing many transactions to be eliminated. This apparently contravened the spirit of fostering transactions; and a system of contract interpretation must be established to allow judicial protection of the contracting parties as well as their transactions.

Some scholars were concerned that allowing courts to interpret contracts would increase the judge's discretion and thus interfere with the parties' free will and interest. Although this opinion was not entirely unreasonable, where there was no system of contract interpretation and the judges were to treat as invalid any contracts that were slightly deficient or unclear, the judges were in fact exercising a greater degree of discretion. Only by providing a system of and clear standards for contract interpretation, can the judge's discretion be appropriately restrained.

The Contract Law now provides for such a system of contract interpretation. Article 41, for example, directs the judges to interpret terms of a form contract by their "prevalent meanings."[82] Where there are two or more equally prevalent meanings, the courts should adopt the one that disfavors the party who provided the form contract.[83] Similarly, Articles 62, 63, and so on, provide concrete guidance on standards to follow where the contract in question is ambiguous as to the quality, price or compensation, location of performance, the time limit for performance, and other components of the contract. These standards for contract interpretation are generally in line with the principle of fostering transactions, as well as those of good faith and freedom of contract.

8 Conditions for terminating a contract where there is a breach

The Contract Law strictly limits the conditions for terminating a contract where there is a breach. In contract law, where one party breaches a contract, the other often has the right to terminate the contract upon the fulfillment of certain legal conditions. Contract breaches therefore form a major cause for contract termination. However, this does not mean that any breach will entail the termination of a contract. Contract termination is, in its nature, the extinction of a transaction. In many situations, if the non-breaching party is willing to accept the breaching party's performance even after the breach, or if continuation of the contract is possible and will not harm the non-breaching party, terminating the contract not only does not add to the protection of the non-breaching party, but also does not reflect the contract law's purpose of fostering transactions. Thus the law must provide clear limitations on contract termination where there is a breach.

In view of the many weaknesses in China's previous contract laws in this regard, many Chinese scholars suggeste d that the new Contract Law should place greater emphasis on the law's function of fostering transactions and allow termination of contract only where the breach has serious consequences.[84] The Contract Law has adopted this opinion, providing that, absent any unreasonable delay of a major obligation (*zhuyao zhaiwu*), only where a party's delay or breach renders the purpose of the contract incapable of being fulfilled can the non-breaching party have a right to terminate the contract.[85] The rationale for this is, where the breach has produced such serious consequences (including damages), the purpose of the non-breaching party in entering the contract may not be materialized and thus the contract may no longer have any substantial significance. Under these circumstances, therefore, the law should allow the non-breaching party to terminate the contract, thus freeing the party from a contract that has been seriously violated. Such limitations on the termination of contact where there is a breach will encourage transactions, as well as avoid property loss and damages that may result from improper termination of contracts.

VI Conclusion

The Contract Law represents a significant improvement over China's previous contract laws. In view of the contradictions and redundancies among the previous contract laws, their lack of basic contract rules (such as those on offer and acceptance), as well as their problematic notion of "economic contract," the Contract Law provides a more advanced, comprehensive, and systematic contract law regime that is better suited to China's transitional economy. The three fundamental principles of the Contract Law, namely, freedom of contract, good faith, and the fostering of transactions, constitute the main spirit of the Contract Law and bring it more in line with international business practice.

As with any complex piece of legislation, of course, there may arise various problems and issues as the Contract Law is being implemented and interacts with various courts, arbitration tribunals, practicing lawyers, as well as particular contracting individuals and entities in their multitude of legal and/or business contexts. To tackle such problems and issues as they emerge, especially when China's business practice is in a flux and rapidly evolving, will undoubtedly be a serious and fascinating challenge.

Notes

1 Zhonghua Renmin Gongheguo Hetong Fa [Contract Law of the People's Republic of China] [hereinafter Contract Law]. For the full text of the Contract Law, as well as an English translation thereof, *see* CCH, *China Laws for Foreign Business – Business Regulation*, Vol. 1, ¶5–650.
2 The Civil Code is currently scheduled to be completed by the year 2010. *See* discussion *infra* Part II, Section D.
3 The few exceptions are contracts or agreements involving the parties' civil status or relationship, such as marriage, adoption and guardianship, which are to be governed by other relevant laws. *See* Contract Law, *supra* note 1, art. 2.
4 These categories include, for example, sales contracts, contracts on the supply of electricity, water, gas or heat, gift contracts, loan contracts, and so on. Those not

enumerated are to be governed by the general provisions (*zongze*) and may be dealt with by reference and analogy to (*canzhao*) the particular provisions (*fenze*) or other laws. *See id.*, art. 124.

5 For a discussion of the Contract Law's drafting process, see Professor Jiang Ping, *Drafting the Uniform Contract Law in China*, 10 Colum. J. Asian L. 245, 245 (1996).

6 Zhonghua Renmin Gongheguo Jingji Hetong Fa [Economic Contract Law of the People's Republic of China] (adopted December 13, 1981, implemented July 1, 1982) [hereinafter Economic Contract Law]. CCH, *China Laws for Foreign Business – Business Regulation*, Vol. 1, ¶5–550

7 Zhonghua Renmin Gongheguo Shewai Jingji Hetong Fa [Foreign Economic Contract Law of the People's Republic of China] (adopted March 21, 1985, effective July 1, 1985) [hereinafter Foreign Economic Contract Law]. CCH, *China Laws for Foreign Business – Business Regulation*, Vol. 1, ¶5–550.

8 Zhonghua Renmin Gongheguo Jishu Hetong Fa [Technology Contract Law of the People's Republic of China] (adopted June 23, 1987, effective November 1, 1987) [hereinafter Technology Contract Law]. CCH, *China Laws for Foreign Business – Business Regulation*, Vol. 1, ¶5–577

9 When it took effect recently on October 1, 1999, the Contract Law according to its Article 428 simultaneously repealed the Economic Contract Law, the Foreign Economic Contract Law, and the Technology Contract Law. *See* Contract Law, *supra* note 1, art. 428.

10 *See* Shangye Bu Difang Gongye Bu dui Muqian Youguan Gongshang Jihua Xianjie Guance Jingji Hetong zhong Ruogan Wenti Guiding de Lianhe Tongzhi [the Ministries of Commerce and Regional Industry Joint Notice on Regulations on Certain Current Questions on Linking up with and Implementing Economic Contracts in Industrial and Commercial Plans], issued in 1956 [hereinafter Joint Notice]. Issued by ministries under the State Council, the joint notice thus was an administrative regulation [*xingzheng fagui*] or rule [*guizhang*] but not a law proper [*falü*], which can only be promulgated by the legislature – i.e., the NPC and its Standing Committee. *Cf. infra* note 25 and accompanying text.

11 Economic Contract Law, *supra* note 6, art. 2. A legal person is an organization that can independently bear civil rights and duties. *See* Article 36, Zhonghua Renmin Gongheguo Minfa Tongze (General Principles of Civil Law of the People's Republic of China) (adopted April 12, 1986, effective January 1, 1987) [hereinafter GENERAL PRINCIPLES OF CIVIL LAW or GPCL].

12 *Cf. supra* note 4.

13 *See supra* note 11 and accompanying text. As distinguished from legal persons, natural persons refer to individual citizens (*gongmin*) in general. *See* GPCL, *supra* note 11, Chapter 11.

14 *Cf.* Liu Ruifu (ed.), Hetongfa Jiaocheng [A Textbook on Contract Law], 25 (Zhongguo Zhengfa Daxue Chubanshe [The Publishing House of the China University of Political Science and Law] 1991).

15 *See* Zhonghua Renmin Gongheguo Jingji Hetong Fa [Economic Contract Law of the People's Republic of China] (revised September 2, 1993) [hereinafter REVISED ECONOMIC CONTRACT LAW].

16 *See supra* note 11.

17 *Cf.* Professor Jiang Ping, *supra* note 5, at 246.

18 *See*, Economic Contract Law, *supra* note 6, art. 31; *Cf.* Liu Zhongya (ed.), Xin Jingh Hetongfa [The New Economic Contract Law], 60 (Zhongguo Shenji Chubanshe [China Audits and Statistics Press] 1990).

19 Technology Contract Law, *supra* note 8, art. 24.

20 *See* Foreign Economic Contract Law, *supra* note 7, art. 2.

21 *See* Technology Contract Law, *supra* note 8, art. 2.

22 *Cf.* Foreign Economic Contract Law, *supra* note 7, art. 2.
23 The Revised Economic Contract Law provided that foreign-related technology contracts were to be governed by the Technology Contract Law. Revised Economic Contract Law, *supra* note 15, art. 46. This temporary make-do was problematic, however, because the Technology Contract Law was generally more restrictive than the Foreign Economic Contract Law. *Cf. supra* note 19 and accompanying text. It was also awkward because Article 2 of the Technology Contract Law explicitly excluded foreign-related technology contracts from its coverage.
24 GPCL, *supra* note 11, art. 4.
25 Liang Huixing, *Cong Sanzudingli Zouxiang Tongyi De Hetongfa [To advance from the three-pillars/laws system to a unified contract law]*, ZHONGGUO FAXUE [CHINESE JURISPRUDENCE], No. 3, 1995, at 9.
26 *Id.*
27 *See, e.g.*, American Law Institute, Restatement of the Law Second, Contracts (1981) [hereinafter RESTATEMENT OF CONTRACTS 2d]; American Law Institute and the National Conference of Commissioners on Uniform State Laws, Uniform Commercial Code (1990) [hereinafter UCC].
28 *See, e.g.*, the United Nations Convention on Contracts for the International Sale of Goods (1980) [hereinafter CISG] and the UNIDROIT Principles of International Commercial Contracts (1994) [hereinafter UNIDROIT Principles].
29 *Cf.* Liang Huixing, *supra* note 25.
30 *Cf.* Yu Liang, *Hetong Xiaoli De Buchong [Supplementation to the effectiveness of a contract]*, ZHENGFA LUNTAN [POLITICAL SCIENCE AND LAW FORUM], No. 4, 1998, at 75–79.
31 *See, e.g.*, Sun Peng, *Qiyuefa De Xiandai Fazhan [Contemporary development of contract law]*, XIANDAI FAXUE [CONTEMPORARY LEGAL STUDIES], No. 4, 1998.
32 See, e.g., E.ALLAN FARNSWORTH, CONTRACTS, 3rd Edition, (Aspen Law & Business, 1998), §1.7, §1.8.
33 *Cf.* Liang Huixing, *Zhongguo Hetongfa Qicao Guochengzhong De Zhenglundian [Issues in the drafting of China's Contract Law]*, FAXUE [THE SCIENCE OF LAW], No. 2, 1996, at 13–15.
34 Jiang Ping et al., *Shichang Jingji He Yisi Zizhi [Market economy and autonomy by parties' free will]*, FAXUE YANJIU [LEGAL STUDIES], No. 6, 1993, at 20–25.
35 Cf. Liu Hainian et al (eds.), YIFA ZHIGUO, JIANSHE SHEHUI ZHUYI FAZHI GUOJIA [ADMINISTERING THE COUNTRY ACCORDING TO LAW, ESTABLISHING A SOCIALIST COUNTRY UNDER THE RULE OF LAW], 25 (Zhongguo Fazhi Chubanshe, 1996).
36 See, e.g., GPCL, *supra* note 11, art. 4. *Cf.* Revised Economic Contract Law, *supra* note 15, art. 5.
37 *Cf.* Liang Huixing, *supra* note 33.
38 See, e.g., Contract Law, *supra* note 1, articles 34 and 79 among the general provisions (*zongze*) and articles 133, 142, 197, 220, 225, etc., among the particular provisions (*fenze*).
39 *See, e.g.*, Economic Contract Law, *supra* note 6, art. 51.
40 Contract Law, *supra* note 1, art. 127.
41 *Id.*, art.12.
42 See Economic Contract Law, *supra* note 6, art. 27(1); Foreign Economic Contract Law *supra* note 7, art. 31(3); Technology Contract Law, *supra* note 8, art. 23.
43 *See* Contract Law, *supra* note 1, art. 93.
44 See Economic Contract Law, *supra* note 6, art. 31; *Cf.* Liu Zhongya, *supra* note 18, at 60.
45 *See* Contract Law, *supra* note 1, art. 114.
46 *See* Wang Yuanzhi and Feng Jinsheng, *Lun Hetong Zhengyi [On contract justice]*, ZHENGFA LUNTAN [POLITICAL SCIENCE AND LAW FORUM], No. 6, 1996.

47 Article 39 requires the party employing a form contract to alert the other party to the contract's indemnification provisions and to explain these provisions at the other party's request. Article 40, by cross-referencing to Articles 52 and 53, invalidates form contracts that harm the State interest or public interest, or improperly shift liabilities to the other party. Article 41 provides that contract interpretation is to disfavor the party employing a form contract. Article 53 invalidates clauses in a contract that indemnify a party against 1) property damages it causes to the other party by its intentional misconduct or gross negligence and 2) personal injury it causes to the other party.

48 *Cf.* MORIDA MITSUO, SAIKENHOU SOURON [A GENERAL INTRODUCTION TO OBLIGATION LAW], 28 (Gakuyou Shobou [Gakuyou Publishing House] 1978).

49 *Cf.* Liang Huixing, *supra* note 33.

50 Contract Law, *supra* note 1, art. 42.

51 *Id.*

52 *See* Contract Law, *supra* note 1, art. 33.

53 *Id.*, art. 43.

54 *See id.*, art. 68.

55 *Cf. id.*, art. 108.

56 *Cf. id.*

57 *See supra* discussion Part IV, Section C.1.

58 Wang Jiafu, ed., MINFA ZHAIQUAN [OBLIGATION RIGHTS IN THE CIVIL LAW], 393 (Falü Chubanshe [Publishing House of Law] 1991).

59 *Cf.* Contract Law, *supra* note 1, art. 94.

60 *See* Zhang Jing, ed., ZHONGHUA RENMIN GONGHEGUO HETONGFA SHIYI (AN INTERPRETATION OF THE CONTRACT LAW OF THE PEOPLE'S REPUBLIC OF CHINA) 159 (Zhongguo Fangzheng Chubanshe [China Fangzheng Press] 1999).

61 Article 92 provides that "[u]pon the termination of contractual rights and duties, the parties shall follow the principle of good faith and fulfill duties such as notification, assistance, confidentiality, etc., in accordance with business customs." Contract Law, *supra* note 1, art. 92.

62 *See* Liang Huixing, ed., SHEHUI ZHUYI SHICHANG JINGJI GUANLI FALÜ ZHIDU YANJIU [RESEARCHING A LEGAL SYSTEM THAT GOVERNS THE SOCIALIST MARKET ECONOMY], 7 (Zhongguo Zhengfa Daxue Chubanshe [The Publishing House of the China University of Political Science and Law] 1991).

63 Wang Weiguo, *Lun Hetong Wuxiao Zhidu [On the system of invalidating contracts],* FAXUE YANJIU [LEGAL STUDIES], No. 3, 1995, at 11–24.

64 *Cf. id.*

65 GPCL, *supra* note 11, art. 58(3).

66 These include contracts 1) that are entered through fraud or duress and harm the State interests; 2) whose parties collude maliciously to harm the interest of the State, the collective or a third party; 3) that conceal an unlawful purpose with a lawful form and 4) that harm the public interest. Contract Law, *supra* note 1, art. 52.

67 *Id.*

68 *See* Contract Law, *supra* note 1, art. 54.

69 *See* Contract Law, *supra* note 1, art. 55.

70 *See* Contract Law, *supra* note 1, art. 54.

71 Cf. ZHOU LINBIN ET AL., BUIAO HETONG FA [COMPARATIVE CONTRACT LAW], 410 (Lanzhou Daxue Chubanshe [Lanzhou University Press] 1989).

72 *See* Contract Law, *supra* note 1, articles 47–51.

73 *See id.*

74 For example, the Gongkuang Chanpin Gouxiao Hetong Tiaoli [Rules on Purchase and Marketing Contracts Concerning Industrial and Mineral Products] provided for 12 necessary terms for contracts involving industrial and mineral products; the Economic

Contract Law listed 5 major terms for economic contracts in general. *See* Economic Contract Law, *supra* note 6, art. 12.

75 *See* Contract Law, *supra* note 1, art. 12.

76 *Id.* articles 13–31.

77 CISG, *supra* note 28, art. 19.

78 *See* Economic Contract Law, *supra* note 6, art. 3; Foreign Economic Contract Law, *supra* note 7, art. 7; Technology Contract Law, *supra* note 8, art. 9.

79 Su Huixiang ed., ZHONGGUO DANGDAI HETONGFA LUN [ESSAYS ON CONTEMPORARY CHINESE CONTRACT LAW], 87 (Jilin Daxue Chubanshe [Jilin University Press] 1992).

80 Contract Law, *supra* note 1, art. 10.

81 These include, for example, Sino-foreign joint venture contracts (*zhongwai hezuo jingying hetong*) and equity joint venture contracts (*zhongwai hezi jingying hetong*). Out of necessity, these contracts have to be in writing when submitted to the relevant registering and approving authorities. *See* Article 7(3), Zhonghua Renmin Gongheguo Zhongwai Hezuo Jingying Qiye Fa [The People's Republic of China Law on Sino-foreign Cooperative Enterprises] (adopted April 13, 1988, effective April 13, 1988) and Article 3, Zhonghua Renmin Gongheguo Zhongwai Hezi Jingying Qiye Fa [The People's Republic of China Law on Sino-foreign Joint Equity Enterprises] (adopted July 1, 1979, effective July 1, 1979). An English translation of these laws can be found in CCH, *China Laws for Foreign Business – Business Regulation*, Vol. 1, ¶6–100(5) and ¶6–500(3), respectively.

82 Contract Law, *supra* note 1, art. 41.

83 *Id.*

84 *See, e.g.*, Cao Shiquan and Zhu Guangxin, HETONG FADING JIECHU DE SHIYOU TANTAO [AN EXPLORATION OF LEGAL CAUSES FOR CONTRACT TERMINATION], ZHONGGUO FAXUE [CHINESE JURISPRUDENCE], No. 4, 1998, at 34–47.

85 *See* Contract Law, *supra* note 1, art. 94(3) and (4).

41

NEW HOPE FOR CORPORATE GOVERNANCE IN CHINA?

James V. Feinerman

Source: *China Quarterly* 191 (2007): 590–612.

Abstract

China's recent revisions to its Company Law and Securities Law have brought new attention to issues of corporate governance in Chinese companies and financial markets. Among the chief criticisms of the earlier laws – in both their provisions and application – were the lack of protection for minority shareholders, the paucity of independent directors, the absence of transparency and inadequate financial disclosure. The acknowledged need for greater congruence between Chinese law and practice and that of countries with more developed capital markets led to the proposal of amendments to China's legislation during the first half of this decade. This article highlights several improvements resulting from the revisions as well as remaining weaknesses in the regulatory framework for corporate enterprises in China.

Corporate governance, *gongsi zhili* (公司治理) has become an increasingly important topic in academic, business and policy discussions in China in the last few years. It is closely related to ongoing economic reform, especially of state-owned enterprises (SOEs), and development of the securities and financial market. Recent revisions of China's Company Law and Securities Law have focused new attention on various aspects of corporate governance, including shareholder voting rights and fiduciary duties. These laws will determine the proper roles of a corporate board and its directors, the rights of shareholders, the fiduciary duties of directors and officers, and the balance between directors' responsibilities and the reasonable protection of directors. While it was not the primary goal in their revision, in their current form they hold out some promise for improving corporate governance in China. Of potentially larger significance are changes they imply for other arenas of life and politics there.

How is corporate governance important for China? Better corporate governance is a vital link in bringing capital to China; affordable capital creates jobs, increases tax revenue, increases shareholder wealth – all leading to an increase in the standard of living. Full disclosure and transparency also serve to promote good corporate governance and capital mobility. In China today it is not possible for any sizeable enterprise to ignore the ramifications of globalization and implications for corporate governance. But there is a conundrum: looking at China, and what it has been able to achieve with relatively poor corporate governance, is there still an argument for a good, or at least better, system? China may present a unique "high risk-high reward" scenario in global corporate governance, with a singular combination of 1.3 billion people, vast resources and economic momentum. Yet the emphasis on the acquisition and deployment of capital raises a question with some salience for China. What makes capital "unaffordable"? In China's case, there are several countervailing forces: scarcity due to policy loans made to underperforming state-owned enterprises; corruption premiums ranging from 20 per cent to as high as 50 per cent for non-transparency[1]; and the basic fact that global demand for capital is greater than the supply.

While there are many factors which influence corporate governance, several important pillars include respect for (and legal protection of): a wide range of stakeholders in the enterprise; the board of directors and its responsibilities; disclosure and transparency; and the rights of shareholders, including their equitable treatment. Yet the essence of corporate governance is doing the right thing whether or not anyone is watching; not doing it because the law says so, but doing it because it's right. Of course, good corporate governance also promotes increased regional and international recognition for Chinese corporations and overall greater prosperity.

As a practical matter, however, there must be incentives to change. For Chinese enterprises, these may include an increasing perception of better performance, higher earnings, more access to affordable capital, reduced tension among stakeholders and other benefits. Legal adjustments may also lead to less government interference with the market mechanisms, which in turn builds trust and confidence by the stakeholders, who will then contribute money, talent and greater vitality to civic life.

This article begins by trying to define (generically and in the Chinese context) corporate governance. A few particular Chinese issues are highlighted, including board issues, shareholders' issues, transparency and disclosure, and monitoring. The article also attempts some preliminary evaluation of the effectiveness of the recently revised Chinese Company Law and Securities Law in dealing with these corporate governance questions.

Defining objective corporate governance standards

Corporate governance relates to the internal means by which corporations are operated and controlled. In the formulation of the Organization for Economic

Co-operation and Development (OECD), an international organization of developed countries that accept the principles of representative democracy and a free market economy:

> Corporate governance is the system by which business corporations are directed and controlled. The corporate governance structure specifies the distribution of rights and responsibilities among different participants in the corporation, such as the board, managers, shareholders and other stakeholders, and spells out the rules and procedures for making decisions on corporate affairs. By doing this, it also provides the structure through which the company objectives are set, and the means of attaining those objectives and monitoring performance.

The corporate governance principles of the OECD[2] are recognized as an influential, objective set of corporate governance principles and represent the first initiative by an inter-governmental organization to develop the core elements of a good corporate governance regime. The principles can be used as a benchmark by governments as they evaluate and improve their laws and regulations. They have also been used by private sector parties that have a role in developing corporate governance systems and best practices.

The OECD principles comprise five themes: protection of shareholders' rights; equitable treatment of all shareholders, including minority and foreign shareholders; recognition of the rights of stakeholders as established by law; ensuring timely and accurate disclosure of all material matters regarding the corporation; and effective monitoring of management by the board, with board accountability to the company and the shareholders. Each of these principles has salience for the current situation in China, since every one of them has proven problematic since the inception of China's corporatizing reforms over the past two decades.

General observations on corporate governance in China

Since China's first Company Law,[3] enacted in 1993 to come into effect in 1994, much has been accomplished in establishing the basic features of corporate governance; however, there is still much to do. While various laws had existed before the Company Law to deal with state, collective and private enterprises and those with foreign investment, the Company Law was the first attempt since 1949 to create limited liability companies without regard to the nature of ownership as part of a modern economic system.[4] In little more than a decade, corporate governance has moved to the centre stage of Chinese enterprise reform. The Fourth Plenum of the Chinese Communist Party's 15th Central Committee held in September 1999 adopted a decision that identified corporate governance as the core of the modern enterprise system. Commitments under the World Trade Organization add some urgency to tackle corporate governance issues in a comprehensive and systematic manner.[5]

However, the current legal framework – even after the recent revisions of the Company Law[6] and the Securities Law[7] – still provides rather limited shareholder protection. In the light of continuing majority government ownership of enterprises, corporations with concentrated ownership still predominate. Small shareholders are inactive in company oversight; government influences management appointments and corporate operations. Too much power remains concentrated in the hands of a few shareholders, and there is – in many instances – a lack of accountability for corporate actions or omissions.

Major issues of corporate governance in Chinese listed companies

The biggest single factor affecting corporate governance in China is state ownership: the Chinese state owns about 50 per cent of all the shares of listed companies. Moreover, during the economy's transition from command to market it is often unclear who represents the state as a shareholder in the listed companies. In addition, transactions between the controlling shareholder (or a group company) and the listed company often disadvantage minority shareholders.

Other issues for corporate governance relate to the directors and officers of Chinese listed companies. For example, most directors are "inside" or executive directors; few companies have many independent directors, leading to insider control. Although Chinese securities regulators attempted to overhaul insider-controlled boards by requiring every listed company to have independent directors forming at least a third of the board, majority power remains extremely concentrated.

Traditionally, executives of PRC companies and other enterprises have been underpaid.[8] Managers of major listed SOEs, still chosen by the government, are often appointed more for political reliability than managerial skill.[9] Lack of a market for professional managers and proper incentives for rewarding performance also influence the quality of management.[10] Information disclosure in many cases is not timely and accurate, and not easily understandable to investors, making it difficult to monitor board and management performance.

The increasing importance of corporate governance reform in China

An overview of China's securities market shows that in December 2006 there were 1,461 companies listed in China.[11] There are two stock exchanges, the Shanghai Stock Exchange and the Shenzhen Stock Exchange, both established in 1990. Total market capitalization reached US$520 billion at the end of 2001, and about US$516 billion by the end of 2002; at the end of 2006, the Shanghai Stock Exchange's capitalization alone was US$915 billion. There were over 65 million investor accounts (5 per cent of the population), 118 securities firms and dozens of fund management firms in China as of mid-2003.[12]

As for the regulatory system, the China Securities Regulatory Commission (CSRC), established in 1992, oversees all the securities business activities in China (including futures). Its headquarters are in Beijing, with 36 regional offices in each province and many major municipalities, and 1,500 employees. The original Securities Law, enacted in July 1999 and significantly amended in 2005 along with the revised Company Law, provides a legal framework for securities regulation. The CSRC's recent and ongoing measures to improve corporate governance include encouraging public companies to get independent directors on board, to adopt a Code of Corporate Governance and to provide better information disclosure. Legal reform protecting shareholder rights through lawsuits, accounting reform and supervision of auditors have also been promoted by the CSRC.

As noted above, one of the chief policies of CSRC regulation was to increase the number of independent directors to company boards.[13] By 30 June 2002, 2,414 independent directors had been elected and appointed by shareholder meetings of listed companies. In a survey of 1,084 firms, 80 per cent appointed two independent directors to their board of directors, and 70 per cent had at least one accounting professional as an independent director.[14]

In 2001, just as the United States was beginning to experience the collapse of a series of corporations from Enron to WorldCom to Global Crossing as a result of corporate governance failures, the exposure of several major Enron-type scandals highlighted the urgency of corporate governance reform in China. The companies involved were leading enterprises and their stock prices performed extremely well before they collapsed. It turns out that profit figures were highly inflated or even fabricated by the directors and management to support the high stock prices and for the purpose of secondary offerings. Subsequent abuses from just one year (2004) included the implosion of the conglomerate D'Long group, the arrest of the chairman and six senior executives of Guangdong Kelon Electrical Holdings for overstating revenues and profits by over 2 billion yuan and a three-year prison sentence for one of China's richest citizens, Zhou Zhengyi, for manipulating share prices and falsifying the registered capital of his company, Nongkai Development Group. Zhou's case also proved an embarrassing setback for the Bank of China's then-recently listed Hong Kong branch and revealed internal-control and governance lapses in the Bank of China Hong Kong branch.[15]

In mid-2006, Guangdong Securities Co. was liquidated after the CSRC lifted its business permit and ordered its closure because of "severe irregularities." The CSRC assigned the China Securities Investors Protection Fund the task of trusteeship and liquidation of Guangdong Securities after share transactions were halted on 4 November 2005. Guangdong Securities was the fifteenth securities firm the CSRC had shut down since August 2004, when it launched a nationwide campaign to crack down on irregularities in the country's problem-plagued securities sector "to protect legitimate rights of investors and creditors."[16]

Even before some of these occurrences, a Code of Corporate Governance for Listed Companies in China had been developed and enforced from January

2002. The Code is mandatory for all listed companies and has been melded into the listing rules of the two stock exchanges. It stipulates the rights and responsibilities of shareholders, directors, the management and stakeholders.[17] In addition, information disclosure is an ongoing responsibility of all the listed companies. All the shareholders have an equal right to receive correct, timely and complete information, and regular disclosure of audited annual reports, mid-year reports and unaudited quarterly reports. Disclosure of corporate governance practices is required in the annual report, along with disclosure of information on the controlling shareholder or the actual controller of the company.[18]

Legal and accounting reform has also been coming to China.[19] Lawsuits have been brought against directors and management. The Supreme People's Court issued provisions in 2001 about procedures for shareholders suing directors and management for losses due to false company disclosure, and the courts have started to accept such cases. Chinese accounting standards are being revised according to international accounting standards.[20] The regulators have strengthened the supervision of auditors, even revoking the licence for the securities business of one of the largest auditing firms in China because of its involvement in a scandal.

Stronger enforcement of existing law and regulations has led to more regular on-site inspection of listed companies concerning accounting, disclosure, related-party transactions and so on. In a given year about 300 firms go through regular inspection; special inspection on compliance with the Code of Corporate Governance has also been enacted. Stronger sanctions include public criticism against violations of laws and regulations; stock exchanges have been given the power to reprimand listed companies publicly for violations of their listing rules. The CSRC has also established a joint Bureau for Investigation of Securities Crimes with the Ministry of Public Security to prosecute violations of the Securities Law.[21]

Training of directors and investor education is also a focus of recent reforms. Monthly classes for independent director candidates in Shanghai and Beijing train about 5,000 candidates during a typical year. Monthly training courses for existing directors were organized by the two stock exchanges in 2003 to train all directors over three years. The CSRC also sponsors investor education sessions in major cities and through the media, including the internet.

Key areas for reform

Comparison of the Chinese market with mature global markets suggests a need for more reform of the system of state asset management to broaden ownership structures and to transform the enterprise management techniques employed by the government from administrative fiat to contract. Easier prospects for listing non-state controlled companies and better procedures for mergers and acquisitions would also be welcome. Regardless of their ownership, listed companies need increased incentives for their management, to expand the management talent pool in China by providing more effective compensation schemes.

Concentrated ownership[22]

In recent years, the three largest shareholders held, on average, about 58 per cent of total shares in listed Chinese companies. In almost half of all firms, the three largest shareholders accounted for 60 to 80 per cent of total shares. In PRC listed companies, the largest shareholder accounts for slightly less than 50 per cent of all shares but controls more than 50 per cent of board seats. Directly or indirectly, the state selects almost 70 per cent of directors of all PRC listed companies. Other jurisdictions recognize a duty of fair dealing by majority shareholders in relation to minority shareholders. Until the most recent reform (and perhaps even afterwards), fiduciary duties of controlling shareholders have not been clearly stipulated in relevant law, and their liabilities for losses incurred by minority shareholders are not obvious.

Recent PRC regulations may introduce this principle implicitly, however, without spelling out liabilities, penalties or the procedures for invoking them. Thus, there continue to be documented abuses by controlling shareholders: taking out soft loans from listed companies on a long-term basis; using listed companies as guarantors for bank loans; and selling assets at unfair prices, usually without an appraisal by an independent evaluator. As noted below, the recently revised Company Law attempts to address these abuses.

Board issues

In general, Chinese directors are insulated from responsibility for their company's economic performance. Their compensation is not linked to it, and they cannot be dismissed prior to the expiration of their terms without "cause," although what constitutes "cause" is not defined. Directors owe duties of good faith and due diligence and care towards the company and its shareholders, although the law does not define these concepts further or create enforcement mechanisms. Compared with practices in other markets, Chinese boards have less decision-making power within the existing legislative framework, while government ministries and commissions, as well as securities regulatory authorities, have substantial decision-making power. Indeed, the range of decisions which must be made by the shareholders' meeting is extraordinarily large by comparison with the corporate law of other jurisdictions, and the discretion left to the board correspondingly narrow.

The Company Law does not stipulate any disclosure obligation on the part of directors or any specific liabilities for directors who fail to perform their obligations. On 16 August 2001 the CSRC issued the Establishment of Independent Director Systems by Listed Companies Guiding Opinion (the Guiding Opinion), requiring that one-third of Board directors be independent. A 1999 survey showed that only about 3 per cent of all directors had some degree of independence; in 2003, following issuance of the Guiding Opinion, the average company still had only three independent directors.[23] Moreover, most listed Chinese companies have no system for establishing board committees, and only a few plan to establish them. Companies that do have them usually have an investment or finance committee, an audit committee, a financial management committee, and/or a strategy committee. They lack nominating committees for directors and corporate governance committees; listed companies do not disclose their procedures for nominating directors or their corporate governance principles. The main functions of the committees that do exist are to decide on major investment projects. Independent committees with supervisory and adulting functions are at an early stage of development. Thus, independent directors would have few opportunities to exercise their independent judgement.

Shareholders' issues

The Company Law requires every company to hold an annual shareholders' general meeting. While every shareholder may attend a general meeting, recent data indicate that most attendees are state representatives and representatives of legal persons. Not all companies comply with this requirement, and there are indications that some boards simply ignore the meeting's decisions. Shareholders' general meetings sometimes check decisions with the board before taking action. Anecdotal evidence suggests that only about 20 per cent of company actions are voted upon at the shareholders' general meeting, despite the very wide range of situations in which such a vote seems to be legally required.

A major disincentive for shareholder protection is the fact that the Supreme People's Court allows courts to hear only a very limited class of securities-related claims as class actions.[24] The remedy the Company Law provides to minority shareholders is application to the courts to prevent the continuation of unlawful conduct by directors and majority shareholders. Existing laws and regulations do not specify penalties for corporations and officers that obstruct shareholders' rights to access information. The Securities Law is unclear as to when and whether investors can take civil action against directors and investment professionals for false or negligent disclosures that result in losses.

On 26 December 2002, the Supreme People's Court promulgated the Several Provisions on Trial of Civil Damages Cases Arising from Misrepresentation in the Securities Market (the Provisions),[25] which entered into effect on 1 February 2003. The Provisions extend the Notice on Questions Concerning the Acceptance of Civil Tort Dispute Cases Arising from Misrepresentation in the Securities Market,[26] issued and effective on 15 January 2002. The Provisions discuss acceptance of cases and jurisdictions, methods of bringing lawsuits, determination of misrepresentation, liabilities determination and exemption, joint tort liability and calculation of loss. As defined in the Provisions, misrepresentation can include fraudulent records, misleading statements, material omissions and improper disclosure. The Provisions deal only with misrepresentation made by public companies and not share price manipulation or insider trading.

The greatest criticism of the Provisions is that they require the Ministry of Finance, the CSRC or other administrative agencies first to determine an administrative penalty declaring that directors, officers or other corporate actors have misbehaved. Once this decision is issued by the appropriate administrative agency the courts are then empowered to take the civil case. As a result, obtaining a civil remedy is so cumbersome that private enforcement may be all but impossible.

Recent amendments to the Company Law

The dilemma in Chinese company law, as in corporate law around the world, is that a majority shareholder or majority of the shareholders have the power to control a company. Corporate law has long recognized the need to counter this right so that majority shareholders do not exercise their control to gain disproportionate benefits at the expense of the corporation or non-controlling shareholders.[27] At the same time, opportunistic behaviour by minority shareholders must also be checked. Therefore, corporate law seeks to provide a sensible balance between the control rights of majority shareholders and protecting minority shareholders from abuse.[28]

Protection of shareholders' rights

The recently amended Company Law makes some considerable progress in this direction but still falls short of protecting minority shareholders in some important respects. This is partly the result of the relatively brief corporate history of post-Mao China: companies are few and only very recently established; most public companies' shares are highly concentrated and have a controlling shareholder (or joint controlling shareholders)[29]; the board of directors is controlled by majority shareholders; PRC courts are inexperienced, ineffective and often corrupt; and market and cultural constraints on the controlling shareholders are weak or absent.[30] Most importantly – and not surprisingly – the managers, directors and controlling shareholders of these new companies remain sheltered with the power of the state, since in most cases these companies are reformulated SOEs or parts thereof. If corporate law reform is to have the transformational effect on Chinese society for which some reformers hope, these features will have to change.

Improved corporate governance is a goal of several adjustments in the new Company Law. In general, the revised Company Law creates better rules about shareholders' meetings; it regulates related-party transactions; it provides minority shareholders with some remedies if they are abused; it ensures information rights for minority shareholders; and it reinforces the power of the board of supervisors or other supervisory authorities. Despite these achievements, the revised Company Law also has several failings. Some are continuing lapses and gaps; others are missed opportunities to remedy deficiencies noted in the earlier

Company Law. Some of these are detrimental to the protection of the minority shareholders; others do not improve the lot of the majority who control the company.

Article 20 establishes the fiduciary duty[31] owed by the majority shareholders to the minority shareholders by providing a cause of action for the minority shareholders against controlling shareholders. It provides: "Where any of the shareholders of a company causes any loss to the company or to other shareholders by abusing shareholder's rights, it shall be liable for compensation." These fiduciary duties are owed to all shareholders; elsewhere, Article 152 allows any shareholder "to bring a suit against any person [including controlling shareholders] who encroaches on the lawful rights and interests of the company and causes losses to the company." Despite a failure to list in the new law what acts constitute "encroachment," it provides both a standard and a legal basis for explicit rights to sue, a conspicuous failing of the earlier law which was even more ambiguous as to whether such a right even existed.

The new Company Law also imposes "duties of loyalty and diligence" upon directors, supervisors and senior managers. Article 149 of the revised law prohibits specific acts, mainly involving self-dealing and the usurpation of corporate opportunities as well as ordinary misappropriation, classic duty-of-loyalty problems. These fiduciary principles are alternatives to precatory language or more specific regulatory monitoring. They also shift from criminal and administrative penalties to the private enforcement (by other shareholders) model found in the United States and other developed countries. They substitute deterrence for prior supervision, resetting the balance between majority and minority shareholders.

Equitable treatment for all shareholders

The revised Company Law seeks to ensure that there are regular shareholders' meetings. Chinese experience has shown that scheduled regular and ad hoc interim meetings can be very useful devices to constrain the board of directors and managers. The original Company Law stipulated that the shareholders' meeting could only be convened by the board of directors and had to be presided over by the chairman of the board of directors.[32] Majority shareholders could refuse to convene or to preside over a meeting to suppress expressions of dissent by minority shareholders. Articles 41 and 102 of the revised Company Law entitle the shareholders above a certain threshold, when the board of directors and board of supervisors do not convene or preside over an interim meeting, to do so themselves. Because an interim meeting convened by other shareholders may affect the majority shareholders adversely, this new rule creates in effect a "demand provision" for the board of directors chosen by majority vote to convene shareholders' meetings or else face the prospect that others might convene one.[33] Article 22 further provides shareholders the right to petition a court to revoke any shareholder or board resolution within 60 days of the resolution's passage, where the procedure for convening that shareholders' meeting violates any law, administrative regulation or the articles of association. So both majority and minority shareholders have an incentive to hold shareholders' meetings in an orderly, predictable and lawful fashion, to avoid unnecessary disputes.[34] In a shareholders' meeting with all parties present, each party wishing to pass a proposal must create mutually acceptable conditions, conducive to a sensible balance between them.

By providing minority shareholders above certain thresholds with the rights to propose an interim meeting[35] and with proposal rights,[36] the revised Company Law may encourage minority shareholders to use the shareholders' meeting to check the illegitimate behaviour of a dominant majority.

The revised law allows shareholders to bring an action against the directors, supervisors or officers of a company for both work-related and non-work-related acts harmful to the company committed in violation of the articles of association, regulations or laws. Shareholders may also bring an action against third parties whose actions damage the interests of the company. Furthermore, the rules provide the means for minority shareholders to oust directors who injure overall company rights by favouring the majority, helpful in creating a disincentive for majority shareholders' abuse of their power.

The proposal rights give minority shareholders the chance to raise their concerns in the shareholders' meeting,[37] without which the agenda and content of the shareholders' meeting might be completely controlled by board of directors. As with the rights to propose an interim meeting, the proposal rights also make it possible for outsiders to acquire some shares and replace directors without having to wait until the directors' tenure expires at the next annual shareholders' meeting, reducing the costs of acquisition and creating market power constraints.

Enabling public companies to adopt cumulative voting, set out in Article 106, provides another important protection for shareholders. Under a straight voting system, any person or bloc who controls a majority of the votes in a particular election can elect all the directors. Cumulative voting allows shareholders to multiply their votes by the number of directors and supervisors to be elected.[38] Furthermore, where a listed company within one year purchases or sells material assets or provides a guarantee in excess of 30 per cent of its total assets, approval of shareholders with no less than two-thirds of voting rights must be obtained. These revised voting rights provide shareholders with large minority stakes a chance to elect at least one or more directors, to affect board and management decisions, and may lead to better corporate governance.

This ability to elect "representative" directors is particularly important in China. There have been many cases where majority shareholders overrode minority shareholders' interests notwithstanding a board with independent directors, the oversight of the board of supervisors and shareholder rights to sue. The root failures lie in the weakness and lack of independence of the judiciary and the high costs of shareholders' suits.[39] Furthermore, independent directors and supervisors are not in the position of shareholders: they have no motivation to supervise a majority-dominated company.[40] In contrast, the directors elected by cumulative voting who represent the minority shareholders have greater incentives to exercise their rights. Minority representation on the board may add independent, critical scrutiny of majority-dominated companies and sometimes presents a prior constraint on illegal behaviour, enhancing the protection of minority shareholders.

Regulation of related-party transactions[41] provides protection from the risk that a corporation may be treated unfairly in such transactions.[42] Legislators cannot expect self-interested directors, for example, to afford primacy to other shareholders' interests.[43] In recent years, many Chinese companies, especially listed companies, have provided illegal guarantees. Article 16 requires that guarantees or investing by a company in related entities must be subject to the determination of the shareholders' meeting, in which the related parties are not eligible to vote.

Normally the majority shareholders hold a high percentage of voting rights; minority shareholders (due to rational apathy) fail to vote; and there is no minimum quorum for a shareholders' meeting of a public company. Thus, even though an investment or a guarantee will substantially injure the interests of the company and minority shareholders, the proposal will be passed. Excluding the votes of related parties can prevent the majority shareholders from engaging in misconduct. If majority shareholders want the company to provide a guarantee, they must provide the same conditions as, or more favourable conditions than, the market requires. For similar reasons, Article 125 states directors of listed companies are ineligible to vote on matters in which they have an interest.

Providing these remedies to aggrieved minority shareholders not only serves to compensate them but may also deter misconduct by majority shareholders. At the same time, to guard against minority shareholders' opportunism and possible harassment of the majority, the Company Law stipulates certain requirements for the minority to exercise their rights.

Article 106 allows cumulative voting as a choice for public companies,[44] but boards of directors will probably continue to be controlled by majority shareholders, allowing continuing injury to a company's interests. Most of the articles of association of the company are determined by the controlling shareholders, and companies may "opt out" of cumulative voting, so majority shareholders can veto a decision in favour of cumulative voting. Some object that cumulative voting may polarize a board and transform it into a contentious group, where constant bickering deflects energies from rational efforts to identify and respond to the corporation's problems and opportunities.[45] Nevertheless, China has introduced independent directors for listed companies to supervise majority shareholders.[46] The independent directors may also fight with inside directors, and supervision may lead to arguments. On the other hand, minority and majority shareholders' interests may "converge to a significant extent."[47] Hence, contention within the board is unlikely to lead to bad results. Moreover, empirical and historical evidence from the United States shows that the elimination of cumulative voting in large public firms has reduced shareholder wealth on average.[48] The benefits brought by cumulative voting will definitely outweigh its costs.

Derivative suits; appraisal rights

Since those controlling a company are unlikely to authorize it to sue them personally, Article 152 establishes a system of derivative suits. It provides a device by which shareholders may enforce claims of the corporation against managing officers and directors of the corporation, who may be dominated by the majority shareholders. In China, where majority shareholders' illegal behaviour is rampant,[49] the derivative suit may prove a very useful weapon for minority shareholders to protect their interests and deter majority shareholders' oppressive behaviour. To provide a minimal basis for standing to sue, Article 152 requires that the minority shareholders must hold 1 per cent or more of the total shares of the company for more than 180 days and must make a demand on the company first. The reason for the demand requirement is to re-emphasize the basic principle that the board of directors, not the shareholders, manages the corporation, and to protect the directors or supervisors from harassment by litigious shareholders.[50]

Article 75 entitles the shareholders in close companies to appraisal rights when they vote against a shareholders' meeting resolution concerning matters which seriously affect shareholders' rights or suffer other arguably oppressive behaviour.[51] These appraisal rights liberalize the rules related to shareholders' approval of fundamental transactions. They may also overcome a requirement for unanimous consent that permits a small minority to block a decision desired by the majority.[52] It gives the majority the right to control the company, while at the same time creating a means for the dissenting shareholders to exit. These appraisal claims, while enhancing fairness, may siphon cash from the corporation; thus, the Company Law stipulates the dissenting shareholders may only exercise the rights in designated circumstances.[53]

Article 183[54] empowers shareholders to apply for the company's dissolution to a People's Court, so long as they successfully prove that the company is encountering serious operating difficulties which will cause substantial and irreparable losses,[55] and the problems cannot be solved by any other means. The remedy of involuntary dissolution serves as protection against majority oppression as well as an incentive for the majority shareholders to exercise their control so as to maintain minority confidence.[56] Since involuntary dissolution may cause hardship to other parties, the Article designates that only in the event of serious deadlock with no other solutions may shareholders invoke the remedy. Moreover, to prevent strike suits,[57] it permits only shareholders who have 10 per cent or more of the shares outstanding to exercise the rights.

To ensure shareholders' rights to information, Article 34(1) and Article 98 entitle the shareholder to consult and copy the articles of association, minutes of the shareholders' meetings, resolutions of the board of directors, resolutions of the board of supervisors, and financial reports.[58] Article 151 empowers the shareholders to elicit accurate information from the directors, the senior officials and supervisors. To protect their interests, the shareholders need to ascertain how the majority-controlled directors and officers conduct the company's business. Without access to information, the deterrent effects of shareholder oversight would be reduced. To prevent harassment of management or theft of corporate secrets, Article 34 requires that shareholders in limited liability companies cannot consult the accounting books unless they make a request in writing which states a "proper purpose."

Effective monitoring of management

The revised Company Law intends to reinforce the power of the board of supervisors. The board of supervisors in China – following the model established in German commercial law and employed in other civil law jurisdictions – was supposed to oversee the work of the board of directors and to provide an additional layer of checks on management. In the past, it played little role as a watchdog and fell short of the expectations of investors and legislators. Thus, the new Company Law provides the board of supervisors with more powers to make it work properly.

Articles 54, 55 and 119 – which give the board of supervisors the right of inquiry and the right to hire an accounting firm (with the relevant expenses being born by the company) – enhance the board of supervisors' ability to get information about the company, help the board better understand corporate information, and set priorities for supervision.[59] Articles 40 and 101 entrust the board of supervisors in close and public companies to propose an interim meeting, and Articles 41 and 102 vest the right to convene a shareholders' meeting in the board of supervisors in the event the board of directors or executive directors fail to do so. These rules make it possible for the board of supervisors to propose, convene and preside over a shareholders' meeting and report what it has found, augmenting the links between it and the shareholders, indirectly increasing the board of supervisors' role as a watchdog, providing greater deterrence to illegal behaviour by the majority and more weapons to protect the minority shareholders.

Nevertheless, the new Company Law has not altered situations where the watchdog functions of the board of supervisors can be stymied. Articles 52 and 118 still require that at least one-third of the board of supervisors must be employee supervisors, elected by employees. Theoretically employee supervisors know the operation better than other supervisors, and are thus better able to supervise the board of directors. In practice, the situation is quite different.[60] Employee supervisors are more likely to be employees whose salaries and promotion are determined by the directors and managers. While employee supervisors have been successful in Europe (in Germany, for example), Asian nations such as South Korea and Taiwan prohibit employees from being supervisors. This is because of the fear that such supervisors, given the hierarchies of Asian societies, would not be able to exercise their rights neutrally.

In addition, Articles 99 and 104 stipulate that supervisors elected by shareholders should be elected by straight voting in public companies, which may also lead to a majority-controlled board of supervisors. Unlike the supervisors in companies in some other Asian countries (Taiwan, Japan and South Korea) those in the PRC cannot act separately and independently.[61] Because of majority shareholders' control of the board of supervisors, the board may not meaningfully protect minority shareholders.

Voting rules still provide various loopholes. The revised Company Law does not mandate cumulative voting and the manner of election of auditors for public companies. Minority shareholders sometimes do not vote in their best interests as a result of information asymmetry, collective action problems or difficulty in judging what arrangements will best suit their interests.[62] Mandatory structural rules may not only help ensure outside directors and large minority shareholders participate in the decision-making process but also protect them against opportunism by insiders.[63]

Article 170 enables a public company to choose the shareholders' meeting or the board of directors to hire or dismiss the accounting firm which audits the company.[64] Independent auditors play a "gatekeeper" role in protecting minority shareholders' interests. Regrettably, in China, there have been many instances where the independent auditors have "cooked the books,"[65] providing further support for the proposition that the watchdogs should not be chosen by those they are supposed to watch.[66] Indeed, mandating that independent auditors must be chosen by the shareholders' meetings does nothing to prevent majority shareholders' opportunistic amendment of the articles to allow the majority-dominated board of directors to choose the independent auditors. It is hard to imagine how the auditors thus chosen will fulfil their gate-keeping responsibility

Article 152 stipulates that defendants in a derivative suit can only be the directors, senior managers and supervisors of a company. An outsider who adversely affects the company's interests – for instance, one who does not pay a debt to the company on time and is not sued by the directors and the supervisors – cannot be sued by the shareholders. As a result, this rule cannot prohibit majority shareholders from utilizing other companies as intermediaries to transfer interests in public companies.

Some elements of the revised Company Law could harm the company and majority shareholders. Article 151[67] demands that directors, senior managers and supervisors must answer shareholders' enquiries. Yet sometimes honest, complete public responses by a director or supervisor may injure the interests of the company; for example, these may involve trade secrets or business strategy. Despite provisions of the Company Law which might hold shareholders liable, the weakness of the courts, the expense of lawsuits and unpredictability of results make any threat of liability highly unlikely.[68]

Articles 34 and 98 give shareholders the right to consult resolutions of meetings of the board of directors, which may also provide access to trade secrets of the company. Minority shareholders may use this right to affect adversely the interests of the company. The Company Law now does not require that shareholders who want to review resolutions of the meetings of the board of directors have a proper purpose.

Executive compensation

Among the issues related to effective monitoring of management by the board of directors, perhaps the most important is executive compensation. Recently this has become a major issue, not only in the United States but in other developed countries. In the United States it is hardly new; as early as 1939, the SEC enacted regulations regarding disclosure of executive compensation.[69] Recently, corporate scandals such as those involving Enron, WorldCom, HealthSouth and Tyco have focused on executive compensation as an important factor in eroding corporate governance. The primary complaint against excessive executive compensation is that in many cases – despite the mantra of pay for performance – executive pay simply does not correlate with performance.[70] The widespread view is that chief executive officers are grossly overpaid[71]: senior managers' pay has increased significantly faster than that of ordinary workers.[72] Moreover, the range of perquisites for high-level executives, including bonuses and special payments, has become excessive.

In China, the development of capital markets and increase in the number of large companies had brought new attention to executive compensation.[73] As in other economies, directors and officers of Chinese companies do not own corporate assets; thus, the economic consequences of their management are felt not by them but by shareholders. To align their interests with those of shareholders and to reduce agency costs, companies create incentives for directors and executives. The most effective, but most often misapplied, incentive is executive compensation.[74]

The revised Chinese Company Law provides that directors, supervisors and management executives must comply with the laws, administrative regulations and corporate charters, and that they owe the duties of loyalty and care. Directors, supervisors and executives may not utilize their power for bribes or other illegal income and may not make personal use of corporate assets.[75] The law further provides that they and controlling shareholders should compensate the company for any losses resulting from abuse of their control positions.[76] As noted above, shareholders' right to file derivative suits is recognized by the law; Article 152 of the Company Law entitles shareholders to sue directors and executives for illegal use of corporate assets.

In most American jurisdictions, suits against executives for excessive compensation rarely succeed. Only where plaintiffs can prove that compensation is unreasonable for the services provided will the courts intervene with their equity power to "prevent a waste of the corporation's assets."[77] If equity requires it, the court will award recovery of excess compensation directly to harmed minority shareholders. The provisions of China's revised Company Law do not explicitly allow a parallel action, so it is difficult to determine whether or not Chinese courts can sustain similar claims.

Increased disclosure of executive compensation has become the norm in developed countries in recent years. The United States Congress passed the Sarbanes-Oxley Act in 2002 which, inter alia, prohibits corporate loans to executives.[78] British and Canadian laws also impose some restrictions on executive compensation; for example, a British corporate reform regulation also passed in 2002 requires an annual shareholder vote on executive compensation practices.[79]

Compared with the law in North America and the United Kingdom, Chinese law has much room for development. Despite China's traditions of centralization and government regulation, the law hardly regulates executive compensation at all. The Company Law treats it entirely as an internal corporate issue, only providing that compensation of directors and supervisors shall be decided by the shareholders' meeting[80] and that compensation of executives shall be decided by the board of directors.[81] After recent revisions, the law prohibits companies from offering loans directly or indirectly through subsidiaries to directors, supervisors and executives.[82] It also requires that companies disclose the compensation of directors, supervisors and executives regularly, similar to provisions of the US Sarbanes-Oxley Act.[83] Yet there have been no implementing rules promulgated by the State Council, the CSRC or other relevant government agencies. It is clear that the system for regulating executive compensation in China will have to be improved in the future, as incentive systems are adopted which attempt to tie managers' take-home pay with job performance. While excessive executive compensation in Chinese listed companies has not proven to be a major problem thus far, experience elsewhere makes clear the need for government regulation of executive compensation to protect vulnerable shareholders – especially small shareholders.[84] Such reforms should do much to increase public confidence in corporate governance and the capital market in China.

Conclusion

Although they fail to address all concerns, the revised Company Law and Securities Law do endeavour to stipulate better rules by taking account of the actual situation of corporate governance in PRC and making use of foreign legislative experience. As for balancing the interests of majority and minority shareholders, especially in attempting to enhance the protection of minority shareholder's interests, the new laws do make some progress. It remains to be seen how effective they will turn out to be in practice.

In the long term, better corporate governance in China will require: clear rules and regulations, including implementing rules for these new laws; certainty in the application of these rules and regulations; fair and consistent enforcement, combined with strong sanction against breaches; and policy initiatives to coordinate reforms necessitated by market developments. Not every observer necessarily applauds the recent trends in China of adopting foreign models of corporate governance to achieve results in the context of the business culture of Chinese enterprises.[85] It remains to be seen how a more characteristically Chinese corporate governance system might evolve.

Moreover, there may be many twists and turns in the process of improving and adjusting the corporate governance regime in China. For example, in 2004 the contentious issue of management buyouts (MBOs) of SOEs was clarified. New State Asset Supervision and Administration Commission (SASAC) regulations temporarily prohibited MBOs at large SOEs, closed a number of loopholes and clarified under which conditions MBOs of smaller enterprises could be carried out.[86] At the time, fears were expressed about the possible abuse of insider information by managers to acquire shares of SOEs at bargain prices. By 2006, however, the government was promising to introduce a stock option scheme for managers at China's overseas-listed SOEs, which analysts then said would be an important step in promoting the healthy growth of Chinese companies in the long run. A management incentive stock option programme for overseas-listed SOEs, drafted by SASAC, was to take effect from 1 March 2006.[87] SASAC relaxed the previous ban on management buyouts in large-scale SOEs, allowing executives in those companies to purchase limited shares of the company in which they work. The relationship between policy experimentation and law reform remains unclear and suggests that transition from the command economy to a market environment will combine legal, economic and policy reforms in unstable combinations until a new model suited to Chinese circumstances is developed.

Notes

1 Transparency International, National Integrity System, Transparency International Country Study Report, *China 2006*: "As China is in the process of unprecedented reform and transition in its economic, political and social systems and a proper legal anti-corruption framework is yet to develop, there are still huge opportunities for corruption. Corruption remains a big challenge in China... . Overregulation of the economy has impeded the private sector and civil society. Extra-budgetary funds provide opportunities for corruption, and government transparency is limited" (http://www. transparency.org/policy_research/nis/regional/asia_pacific China_nis_2006. pdf, p. 8). Cf. Bernard Black, "The corporate governance behavior and market value of Russian firms," *Emerging Markets Review*, Vol. 2, No. 2 (2001), pp. 89–108. (Study of Russian firms showed that a worst-to-best improvement in corporate governance predicted an astronomical 700-fold (70,000%) increase in firm value!) See also International Finance Corporation, "The irresistible case for corporate governance," March 2006, http://www.ifc.org/ifcext/pepse.nsf/AttachmentsByTitle/IrresistibleCase4CG.pdf/$FILE/IrresistibleCase4CG.pdf.
2 Available at http://www.oecd.org/dataoecd/32/18/31557724.pdf.
3 The Company Law of the People's Republic of China, *Zhonghua renmin gongheguo gongsi fa*, adopted by the Fifth Session of the Standing Committee of the Eighth National People's Congress, 29 December 1993, effective 1 July 1994; revised at the 18th Meeting of the Standing Committee of the Tenth National People's Congress, 27 October 2005, according to the Decision on Revising the Company Law of the People's Republic of China, at the 11th Meeting of the Standing Committee of the Tenth People's Congress, 28 August 2004.

4 But see James Feinerman, "Backwards into the future (Securities Law in the People's Republic of China)," *Law and Contemporary Problems*, Vol. 52, No. 3 (1989) pp. 169–84, describing institutions in existence before the enactment of enabling legislation such as the 1994 Company Law and 1999 Securities Law.

5 A study based on empirical evidence and survey data on Shanghai's publicly listed companies concluded that China's approach to corporate governance development may be failing to achieve its objectives and outcomes. These data – gathered before Chinese accession to the WTO – showed the adoption of Anglo-American external market-based models: i.e. a top-down legalistic approach to mandate formal corporate governace structures as the major means to develop modern corporate forms. It remains to be seen whether the problem lies in choosing the wrong model or incomplete implementation of the model chosen. O.K. Tam, "Models of corporate governance for Chinese companies," *Corporate Governance: An International Review*, Vol. 8, No. 1 (2000), pp. 52–64.

6 Revised for the third time at the 18th Session of the Tenth National People's Congress, 27 October 2005.

7 The Securities Law of the People's Republic of China, *Zhonghua renmin gongheguo zhengquan fa*, adopted at the Sixth Meeting of the Standing Committee of the Ninth National People's Congress, 29 December 1998, effective 1 July 1999; revised at the 18th Meeting of the Standing Committee of the Tenth National People's Congress, 27 October 2005 according to the Decision on Revising the Securities Law of the People's Republic of China, at the 11th Meeting of the Standing Committee of the Tenth People's Congress, 28 August 2004.

8 Oliver Rui, Michael Firth and Peter Fung, "Corporate governance and CEO compensation in China" (September 2002). Available at SSRN: http://ssrn.com/abstract=337841.

9 Despite attempts to export Western management techniques and training, it has been suggested that the nature of management tasks and the skills required to run Chinese enterprises may entail different learning. Sue Newell, "The transfer of management knowledge to China: building learning communities rather than translating Western textbooks?" *Education & Training*, Vol. 41, No. 67 (1999), pp. 28–29.

10 While in many cases in other countries the primary problem is excessive executive compensation, in China the opposite problem may be more significant: under-compensation of senior managers which would provide a greater incentive to maximize returns for all shareholders. Takao Kato and Cheryl Long, "Executive compensation, firm performance, and corporate governance in China: evidence from firms listed in the Shanghai and Shenzhen Stock Exchanges," IZA Discussion Papers 1767, Institute for the Study of Labor (IZA) (2005).

11 China Securities Regulatory Commission, Statistical Information, http://211.154.210.238/en/statinfo/ index_en. China Enterprise Confederation and China Enterprise Directors Association, *China Top 500 Enterprises 2006 Analysis Report*, revealed that 349 enterprises were state owned, nearly 70% of the total. Their combined assets reached 39 trillion yuan (US$4.87 trillion) at the end of 2005, 95% of the total. The state-owned economy remains dominant and controls the leading industries in the national economy. 2 September 2006 http://news3.xinhuanet.com/english/2006–09/02/content_5040531.htm.

12 OECD, "China's securities market," http://www.oecd.org/dataoecd/5/32/18469881.pdf.

13 Donald Clarke, "The independent director in Chinese corporate governance," *Delaware Journal of Corporate Law*, Vol. 36, No. 1 (2006) pp. 125–228.

14 See also "China issues new guidelines for listed companies," www.chinaview.cn, 21 March 2006. The China Securities Regulatory Commission (CSRC) issued amended guidelines for the charters of listed companies, first published in 1997. The new guidelines seek to improve corporate governance by limiting the power of executives in order

to prevent power abuse or fraudulent transactions. It states that the highest authority in a listed company is the shareholders' meeting, not the board chairman, and that any major decisions must be approved by the shareholders' meeting. Senior managers and employees' representatives must not account for more than half of the directors. Shareholders cannot vote on transactions in which they are involved, and only the shareholders' meeting can appoint accounting firms. Board members, supervisors and senior executives were formerly banned from selling their shares during their tenure. Now they are allowed to sell them one year after the stocks are listed or six months after termination of service. In any given year, they cannot sell more than 25% of their shares.

15 M. O'Neill, "Shame and scandal on the road to riches," *South China Morning Post*, 7 August 2006.

16 Xinhua "Liquidation going on with Guangdong Securities Co.," http://english.people. com.cn/200511/ 08/eng20051108_219901.html.

17 CSRC, "Code of corporate governance for listed companies in China," 7 January 2001 (Zhengjianfa No.1 of 2002). Available in English at http://www.csrc.gov.cn.

18 Yet as Benjamin Liebman has pointed out, the Chinese media, including the business press, often fail to provide an independent source of information despite some de facto autonomy. Commercialization of the media may create conflicting pressures to highlight sensational cases of abuse and at the same time to suppress unfavourable information about potential advertisers and locally important enterprises. Liebman, "Watchdog or demagogue? The media in the Chinese legal system," *Columbia Law Review*, Vol. 105, No. 1 (2005), pp. 1–157.

19 Jason Z. Xiao, Yikuan Zhang and Zhihua Xie, "The making of independent auditing standards in China," *Accounting Horizons*, Vol. 14, No. 1 (2000), p. 69.

20 Nevertheless, studies have found that China's efforts to improve auditing standards were resisted by companies that prefer small local auditors whose political connections may be helpful in gaining regulatory approvals. Qian Wang, T.J. Wong and Lijun Xia, "State ownership, institutional environment and auditor choice: evidence from China" (September 2005), http://www.baf.cuhk.edu.hk/research/cig/pdf_download/WangWongXia.pdf.

21 The CSRC has been quick to impose fines under the new Securities Law, which came into effect on 1 January 2006. Maximum fines are between 300,000 and 600,000 yuan. More specifically, in early July 2006, Kelon was fined 600,000 yuan (US$75,000) for providing false information and other offences; its former chairman, Gu Chujun, was fined 300,000 yuan (US$37,500) in mid-July 2006 for a number of "economic crimes."

22 Grace Hu and Marc Goergen, "A study of ownership concentration, control and evolution of Chinese IPO companies," available at SSRN: http://ssrn.com/ abstract=286612.

23 Cf. Tong Lu, "Development of system of independent directors and the Chinese experience," http://www.cipe.org/china/development.htm. The author suggests companies facing the new rules established by the CSRC were seeking methods for nominal compliance without implementing the system completely.

24 Binglan Xu, "Securities legislation protects investors," *China Daily*, 28 February 2005, http://www. chinadaily.com.cn/english/doc/2005–02/28/content_419958.htm. "In 2003, the Supreme People's Court promulgated a set of guidelines on [class actions], which said the local courts can only accept cases about fabricated statements, which basically ruled out investors' chances for taking listed companies to court for other misbehaviour."

25 "Zuigao renmin fayuan guanyu shenli zhengquan shichang yin xujia chenshu yinfade minshi peichang anjian de ruogan guiding" ("Several provisions on civil compensation cases arising from misrepresentation in the securities market"), 26 December 2002, available at http://xinhuanet.org.

26 "Zuigao renmin fayuan guanyu shouli zhengzhuan shichang yin xujia chenshu yinfa de minshi qinfan jiufen anjian youguan wenti de tongzhi" ("Notice on questions concerning the acceptance of civil tort dispute cases arising from misrepresentation in the securities market"), *Fazhi ribao* (*Legal Daily*), 16 January 2002.

27 See e.g. James Cox, Thomas Hazen and F. Hodge O'Neal, *Corporations* (New York: Aspen Law & Business, 1997), pp. 250–58.

28 Bernard Black and Reinier Kraakman, "A self-enforcing model of corporate law," *Harvard Law Review*, Vol. 109, No. 8 (1996) pp. 1911–82.

29 In June 2004, CSRC statistics stated that China had 1,324 listed companies. Of those, one shareholder held more than 50% of the issued shares of 486 companies, and one shareholder held between 20 and 50% of 724 companies. Nicholas C. Howson, "Regulation of companies with publicly listed share capital in the People's Republic of China," *Cornell International Law Journal*, Vol. 38, No. 1 (2005) pp. 237–49.

30 Xiaonian Xu and Yan Wang, "Ownership structure and corporate governance in Chinese stock companies," *China Economic Review*, Vol. 10, No. 1 (1999) pp. 75–98.

31 A fiduciary is held to a standard of conduct above that of a stranger or casual business person and must avoid "self-dealing" or "conflicts of interests" where his potential benefit conflicts with what is best for the person who trusts him. Commonly as a legal matter, these are duties of care and loyalty on the part of the fiduciary.

32 The 1994 Company Law of China, Articles 10(1) and 43(3).

33 In most legal systems, company law requires that before shareholders can sue derivatively or on their own behalf they must make an explicit written demand that the board of directors take appropriate legal action to safeguard the corporation's and shareholders' interests. The demand may be excused if to do so would be futile.

34 Stephen Green and Ming He, "China's stock market: out of the valley in 2004?" Royal Institute of International Affairs, Briefing Paper No. 1, February 2004.

35 Article 40 reduces the threshold from 25% to 10% of voting rights to call a special meeting in a close corporation. Article 101 further enables the articles of association of a company to specify the requirements for calling a special meeting of a public company. Articles 41 and 102 designate that in case the board of directors and board of supervisors does not convene or preside over the shareholders' meeting, any shareholder possessing 10% or more voting rights and the shareholders separately or aggregately holding 10% of the shares can do so.

36 Article 103(2); The shareholders separately or aggregately holding 3% or more of the shares of the company may put forward a written interim proposal to the board of directors ten days before a shareholders' meeting is held. The board of directors may notify other shareholders within two days and submit the interim proposal to the shareholders' meeting for deliberation. The contents of an interim proposal shall fall within the scope to be decided by the shareholders' meeting, and the interim proposal shall have a clear topic for discussion and matters to be decided.

37 Frank Easterbrook and Daniel Fischel, "Voting in corporate law," *Journal of Law & Economics*, Vol. 26 (1983) pp. 395–427.

38 Cumulative voting helps strengthen the ability of minority shareholders to elect a director, allowing shareholders to cast all their votes for a single nominee for the board of directors when the company has multiple openings on its board. For example, if an election is for four directors and a shareholder holds 500 shares (one vote per share), under straight voting they have a maximum of 500 shares for any one candidate (2,000 votes total, 500 votes for each of the four candidates). With cumulative voting, all 2,000 votes could be for one candidate, 1,000 each to two candidates, or otherwise divided whichever way they chose.

39 The minority shareholders need to bear costs of the suit, and have the burden of proof, as a matter of Chinese civil procedure.

40 See Armen Alchian and Harold Demsetz, "Production, information costs, and economic organization," *American Economic Review*, Vol. 62, No. 5 (1972), pp. 777–95.

41 Transactions conducted between related parties are sometimes called "connected transactions" in Chinese parlance.

42 Cox, Hazen and O'Neal, *Corporations*, pp. 204–15.

43 Huan, "Shareholders' rights in China: an analysis of private equity in former state-owned enterprises," *Singapore Academy of Law Journal*, Vol. 12 (2000), p. 428.

44 Article 106: When the shareholders' assembly elects directors or supervisors, it may, under the articles of association or resolution of the shareholders' assembly, adopt a cumulative voting system.

45 See Robert Charles Clark, *Corporate Law* (Boston: Little, Brown 1986), pp. 362–64.

46 See China Securities Regulatory Commission, "Guanyu zai shangshi gongsi jianli duli dongshi zhidu de zhidao yijian" ("Guidelines regarding establishing the rule of independent directors"), 21 August 2001, http://www.cas.cn/html/Dir/2001/08/21/5860.htm.

47 See Melvin Eisenberg, "The structure of corporation law," *Columbia Law Review*, Vol. 89, No. 7 (1989), pp. 1461–1525.

48 See Jeffery Gordon, "Institutions as relational investors: a new look at cumulative voting," *Columbia Law Review*, Vol. 94, No. 1 (1994), pp. 124–92.

49 Gregory Chow, "Corruption and China's economic reform in the early 21st century," Princeton University CEPS Working Paper No. 116, October 2005, http://www.princeton.edu/~ceps/workingpapers/116chow.pdf.

50 See Clark, *Corporate Law*, p. 641. In the United States, the demand requirement, minimum shareholdings and posting of bond as security for the expenses of litigation are all features of shareholder derivative litigation.

51 Article 75: Under any of the following circumstances, a shareholder who votes against the resolution of the shareholders' meeting may request the company to purchase its stock rights at a reasonable price: (1) The company has not distributed any profit to the shareholders for five consecutive years, but it has made profits for five consecutive years and conforms to the profit distribution conditions as prescribed in this Law; (2) The merger, split-up, or transfer of the main properties of the company; (3) When the business term as specified in the articles of association expires or other reasons for dissolution as prescribed in the articles of association occur, the shareholders' meeting makes the company continue existing by adopting a resolution on modifying the articles of association.

52 See Cox, Hazen and O'Neal, *Corporations*, pp. 595–606. In corporate law, the appraisal remedy – typically viewed as a form of protection for minority shareholders – gives shareholders the right to dissent from corporate transactions and to obtain payment for their shares from the corporation.

53 See Article 75.

54 Article 183: Where any company meets any serious difficulty in its operations or management so that the interests of the shareholders will face heavy loss if it continues to exist and it cannot be solved by any other means, the shareholders who hold 10% or more of the voting rights of all the shareholders of the company may plead the people's court to dissolve the company.

55 See Alan Wang, "Redressing the rights of shareholders in corporate fraud," http://www.chinalawandpractice.com/default.asp.

56 See Cox, Hazen and O'Neal, *Corporations*, pp. 679–89.

57 The purpose of a strike suit, brought by someone who owns very few shares, is to gain a private settlement before going to court that would cost the company less than defending the suit. The suit itself does not benefit the company or other shareholders.

58 Article 98 also entitles shareholders to consult records relating to corporate bonds.

59 Under provisions of the US Sarbanes-Oxley legislation, a corporation's audit committee also has the authority to retain independent legal, accounting and other consultants to advise the committee.

60 Articles 52 and 124 of the 1994 Company Law also required that some supervisors be employees, but in public companies there were few employee supervisors who fulfilled their responsibility to protect minority shareholders from oppression.

61 Articles 54, 55, 56, 57, 118, 119 and 120 of the Company Law require the supervisors in a company to act collectively, except when attending the meeting of the board of directors.

62 Eisenberg, "The structure of corporation law," p. 1461.

63 Jeffery Gordon, "The mandatory structure of corporate law," *Columbia Law Review*, Vol. 89, No. 7 (1989) pp. 1549–98.

64 Article 170 enables both close companies and public companies to choose whether the shareholders' meeting or the board of directors determines hiring or dismissing independent auditors.

65 Yuan Ding, Hua Zhang and Honghui Zhu, "Accounting failures in Chinese listed firms: origins and typology," *International Journal of Disclosure and Governance*, Vol. 2, No. 4, (2005) pp. 395–412. Z. Jun Lin and Feng Chen, "An empirical study of audit 'expectation gap' in the People's Republic of China," *International Journal of Auditing*, Vol. 8, No. 2 (2004), pp. 93–115.

66 See Clark, *Corporate Law*, p. 375.

67 Article 151: If the shareholders' meeting or shareholders' assembly demands a director, supervisor or senior manager attend the meeting as a non-voting representative, he shall do so and shall answer shareholders' inquiries.

68 Cindy Schipani and Junhai Liu, "Corporate governance in China: then and now," *Columbia Business Law Review*, Vol. 2002 (2002), pp. 1–69.

69 Tracy Scott Johnson, "Pay for performance: corporate executive compensation in the 1990s," *Delaware Journal of Corporate Law*, Vol. 20 (1995), p. 183.

70 *Ibid.* p. 214.

71 Stephen M. Bainbridge, "Book review essay: executive compensation: who decides? Pay without performance: the unfulfilled promise of executive compensation," *Texas Law Review*, Vol. 83 (2005), pp. 1615–62.

72 According to the Institute for Policy Studies, the ratio in pay between CEOs covered in *Business Week's* survey and the average production worker reached 301 to 1 in 2003. In 2002, the ratio stood at 282 to 1. Estimates more recently suggest the ratio is now over 400 to 1. Institute for Policy Studies and United for a Fair Economy, *Executive Excess 2004* (2004).

73 Kato and Long, "Executive compensation, firm performance, and corporate governance," pp. 945–83.

74 See e.g. D. Quinn Mills, "Paradigm lost: the imperial CEO," *Directors and Boards*, Vol. 27, No. 4 (2003), pp. 41–42.

75 Article 148.

76 Article 21.

77 Such lawsuits were successfully prosecuted in the Tyco case. Yet courts often uphold huge compensation for executives. See *In re The Walt Disney Co. Derivative Litigation*, Delaware No 411, 2005 (8 June 2006), where the Delaware Supreme Court upheld a severance package of $130 million after only 14 months' work for Michael Ovitz, which withstood a shareholder challenge, *In re The Walt Disney Co. Derivative. Litigation*, Delaware No. 15452 (9 August 2005) (Chandler, C.).

78 Sean A. Power, "Comment, Sarbanes-Oxley ends corporate lending to insiders: some interpretive issues for executive compensation surrounding the Section 402 loan prohibition," *University of Missouri Kansas City Law Review*, Vol. 71 (2003), p. 911.

79 Joanna L. Ossinger, "Regarding CEO pay, why are the British so different?" *Wall Street Journal*, 10 April 2006.

80 Article 37 (2).

81 Article 46 (9).

82 Article 116.

83 Article 117.

84 But see Dapeng Cai and Jie Li, "A theoretical investigation of agent corruption in Chinese SOEs: causes, effects, and its prevention," taweb.aichi-u.ac.jp/kurihara/jsie8ab.pdf. The authors find increasingly pervasive corruption by SOE managers, especially in large and medium-sized SOEs which have begun to access global capital markets. Others suggest that Chinese managers may need different incentives, such as stock options (which are rarely granted in China), as an inducement to better corporate governance. See Rui, Firth and Fung, "Corporate governance and CEO compensation," p. 20.

85 See e.g. Yu Guanghua, "Takeovers in China: the case against uniformity in corporate governance," *Common Law World Review*, Vol. 34, No. 2 (2005) pp. 169–98. Hui Huang, "The regulation of insider trading in China: a critical review and proposals for reform," *Australian Journal of Corporate Law*, Vol. 17 (2005), pp. 281–322.

86 Barry Naughton, "SASAC rising," *China Leadership Monitor*, No. 14 (2005), Hoover Institution, http://www.chinaleadershipmonitor.org/20052/bn.html.

87 Zheng Lifei, "State firm executives to get stock options from March 1," *China Daily*, 23 February 2006. "The application of (the management stock options incentive) scheme in overseas-listed SOEs is an important step to improve their corporate governance," said Wang Zhigang, director of the Company Reform and Development Studies at a think-tank affiliated to SASAC.

42

ONE HUNDRED YEARS OF PROGRESS

The development of the intellectual property system in China

Handong Wu

Source: *WIPO Journal* 1 (2009): 117–124.

As the ideal of a global economy meanders toward reality, the world is moving steadily toward a unified global system of intellectual property protection. From an international view, IPR has become a set of game rules with universal binding force. In the meantime, the systematisation and codification of IPR have also shown some indications. In the complicated international background, the construction of an IPR system in modern countries has vivid characteristics of the present time which, not only concerns the strategic policy consideration of facilitating economic and social development, but also with the rational arrangement made in pursuit of a systematisation of legal norms.

The system of intellectual property rights results from the development of modern commerce, economy and science and technology. It was during the 17th to 18th century that western, developed countries commenced to make IP legislation, which is 200 to 300 years older than that in China. Even some developing countries, such as India and Brazil, built the system of intellectual property rights 100 years earlier than China. China has experienced a history from "being forced to apply" into "being willing to apply" in terms its development of an IPR system.

A century's history of the development of China's IPR system can be divided into four stages as below:

Passive acceptance

Generally speaking, China's intellectual property protection began in the late Qing Dynasty. It resulted very much from the pressure imposed by the imperialists rather than learning from the west. In 1898, the first patent law in history was enacted as a result of political reform, which is called the Statute of

Encouraging Arts and Crafts; however it came to an untimely end due to the failure of "Wu Xu Reform". Hereafter, in light of the intellectual property clauses contained in the Sino-British Treaty of Commerce and Navigation of 1902 and the Sino-American Commercial Navigation Treaty of 1903, the Qing Government separately enacted the Statute of Trademark Registration in 1904 and Copyright Law of the Qing Dynasty in 1910 with the help of foreigners. The two statutes were applicable from the late Qing to the early Republic of China. The later Beiyang Government (the Northern Warlord Government) and the Kuomintang Government had instituted copyright, patent and trade mark laws, which were derived from foreign law. This passive legal transplant was quite common in developing countries. Those British colonies, such as India, all directly applied UK copyright law. India Copyright Law of 1914 originated from UK Copyright Law of 1911. At that time, it was usually very late for developing countries to build their IPR systems, which, meanwhile were strongly influenced by outside pressure. Under these circumstances, it was very difficult for developing countries to institute the needed legislation to reflect the overall goal of domestic social development.

2 Selective arrangement

Since the founding of New China, the Central Government once enacted several administrative regulations to protect intellectual property. In a strict sense, however, IP legal system had not yet been established. Since the adoption of its reform and open-up policy, especially from the late 1970s to the early 1990s, China enhanced IP legislation, enacting the Trademark Law of the China (1982), the Patent Law of China (1984) and the Copyright Law of China (1990). A preliminary IPR system has been built, the IP legislation at this stage can be concluded as a selective arrangement. In my view, there are three reasons. First, due to the difficulty and insufficient preparation in drafting legislation, China has drafted some main intellectual property laws while failing to consider other IP laws.

Secondly, in view of the current situation of domestic economy, science and technology, its IP protection level is not high. For instance, the scope of patent is quite limited; the universal international standard has not yet applied in computer software protection. Finally, due to the imbalance of international cultural exchange and short-term implementation of the Copyright Law, China did not participate in co-operation of international copyright matters.

Accordingly, it was beneficial for China to make the said selective arrangement in light of domestic development. There are many similar worldwide precedents to be followed. For example, the US enacted the US Copyright Law in 1790. For an extended period of time, the US did not offer protection to foreign works, taking the view that its culture and education lagged behind those of European countries. As a result the US strayed away from the Berne Convention for the Protection of Literary and Artistic Works (1886) for 102 years. Not until 1988 did it declare its accession to the Berne Convention. Japan is another case.

Patent Law was enacted in 1885 after the Meiji Restoration in Japan, in which the level for patent protection is basically lower. In order to facilitate domestic industries to absorb foreign technology, drugs and chemical substances are excluded from patent protection for 50 years. It shows that any country experiences a transitional stage from "selective protection" to "absolute protection", and from "low-level protection" to "high-level protection" in terms of the history of its IPR system. In the case of low level of domestic development in economy and society, this stage characterised by low-level IPR protection is significantly essential.

3 Modulated application

From the early 1990s to the early part of this new century, China has entered into an important stage in terms of development and perfection of its IPR system. Before acceding to WTO, China had completely modified the Copyright Law (1991, 2001), the Patent Law (1993, 2001) and the Trademark Law (1993, 2001), and had enacted the Regulations for the Protection of New Varieties of Plants (1997) and the Regulations for the Protection of Layout-design of Integrated Circuits (2001). China ultimately met the requirement of TRIPS Agreement in terms of IP protection standard and level. In a word, it took China only just over 10 years to achieve the transition of IP protection from low level to high level and from localisation to internationalisation.

The reasons therein include not only the promise that China agrees to perform duties contained in international conventions, but also the domestic need for development. Internationally, the Sino-American Memorandum of Understanding on the Protection of Intellectual Property of 1992 and the Sino-American Intellectual Property Agreement of 1995 significantly quickened the process of internationalisation in respect of intellectual property protection in China. In particular, the TRIPS Agreement promulgated by the WTO in 1994 produced a direct influence on China's IP legislation. With the internationalization of IPR, it was impossible for China not to protect foreigners' intellectual property for the purpose of developing its domestic economy, science, technology and culture. Meanwhile, with the increasingly intellectualization of international trade it is impossible for China to either isolate itself from the world or get rid of the pattern of developed-country-led international protection of IPR. At home, for the purpose of boosting economic development and scientific and technological advances, it is for China as a rising industrial country which had an internal need to strengthen IP protection. In terms of the arrangement, it is a necessary choice for an economically-advancing country to modulate its domestic legislation.

Legislative revision initiated during this stage was the result of system innovation. Revision of the Copyright Law in 2001 focused on expanding objects namely, reviewing practical art work and acrobatics art work in the scope of protected objects, enhancing protection of computer program, and adding the right to lease and the right to diffuse information network to the scope of protected rights. Revision of Patent Law (1993, 2001) engaged in promoting the development of science and technology and innovation, creating more favourable conditions for deepening the reform and open-up policy, intensifying protection and improving judicial and administrative enforcement. The revision also streamlined procedures for examination and granting and maintaining the legal rights of patent holders, furthering the reform and open-up policy for China's entry to the WTO and compliance with the TRIPS Agreement while establishing a diligent, incorrupt, pragmatic and highly efficient workforce for patent examination and granting. Revision of Trademark Law (1993, 2001) focused on extending protection scope of trade mark right to service trade mark, adding registered trade mark and registrant into the application scope, and strengthening the protection of famous brands. Moreover, the Regulations for the Protection of New Varieties of Plants (1997) and the Regulations for the Protection of Layout-design of Integrated Circuits (2001) have been enacted. We can safely conclude that China's IPR legislation is designed with concern for modern scientific and technological development, and it makes greater efforts to promote the modernisation of science and technology through the modernisation of its legislation.

4 Active decision-making

In order to intensively protect intellectual property and promote the building of the IPR system, China has separately set up the National Working Group for Intellectual Property Rights Protection in 2001 and the Leading Group for National Intellectual Property Strategy Formulation in 2005. Since then, China has entered a new phase of stratagem initiative in terms of IP system building. In January 2006, Chinese President Hu Jintao put forward the strategic object of building an innovative society in China's Science and Technology Conference. In May 2006, President Hu made remarks in the Group Study of the Political Bureau of the Central Committee of CPC:

> "Strengthening the building of China's system of intellectual property right and vigorously upgrading the capacity of creation, management, protection and application regarding intellectual property are our urgent need for the purpose of enhancing independent and self-driven innovation capabilities and building an innovation-oriented country".

His remarks reveal that China has reconsidered the role and position that the IPR system plays and strays from the viewpoint of its national strategy. Based on the development trend of international science, technology and economy, as well as the development of innovative countries, China will build and implement a national intellectual property strategy and effectively develop the IPR system for the purpose of reducing differences between China and developed countries and realising the spancentered developing mode for decision-making.

IP policy-making is done on the basis of overall national objective of building an innovation-oriented country. An innovative country refers to a country whose basic strategy is to enhance scientific and technological innovation, to enormously boost innovative capacity in science and technology and thereupon build its competitiveness advantage. At present, there are about 20 countries which are recognised worldwide as innovative countries, including the United Kingdom, Japan, Finland, Korea, etc. The common characteristics of these countries are: integrated innovation index is obviously higher than that in other countries; contribution ratio of scientific and technological advance committed to economic growth is above 70 per cent; R&D investment is above 2 per cent in domestic gross productivity; and the degree of dependence on foreign technology is below 30 per cent.[1]

In order to build an innovative country and to realise the objective of long-term sustainability for development, China will have to make choices about its development mode. In the past, China participated in international specialization through labourintensive industries, which has played an important role in accelerating economic growth and enlarging employment. However, with the escalating costs of labour and environmental resources, an increasingly acute issue concerning low valued-added products appeared. For example, China's per capita natural resource is comparatively rare: plowland resource is only one-third of the world's per capita level, freshwater resource is one-fourth, oil resource is 17 per cent, and natural air resource is 13 per cent. Relatively sufficient coal resource is only 42 per cent of world per capita level.[2] These data reveal that China shall never follow the path of development that consumes a considerable amount of resources. Meanwhile, in the international economic framework in which "developed countries offer technology and knowledge while developing countries provide labor and resource", western developed countries are reluctant to transfer their core technology to China due to either the consideration of benefits of keeping its own technology or prejudice on China's political ideology. China's investment in R&D is only 1.3 per cent of GDP whereas its dependence on foreign technology is above 50 per cent. Due to its lack of core technology, China's enterprises have to pay to foreign patent holders 20 per cent of the selling price for a domestically-made cell phone, 30 per cent of the selling price of a computer and 20–40 per cent of the selling price of a numerical-controlled machine tool. One of four computers in worldwide production is from Jiangsu. However, after paying technology licence charges to Intel and Microsoft, what China's enterprises earn from each computer is only equal to the price of 10 apples. The said examples reveal that it is impossible for China to follow the path of technology-dependent development; instead it should follow the path of technology-advanced and knowledge-innovated mode.

However, technological, cultural or knowledge-based innovation must depend on system innovation. China has witnessed that those countries and multinational corporations that have stronger self-driven innovation capacities all hold their own core technology and stress applying intellectual property to promote technology research, development and update for the purpose of strengthening national core competitiveness and boosting market competitiveness for enterprises. For example, the US ranks first in terms of its innovative capacity, especially in the fields of computer technology, internet technology, biotechnology, etc. With powerful support from the IPR system, the "sunrise industries of the US", such as electronic, software, bioengineering and internet industries, rapidly develop and expand. Meanwhile, those MNCs which have stronger technological innovative capacity always hold the representative technologies which are all centred on self-driven intellectual property, such as micromationed electronic technology in Sony, optics medium technology in Philips, CPU producing technology in Intel, etc. IBM, called Big Blue, has gained nearly 30,000 patented technologies in a few recent years. The big gap between China and developed countries mainly exists in terms of technological capacity and innovative capacity, in terms of difference in the quantity and quality of self-driven intellectual property. China has the biggest population in the world; however, the rich labour force has not been transformed into intellectual resources. China is the biggest manufacturing country in the world in which there are nearly 200 goods ranking the first in output; however, its industry preponderance is not striking. Compared to developed countries, the relative preponderance for China's industries lies in a cheap labour force, whereas the biggest gap lies in the lack of scientific and technological strength and innovative capacity. In summary, China is short of core-technology patent, copyright and internationally famous brands. Up to 2005, only 37 per cent of applications submitted in China by Chinese citizens have been granted an invention patent. In the field of high technology, such as automobile, aeroplane, instrument, information, bioengineering, new material, etc. patents granted by China almost go solely to foreign companies, accounting for 80–90 per cent of the total granted patents.

Since the implementation of the Patent Law, although the amount of domestic brand registration has increased dramatically, there are very few internationally well-known brands owned by Chinese enterprises. Among China's top 200 export enterprises, 80 per cent use foreign brands. In recent public appraisals of the worldwide top 100 international famous brands, none of the Chinese brands were included. At present, China is making great efforts to restructure industries, change the mode of growth, upgrade technology and reform enterprises. Under these circumstances, it has significant strategic plans to finish the transition from the mode of "imitated by China" to the mode of "made in China" and ultimately to the mode of "created by China".

Seeing the development trend of international protection of IPR and general experience of building an IPR system of each country, I believe it is necessary to further enrich, adjust and improve China's intellectual property policy. Thereupon, I specially put forward some proposals as follows:

* Revising and perfecting IPR legislation closely depending on China's actual situation and practical experience. China's current IPR legislation basically

accords with actual situation and international rules; however, some imperfections still exist. At present, China should revise its Patent Law, Copyright Law, Trademark Law and Anti-Unfair Competition Law, improve the review and authorisation mechanisms for granting design patents, perfect the search and report system for utility model and clarify the standard for recognizing torts. China should issue the Anti-Monopoly Law and the Business Secret Protection Law, enact some regulations such as the Statute of Protecting Folklore in Art for the purpose of offering domestic legal protection to "expressions of folklore" art-literature and traditional knowledge. China should make full use of related rules on intellectual property abuse and limiting competition practice in licensing trade, pay attention to prevent intellectual property abuse and build mechanism of defining, restricting and punishing intellectual property abuses.

- Establishing IP-oriented public policy system is closely dependent on the national intellectual property strategy. This strategy is a strategy for holistic, long-term and national policy development, which embodies that a country should promote and pilot self-driven innovations through the IPR system. Hereupon, a harmonised and integrated strategy shall be built based on the combination of government, enterprises, industries and society. Piloted by the national IP strategy, the IPR system shall co-operate with national science and technology policy, industry policy, cultural policy, educational policy and foreign trade policy, incorporating in particular intellectual property clauses into these related policies. In terms of industry policy, China should emphasise the restricting of reconstructing industry structure and the facilitation of the industrialisation of intellectual property. In terms of science and technology policy, China should intensify the strength of protection for inventors and promote the industrialisation of scientific and technological products. In terms of foreign trade, China should change the mode to increase foreign trade, optimise the structure of imported and exported goods, and support the export expansion for goods having independent intellectual property and an independent brand identity. In terms of cultural and educational policy, we should encourage cultural innovation and boost copyright-granted culture into the market. In terms of investment policy, China should strengthen investment on innovation fund and intensify financial support for R&D.
- Reinforcing exchange and co-operation with regard to IPR international affairs, closely depending on the latest reforms on the international IPR system. As a big country which is playing an important political role in the world, China should conduct dialogues and communications with other countries, international organisations and foreign enterprises in the field of intellectual property. At present, China should pay particular attention to playing a constructive role in the new round of TRIPS negotiation and make efforts to express concerns about benefits in the process of revising and making IPR international protection rules.

China's first concern is to strengthen legal protection on traditional resources (including traditional knowledge and inherited resources) and geographical indications. China should enhance international protection of traditional medicine, "expressions of folklore" art-literature, inherited resource, biological diversity and geographical indications in which China has an advantage and reduce the protection level for some intellectual products in which China is in an inferior position to create. The second concern is to attach importance to the benefits in maintaining the balance between developing and developed countries. In constructing an international IPR system, China should consider the phase of scientific, technological, economic and social development for developing countries, and increase technological transformation and assistance which is closely related to the benefits for developing countries. Finally, the last concern is to promote the harmonised development of intellectual property and human rights. China should closely combine IPR international protection with human rights and try to implement the harmonised development in terms of IPR protection and human rights, such as the right to free expression, privacy, right to health and development.

Notes

1 Based on following minimum protection standard provided in international conventions, developing countries should combine the "Phase Theory" with the "Scope Theory" in making choices with regard to the IPR system. The "Phase Theory" states the IPR protection level in one country should conform to its domestic economic and social developing levels, namely, it shouldn't lag behind or go beyond its scientific, technological and economic development in a certain phase. The "Scope Theory" states that IPR protection scope in one country should conform to its domestic economic and social development, namely, it shouldn't inappropriately reduce or expand the scope.
2 See Jean-Eric Aubert, *Promoting Innovation in Developing Countries: A Conceptual Framework*, (Washington D.C.: World Bank, 2005).